The Satipaṭṭhānasutta with Pemasiri Thera's Commentary

The Satipaṭṭhānasutta with Pemasiri Thera's Commentary

Edited, Translated and Annotated
by Tamara Ditrich

equinox

SHEFFIELD UK BRISTOL CT

Published by Equinox Publishing Ltd.
UK: Office 415, The Workstation, 15 Paternoster Row, Sheffield, South Yorkshire S1 2BX
USA: ISD, 70 Enterprise Drive, Bristol, CT 06010
www.equinoxpub.com

British Library Cataloguing-in-Publication Data
A catalogue record for this book is available from the British Library.

ISBN-13	978 18005039 39	(hardback)
	978 18005039 46	(paperback)
	978 18005039 53	(pdf)
	978 180050 613 8	(ePub)

Library of Congress Cataloging-in-Publication Data

Names: Ditrich, Tamara, translator, editor. | Pemasiri, Thera, 1942- commentator.
Title: The Satipaṭṭhānasutta with Pemasiri Thera's commentary/ by Tamara Ditrich.
Other titles: Tipiṭaka. Suttapiṭaka. Majjhimanikāya. Satipaṭṭhānasutta. English. | Tipiṭaka. Suttapiṭaka. Majjhimanikāya. Satipaṭṭhānasutta.
Description: Bristol : Equinox Publishing Ltd, 2024. | Includes bibliographical references and index. | Summary: "The book presents a comprehensive guide for understanding mindfulness by situating it within the larger Theravāda doctrinal framework in a way accessible to contemporary readers. The book will appeal to general and scholarly readers interested in any aspects of the theory and practice of mindfulness, Buddhist teachings or Pāli studies"-- Provided by publisher.
Identifiers: LCCN 2023044115 (print) | LCCN 2023044116 (ebook) | ISBN 9781800503939 (hardback) | ISBN 9781800503946 (paperback) | ISBN 9781800506138 (epub) | ISBN 9781800503953 (pdf)
Subjects: LCSH: Meditation--Theravāda Buddhism. | Mindfulness (Psychology)
Classification: LCC BQ1320.S2522 E57 2024 (print) | LCC BQ1320.S2522 (ebook) | DDC 294.3/91--dc23/eng/20231023
LC record available at https://lccn.loc.gov/2023044115
LC ebook record available at https://lccn.loc.gov/2023044116

Edited and Typeset by Queentson Publishing, Hamilton, Canada

Contents

Acknowledgements vii

Abbreviations ix

Introduction 1

Note 9

Chapter I Introducing the four foundations of mindfulness (*cattāro satipaṭṭhānā*) 13

Chapter II Contemplation of the body (*kāyānupassanā*) 33

- II 1 Mindfulness of breathing (*ānāpānasati*) 33
- II 2 Ways of movement (*iriyāpatha*) 48
- II 3 Clear comprehension (*sampajañña*) of bodily activities 50
- II 4 Reflection on the troublesomeness (*paṭikkūlamanasikāra*) of the body 53
- II 5 Reflection on the four elements (*catudhātumanasikāra*) 57
- II 6 Nine cemetery contemplations (*navasīvathikā*) 63

Chapter III Contemplation of feelings (*vedanānupassanā*) 69

Chapter IV Contemplation of the mind (*cittānupassanā*) 81

Chapter V Contemplation of phenomena (*dhammānupassanā*) 99

- V 1 Five hindrances (*pañca nīvaraṇāni*) 99
- V 2 Five aggregates of clinging (*pañcas'upādānakkhandhā*) 115
- V 3 Six sense spheres (*cha āyatanāni*) 125
- V 4 Seven factors of awakening (*satta bojjhaṅgā*) 139
- V 5 Four noble truths (*cattāri ariyasaccāni*) 157

Chapter VI Conclusion 173

Bibliography 177

Glossary 179

Discourse on the Foundations of Mindfulness (*Satipaṭṭhānasutta*) 187

Index 205

Acknowledgements

Many people have helped in all kinds of ways to prepare this material for publication: I am grateful to each and every one of them. First, my deepest gratitude goes to my lifelong *kalyāṇamitta*, Pemasiri Thero of Kanduboda (Sri Lanka), a traditional Pāli scholar in the Theravāda tradition and experienced meditation teacher. During my multiple retreats in Sri Lanka over the last two decades, on my request, he agreed to prepare and deliver multiple talks explaining the *Satipaṭṭhānasutta* and related topics. He also generously responded to my numerous questions with comprehensive explanations and clarifications. Pemasiri Thera's commentaries on the *Satipaṭṭhānasutta* were delivered orally in Sinhalese, with local volunteers translating the highly technical presentations into English on the spot. Among them, I am particularly thankful to Anil Ratwatte who aptly and accurately translated most of the talks that I recorded. Among the other translators, I would also like to sincerely acknowledge the late Venerable Chandra, Komi Mendis, Dilrukshi Samaraweera and Indunil Abeyesekere. I thank all of them, not only for their translation work but also for their kindness, generosity and help over the years.

I received extensive assistance in transcribing the many hours of recordings of Pemasiri Thera's discourses. I gratefully acknowledge the work of the late Sue Sawyer, Royce Wiles and Ana Bajzelj who accurately and patiently typed a great number of talks. After I had compiled and edited the talks into a book, several people read the manuscript. I am much indebted and thankful to Royce Wiles for his generosity, friendship and encouragement from the very beginning of this project as well as for his careful reading of the manuscript: he provided many valuable suggestions, comments and corrections. I am also grateful to my Australian friends, especially to Charles Wang and Pilar Helmers for their friendly support during the writing of this book. In addition, I sincerely thank Victoria Grace for her excellent and meticulous editing work and the Equinox editor Valerie Hall for her help. I remain entirely responsible for any mistakes and misinterpretations in this book, which are due to my limited knowledge and understanding of the Buddhist teachings.

Finally, I dedicate this book to the memory of my late husband, Primoz Pecenko, whose lifelong enthusiasm for and knowledge of both Buddhist theory and practice has been a great source of inspiration throughout my life.

Abbreviations

The abbreviations of Pāli sources and the quotation system follow the *Critical Pāli Dictionary* (Epilegomena to vol. 1, 1948, 5*–36* and vol. 3, 1992, II–VI). The numbers in the quotations of Pāli sources refer to the volume and page of the PTS edition (e.g., M I 21 refers to the *Majjhima Nikāya*, vol 1, 21).

A *Aṅguttaranikāya*. [1885–1900] 1999–2013. Ed. by R. Morris and E. Hardy. 5 vols. PTS.

As *Atthasālinī*. [1897] 2011. Ed. by E. Müller, rev. by L. S. Cousins. PTS.

D *Dīghanikāya*. [1890–1911] 1995–2007. Ed. by T. W. Rhys Davids and J. E. Carpenter. 3 vols. PTS.

Dhp *Dhammapada*. [1994] 2014. Ed. by O. von Hinüber and K. R. Norman. 2nd ed. (with Indexes by Yamazaki, Ousaka and Miyao). PTS.

Dhp-a *Dhammapadaṭṭhakathā*. [1906–1952] 1993–2018. Ed. by K. R. Norman and Helmer Smith. PTS.

Dhs *Dhammasaṅgaṇi*. [1885] 2001. Ed. by Edward Müller. PTS.

DP *A Dictionary of Pāli*. 2001–. Ed. by Margaret Cone. 3 vols. PTS.

It-a *Itivuttaka Commentary* [1934–1936]. 1977. Ed. by M. Bose. 2 vols. PTS.

M *Majjhimanikāya*. [1888–1902] 2013. Ed. by V. Trenckner and R. Chalmers. 3 vols. PTS.

Mil *Milindapañhā*. [1880] 1986. Ed. by V. Trenckner. PTS.

Mp *Manorathapūraṇī*. [1924–1957] 1968–1977. Ed. by M. Walleser and H. Kopp. 5 vols. PTS.

MW Monier-Williams, M. [1899] 1988. *A Sanskrit-English Dictionary*. Oxford: Oxford University Press. Reprinted, Delhi: Motilal Banarsidass.

Nidd I *Mahāniddesa*. [1916–1917] 2001. Ed. by L. de la Vallée Poussin and E. J. Thomas. PTS.

Nidd II *Cullaniddesa*. [1918] 1988. Ed. by W. Stede. PTS.

Paṭis *Paṭisambhidāmagga*. [1905–1907] 2003. Ed. by Arnold C. Taylor. 2 vols. PTS.

PED *Pāli-English Dictionary*. 1921–1925. T. W. Rhys Davids and W. Stede. PTS.

Ps *Papañcasūdanī, Majjhimanikāyāṭṭhakathā* of Buddhaghosa. [1922–1938] 1976–1979. Ed. by J. H. Woods, D. Kośambi and I. B. Horner. 5 vols. PTS.

S *Saṃyuttanikāya*. [1884–1898] 1975–2006. Ed. by L. Feer. 5 vols. PTS.

Sn *Suttanipāta*. [1913] 2017. Ed. by D. Andersen and H. Smith. PTS.

Spk *Sāratthappakāsinī*. [1929–1937] 1977. Ed. by F.L. Woodward. PTS.

Sv *Sumaṅgalavilāsinī*. [1929–1932] 1968–1971. Ed. by T. W. Rhys Davids, J. E. Carpenter and W. Stede. 3 vols. PTS.

Th *Thera- and Therī-gāthā*. [1883] 1999. Ed. by H. Oldenberg and R. Pischel. PTS.

Th-a *Theragāthā* Commentary (*Paramatthadīpanī* V). 1940–1984. Ed. by F. L. Woodward. 3 vols. PTS.

Ud *Udāna*. [1885] 2017. Ed. by Steinthal. PTS.

Vibh *Vibhaṅga*. [1904] 2003. Ed. by C. A. F. Rhys Davids. PTS.

Vibh-a *Sammohavinodanī*. [1923] 1980. Ed. by A. Buddhadatta. PTS.

Vism *Visuddhimagga*. [1920–1921] 1975. Ed. by C.A.F. Rhys Davids. PTS.

Vism-a *Visuddhimaggassa Atthasaṃvaṇṇanābhūtā Bhadantācariyadhammapālattherena katā Paramatthamañjūsā nāma Visuddhimaggamahāṭīkā*. 2008. 2 vols. Ṭīkā Series 25–26. Yangon, Myanmar: Buddhasāsana Society.

Introduction

Many books have been written about the *Satipaṭṭhānasutta* ('Discourse on the Foundations of Mindfulness'), especially since the late nineteenth century when it was positioned as the foundational text of mindfulness practice and *vipassanā* meditation.[1] There are numerous versions of the *Satipaṭṭhānasutta* in the Pāli canon of the Theravāda and other Buddhist textual traditions. The text has also been the subject of traditional commentaries, and since the late nineteenth century, many translations and scholarly works have been published, among which the commentary of Anālayo (2003) is especially noteworthy on account of its thorough analysis of the *sutta* and review of previous research. Despite these many studies, the *sutta* nevertheless remains quite enigmatic, being open to multiple interpretations and practical applications. The translation and commentary of the *sutta* offered in this book bring to light previously unexplored facets, approaches, understandings and elucidations, which undoubtedly prompt new avenues of inquiry and ways of exploring this unique text; these can in turn reinvigorate research and inspire the investigation of the Dhamma itself through meditation practice.

The primary aim of this book is to record an authentic contemporary commentary on the *Satipaṭṭhānasutta* by Pemasiri Thera, a traditional Pāli scholar in the Theravāda tradition and an experienced meditation teacher from Kanduboda (Sri Lanka). He makes a particularly valuable contribution to interpreting key concepts in this *sutta* by linking them to meditation practice, often in an innovative manner, while also drawing from the Pāli canon and its commentaries to lend support to his understanding.

Translating an ancient traditional text such as the *Satipaṭṭhānasutta* from Pāli—the Indian scholastic language of the Theravāda school of Buddhist thought—into modern European languages is fraught with difficulties and highly problematic. In addition to the difficulties inherent in the translation of any text, the key Buddhist terminology presents significant challenges when bridging two fundamentally different discourses, namely, the ancient Indian and modern Western ones. By revisiting the commonly accepted translations and interpretations of key terms in the *Satipaṭṭhānasutta*, Pemasiri Thera's commentary sheds new light on many issues involved in understanding (and therefore translating) the original Pāli. In addition, I believe that it is never superfluous, neither for scholars nor for meditation practitioners, to discuss mindfulness (*sati*), as it is one of the key components of the Buddhist path (*magga*)

1. For the modern history of mindfulness and insight meditation, see Sujato 2005; McMahan 2008; Braun 2013; Ditrich 2016a.

positioned at the fore of Buddhist teachings, as stated in the *Ādittapariyāyasutta* in the *Bojjhaṅga-saṃyutta*, 'but mindfulness, monks, I say, is always useful.'[2]

The idea of writing this book was born long ago, well before mindfulness in its new contexts and interpretations had become such a widespread and popular modern phenomenon. The accumulation of material in this volume is the outcome of my protracted questioning of Pemasiri Thera during multiple personal meditation retreats in Sri Lanka and elsewhere from the 1970s onwards. To this day, I remain particularly interested in the ways of linking experiences in meditation practice to the textual records in the Pāli canon, notably with the contents of the *Satipaṭṭhānasutta* and other related texts. To address my questions, Pemasiri Thera would every now and then give a series of talks in Sinhala on the *Satipaṭṭhānasutta*, which I started to record in the 1990s. As I kept visiting Sri Lanka, I returned to him with new questions relating to the *sutta*, which were then duly addressed in further talks. I eventually ended up with several hundred hours of recorded talks by Pemasiri Thera, discussing a wide range of topics relating to the theory and practice of meditation, with a specific focus on the *Satipaṭṭhānasutta*. In the beginning, the recordings were intended solely for my personal use, but later and with Pemasiri Thera's permission, I decided to compile them into a book to make these teachings available to others.

As a well-read traditional scholar of Buddhist texts, Pemasiri Thera made considerable use of the Theravāda canon and its commentaries to respond to my questions about the terms in the *Satipaṭṭhānasutta*. He does not read English and so his comments are, for the most part, not directly influenced by contemporary writings on the *sutta* in English or other Western languages. Pemasiri Thera's commentaries were given exclusively in Sinhalese, with frequent references to Pāli terminology and the recitation of passages from the *Tipiṭaka*; each talk was accompanied by an on-the-spot oral English translation made by one of several local volunteer translators. For this book, I initially only selected the discussions relating directly to the *Satipaṭṭhānasutta*, which amounted to several hundred recordings, each about an hour long. My original intention was to simply transcribe the oral English translation of the talks, edit them and then publish them as a commentary on the *Satipaṭṭhānasutta*. However, when I started editing, I realised that most of the talks contained abundant material that was not directly linked to the *Satipaṭṭhānasutta*, including discussions on diverse subjects and aspects of Buddhist teachings as well as anecdotes and personal stories. Conversely, many other discussions by Pemasiri Thera, which I had not initially planned to include, presented useful material on aspects of the *Satipaṭṭhānasutta*. I decided to draw relevant materials from all the recorded talks and insert them under the corresponding sections of the *Satipaṭṭhānasutta*, thus retaining the structure of the *sutta* itself. The compilation process therefore required a great deal of selecting, restructuring and editing; almost every sentence had to be reformulated to provide a continuous text, with paragraphs rearranged multiple times, inevitably sacrificing the completeness of the individual talks, which would commonly include diversions away from the topic in question via various narratives relating to Pemasiri Thera's personal experience as a monk and other anecdotes. Because of this editorial decision, the lively spirit of the individual talks has no doubt been lost, and it cannot be said that Pemasiri Thera presented all this material at one time in exactly this sequence. Here I have adopted a more systematic analytical approach, closely following the structure of the *Satipaṭṭhānasutta* itself to unify the material and dividing it into smaller sections, each followed by the relevant commentaries of Pemasiri Thera.

2. S V 115: *Satim ca kvāham bhikkhave sabbatthikaṃ vadāmīti.*

In the main text of this book, the presentation of the *Satipaṭṭhānasutta* follows, to some extent, the standard model of ancient Indian textual transmission, namely, starting with short segments of the text in Pāli followed by comments. For the Pāli text, I have used the version of the *Satipaṭṭhānasutta* from the *Majjhima Nikāya* (M I 55–63).[3] To make the material more accessible, I subdivided the *sutta* into smaller segments that each represent a meaningful unit, usually just a few sentences; thus, I generally followed the standard subdivisions found in most modern English translations of the text. I then rendered the Pāli text into English, largely adopting the translation of Ñāṇanamoli and Bodhi (1995, 145–155), which I occasionally modified in the light of Pemasiri Thera's comments and my own understanding of the teachings.

The Pāli text and English translation of each segment of the *sutta* are followed by Pemasiri Thera's comments, which are drawn directly from the recorded and transcribed talks. The main foci of his comments are the discussion and interpretation of key Pāli terms from the *sutta* (reflecting my own questions at the time, which mainly centred on understanding the Pāli technical terminology) and other topics related to the four foundations of mindfulness. Although I have used English renderings for all the key Buddhist concepts discussed—presuming that not all readers are familiar with Pāli—I have consistently and purposefully added, whenever they occur, the original Pāli words in parentheses in order to avoid the ambiguity of English translations and familiarise readers with the fundamental terms of the *Satipaṭṭhānasutta*, which appear in a variety of contexts with a broad semantic range.[4] I believe that retaining a closer link between Pāli words and their English translations will help promote clarity about and familiarity with key Pāli technical terms occurring in different contexts; this is vital in light of the numerous challenges posed by the linguistic and cultural translations of ancient Indian texts. There is mostly no adequate or precise equivalent for key Pāli terms in English, since their signification (with the associated spectrum of connotations) stems from a discourse very different from any Western one; the clarity of the original Pāli is thus often lost in translation. An additional point is that the terminology relates to subtle cognitive processes and mind states rather than shared external events or experiences, and so even native English speakers discussing internal experiences run into issues of precision and clarity when attempting to talk about such topics. Being acutely aware of the problems relating to the translation of Buddhist texts from Pāli, especially regarding key terms without appropriate equivalents in modern English, I have endeavoured to use well-established translations such as 'knowledge' for *ñāṇa*, 'wisdom' for *paññā* and 'clear comprehension' for *sampajañña*, to avoid creating further obscurity by translating key Pāli terminology with new English terms.

All translations of Pāli passages into English in this book are my own; however, I have drawn on existing translations, especially the English renderings of the Nikāya passages, mainly based on the translations of Bodhi (2000; 2012), Ñāṇanamoli and Bodhi (1995) and Walshe (1995), although in my attempts to clarify the meaning, I diverge much more in my translations of the Abhidhamma texts.

3. Several texts in the *Tipiṭaka* describe or prescribe the practice of the four *satipaṭṭhānas*; the longest and most detailed are the *Mahāsatipaṭṭhānasutta* in the *Dīgha Nikāya* (D II 290–315) and the *Satipaṭṭhānasutta* in the *Majjhima Nikāya* (M I 55–63). Shorter versions are also recorded in A III 450; D II 290–315; M I 55–63; M III 111–112; S V 143, 294–297; Nidd 1 1, 28, 63, 72, 78, 99; 340, 354, 370, 387; Nidd 2 78, 124, 128.

4. Individual Pāli words (including compounds) are written in their stem form, whereas groups of words and phrases are cited in the appropriate cases found in the text.

To Pemasiri Thera's commentaries, I have added my own explanatory comments, links to the Pāli sources and extensive footnotes. To maintain a clear distinction between Pemasiri Thera's comments and my own analysis, my comments are placed in brackets, with additional quotations from the primary sources. I have also occasionally added diagrams and tables in the main body of the book to systematically present some of the main features of the *Satipaṭṭhānasutta* that were commented on or mentioned by Pemasiri Thera, who himself often uses charts, tables and drawings in his talks to visually present the teachings; furthermore, I also drew inspiration from Anālayo (2003) when designing the tables. In the footnotes, I primarily endeavoured to contextualise and situate Pemasiri Thera's commentaries within the broader range of Theravāda canonical and post-canonical texts by identifying the Pāli passages that he quoted, referred to or drew from in his discussions. I have also provided explanations of the basic doctrinal aspects in question or suggested references for further details on the topic. In addition, I occasionally annotated Pemasiri Thera's interpretations that throw new light on (or suggest alternative approaches to) traditional interpretations of Buddhist teachings, especially those of the orthodox Theravāda commentator Buddhaghosa, and I have tried to connect the wording or contextualise the concepts within the Theravāda textual sources. Several footnotes that provide important references or clarification are occasionally repeated for the sake of clarity, as I consider these to proffer valuable information; I also presume that the reader will not necessarily read this book from start to finish in one sitting.

My annotations are not intended to be exhaustive but rather indicative, mostly referring to a few notable examples from the Pāli canonical texts and commentaries and inevitably reflecting my own personal interests, especially in the Abhidhamma literature, which I cite frequently. Only very occasionally do I refer to relevant modern scholarly works in English; my engagement with modern scholarship in relation to this *sutta* is minimal by design, as my main focus is to explain and contextualise Pemasiri Thera's commentaries by linking them to the traditional Pāli textual sources. Connecting Pemasiri Thera's views on these traditional teachings to contemporary mindfulness literature is a separate project. To restate my purpose and method, this book represents an attempt to meld two approaches for the study of the *Satipaṭṭhānasutta*: on the one hand, it captures a traditional approach articulated through the orally transmitted comments of Pemasiri Thera, a traditional Theravāda scholar and practitioner, and on the other hand, it epitomises a modern Western approach, mainly '*explication de texte*,' through the textual analysis in my extensive footnotes, with a special focus on the interpretation and contextualisation of the key Pāli terms in the *sutta*.

In my annotations, I refer to the Pali Text Society (PTS) editions of the Pāli canon and its commentaries. As is standard for academic approaches to these texts, the numbers in the quotations of Pāli sources refer to the volume and page number of the PTS edition (see the section on Abbreviations). Readers who do not read Pāli may nevertheless find these references to the Pāli texts in existing English translations, especially in the translations of the *Nikāyas* (Bodhi 2000; 2012; Ñāṇanamoli and Bodhi 1995; Walshe 1995) and other English translations published by PTS, in which the references to the original Pāli sources are marked by numbers [in square brackets] inserted within the English text.

Although Pemasiri Thera's commentaries largely follow and reflect traditional Theravāda teachings, he frequently proposes new angles or elucidations in his interpretations. Some of his innovative approaches stem from his meditation practice, while others provide new links between the various Pāli textual sources in ways that are not usually presented in other modern translations and interpretations of the *Satipaṭṭhānasutta*. Before providing a few examples of his interpretations of the *sutta*, it should be mentioned that Pemasiri Thera was from the 1950s onwards mainly trained in the meditation tradition popularised by Mahāsi Sayadaw. His main teacher was a very respected meditation master Sumatipāla Mahāthera of the Siyane Vipassanā Meditation Centre in Kanduboda, Sri Lanka, who belonged to the Burmese lineage of Mahāsi Sayadaw. Pemasiri Thera also studied with Webu Sayadaw, U Pandita and other meditation masters, especially in Burma (Myanmar) and India. He is currently the Abbot and the main meditation teacher at Sumathipāla Nā Himi Senasunārana in Sri Lanka.

As a highly experienced practitioner and meditation teacher whose experience in teaching meditation spans over fifty years, he frequently links his interpretations of the *Satipaṭṭhānasutta* to meditation practice. For example, in the passage about the ways in which contemplation, as presented in this *sutta*, should be conducted, he questions the traditional understanding of the terms 'internally' (*ajjhattam*) and 'externally' (*bahiddhā*) as referring to 'oneself' and 'others,' respectively, which was largely established by Buddhaghosa and is subsequently followed by most modern interpreters. Pemasiri Thera instead proposes an interpretation drawn from meditation practice, arguing that when the phenomena or processes experienced in meditation are understood and noted with an inherent idea of an 'I' or 'myself,' the contemplation is conducted internally (*ajjhattam*). Conversely, if the meditator develops an insight that there is no 'I' but only a flow of experienced objects and processes, the contemplation takes place without the sense of an 'I' or 'knower'. In other words, there is just knowing and an object that is known, and such a contemplation can be understood to be carried out externally (*bahiddhā*).[5]

To give another example, Pemasiri Thera draws from his experience as a meditation teacher in his interpretation of the phrase *vineyya abhijjhādomanassaṃ*, usually translated into English as 'having abandoned desire and discontent.' He points out that meditators often base their understanding of renunciation or abandonment on dislike, albeit at times a very slight aversion of which they are unaware. To highlight and avoid this potential misunderstanding in the cultivation of mindfulness, he suggests an expanded interpretation of the phrase *vineyya abhijjhādomanassaṃ*, as 'having *recognised* desire and discontent and then put them away.' This means that the meditator first has to see and recognise desire (*abhijjhā*) and discontent (*domanassa*) in order to understand how troublesome they can be; only then can they be abandoned. He further argues that if only 'abandoning' was meant here, another Pāli word would have been used such as *pajahati*, which means 'gives up, renounces, gets rid of.'[6]

In yet another example, Pemasiri Thera interprets the phrase 'experiencing the whole body' (*sabbakāyapaṭisaṃvedī*) from the perspective of an experienced meditator: he argues that the word 'body' (*kāya*) does not necessarily refer just to the physical body or the body of the whole breath but also to the 'mental body' (*nāmakāya*), that is, the body of mental concomitants (*cetasika*).

5. Although this explanation seemingly does not appear in traditional commentaries, I identified one instance in the *Tipiṭaka* (i.e., Vibh 194) in which this interpretation is implied. For details, see Chapter II, under the subheading 'Internally (*ajjhattam*), externally (*bahiddhā*) and internally and externally (*ajjhattabahiddhā*).'

6. Although I am not aware of such an explicit explanation of the phrase *vineyya abhijjhādomanassaṃ* in the Pāli canon or its commentaries, this meaning is implicitly understood in many contexts in the textual sources, especially around the ideal of renunciation (*nekkhamma*), which is always linked to wholesome states (*kusala*) and thus reflects an understanding of the nature of desire and discontent (e.g., Vibh 86). For details, see Chapter I, under the subheading 'Having abandoned desires and discontent in regard to the world (*vineyya loke abhijjhādomanassaṃ*).'

As a result, the term *sabbakāyapaṭisaṃvedī* could be rendered as 'experiencing the whole mental body,' i.e., the mental concomitants (*cetasika*).[7]

Pemasiri Thera often highlights links between various key concepts or doctrinal models in ways that are not usually presented in modern studies of the *Satipaṭṭhānasutta*. His comments frequently draw from the Theravāda *Abhidhamma*, as he explains key Pāli terms from the viewpoint of Abhidhammic categories such as the mental concomitants (*cetasika*) and the mind (*citta*), which are then connected to other doctrinal models such as the five aggregates (*khandha*) and the formula of dependent origination (*paṭiccasamuppāda*). His comments are consistently grounded in and refer to one of the most foundational Buddhist teachings, namely, non-self (*anattā*), especially when meditation practice is discussed.

Often using references to the primary Pāli sources, he clearly elucidates many key terms that are often used indistinctly and ambiguously in both modern English translations of Pāli texts and the secondary literature on Buddhist meditation. For example, in Chapter I, he comprehensively discusses the distinction between attention (*manasikāra*), wise attention (*yoniso manasikāra*) and mindfulness (*sati*),[8] and the role of clear comprehension (*sampajañña*) in the transition from calm (*samatha*) to insight (*vipassanā*) meditation, while linking them to the insight into non-self (*anattā*).[9] Further on, he delineates the relationship between the concepts of clear comprehension (*sampajañña*), wisdom (*paññā*), investigation of *dhammas* (*dhammavicaya*) and investigative inquiry or discernment (*vimāṃsā*).[10]

In Chapter III on the contemplation of feeling (*vedanānupassanā*), Pemasiri Thera discusses feeling (*vedanā*) within the Buddhist foundational framework of dependent origination (*paṭiccasamuppāda*) and links this discussion to the insight into non-self (*anattā*).[11] In this chapter, he also distinguishes between the terms neither-unpleasant-nor-pleasant feeling (*adukkhamasukhavedanā*) and equanimity (*upekkhā*). He proposes that the difference between the usage of these two terms can be explained in the context of two types of meditation: on the one hand, the cultivation of the four foundations of mindfulness (*satipaṭṭhāna*) in which neither-unpleasant-nor-pleasant feeling (*adukkhamasukhavedanā*) is experienced, and on the other, calm meditation (*samatha*) in which the meditator experiences equanimity (*upekkhā*). As shown in my annotations, although this distinction is not directly articulated in the Pāli sources, it is clearly indicated in several canonical and post-canonical texts.[12]

Another example of Pemasiri Thera's original contribution is his discussion on the relationship between *citta*, *viññāṇa* and *mano*—three Pāli terms that are often ambiguously and inconsistently translated as 'mind' or 'consciousness.' Pemasiri Thera clearly delineates the semantic ranges of each concept and contextualises them within several doctrinal models.[13] In his comments, Pemasiri Thera frequently and consistently highlights the insight into non-

7. See Chapter II, under the subheading 'Experiencing the whole body (*sabbakāyapaṭisaṃvedī*).'
8. See Chapter I, under the subheadings 'Mindful (*satimā*),' 'Four foundations of mindfulness (*cattāro satipaṭṭhānā*)' and 'Clearly comprehending (*sampajāno*).'
9. See Chapter I, under the subheadings 'Four foundations of mindfulness (*cattāro satipaṭṭhānā*)' and 'Clearly comprehending (*sampajāno*).'
10. See Chapter V.4, under the subheading 'Investigation-of-*dhammas* factor of awakening (*dhammavicayasambojjhaṅga*).'
11. See Chapter III, under the subheading 'Pleasant feeling (*sukhavedanā*) and unpleasant feeling (*dukkhavedanā*).'
12. See Chapter III, under the subheading 'Neither-unpleasant-nor-pleasant feeling (*adukkhama-sukhavedanā*).'
13. For a detailed discussion, see Chapter IV, under the subheading 'Mind (*citta*).'

self (*anattā*) as the key component in the cultivation of the meditation path, in this way linking it to the development of wisdom (*paññā*) and the investigation of *dhammas* (*dhammavicaya*), which he then interprets in light of dependent origination (*paṭiccasamuppāda*).

For most of Pemasiri Thera's comments on the terms, concepts and doctrinal aspects, I was able to find explicit or implicit references in the Pāli canon and its commentaries. However, many of his interpretations are innovative in the sense that they are not articulated in most of the secondary modern literature on the *Satipaṭṭhānasutta*. For example, in the section on the five aggregates (*khandha*),[14] Pemasiri Thera discusses three concepts—*kamma*, mental formations (*saṅkhāra*) and volition (*cetanā*)—and situates them within the framework of three prevalent doctrinal models presented in the Pāli canon—i.e., the five aggregates (*khandha*), the Abhidhammic model of the four categories of *dhammas* and dependent origination (*paṭiccasamuppāda*)—while viewing them from the perspective of non-self (*anattā*) and highlighting their intrinsically empty nature. He explains that *kamma* does not arise with every volition (*cetanā*) but only when perception (*saññā*) and feeling (*vedanā*) are sufficiently strong to create mental formations (*sankhāra*) along with the other mental concomitants (*cetasika*). In other words, when volition (*cetanā*), a mental concomitant (*cetasika*) in Abhidhammic analysis, becomes strengthened, it may result in *kamma*, thus creating mental formations (*saṅkhāra*), which are comprised of various groups of mental concomitants (*cetasikas*). He then situates mental formations (*saṅkhāra*) in the context of dependent origination (*paṭiccasamuppāda*) as a condition for consciousness (*viññāṇa*) to arise. Similarly, Pemasiri Thera comments on the six sense spheres (*āyatana*) in the context of dependent origination (*paṭiccasamuppāda*) while focusing on the role of ignorance (*avijjā*), which conditions contact (*phassa*) with an object and may lead to craving (*taṇhā*), the creation of a 'person' or an 'I' and thus the continuation of the process of becoming (*bhava*).[15]

In conclusion, a question may be asked about the intended audience for this commentary. The book, which assumes some previous knowledge of Theravāda Buddhism[16] and familiarity with the *Satipaṭṭhānasutta,* is addressed to a broad range of readers: more generally, anyone interested in the theory and practice of mindfulness as traditionally presented in the *sutta* and, more specifically, students and scholars of Buddhism and Pāli. But above all, it is dedicated to the transmitters and practitioners of Buddhist meditation with the hope that they may benefit from and be inspired by Pemasiri Thera's commentaries on the meaning and practice of the four *satipaṭṭhānas.*

14. See Chapter V.2, under the subheading 'Mental formation (*saṅkhāra*) and consciousness (*viññāṇa*).'

15. He then adds that there is no such thing as ignorance (*avijjā*) and that we only discuss this concept because of the first nine fetters (*saṃyojana*). Once they are relinquished, there is no experience or object that can arise with ignorance (*avijjā*) alone. See Chapter V.3, under the subheading 'Fetter (*saṃyojana*).'

16. For a better understanding of the topics raised in this book, the following preliminary sources will be helpful to readers: Gethin (1998) and Harvey (2013) for an overview of general Buddhist teachings; Nyanaponika (1965), Bodhi (1993), Nyanatiloka (2008) and Karunadasa (2010) for the foundations of Theravāda *Abhidhamma.*

Note

The *Satipaṭṭhānasutta*, translated into English as 'Discourse on the foundations of mindfulness,'[1] is presented in this book in six sections, each treated in a separate chapter: the introductory chapter of the *sutta* is followed by four chapters on the four foundations of mindfulness, and at the end, a concluding chapter. Each chapter is further divided into smaller segments marked by headings, usually comprising a few sentences from the *sutta* that constitute a meaningful unit.

As mentioned in the Introduction, the Pāli text used here is the *Satipaṭṭhānasutta* version from the *Majjhima Nikāya* (MN I 55–63), followed by an English translation, which largely follows that of Ñāṇanamoli and Bodhi (1995, 145–155) with a few modifications. The Pāli text and the English translations of each segment of the *sutta* are followed by Pemasiri Thera's commentary. This material was taken from various talks given by Pemasiri Thera, mainly between 2002 and 2015, all of which were orally translated into English as he spoke by a number of local translators. I then edited the transcribed recordings of these talks, which involved paraphrasing most sentences, restructuring sections and paragraphs and making numerous other changes. I added the Pāli original (in parentheses) for all the technical terms used in the *sutta*, as well as the many annotations, references and quotations from the Pāli canon and its commentaries to which Pemasiri Thera referred or alluded. In addition, I inserted into the footnotes various references or parallels to relevant passages from the canonical and post-canonical literature, either as direct quotations (in Pāli and English) or, in the case of longer passages, as abridged translations. My references to the Pāli sources refer to the PTS editions (following their individual styles of presenting the Pāli), whereas the English translations are my own, though largely drawing from the existing PTS translations in English with a few modifications to reflect Pemasiri Thera's comments and my own research. At the same time, I tried to carefully convey the gist of Pemasiri Thera's teachings and retain, where possible, his style and expressions.

1. In this book, I have kept the commonly used English translation of the title of the *Satipaṭṭhānasutta*, namely, 'Discourse on the foundations of mindfulness' (i.e., *sati+paṭṭhāna*), which is based on canonical commentaries like the *Papañcasūdanī* (Ps I 238). However, other interpretations of this title are also possible; for example, it could be read as *sati-upaṭṭhāna*, meaning 'attendance or presence of mindfulness.' Yet another perspective could be added to the interpretation of these rather unusual elements of the title: in personal correspondence, Royce Wiles informed me that in Jain texts, the related Prakrit terms *uvaṭhāṇa/uvaṭṭhāvaṇa* (and derivatives) refer to the formal induction or initiation into monkhood (Poddar, 2013–2014, vol. 5, 1609); thus, if we draw on these parallels from Jainism—a separate ancient Indian ascetic (*samaṇa*) tradition also active at the time of the Buddha—the title of the *Satipaṭṭhānasutta* could perhaps be understood as an induction or initiation into mindfulness (*sati*), which would present and list all the domains involved in its cultivation.

Let me reemphasise for absolute clarity: Pemasiri Thera did not present the comments here in the format laid out in this book; instead, he gave many series of talks in Sinhala over a number of years. Based on the transcriptions of the oral translations made simultaneously by some Sri Lankan meditators, I chose to restructure the relevant material to present here Pemasiri Thera's thought-provoking comments in the same sequence as found in the Pāli text of the *sutta*. I sincerely hope to have weeded out most of my own or the translators' misunderstandings.

In the Pāli text and the English translation, bold is used to indicate the words and phrases that are expounded in further detail. The comments made by Pemasiri Thera frequently relate to the key Pāli (technical) terms occurring in the *sutta*, with each term usually being discussed under a separate subheading. Some key Pāli terms such as mindfulness, attention, clear comprehension and wisdom are discussed at length and in greater depth, whereas other sections of the text receive rather scant comment, thus reflecting the variable nature and scope of Pemasiri Thera's talks.

Table 1 Outline of the *Satipaṭṭhānasutta* indicating terms and phrases commented on in this book.

I Introducing the four foundations of mindfulness (*cattāro satipaṭṭhānā*)
- Mindful (*satimā*)
- Four foundations of mindfulness (*cattāro satipaṭṭhānā*)
- Contemplating (*ānupassī*)
- Abides (*viharati*)
- Ardent (*ātāpī*)
- Clearly comprehending (*sampajāno*)
- Having abandoned desires and discontent in regard to the world (*vineyya loke abhijjhādomanassaṃ*)

II Contemplation of the body (*kāyānupassanā*)

II 1 Mindfulness of breathing (*ānāpānasati*)
- Contemplating the body (*kāyānupassī*)
- Gone to the forest (*araññagato*)
- Having folded his legs crosswise (*pallaṅkaṃ ābhujitvā*)
- In front (*parimukham satim upaṭṭhapetvā*)
- He knows (*pajānāti*)
- Experiencing the whole body (*sabbakāyapaṭisaṃvedī*)
- He trains (*sikkhati*)
- Calming the body formations (*passambhayaṃ kāyasaṅkhāra*)

Recurring passage indicating the ways to approach the contemplation
- Internally (*ajjhattam*), externally (*bahiddhā*) and internally and externally (*ajjhattabahiddhā*)
- Contemplating the arising of phenomena (*samudayadhammānupassī*), contemplating the passing away of phenomena (*vayadhammānupassī*) and contemplating the arising and passing away of phenomena (*samudayavayadhammānupassī*)
- To the extent necessary for knowledge and mindfulness (*yāvadeva ñāṇamattāya patissatimattāya*)

II 2 Ways of movement (*iriyāpatha*)
- Walking (*gacchanto*), standing (*ṭhito*), sitting (*nisinno*) and lying down (*sayāno*)
- Recurring passage

II 3 Clear comprehension (*sampajañña*) of bodily activities
- Acts with clear comprehension (*sampajānakārī*)
- Recurring passage

II 4 Reflection on the troublesomeness (*paṭikkūlamanasikāra*) of the body
- Troublesomeness (*paṭikkūla*) of the body
- Recurring passage

II 5 Reflection on the four elements (*catudhātumanasikāra*)
- Earth element (*paṭhavīdhātu*), water element (*āpodhātu*), fire element (*tejodhātu*) and air element (*vāyodhātu*)
- Recurring passage

II 6 Nine cemetery contemplations (*navasīvathikā*)
- Approaches (*upasaṃharati*)
- Nine recurring passages (each following a contemplation)

III Contemplation of feeling (*vedanānupassanā*)
- Pleasant feeling (*sukhavedanā*) and unpleasant feeling (*dukkhavedanā*)
- Neither-unpleasant-nor-pleasant feeling (*adukkhamasukhavedanā*)
- Worldly (*sāmisa*) and unworldly (*nirāmisa*) feeling
- Recurring passage

IV Contemplation of the mind (*cittānupassanā*)
Mind (*citta*)
Mind with desire (*sarāgacitta*) and mind without desire (*vītarāgacitta*)
Mind with aversion (*sadosacitta*) and mind without aversion (*vītadosacitta*)
Mind with delusion (*samohacitta*) and mind without delusion (*vītamohacitta*)
Contracted mind (*saṅkhittacitta*) and distracted mind (*vikkhittacitta*)
Exalted mind (*mahaggatacitta*) and unexalted mind (*amahaggatacitta*)
Surpassable mind (*sa-uttaracitta*) and unsurpassable mind (*anuttaracitta*)
Concentrated mind (*samāhitacitta*) and unconcentrated mind (*asamāhitacitta*)
Liberated mind (*vimuttacitta*) and unliberated mind (*avimuttacitta*)
Recurring passage
V Contemplation of phenomena (*dhammānupassanā*)
V 1 Five hindrances (*pañca nīvaraṇāni*)
Contemplating phenomena (*dhammānupassī*)
Sense desire (*kāmacchanda*)
Ill will (*vyāpāda*)
Sloth and torpor (*thīnamiddha*)
Restlessness and worry (*uddhaccakukkucca*)
Doubt (*vicikicchā*)
Recurring passage
V 2 Five aggregates of clinging (*pañcas'upādānakkhandhā*)
Five aggregates (*pañca khandhā*) and the five aggregates of clinging (*pañcas'upādānakkhandhā*)
Materiality (*rūpa*)
Feeling (*vedanā*) and perception (*saññā*)
Mental formations (*saṅkhāra*) and consciousness (*viññāṇa*)
Recurring passage
V 3 Six sense spheres (*cha āyatanāni*)
Sense spheres (*āyatana*)
Fetter (*saṃyojana*)
Ten fetters (*saṃyojana*)
Recurring passage
V 4 Seven factors of awakening (*satta bojjhaṅgā*)
Seven factors of awakening (*satta bojjhaṅgā*)
Mindfulness factor of awakening (*satisambojjhaṅga*)
Investigation-of-*dhammas* factor of awakening (*dhammavicayasambojjhaṅga*)
Energy factor of awakening (*viriyasambojjhaṅga*)
Joy factor of awakening (*pītisambojjhaṅga*)
Tranquillity factor of awakening (*passaddhisambojjhaṅga*)
Concentration factor of awakening (*samādhisambojjhaṅga*)
Equanimity factor of awakening (*upekkhāsambojjhaṅga*)
Recurring passage
V 5 Four noble truths (*cattāri ariyasaccāni*)
Four noble truths (*cattāri ariyasaccāni*)
Suffering (*dukkha*)
Origin of suffering (*dukkhasamudayo*)
Cessation of suffering (*dukkhanirodho*)
Path leading to the cessation of suffering (*dukkhanirodhagāminī paṭipadā*)
Moral virtue (*sīla*)
Wisdom (*paññā*)
Meditation (*samādhi*)
Recurring passage
VI Conclusion

— I —

Introducing the Four Foundations of Mindfulness (*Cattāro Satipaṭṭhānā*)

Evaṃ me sutaṃ. Ekaṃ samayaṃ Bhagavā Kurūsu viharati Kammāssadhammaṃ nāma Kurūnaṃ nigamo. Tatra kho Bhagavā bhikkhū amantesi Bhikkhavo ti. Bhadante ti te bhikkhū Bhagavato paccassosum. Bhagavā etadavoca:

Ekāyano ayaṃ bhikkhave maggo sattānaṃ visuddhiyā sokapariddavānaṃ samatikkamāya dukkha-domanassānaṃ atthagamāya ñāyassa adhigamāya nibbānassa sacchikiriyāya yadidaṃ ***cattāro sati-paṭṭhānā****. Katame cattāro? Idha bhikkhave bhikkhu kāye kāy****ānupassī viharati ātāpī sampajāno satimā vineyya loke abhijjhādomanassaṃ****, vedanāsu vedanānupassī viharati ātāpī sampajāno satimā vineyya loke abhijjhādomanassaṃ, citte cittānupassī viharati ātāpī sampajāno satimā vineyya loke abhijjhādomanassaṃ, dhammesu dhammānupassī viharati ātāpī sampajāno satimā vineyya loke abhijjhādomanassaṃ.*

Thus have I heard. Once the Blessed One was staying in the Kuru country, in a town of the Kurus called Kammāsadhamma. There he addressed the monks thus: 'Monks.' 'Venerable sir,' they replied. The Blessed One said this:

> 'Monks, this is the direct path for the purification of beings, for the overcoming of sorrow and lamentation, for the disappearance of suffering and grief, for the attainment of the right path, for the realisation of *nibbāna*, namely, the **four foundations of mindfulness**. What are the four? Here, monks, a monk **abides contemplating** the body as a body, **ardent, clearly comprehending, mindful, having abandoned desires and discontent in regard to the world.** He abides contemplating feelings as feelings, ardent, clearly comprehending, mindful, having abandoned desires and discontent in regard to the world. He abides contemplating mind as mind, ardent, clearly comprehending, mindful, having abandoned desires and discontent in regard to the world. He abides contemplating phenomena as phenomena, ardent, clearly comprehending, mindful, having abandoned desires and discontent in regard to the world.'

Pemasiri Thera's commentary

'Mindful' (*satimā*)

As the entire *Satipaṭṭhānasutta* talks about mindfulness (*sati*), a few clarifications are first needed about this essential concept. Mindfulness (*sati*) only occurs in mental states that are wholesome (*kusala*), without greed (*lobha*) or aversion (*dosa*).[1] Today, mindfulness (*sati*) is often

1. Here Pemasiri Thera refers to the Theravāda *Abhidhamma* tradition in which mindfulness (*sati*) is listed among the wholesome mental concomitants (*cetasika*), which only occur with wholesome (*kusala*) mental states (Dhs 9). In summary, the Theravāda *Abhidhamma* systematically presents the structural foundations

understood and taught as a practice of paying attention to one's actions and thoughts from moment to moment; however, from the Buddhist perspective, this would actually be training in attention (*manasikāra*),[2] just attentively noting one object after another as they arise. Although such noting practice is not yet mindfulness (*sati*), it should be stressed that training in attention (*manasikāra*) is an important preliminary aid for the subsequent emergence of mindfulness (*sati*).[3] Attention (*manasikāra*) is like the support needed by a child who cannot yet walk on her or his own, whereas mindfulness (*sati*) is the stage at which the child starts walking. When one is well trained in paying attention (*manasikāra*), mindfulness (*sati*) may simultaneously occur. In other words, after continuously training in and practising the faculty of attention (*manasikāra*), the time may come when the mind reverts to the object of attention without greed (*lobha*) or aversion (*dosa*)—and at this point, mindfulness (*sati*) can be said to have arisen (along with attention). Thus, mindfulness (*sati*) and paying attention (*manasikāra*) to the present moment are two different things. During the early stages of meditation, one develops attention (*manasikāra*), which may gradually produce some tranquillity (*passaddhi*) and focus or one-pointedness (*ekaggatā*) and after some time, mindfulness (*sati*) may arise; in this case, the practice is inclined towards concentration (*samādhi*) and eventually meditative absorption (*jhāna*) may be reached.[4] If attention (*manasikāra*) and mindfulness (*sati*) are well established and are then joined by clear comprehension (*sampajañña*), the practice becomes insight (*vipassanā*) meditation.[5] So the establishment of mindfulness (*satipaṭṭhāna*) has two aspects to it—concentration (*samādhi*) and insight (*vipassanā*).

---

of Buddhist analysis of human cognitive processes; in doing this, it identifies a number of fundamental components called *dhammas* that are involved in or condition all mental and physical phenomena arising moment to moment. The entire Abhidhammic structure is presented under four overarching categories: the mind (*citta*), mental constituents or concomitants (*cetasika*), materiality (*rūpa*) and *nibbāna*. The mind (*citta*) is defined as the 'knowing' of an object (As 63); it arises every moment in conjunction with a group of mental concomitants (*cetasika*), which determine how the object is known. The *Abhidhamma* lists over fifty such mental concomitants (*cetasika*) that can occur in various groupings and are classified, on an ethical basis, as wholesome, unwholesome or variable. Wholesome concomitants always appear together in a group and are not compatible with unwholesome ones and vice versa. Mindfulness (*sati*) is listed as one of the wholesome concomitants (*cetasika*), always arising with other wholesome ones such as trust (*saddhā*), non-greed (*alobha*), non-aversion (*adosa*) or peace (*passaddhi*). All the mental concomitants (*cetasika*) are listed in Table 6 below. For further details on the Theravāda *Abhidhamma*, see Nyanaponika (1965), Bodhi (1993), Nyanatiloka (2008) and Karunadasa (2010).

2. Attention (*manasikāra*) makes the mind attentive to the object. It is described in the *Atthasālinī* (As 133) and *Visuddhimagga* (Vism 466) as 'making (i.e., placing) in the mind' (*manamhi kāro*); its characteristic is to drive the associated states towards the object, its function is to link the associated states to the object and it is manifested as facing the object (Vism 466: *So sāraṇalakkhaṇo, sampayuttānaṃ ārammaṇe saṃyojanaraso, ārammaṇābhimukhabhāvapaccupaṭṭhāno*).

3. Mindfulness (*sati*) is presented in the *Visuddhimagga* as remembering; its characteristic is not wobbling, its function is not forgetting and it is manifested as protection (Vism 464: *Saranti tāya, sayaṃ vā sarati, saraṇamattam eva vā, esā ti sati. Sā apilāpanalakkhaṇā, asammoharasā, ārakkhapaccupaṭṭhānā*).

4. The term *jhāna* refers to the stages of high concentration when the mind is absorbed in the object of meditation. Descriptions of the absorptions (*jhāna*) in the realm of form (*rūpa*) as well as formless (*arūpa*) absorptions (*jhāna*) and their components are found in many canonical texts (e.g., M I 40-41; A IV 438–448; S IV 217; D I 73–74; Dhs 31–56). A comprehensive presentation of the absorptions (*jhāna*) is given in the *Visuddhimagga* (Vism 122–169; 326–340); for an overview, see Bodhi (1993, 52–64) and Bucknell (1993).

5. For a discussion on the meaning of the term 'clear comprehension' (*sampajañña*), see Chapter I, under the subheading 'Clearly comprehending (*sampajāno*).'

The foundation of mindfulness (*satipaṭṭhāna*) is only established when attention (*manasikāra*) and mindfulness (*sati*) work together—it is as if attention (*manasikāra*) is in the centre with mindfulness (*sati*) surrounding it on all sides, or put another way, the strengthening of attention (*manasikāra*) allows for the possibility of mindfulness (*sati*) to arise. Without strong attention (*manasikāra*), there is no basis on which mindfulness (*sati*) can be established. Attention (*manasikāra*) is thus the very foundation on which mindfulness (*sati*) is built, with the latter acting on the former as a lid on top of a bowl. Attention (*manasikāra*) is a mental factor or concomitant (*cetasika*) with no inclination towards wholesome (*kusala*) or unwholesome (*akusala*) states; it is defined as a neutral mental concomitant.[6] When mindfulness (*sati*) is absent, attention (*manasikāra*) can incline towards unwholesome (*akusala*) states; for example, even a thief can have strong attention (*manasikāra*), but it arises in conjunction with greed or fear.

When attention inclines towards wholesome (*kusala*) states, then mindfulness (*sati*) may occur, and at such moments, unwholesome states are (temporarily) abandoned and wholesome ones developed. Mindfulness (*sati*) is like the guardian at a city gate who checks everyone wanting to enter;[7] his only duty is to remain wakeful at the gate, as he does not go inside the city or outside onto the road. If a robber comes and sees the guardian at the gate, he will go away and even if he repeatedly returns, he will eventually stop coming. But if the robber goes through the gate without being caught by the guardian, then many more robbers may enter. Thus, the function of mindfulness (*sati*) is not limited to a bare noting of the object as it arises but, importantly, knowing whether the object arises with or without greed (*lobha*) or aversion (*dosa*).

As soon as any sense of a person or an 'I' is present, mindfulness (*sati*) is lost. When one thinks '*I* see, *I* hear, *I* am feeling, *I* am not concentrated, *my* mind is wandering, *my* meditation practice is not good', an 'I' has arisen, has been created and at that very moment, mindfulness (*sati*) is not present, it has gone. When mindfulness (*sati*) is absent, greed (*lobha*) and aversion (*dosa*) tend to arise and the meditator may say: '*I* should calm down, *I* should be concentrated' and usually focuses, in response, on the body, the breathing or some other object. Then the subtle aspects of the body and mind cannot be seen and the mind moves away from contemplation and insight meditation (*vipassanā*) and instead focuses on the object of meditation, thus engaging in calm meditation (*samatha*). But if mindfulness (*sati*) is present—and thus no 'I' arises or is created in this process—clear comprehension (*sampajañña*) may arise, which apprehends or knows the

6. In cognitive processes (as analysed by the Theravāda *Abhidhamma*), attention (*manasikāra*) is present at every moment of cognition, in any mental state whether wholesome or not; by contrast, mindfulness (*sati*) only occurs in wholesome, skilful (*kusala*) states (see Table 6; Vism 466; Bodhi 1993, 79). The aim of mindfulness practice then, as presented in the Pāli canon, is not solely paying attention as such but rather cultivating (*bhāvanā*) skilful 'wise attention' (*yoniso manasikāra*), which arises together with wholesome mental components and is the foundation for wisdom (*paññā*) to arise. For example, it is said in the *Mahāpadānasutta* that wisdom (*paññā*) is founded on wise attention (*yoniso manasikāra*), leading to an understanding of dependent origination (*paṭiccasamuppāda*) (D II 33: *yoniso manasikārā ahu paññāya abhisamayo: Bhave kho asati jāti na hoti, bhave nirodhā jāti nirodho ti*).

7. This metaphor is frequently used in the Pāli canon; for example, in the *Nagarasutta*: 'Like the guardian in the king's town who is skilled, clever and intelligent, one who keeps out strangers and lets enter the well-known in order to protect the inhabitants and ward off outsiders, so too, monks, the noble disciple is mindful, endowed with supreme mindfulness and discrimination' (A IV 110–111: *eyyathā pi bhikkhave rañño paccantime nagare dovāriko hoti paṇḍito vyatto medhāvī aññātānaṃ nivāretā ñātānaṃ pavesetā abbhantarānaṃ guttiyā bāhirānaṃ paṭighātāya, evam eva kho bhikkhave ariyasāvako satimā hoti paramena satinepakkena samannāgato*). See also the metaphor of the town in the *Kiṃsukasutta* (S IV 194.)

aggregates (*khandha*),[8] elements (*dhātu*)[9] and six sense spheres (*āyatana*)[10] in the process of cognition.[11] Clear comprehension (*sampajañña*) is built on or arises through mindfulness (*sati*). When clear comprehension (*sampajañña*) is present, dependent origination (*paṭiccasamuppāda*)[12] can be understood, views can be purified and insight meditation (*vipassanā*) can start developing.

It can be said that clear comprehension (*sampajañña*) is the first stage of wisdom (*paññā*).[13] When mindfulness (*sati*) is established, concentration (*samādhi*) increases and clear comprehension (*sampajañña*) can emerge. At that point, the meditator has no expectations and so can clearly note any phenomenon that arises and passes away with concentration (*samādhi*), clear comprehension (*sampajañña*), energy (*viriya*) and trust (*saddhā*). Then the right condi-

---

8. The five aggregates (*khandha*) are materiality (*rūpa*), feeling (*vedanā*), perception (*saññā*), mental formations (*saṅkhāra*) and consciousness (*viññāṇa*).

9. The term *dhātu* has a very broad semantic range (DP, *s.v.*); it is explained in the *Bahudhātukasutta* (M III 61–63) in several ways:

   1) eighteen elements of cognition: i.e., the elements of the five physical senses with their respective objects and consciousness as well as the mind element (*manodhātu*) with mental objects (*dhammadhātu*) and mind-consciousness elements (*manoviññāṇadhātu*);
   2) six elements: i.e., the elements of earth (*paṭhavīdhātu*), water (*āpodhātu*), air (*vāyodhātu*), fire (*tejodhātu*), space (*ākāsadhātu*) and consciousness (*viññāṇadhātu*);
   3) three elements: i.e., the elements of the sense sphere (*kāmadhātu*), fine material (*rūpadhātu*) and immaterial elements (*arūpadhātu*); or
   4) two elements: i.e., the conditioned (*saṅkhatā*) and unconditioned (*asaṅkhatā*) elements.

   In the *Satipaṭṭhānasutta*, the term *dhātu* occurs in the section on the contemplation of the body (*kāyānupassanā*) as four basic qualities of materiality or elements (*dhātu*), namely, the earth element (*paṭhavīdhātu*), water element (*āpodhātu*), fire element (*tejodhātu*) and air element (*vāyodhātu*) (M I 157). For a more detailed analysis of the elements, see the *Vibhaṅga* (Vibh 82–98) and *Visuddhimagga* (Vism 484–490).

10. The six sense spheres (*saḷāyatana*) encompass the six sense organs and six sense objects: eye (*cakkhu*) and visible form (*rūpa*); ear (*sota*) and sounds (*sadda*); nose (*ghāna*) and smell (*gandhā*); tongue (*jivhā*) and taste (*rasā*); the body (*kāya*) and tangible object (*phoṭṭhabba*); and the mind (*mano*) and mental phenomena (*dhamma*). See the *Saḷāytanasaṃyutta* (S IV 1–203).

11. The *Papañcasūdanī* commentary explains that the contemplation of the aggregates (*khandha*), elements (*dhātu*), sense spheres (*āyatana*), three characteristics (i.e., impermanence (*anicca*), unsatisfactoriness (*dukkha*) and non-self (*anattā*)) and foundations of mindfulness (*satipaṭṭhāna*) are the 'highest teaching' (*paramatthadesanā*) of the Buddha (Ps 137: *Aniccaṃ dukkhaṃ anattā, khandhā dhātū āyatanāni satipaṭṭhānā ti evarūpā paramatthadesanā*). For details, see Chapters V.2. Five aggregates and V.3. Six sense spheres.

12. The Buddhist doctrine referred to as 'dependent origination' (*paṭiccasamuppāda*) is fundamental to understanding the comments and clarifications put forward by Pemasiri Thera throughout this book. This doctrine is usually presented in Pāli texts as the following twelvefold formula: conditioned by (1) ignorance (*avijjā*) are (2) mental formations (*saṅkhāra*); conditioned by mental formations is (3) consciousness (*viññāṇa*); conditioned by consciousness are (4) mentality and materiality (*nāmarūpa*); conditioned by mentality and materiality are (5) sense bases (*saḷāyatana*); conditioned by sense bases is (6) contact (*phassa*); conditioned by contact is (7) feeling (*vedanā*); conditioned by feeling is (8) craving (*taṇhā*); conditioned by craving is (9) clinging (*upādāna*); conditioned by clinging is (10) becoming (*bhava*); conditioned by becoming is (11) birth (*jāti*); conditioned by birth are (12) ageing, death, suffering, lamentation, pain, displeasure and despair (*jarāmaraṇaṃ sokaparidevadukkhadomanassupāyāsā*) (S II 1).

13. The Pāli word *paññā* is described in the Buddhist texts in many ways (see PED, *s.v.*); it is often presented as the mental component that understands the three characteristics (*tilakkhaṇa*), namely, impermanence (*anicca*), unsatisfactoriness (*dukkha*) and non-self (*anattā*) (S V 199; Vism 436–437); or it is equated with the understanding of the four noble truths (M I 292; M III 245; S II 32). For a detailed discussion on *paññā*, see Chapter V.4. Seven factors of awakening, under the subheading 'Investigation-of-*dhammas* factor of awakening (*dhammavicayasambojjhaṅga*).'

tions are set up for wisdom (*paññā*) to arise.[14] To illustrate this, let us imagine that we have to pass a thread through the eye of a needle.[15] The whole needle refers to trust (*saddhā*), the needle's body to energy (*viriya*), the needle's eye to mindfulness (*sati*) and the thread to wisdom (*paññā*).[16] With right concentration and attention, the thread (i.e., wisdom) will pass through the eye of the needle; however, this will only happen if there is no obstruction or object blocking the eye of the needle. In this case, it is mindfulness (*sati*) that prevents obstructions. Only when mindfulness (*sati*) has no chosen object can wisdom (*paññā*) arise. However, if the meditator attempts to cultivate mindfulness (*sati*) along with a chosen object, the meditation practice becomes too gross to allow wisdom (*paññā*) to emerge; or in the words of the metaphor, the thread is too thick to pass through the eye of the needle.

To recapitulate, when mindfulness (*sati*) is present, there is no greed (*lobha*), no aversion (*dosa*), no expectation. As the meditator understands that whatever arises also passes away, she or he does not attempt to remain with an object. Only if the meditator subsequently directs thought towards the arisen object and holds onto it, does an idea occur that the object persists, and consequently, the sense of 'I' arises. For example, suppose I am putting a pen on the table with full attention (*manasikāra*) being paid to the actual movement of the hand, touching the pen, picking it up, lifting it, moving the arm and placing it on the table. Although I put the pen on the table with full attention (*manasikāra*), I may act, for example, with the thought that I am leaving the pen there in order to use it tomorrow. In this case, though I have strong attention (*manasikāra*), mindfulness (*sati*) has not arisen since a 'self' or an 'I' was created in relation to this act, projected to tomorrow; thus, a 'future' was created. Let us say that tomorrow I will be here to teach Dhamma, but the pen is missing. Consequently, I may become upset and negative states may arise in the mind; at that moment I will create a 'yesterday.' Thus, today's thought that this pen is put here for the future also creates the past. Although the pen may have been left on the table with a wholesome purpose, such as using it to write Dhamma teachings on the board the following day, it may bring about unwholesome states, create an 'I' and construct both tomorrow and yesterday.

But if the pen is placed on the table with mindfulness (*sati*), without a purpose, without the additional thought of 'I' and 'pen,' there is only an activity, a wholesome process and therefore no tomorrow and no yesterday are created. This is why it is said that mindfulness (*sati*) does not have a chosen object; it is without greed (*lobha*) or aversion (*dosa*) and without the concept of an 'I' or a 'pen.' There is just an act or process without pointing anywhere, not to the future, past or anywhere else.

As I said before, all wholesome states involve mindfulness (*sati*).[17] The development of virtue (*sīla*) or generosity (*dāna*) is accompanied by mindfulness (*sati*) provided that the mind is free

14. Here Pemasiri Thera refers to the five faculties (*indriya*)—i.e., (1) trust (*saddhā*), (2) energy (*viriya*), (3) mindfulness (*sati*), (4) concentration (*samādhi*) and (5) wisdom (*paññā*)—and explains how the first four should be developed and well established to allow the fifth, wisdom (*paññā*), to emerge.

15. The metaphor of the thread is used several times in the Pāli texts: for example, the *Sāmaññaphalasutta* (D I 76), where the purified and concentrated mind is compared to a string threaded through a perfectly clear and pure gem.

16. In this metaphor, Pemasiri Thera again refers to the role of mindfulness (*sati*) in the development of the five faculties.

17. In the Theravāda tradition, mindfulness (*sati*) is considered one of the so-called universal good or beautiful (*sobhanasādhāraṇa*) mental concomitants (*cetasika*) that accompany every wholesome mental state (Dhs 9; cf. Bodhi 1993, 79).

from greed (*lobha*), aversion (*dosa*) and delusion (*moha*) at that particular moment. However, if the giver has an expectation of gaining something from an act of generosity, then mindfulness (*sati*) is absent. Mindfulness (*sati*) is also present in the practice of calm meditation (*samatha*); in this case, greed (*lobha*) and aversion (*dosa*) are temporarily absent or suppressed to a greater extent than in the case of generosity (*dāna*) or virtue (*sīla*), and mindfulness (*sati*) thus advances more deeply and continuously. Therefore, mindfulness (*sati*) is like a vessel that contains all wholesome states such as virtue (*sīla*), generosity (*dāna*), as well as calm (*samatha*) and insight (*vipassanā*) meditation.

In everyday worldly life, one experiences many wholesome states when fulfilling one's responsibilities, taking care of elders and helping people in need. In the act of generosity (*dāna*), for example, when offering food, mindfulness (*sati*) is usually only connected with the act of offering, although it cannot be said that all bodily activities involved in the process of preparing the food were done mindfully. For mindfulness (*sati*) to emerge in every activity or process, the four foundations of mindfulness (*satipaṭṭhāna*)[18] should be cultivated, which means that all bodily activities and mental states are to be wholesome, without greed (*lobha*) or aversion (*dosa*). This practice of mindfulness is then called right mindfulness (*sammā sati*).

Every action performed or process experienced with mindfulness (*sati*) eventually leads to liberation (*nibbāna*). For example, let us say that the sun is *nibbāna* and a dew drop on the tip of a grass blade is mindfulness (*sati*). In the early morning, the rising sun falls on a dew drop and makes it shine radiantly. Despite the minute quantity of water, it shines with the brightness of the sun. The sunlight may fall on other dewdrops as well, but they may not shine because dust or mud contaminates them. Similarly, mindfulness (*sati*) may arise for some time with virtue (*sīla*), generosity (*dāna*) and other wholesome acts, and the mind may be temporarily free from greed (*lobha*) or aversion (*dosa*), but it can be intermittently contaminated with other unwholesome components such as delusion (*moha*). When the four foundations of mindfulness (*satipaṭṭhāna*) are practised properly, performed without any expectations, mindfulness (*sati*) is not contaminated by unwholesomeness. This is therefore called right mindfulness (*sammā sati*).

To summarise, in the initial stages, only attention (*manasikāra*) is practised, which supports the development of focus or one-pointedness (*ekaggatā*). If mindfulness (*sati*) joins attention (*manasikāra*) and one-pointedness (*ekaggatā*), the practice is called calm (*samatha*) meditation, which can lead to meditative absorptions (*jhāna*). The meditator becomes very calm and content and has no problems in the mind, because no tendencies towards greed (*lobha*) and aversion (*dosa*) arise. If mindfulness (*sati*) is joined by clear comprehension (*sampajañña*), the meditator begins to clearly perceive every phenomenon in a state of change, while any ideas or thoughts referring to oneself or the sense of an 'I' no longer occur in the mind; this stage is called contemplation (*anupassanā*),[19] and the practice becomes insight meditation (*vipassanā*).

Some meditators begin their practice with calm (*samatha*) meditation and others with insight (*vipassanā*) meditation. Those who have been practising insight (*vipassanā*) for a long time cannot usually begin with calm (*samatha*) meditation straight away, because the old habits of insight keep coming back. They are also often reluctant to start with calm (*samatha*)

18. The four foundations of mindfulness include mindfulness of the body (*kāya*), feeling (*vedanā*), the mind (*citta*) and phenomena (*dhamma*). For a further discussion, see Chapter I, under the subheading 'Four foundations of mindfulness (*cattāro satipaṭṭhānā*).'

19. For a discussion on the term 'contemplation' (*anupassanā*), see Chapter I, under the subheading 'Contemplation' (*anupassanā*).

meditation because the concentration (*samādhi*) attained through well-established insight (*vipassanā*) meditation is stronger and more stable than that achieved through calm (*samatha*) meditation. Thus, it might take the practitioner some time to settle into the new practice of calm (*samatha*) meditation.

When the meditative absorptions (*jhāna*) are cultivated through the practice of the foundations of mindfulness (*satipaṭṭhāna*), the meditator can see the drawbacks associated with a particular absorption (*jhāna*) and then moves to higher stages up to the final liberation. This is described in many *suttas* such as the *Tapussasutta*, where the Buddha narrates how, while still a *bodhisatta*, he saw and understood the drawbacks of even the highest absorption (*jhāna*) of neither-perception-nor-non-perception (*nevasaññāsaññāyatana*) and thus says:

> Then, Ānanda, by completely transcending the base of neither-perception-nor-non-perception, I entered and dwelled in the cessation of feeling and perception (*saññāvedayitanirodha*) and having seen with wisdom, my taints (*āsava*)[20] were completely eradicated. (A IV 448)[21]

Without practising the foundations of mindfulness (*satipaṭṭhāna*), the meditator becomes too attached to the pleasures derived from the absorptions (*jhāna*); this is why attachment to the absorptions (*jhāna*) is called a fetter (*saṃyojana*).[22] Absorptions (*jhāna*) developed through insight (*vipassanā*) meditation can lead to liberation. Therefore, it is usually easier for both the meditator and the teacher to introduce calm (*samatha*) meditation after developing a solid practice of insight (*vipassanā*) rather than vice versa. Those who have trained in calm (*samatha*) meditation for a long time and achieved a high level of tranquillity or meditative absorption (*jhāna*) often find it very difficult, or even impossible, to practise insight (*vipassanā*) meditation due to their enjoyment of the benefits of calm (*samatha*) practice such as one-pointedness (*ekaggatā*), happiness (*sukha*) and equanimity (*upekkhā*) and also because they do not yet know about the accomplishments and rewards of insight (*vipassanā*) meditation.

In both practices, a neutral mental state is sought. It is difficult to cognise a neutral state, as usually only wholesome or unwholesome states can be clearly observed. In the case of calm (*samatha*) meditation, in the state of absorption (*jhāna*), a sort of neutral state is experienced because the mental formations (*saṅkhāra*) function at a minimal level, the person called 'I' is temporarily dropped and cause and effect are concealed. On reflection after this experience, the meditator can recognise whether it was an absorption (*jhāna*) or not. Conversely, in insight (*vipassanā*) meditation, at path knowledge (*maggañāṇa*),[23] the person called 'I' is also

20. The term 'taint' (*āsava*) refers to predispositions such as sense desire (*kāma*), becoming (*bhava*), ignorance (*avijjā*) and views (*diṭṭhi*), which obstruct liberation and motivate further existence (see DP, *s.v.*) According to the *Atthasālinī*, the term *āsava* refers to deeply rooted corruptions, defilements, or 'intoxicants,' which flow through the five senses and the mind (As 48).

21. A IV 448: *So kho ahaṃ Ānanda aparena samayena sabbaso nevasaññānāsaññāyatanaṃ samatikkamma saññāvedayitanirodhaṃ upasampajja viharāmi, paññāya ca me disvā āsavā parikkhayaṃ agamaṃsu.*

22. Pāli canonical texts (e.g., S V 61) often list the following ten fetters (*saṃyojana*): (1) personality or identity view (*sakkāyadiṭṭhi*), (2) doubt (*vicikicchā*), (3) attachment to rites and rituals (*sīlabbataparāmāsa*), (4) sense desire (*kāmacchanda*), (5) ill will (*vyāpāda*), (6) desire for material existence (*rūparāga*), (7) desire for immaterial existence (*arūparāga*), (8) conceit (*māna*), (9) restlessness (*uddhacca*) and (10) ignorance (*avijjā*). For a discussion on the fetters, see Chapter V.3. Six sense spheres, under the subheading 'Fetter (*saṃyojana*).'

23. Path knowledge (*maggañāṇa*) occurs when insight (*vipassanā*) developed through wisdom (*paññā*) deepens and matures and a supramundane mind state (*maggacitta*) emerges, taking *nibbāna* as its object. Four progressing stages of the supramundane path knowledges are listed in the texts, namely: (1) stream entry (*sotāpatti*), (2) once-returning (*sakadāgāmi*), (3) non-returning (*anāgāmi*) and (4) arahantship (*arahatta*). For further

dropped and cause and effect stop functioning. This is also recognised by the meditator on reflection after the experience. The difference between the experience of absorption (*jhāna*) in calm (*samatha*) meditation and the path (*magga*) in insight (*vipassanā*) meditation is that feeling (*vedanā*) and perception (*saññā*) are temporarily concealed in the former, whereas they are completely absent in the latter.[24]

After prolonged training, some meditators can become equally well versed in both methods—i.e., calm (*samatha*) and insight (*vipassanā*) meditation—and can easily alternate between the two; for example, they dedicate one hour to calm and another hour to insight meditation throughout the day. Such a meditator is called *yuganaddha*,[25] i.e., one who practises both *samatha* and *vipassanā* congruously. In the *Yuganaddhasutta*, four possible paths for attaining liberation are listed, namely:

1. the path that begins with calm (*samatha*) and then develops insight (*vipassanā*);
2. the path that begins with insight (*vipassanā*) and then develops calm (*samatha*);
3. the development of both calm and insight (*samathavipassanaṃ yuganaddhaṃ*); and
4. the path that involves restlessness in the mind concerning the *dhamma* (*dhammuddhaccamānasa*) until, with practice, it settles down.[26]

In the fourth type of practice, the meditator has restlessness (*uddhacca*) in the mind in regard to the insight knowledges (*vipassanāñāṇa*); this happens when a kind of conceit (*māna*) arises along with the ten corruptions of insight (*dasa vipassan'upakilesā*), which can prevent the meditator from progressing.[27] This particular kind of restlessness occurs at some stage between the insight knowledge of arising and passing away (*udayabbayañāṇa*) and the knowledge of equanimity of formations (*saṅkhār'upekkhāñāṇa*), most commonly during the former. It is important that the teacher recognises this type of practitioner and helps them to move forward.

For the cultivation of both types of meditation—i.e., calm (*samatha*) and insight (*vipassanā*)—it is essential to establish mindfulness (*sati*). In both practices, the function of mindfulness (*sati*) is to keep the mind free from greed (*lobha*) and aversion (*dosa*). However, mindfulness (*sati*) functions differently in the two practices: in insight (*vipassanā*) meditation, it can arise along with wisdom (*paññā*), whereas in calm (*samatha*) meditation, it does not. In the case of insight (*vipassanā*) practice, for example, mindfulness (*sati*) may recognise restlessness (*uddhacca*), that is, a scattered state of mind. When the meditator cannot remain with or grasp an object due to restlessness, she or he starts to realise that this is because of impermanence (*anicca*). Then

details, see the *Visuddhimagga* (Vism 672–697). At each successive stage, a number of fetters (*saṃyojana*) are eradicated; see Chapter V.3 The six sense-bases, under the subheading 'Fetter (*saṃyojana*).'

24. This distinction is mentioned in several *suttas* such as the *Ariyapariyesanāsutta* (M I 160–175) or the *Tapussasutta* (A IV 438–448).

25. *Yuganaddha* literally means that the two practices are put under one yoke.

26. A II 157: *Idha āvuso bhikkhū samathapubbaṅgamaṃ vipassanaṃ bhāveti, tassa samathapubbaṅgamaṃ vipassanaṃ bhāvayato maggo sañjāyati. ... Puna ca paraṃ āvuso bhikkhu vipassanāpubbaṅgamaṃ samathaṃ bhāveti, tassa vipassanāpubbaṅgamaṃ samathaṃ bhāvayato maggo sañjāyati. ... Puna ca paraṃ āvuso bhikkhu samathavipassanāyuganaddhaṃ bhāveti, tassa samathavipassanaṃ yuganaddhaṃ bhāvayato maggo sañjāyati. ... Puna ca paraṃ āvuso bhikkhuno dhammuddhaccaviggahītamanā hoti, so āvuso samayo yan taṃ cittaṃ ajjhattaṃ yeva santiṭṭhati sannisīdati ekodihoti samādhīyati, tassa maggo sañjāyati.*

27. The interpretation of the fourth path is problematic. Pemasiri Thera here follows the commentaries that link it to the ten corruptions of insight (*dasa vipassan'upakilesā*), which are described in more detail in the *Visuddhimagga* (Vism 633–638).

the meditator understands that despite wanting to remain with the object of meditation, this cannot occur because of non-self (*anattā*). Following this insight, disappointment may arise in the meditator, which means that she or he experiences unsatisfactoriness (*dukkha*). To see these three characteristics (*tilakkhaṇa*) (i.e., impermanence, non-self and unsatisfactoriness) within restlessness (*uddhacca*), the meditator must develop strong and sharp mindfulness (*sati*). The practitioner who clearly sees and comprehends these three characteristics in restlessness (*uddhacca*) can become an *arahant*. In other words, when the five hindrances (*pañca nīvaraṇāni*)[28] arise and are recognised by mindfulness (*sati*), this facilitates wisdom (*paññā*) by seeing them as they are and comprehending their three characteristics (*tilakkhaṇa*). Thus, in insight (*vipassanā*) meditation practice, mindfulness (*sati*) creates the necessary space for wisdom (*paññā*), which is the portal for liberation.

'Four foundations of mindfulness' (*cattāro satipaṭṭhānā*)

At the beginning of the *sutta*, it is said that the four foundations of mindfulness (*cattāro satipaṭṭhānā*) are the direct path to liberation from suffering and the realisation of *nibbāna*. Although all wholesome (*kusala*) states of mind like generosity (*dāna*) or virtue (*sīla*) are accompanied by mindfulness (*sati*), they cannot be called the foundations of mindfulness (*satipaṭṭhāna*). When cultivating the four foundations of mindfulness (*cattāro satipaṭṭhānā*), mindfulness (*sati*) must be founded on itself. Irrespective of which of the four domains the practice begins with, mindfulness (*sati*) builds upon and strengthens the preceding moment of mindfulness (*sati*). It is like a mason who lays brick upon brick: the first brick is mindfulness (*sati*), the second brick is mindfulness (*sati*) and the cement in the middle is attention (*manasikāra*), which is called wise attention (*yoniso manasikāra*) in this case.[29] When cultivating the four foundations of mindfulness (*cattāro satipaṭṭhānā*), no object can be seen to persist if perceived with mindfulness (*sati*) and clear comprehension (*sampajañña*), because desires and discontent are abandoned (*vineyya loke abhijjhādomanassaṃ*).

Whatever type of meditation practice one begins with, a precondition is the development of virtue (*sīla*). When virtue (*sīla*) is maintained, the mind becomes calm, at least to some extent. But virtue (*sīla*) alone is not sufficient for the cultivation of mindfulness (*sati*). For the establishment of mindfulness (*satipaṭṭhāna*), an object is initially required for the cultivation of concentration (*samādhi*); hence, one initially practises calm (*samatha*) meditation. Mindfulness of breathing (*ānāpānasati*) or any of the fourteen other objects of contemplation of the body (*kāyānupassanā*)[30]

28. The five hindrances (*nīvaraṇa*) are (1) sensory desire (*kāmacchanda*), (2) ill-will (*vyāpāda*), (3) sloth and torpor (*thīnamiddha*), (4) restlessness and worry (*uddhaccakukkucca*) and (5) doubt (*vicikicchā*).

29. The cultivation of wise attention (*yoniso manasikāra*) is an essential quality on the path to liberation; for example, it is said in the *Sabbāsavasutta* that the deepest defilements, the so-called taints (*āsava*), can be extinguished through wise attention (*yoniso manasikāra*): 'With wise attention, monks, unarisen taints do not arise and arisen taints are abandoned' (M I 7: *yoniso ca bhikkhave manasikaroto anuppannā c'eva āsavā na uppajjanti uppannā ca āsavā pahīyanti*).

30. In the *Satipaṭṭhānasutta*, fourteen areas are listed under the contemplation of the body (*kāyānupassanā*):
    - mindfulness of breathing
    - ways of movement (four postures of the body)
    - clear comprehension of bodily activities
    - reflection on the troublesomeness of the body (thirty-one parts of the body)
    - reflection on the four elements
    - nine cemetery contemplations (M I 56–59).

    For further discussion, see Chapter II. Contemplation of the body (*kāyānupassanā*).

can initially be the object of calm (*samatha*) meditation. Only when clear comprehension (*sampajañña*) is activated does the practice turn towards insight (*vipassanā*) meditation. As clear comprehension (*sampajañña*) strengthens, the meditator begins to see the arising and passing phases of objects. In this transition towards insight (*vipassanā*) meditation, the meditator still sometimes relates to the objects in terms of 'I' but at other times without the sense of self.

For example, if one begins with mindfulness of breathing (*ānāpānasati*), after some time, one will reach a stage described in the *Ānāpānasatisutta* as follows:

> He trains thus: "I shall breathe in tranquillising the body formations," he trains thus: "I shall breathe out tranquillising the body formations." (M III 82)[31]

This means that greed (*lobha*), hatred (*dosa*) and delusion (*moha*) are diminished, and the meditator begins to observe the breath with great tranquillity. At this point, mindfulness (*sati*) is well established, and if clear comprehension (*sampajañña*) has not yet joined mindfulness (*sati*), the practice falls within the domain of calm (*samatha*) meditation. However, if clear comprehension (*sampajañña*) emerges and the meditator begins insight meditation (*vipasssanā*), the practice of the four foundations of mindfulness (*cattāro satipaṭṭhānā*) will lead up to the development of the seven awakening factors (*bojjhaṅga*) and liberation, as said in the *Ānāpānasatisutta*:

> When mindfulness of breathing is repeatedly practised and cultivated, it fulfils the four foundations of mindfulness. When the four foundations of mindfulness are repeatedly practised and cultivated, they fulfil the seven awakening factors. When the seven awakening factors are repeatedly practised and cultivated, they fulfil highest wisdom and liberation. (M III 82)[32]

Mindfulness of breathing (*ānāpānasati*) can thus be the foundation of final liberation. Although the meditation commences with the primary object of breathing (*ānāpānasati*), to cultivate the four foundations of mindfulness (*satipaṭṭhāna*) one should not only remain with the main object but also note all other phenomena as they arise and pass away. The primary object is merely an aid during the initial stages of practice. Many meditators think that it is good to remain with the primary meditation object such as the breath and if pains arise in the body, they consider them to be a drawback in their practice. But the opposite is true; pains are a great gift for the meditator, as they should be patiently noted. If one only stays with the primary object and does not note any other objects, one merely remains at the initial steps in the cultivation of mindfulness of breathing (*ānāpānasati*).

When clear comprehension (*sampajañña*) enters the meditation process, the meditator begins to see the arising and passing away of objects and becomes established in the four foundations of mindfulness (*cattāro satipaṭṭhānā*).[33] Here, the mind is very tranquil, the five hindrances (*pañca nīvaraṇāni*) (i.e., sense desire, ill will, sloth and torpor, restlessness and worry, and

31. M III 82: *Passambhayaṃ kāyasaṃkhāraṃ assasissāmīti sikkhati. Passambhayaṃ kāyasaṃkhāraṃ passasissamīti sikkhati.*

32. M III 82: *Ānāpānasati, bhikkhave, bhāvitā bahulīkatā mahapphalā hoti mahānisaṃsā; ānāpānasati, bhikkhave, bhāvitā bahulīkatā cattāro satipaṭṭhāne paripūreti; cattāro satipaṭṭhānā bhāvitā bahulīkatā satta bojjhaṅge paripūrenti; satta bojjhaṅgā bhāvitā bahulīkatā vijjāvimuttiṃ paripūrenti.*

33. It is frequently stated in the Pāli texts like the *Avijjāsutta* that mindfulness (*sati*) and clear comprehension (*satisampajañña*) are the foundation for the establishment of the four domains of mindfulness (*cattāro satipaṭṭhānā*), which, in turn, lead to the development of the seven factors of awakening (*satta bojjhaṅgā*) and then final knowledge and liberation (*vijjāvimutti*) (A V 115).

doubt) are suppressed and wrong view (*micchā diṭṭhi*)[34] is inactive, though not yet eradicated. One can clearly see and note objects, which mainly arise at the mind door and much less at the five physical sense doors.[35] Commonly, the meditator sees many images and visions, often dreamlike, arising at the mind door; in Buddhist countries like Sri Lanka, meditators often have visions of the Buddha, deities, or *arahants* because of their trust or faith (*saddhā*) in the Buddhist teachings. At this stage, the practice has turned into insight (*vipassanā*) meditation, as both the arising and passing away of objects are clearly noted, while cause and effect are understood.

Entering the domain of insight knowledges (*vipassanāñāṇa*),[36] the meditator can discern mental and physical phenomena and understand their conditionality and the three characteristics (*tilakkhaṇa*). Mindfulness (*sati*) and clear comprehension (*sampajañña*) are now highly developed, the sense of 'I' does not arise in regard to objects of experience and the meditator is no longer deceived or carried away by various experiences, however attractive they may be. Gradually, the meditator reaches the insight knowledge of arising and passing away (*udayabbayañāṇa*). The five faculties (*pañc'indriyāni*) become very strong and start functioning at the level of the five powers (*pañcabalāni*),[37] which keep mindfulness (*sati*) stable so that it cannot be easily disrupted. The meditator feels very comfortable, the body seems as light as a cotton ball and she or he experiences extreme peace and pleasure. Sometimes the meditator wrongly believes that she or he has achieved *nibbāna*, a state of liberation, and is reluctant to practise beyond this stage. A good teacher (*kalyāṇamitta*)[38] is needed here to encourage and guide the meditator to continue, otherwise she or he may regress.

At the next stage of insight (*vipassanā*) meditation, the meditator no longer sees the arising of objects but only their passing away; it seems that the object disappears before the mind can even note it. Although the insight into impermanence (*anicca*) is now well established, the meditator becomes disappointed and feels that concentration (*samādhi*) has diminished. However, in reality, the opposite is true, as concentration (*samādhi*) is much stronger than before. All the pleasant feelings and comfort that were previously experienced now disappear.

34. Wrong view (*micchā diṭṭhi*) is described in the *Visuddhimagga*: 'Its characteristic is unwise inclination, its function is holding onto, it is manifested as wrong interpreting, and its proximate cause is unwillingness to see Noble ones and so on. It should be regarded as the greatest fault' (Vism 468–469: *Sā ayoniso abhinivesalakkhaṇā, parāmāsarasā, micchābhinivesapaccupaṭṭhānā, ariyānaṃ adassanakāmatādipadaṭṭhānā, paramaṃ vajjan ti daṭṭhabbā*). Wrong view (*micchā diṭṭhi*) is discussed in many *suttas*; for example, in the *Brahmajālasutta* (D I 1–46), the *Cūḷamāluṅkyasutta* (M I 426–432), and the *Aggivacchagottasutta* (M I 483–489).

35. A discussion on mindfulness in relation to the six sense spheres is given in Chapter V.3. Six sense spheres.

36. The insight knowledges are outlined in several sources; for example, in the *Visuddhimagga* (Vism 628–671) and Mahāsi Sayadaw's *Manual of Insight* (2016, 303–466). Here Pemasiri Thera briefly summarises them.

37. The five faculties (*indriya*) and powers (*bala*) are (1) trust (*saddhā*), (2) energy (*viriya*), (3) mindfulness (*sati*), (4) concentration (*samādhi*), and (5) wisdom (*paññā*). When the five faculties (*indriya*) are well established, stable, and strengthened, they are called the five powers (*bala*); for a discussion on power (*bala*), see Gethin (2001, 140–145).

38. The term *kalyāṇamitta* frequently refers to a meditation teacher, a virtuous companion, a spiritual guide, or a good friend; in the *Upaddhasutta*, it is said that a virtuous friend (*kalyāṇamitta*) represents the entire path to liberation, and in such company, one can develop and cultivate the noble eightfold path (S V 2: *Evaṃ kho Ānanda bhikkhu kalyāṇamitto kalyaṇasahāyo kalyāṇasampavaṅko ariyam aṭṭhaṅgikaṃ maggam bhāveti ariyam aṭṭhaṅgikam maggam bahulīkaroti*). In the *Suriyassa-upamāsutta*, it is said that a monk who has a virtuous friend develops and cultivates the seven factors of awakening (S V 79: *bhikkhu kalyāṇamitto satta bojjhaṅge bhāveti satta bhojjhaṅge bahulīkarotīti*).

This stage is known as the knowledge of dissolution (*bhaṅgañāṇa*). Any phenomenon or object as well as the noting mind simply vanish. This further intensifies until it is no longer possible to note any object at all.

Fear then arises in the meditator, because she or he can no longer relate to or even note anything. The meditator realises that there is no phenomenon worth attaching to in this world, as they all rapidly pass away. This kind of insight is called the knowledge of fear (*bhayañāṇa*). Meditation practice becomes very difficult at this point and at least half of meditators want to abandon it all. The meditator becomes unhappy and starts seeing phenomena as dangerous and oppressive; often painful sensations can start arising in the body and become increasingly intense. The hindrances (*nīvaraṇa*), until now mostly suppressed, emerge once again and the meditator thinks that the practice is deteriorating. This stage of insight meditation is called the knowledge of danger (*ādīnavañāṇa*). At this point, the teacher should be very kind and encouraging, giving small hints about what to expect next to make it easier for the meditator to handle the situations as they arise.

Now everything seems increasingly unpleasant, disagreeable and unattractive to the meditator and it becomes very difficult to maintain the practice; the meditator wants to sleep more and starts to feel physically ill. This stage is called the knowledge of disenchantment or disgust (*nibbidāñāṇa*). Here again, about half of all meditators drop the practice and leave. With the teacher's encouragement, the meditator needs to increase mindfulness (*sati*) and clear comprehension (*sampajañña*) and then as concentration (*samādhi*) strengthens, the meditator may wish to escape from all the objects and the knowing mind; thus, the insight knowledge of desire for deliverance (*muñcitukamyatāñāṇa*) emerges. Here concentration may start fluctuating; sometimes in the same sitting session, it will suddenly drop completely and the mind will become very scattered. Then, concentration (*samādhi*) will increase for some time and drop again. Confusion sets in, and all kinds of experiences from the earlier stages of practice can re-occur, including strong pains never previously experienced. This is the most difficult stage, known as the knowledge of re-observation (*paṭisaṅkhāñāṇa*). Some meditators remember experiences from early childhood, before birth, or even past lives if mindfulness (*sati*) and clear comprehension (*satisampajañña*) are very strong. The meditator feels dejected and the teacher may have to meet with her or him frequently, sometimes even several times a day.

As the practice continues, equanimity (*upekkhā*) gradually evolves, and a sense of lightness emerges, much more pronounced than at the stage of the knowledge of arising and passing away (*udayabbayañāṇa*). This level of practice is called the knowledge of equanimity about formations (*saṅkhār'upekkhāñāṇa*). Some meditators reach this level and never return to the lower levels of practice, even though they do not progress further towards path knowledge (*maggañāṇa*). Now, the teacher can recognise a person who aspires to be a *buddha* or *bodhisatta,* which may explain why the practice remains at this level without regressing or progressing. Many meditators remain at the knowledge of equanimity about formations (*saṅkhār'upekkhāñāṇa*) for a while and then regress to the lower levels of insight. In this case, the teacher must find out why this is happening (perhaps due to external disturbances, conversations with others or unsuitable food) and help the meditator to remove the obstruction and progress beyond this towards path knowledge (*maggañāṇa*).

To summarise, by establishing the four foundations of mindfulness (*cattāro satipaṭṭhānā*), the process of insight (*vipassanñāṇa*) meditation begins, with the meditator contemplating various aspects of the three characteristics (*tilakkhaṇa*) of all phenomena until path knowledge (*maggañāṇa*) is reached. In the early stages of insight meditation, the mediator contemplates impermanence (*anicca*), while the sense of 'I' may still occasionally occur; for example, sometimes the mind seems to be without an owner or a person behind it, but at other times, the idea of a person noting objects may arise. But when the meditator clearly sees that all phenomena are impermanent (*anicca*) and that wanting something to be permanent only causes unsatisfactoriness or suffering (*dukkha*), she or he understands that things cannot be how one would like them to be, which means that an insight into non-self (*anattā*) begins to emerge. As the practice advances further, especially in the contemplation of phenomena (*dhammānupassanā*), the understanding of non-self (*anattā*) deepens. To the meditator, it seems as though there is only consciousness without any object, or conversely, they cannot see consciousness or determine where it is, trying to search for it in vain. The meditator then comprehends that consciousness cannot be located in a specific place, that it is not a person called 'I'; the insight into non-self (*anattā*) thus deepens. As the meditator no longer has any stable object to note, she or he sees the act of only passing away instead of an object that passes away. It seems that there is nothing to be noted; unsatisfactoriness (*dukkha*) then becomes prominent. Subsequent insight knowledges deepen this experience of unsatisfactoriness (*dukkha*) until the knowledge of equanimity about formations (*saṅkhār'upekkhāñāṇa*) is reached, where all three characteristics (*tilakkhaṇa*) are comprehended. From there, one of the three characteristics is seen more markedly than the other two, and the meditator may move towards path knowledge (*maggañāṇa*).

'Contemplation' (*anupassanā*)

In the *Satipaṭṭhānasutta,* it is said that a monk abides contemplating the body (*kāyānupassī*), feeling (*vedanānupassī*), the mind (*cittānupassī*) and phenomena (*dhammānupassī*). Here contemplation (*anupassanā*) refers to mindful observation along with the comprehension (*sampajañña*) of the aggregates (*khandha*), elements (*dhātu*) and six sense spheres (*āyatana*).[39] If the phenomena are observed with clear comprehension (*sampajañña*) and the ever-changing processes are understood as events within the domains of the aggregates, elements and sense spheres, the meditator is said to be engaged in contemplation (*anupassanā*), irrespective of the domain of mindfulness (i.e., the body, feeling, mind, or phenomena) she or he is engaged with.[40] Thus, contemplation (*anupassanā*) takes place when the meditator notes phenomena like the breath without the idea of a person who observes; this is how mindfulness (*sati*) becomes established. But if the meditator has a goal or seeks pleasure or comfort in the practice and has previously experienced unified and tranquil mental states, then she or he may dislike such contemplation, instead preferring to return to the seemingly unchanging peaceful state. However, persistence

39. The contemplation (*anupassanā*) of the aggregates (*khandha*), elements (*dhātu*) and sense spheres (*āyatana*) along with the three characteristics and the foundation of mindfulness (*satipaṭṭhānā*) is considered the 'highest teaching' (*paramatthadesanā*) (Ps 137).

40. The term contemplation (*anupassanā*) occurs in the Pāli canon and its commentaries in several contexts, frequently in relation to the contemplation of the three characteristics; for example, the *Visuddhimagga* explains contemplation (*anupassanā*) as follows: 'he sees repeatedly in various ways, ... he contemplates [the object] as impermanent and so on' (Vism 642: *ettha ca anupassatī ti anu-anupassati; anekehi ākārehi punappunaṃ passatī ti attho ... Aniccato anupassatī ti ādi*). Cf. A V 359; S III 179–180. In the *Vibhaṅga*, contemplation (*anupassanā*) is equated with wisdom (*paññā*), understanding (*pajānanā*), absence of delusion (*amoha*), investigation of *dhammas* (*dhammavicaya*), and right view (*sammādiṭṭhi*) (Vibh 194: *Yā paññā pajānanā ... amoho dhammavicayo sammādiṭṭhi: ayaṃ vuccati anupassanā*). Contemplation (*anupassanā*) is also linked to mindfulness (*sati*) and knowledge (*ñāṇa*); for example, in the *Visuddhimagga*, it is said that the meditator 'contemplates the body by means of mindfulness and knowledge' (Vism 273: *tāya satiyā, tena ñāṇena taṃ kāyaṃ anupassati*).

in contemplative practice (*anupassanā*), though not always comfortable, will eventually bring true comfort and benefit.

All four areas of contemplation (*anupassanā*) are interrelated, although the practice may incline more towards one area due to individual differences in the level and strength of mental faculties such as trust (*saddhā*) and wisdom (*paññā*). It is not possible to keep contemplating a single domain; all four have to be developed. For example, mindfulness of breathing (*ānāpānasati*) falls within the domain of the contemplation of the body (*kāyānupassanā*). However, a pain may occur in the body during this practice, thus giving rise to an unpleasant feeling, or conversely, a comfortable pleasant feeling may occur; if the feeling is noted and comprehended as such, then one practises contemplation in the domain of feeling (*vedanānupassanā*). Then, for example, while meditating, a thought, memory, or old perception may arise, and if it is immediately noted, then one is in the domain of the contemplation of the mind (*cittānupassanā*). While mindful of breathing, the meditator may hear a bird call; if she or he does not think about the bird or try to recognise it but simply notes the hearing and comprehends it as a sound, then their contemplation is in the domain of phenomena (*dhammānupassanā*). Or to give another example, the meditator is eating mindfullly, thus practising in the domain of the contemplation of the body (*kāyānupassanā*). In this process, various feelings may arise depending on whether the food is liked or disliked, and if noted, she or he then contemplates in the domain of feeling (*vedanānupassanā*). Then a thought may arise in relation to the food, such as thinking that the meal is tasty, and if properly noted, the practice occurs in the domain of the contemplation of the mind (*cittānupassanā*). However, frequently such thoughts are not noted, meditators tend to believe that their main practice is sitting meditation and are less attentive in other activities. When the meditator is mindful of tasting the food, their practice is the contemplation of phenomena (*dhammānupassanā*). Thus, all four domains of contemplation develop simultaneously; the four foundations of mindfulness (*cattāro satipaṭṭhānā*) cannot in practice be separated.

The worlds of the body (*kāya*), feeling (*vedanā*), mind (*citta*) and phenomena (*dhamma*) are similar, as they incessantly arise and pass away. No component in our bodies or minds lasts or remains the same for even a moment, but because the processes occur very quickly, we cannot perceive these minute changes, and hence we maintain the idea of a person called 'I.' As stressed earlier, as soon as any view of the existence of a person is created, at that very moment mindfulness (*sati*) is lost, and consequently greed (*lobha*) and aversion (*dosa*) appear again, even if only at a subtle level. Only when the 'I' does not arise is there mindfulness (*sati*) and clear comprehension (*sampajañña*), which allow the meditator to understand the aggregates (*khandha*), elements (*dhātu*) and sense spheres (*āyatana*) as they really are; such practice is known as contemplation (*anupassanā*). Then dependent origination (*paṭiccasamuppāda*) can be comprehended and one's views purified.

To summarise, the aim of training in contemplation (*anupassanā*) is to be without greed (*lobha*) and aversion (*dosa*) in relation to the body and mind. When the meditator lives mindfully, observing and understanding the nature of the body, wisdom (*paññā*) arises, which in turn frees her or him from ignorance (*avijjā*) and can lead to liberation.

'Abides' (*viharati*)

In the *Satipaṭṭhānasutta*, it is said in the beginning that 'a monk abides contemplating the body as a body,' and then the same is stated for feeling, the mind, and phenomena. When the word 'abides' (*viharati*) is used in the context of meditation, it refers to the meditation object; it means that the meditator dwells in or abides with the object of contemplation.[41] In other words, the term denotes that the meditator trains or is restrained (*sikkhati*) and clearly comprehends (*pajānāti*) the object with mindfulness (*sati*).

'Ardent' (*ātāpī*)

Further on, it is said that a monk who abides in contemplation is 'ardent' (*ātāpī*). Here ardour or diligence refers to the energy or effort required to burn the defilements (*kilesa*).[42] Thus, it is not the physical effort required to maintain the meditation posture but rather the mental energy (*viriya*)[43] directed towards the development and maintenance of wholesome mental states.[44] Ardour or diligence is the energy (*viriya*) required to maintain the practice and stabilise mindfulness (*sati*), without letting it go, without any thought of an 'I' arising in the process. When the meditator is ardent (*ātāpī*), it means that her or his energy (*viriya*) is well established and balanced with the four other faculties (*indriya*). Along with mindfulness (*sati*) and clear comprehension (*sampajañña*), ardour contributes to the right conditions for wisdom (*paññā*) to arise. With ardour, clear comprehension (*sampajañña*) and mindfulness (*sati*), the practice becomes stable.

In the *Mahāparinibbanāsutta*, the last words ascribed to the Buddha were: 'All conditioned things are subject to decay—strive on earnestly.'[45] The Buddha asked the monks to practise earnestly and diligently, with zeal (*appamāda*), cultivating the energy, understanding and mindfulness required to attain liberation from suffering.[46] In the context of the *Satipaṭṭhānasutta*, being ardent (*ātāpī*) refers to energy (*viriya*), which is a component of striving or diligence (*appamāda*).

'Clearly comprehending' (*sampajāno*)

In the introductory section of the *Satipaṭṭhānasutta,* a monk is instructed to be ardent, mindful and clearly comprehending (*sampajāno*). As mentioned earlier, in the practice of the four foundations of mindfulness (*satipaṭṭhāna*), clear comprehension (*sampajañña*) has to appear together with mindfulness (*sati*). For both of them to arise together (i.e., *satisampajañña*), wise attention (*yoniso manasikāra*) first has to develop. In the beginning, the meditator trains in the

41. The verb 'abides' (*viharati*) is similarly explained in relation to meditation in the *Vibhaṅga* in the section on *jhānas*: '[The monk] assumes the posture, keeps going, holds, continues, maintains, goes on, dwells' (Vibh 252: *iriyati vattati pāleti yapeti yāpeti carati viharati, tena vuccati viharatīti*).

42. Defilements (*kilesa*) are variously presented in the Pāli texts, most frequently as a group of ten: (1) greed (*lobha*), (2) aversion (*dosa*), (3) delusion (*moha*), (4) conceit (*māna*), (5) views (*diṭṭhi*), (6) doubt (*vicikicchā*), (7) sloth (*thīna*), (8) restlessness (*uddhacca*), (9) shamelessness (*ahirika*) and (10) lack of fear of doing wrong (*anottappa*) (Dhs 257; Vism 683).

43. Energy (*viriya*) is a very important term in the Buddhist discourse: it is one of the faculties (*indriya*) and powers (*bala*) as well as one of the seven factors of awakening (*bojjhaṅgā*). It is discussed in Chapter V.4, under the subheading 'Energy factor of awakening (*viriyasambojjhaṅga*).'

44. Here Pemasiri Thera follows the commentary on the *Satipaṭṭhānasutta*, the *Papañcasūdani*, where the term 'ardent' (*ātāpī*) is explained as energy (*viriya*) that burns (*ātāpeti*) the defilements of the three planes (Ps I 244: *tīsu bhavesu kilese ātāpetīti ātāpo, viriyassetaṃ nāmaṃ*). Cf. Vibh 194.

45. D II 156: *Vayadhammā saṅkhārā, appamādena sampādethāti.*

46. In the *Sumaṅgalavilāsinī* commentary on the *Mahāparinibbanāsutta*, the phrase is explained as 'striving to accomplish all that needs to be done with mindfulness and care' (Sv II 593: *Appamādena sampādethāti sati-avippavāsena sabbakiccāni sampādeyyātha*). Diligence (*appamāda*) is explained in the commentary on the *Itivuttaka* as the four mental aggregates (i.e., feeling, perception, mental formations and consciousness) in conjunction with mindfulness and clear comprehension (It-a I 80: *satisampajaññayogena pavattā cattāro arūpino khandhā appamādo*).

cultivation of attention (*manasikāra*); when attention arises for some time along with wholesome objects or mental states, it is called wise attention (*yoniso manasikāra*), which moves from one wholesome object or state to another. The function of wise attention (*yoniso manasikāra*) is to recognise what is wholesome (*kusala*) and what is not, as stated in the *Viriyārambhavagga*:

> Monks, I do not regard anything by which unarisen wholesome qualities arise and arisen unwholesome qualities decline other than wise attention. (A I 13)[47]

Conversely, unwise attention (*ayoniso manasikāra*) occurs when the mind is entangled with the five hindrances (*pañca nīvaraṇāni*); it is only through wise attention (*yoniso manasikāra*) that a meditator can break free from them. However, wise attention (*yoniso manasikāra*) is not *necessarily* accompanied by mindfulness (*sati*) and clear comprehension (*sampajañña*); the latter does not usually appear in wholesome worldly activities but only in the practice of insight meditation (*vipassanā*). The concepts of mindfulness (*sati*), attention (*manasikāra*) and wise attention (*yoniso manasikāra*) are closely related but not synonymous. The Buddha rarely used synonyms; every term has a specific meaning and function.

When wise attention (*yoniso manasikāra*) has been present for some time, while maintaining the state of wholesomeness, mindfulness (*sati*) may arise along with clear comprehension (*satisampajañña*). Clear comprehension (*sampajañña*) can be understood as an early stage in the development of wisdom (*paññā*).[48] Through clear comprehension (*sampajañña*), the meditator begins seeing the three characteristics of all phenomena (*tilakkhaṇa*) and thus enters into insight (*vipassanā*) meditation.[49] In other words, wise attention (*yoniso manasikāra*) is the condition necessary for the arising of mindfulness (*sati*) and clear comprehension (*sampajañña*), which, in turn, are the foundation for the development of other qualities necessary for liberation. This is explained in the *Avijjāsutta*, where wise attention (*yoniso manasikāra*) is situated in relation to mindfulness (*sati*) and clear comprehension (*sampajañña*) as well as other components on the path to liberation; each component, when fulfilled, leads to the next in the following sequence:

> Association with good people (*sappurisasaṃseva*) leads to hearing the good Dhamma (*saddhammasavana*), this in turn leads to trust (*saddhā*), wise attention (*yoniso manasikāra*), mindfulness and clear comprehension (*satisampajañña*), restraint of the sense faculties (*indriyasaṃvara*), three kinds of good conduct (*tīṇi sucaritāni*), four foundations of mindfulness (*cattāro satipaṭṭhānā*), seven factors of awakening (*satta bojjhaṅgā*), and true knowledge and liberation (*vijjāvimutti*).
> (A V 115)[50]

47. A I 13: *Nāhaṃ bhikkhave aññaṃ ekadhammam pi samanupassāmi yena anuppannā vā kusalā dhammā uppajjanti uppannā vā akusalā dhammā parihāyanti yathayidaṃ bhikkhave yoniso manasikāro*. Similarly, the *Sabbāsavasutta* (M I 7) states that wise attention (*yoniso manasikāra*) prevents unarisen taints (*āsava*) and abandons the arisen ones. For further discussion on wise attention (*yoniso manasikāra*), also see the *Maggasaṃyutta* (S V 31–35).

48. In the *Abhidhamma* texts, clear comprehension (*sampajañña*) is often linked to wisdom (*paññā*); for example, the *Vibhaṅga* explains it as 'wisdom, understanding, absence of delusion, investigation of phenomena and right view' (Vibh 194: *... paññā ... amoho dhammavicayo sammādiṭṭhi — idaṃ vuccati sampajaññaṃ*); cf. Dhs 16.

49. The commentaries link clear comprehension (*sampajañña*) to insight (*vipassanā*); for example, in the *Sammohavinodanī*, it is said that 'it should be understood that by clear comprehension is [meant] insight' (Vibh-a 263: *sampajaññena vipassanā ... veditabbaṃ*). The *Sammohavinodanī* lists four kinds of clear comprehension: (1) clear comprehension of purpose (*sātthakasampajañña*), (2) clear comprehension of suitability (*appāyasampajañña*), (3) clear comprehension of resort or domain of meditation (*gocarasampajañña*) and (4) clear comprehension of non-delusion (*asammohasampajañña*); the latter is then explained as the understanding of non-self (Vibh-1 247–355).

50. A V 115: *Iti kho bhikkhave sappurisasaṃsevo paripūro saddhammasavanaṃ paripūreti, saddhammasavanaṃ paripūraṃ*

To summarise, mindfulness (*sati*) and clear comprehension (*satisampajañña*) are central components on the path to final liberation. One of the functions of mindfulness (*sati*) is to bring the object of contemplation close, to see it clearly, without being deceived by anything else. For example, mindfulness (*sati*) looks at pain but keeps the mind free from suffering; this means that the object can be seen clearly and very closely, without being distorted by greed (*lobha*) or aversion (*dosa*). When mindfulness (*sati*) is supported by clear comprehension (*sampajañña*), a meditator can remain in the state of wholesomeness for long periods. Clear comprehension (*sampajañña*) is like a mother and mindfulness (*sati*) like a child: clear comprehension (*sampajañña*) supports mindfulness (*sati*), allowing it to evolve and continue its progress, whereas mindfulness (*sati*) is the condition for clear comprehension (*sampajañña*) to arise; hence, they are mutually interdependent. If mindfulness (*sati*) and clear comprehension (*sampajañña*) are absent, then one practises only attention (*manasikāra*). For example, if the meditator, while attentively observing the breath, is simultaneously aware of and thinks about another meditator sitting close by, she or he has neither mindfulness (*sati*) nor clear comprehension (*sampajañña*) despite perhaps sitting in meditation for many hours. It would instead be better to practise meditation for only five minutes with both mindfulness (*sati*) and clear comprehension (*sampajañña*).

Mindfulness (*sati*) sees all objects without greed (*lobha*) or aversion (*dosa*), whereas clear comprehension (*sampajañña*) understands the changes taking place in the arising and passing away of objects. In the *Satipaṭṭhānasutta*, it is said that mindfulness (*sati*) can be cultivated in regard to the body (*kāya*), feeling (*vedanā*), the mind (*citta*) and phenomena (*dhamma*); however, instructions for the practice of clear comprehension (*sampajañña*) frequently focus on bodily activities alone. For example, the instructions on the cultivation of mindfulness in the *Satipaṭṭhānasutta* and the *Satipaṭṭhānasaṃyutta* state:

> And how, monks, is a monk clearly comprehending? Here, monks, a monk acts with clear comprehension when going forward and returning; when looking ahead and aside; when bending and stretching the limbs; when wearing his robes and carrying his outer robe and bowl; when eating, drinking, chewing and tasting; when defecating and urinating; when walking, standing, sitting, falling asleep, waking up, speaking and keeping silent. In this way, monks, a monk is clearly comprehending. (M I 57; S V 142)[51]

In the case of bodily activities, clear comprehension (*sampajañña*) is used to protect wholesomeness (*kusala*) and mindfulness (*sati*). For example, if the meditator is mindfully eating in such a way that no unwholesome states arise while observing the changes in this activity, it can be said that she or he is clearly comprehending. But if while slowly eating with full attention (*manasikāra*), a thought arises that 'I am eating in the right way with attention,' and then looking at another person and thinking that she or he is not eating properly, perhaps too

saddhaṃ paripūreti, saddhā paripūrā yonisomanasikāraṃ paripūreti, yonisomanasikāro paripūro satisampajaññaṃ paripūreti, satisampajaññaṃ paripūraṃ indriyasaṃvaraṃ paripūreti, indriyasaṃvaro paripūro tīṇi sucaritāni paripūreti, tīṇi sucaritāni paripūrāni cattāro satipaṭṭhāne paripūrenti, cattāro satipaṭṭhānā paripūrā satta bojjhaṅge paripūrenti, satta bojjhaṅgā paripūrā vijjāvimuttiṃ paripūrenti.

51. M I 57; S V 142: *Kathañca bhikkhave bhikkhu sampajāno hoti? Idha bhikkhave bhikkhu abhikkante paṭikkante sampajānakārīhoti ālokite vilokite sampajānakārī hoti, sammiñjite pasārite sampajānakārī hoti, saṅghāṭi pattacīvaradhāraṇe sampajānakārī hoti, asite pīte khāyite sāyite sampajānakārī hoti, uccārapassāvakamme sampajānakārī hoti, gate ṭhite nisinne sutte jāgarite bhāsite tunhībhāve sampajānakārī hoti. Evaṃ kho bhikkhave bhikkhu sampajāno hoti.*

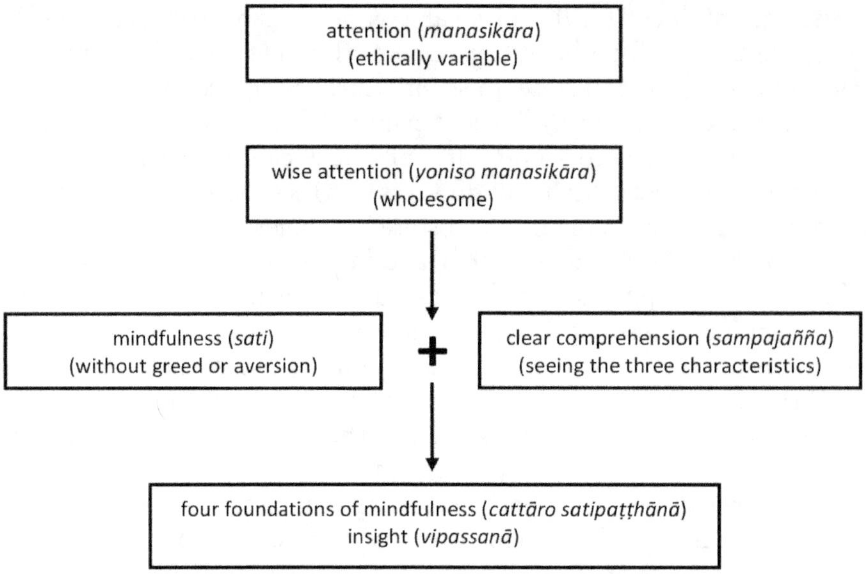

Figure 1 Relationship between attention, wise attention, mindfulness and clear comprehension in the cultivation of the four foundations of mindfulness (*cattāro satipaṭṭhānā*).

quickly or too loudly, clear comprehension (*sampajañña*) is no longer present.

The function of clear comprehension (*sampajañña*) is to clearly see the changes taking place in the object of attention. It is therefore not limited only to the contemplation of the body (*kāyānupassanā*) but is also involved with the three other domains of mindfulness (*satipaṭṭhāna*). Thus, for example, it is said in the *Satisutta* of the *Satipaṭṭhānasaṃyutta*:

> And how, monks, is a monk clearly comprehending? Here, monks, a monk comprehends feelings as they arise, comprehends as they remain, comprehends as they pass away; comprehends thoughts as they arise, as they remain, as they pass away; comprehends perceptions as they arise, as they remain, as they pass away. In this way, monks, a monk is clearly comprehending.
>
> (S V 180–181)[52]

Clear comprehension (*sampajañña*) means seeing the change, that is, impermanence (*anicca*) as well as the two other characteristics, namely, unsatisfactoriness (*dukkha*) and non-self (*anattā*). For example, when stretching out her or his arm, the meditator sees the rapid changes as if there were a series of many arms, rapidly arising and passing away, or when turning the head, the meditator sees numerous phases of movement, as if many heads are being turned. In a similar way, feelings, perceptions and thoughts can be seen in a rapid sequence as they arise, stay for a moment and cease. Initially, it is easier to see these changes in bodily activities, since the meditator is more readily deceived by feelings, thoughts and perceptions. When mindfulness (*sati*) is supported by clear comprehension (*sampajañña*), there is no greed (*lobha*) or aversion (*dosa*) towards the object, because clear comprehension (*sampajañña*) sees the object changing so rapidly that there is nothing to attach to or be repelled by. Through

52. S V 180–181: *Kathañca bhikkhave bhikkhu sampajāno hoti? Idha bhikkhave bhikkhuno viditā vedanā uppajjanti, viditā upaṭṭhahanti viditā abbhatthaṃ gacchanti. Viditā vitakkā uppajjanti, viditā upaṭṭhahanti, viditā abbhattham gacchanti. Viditā saññā uppajjanti, viditā upaṭṭhahanti, viditā abbhatthaṃ gacchanti. Evaṃ kho bhikkhave bhikkhu sampajāno hoti.*

clear comprehension (*sampajañña*), the conditionality of all phenomena is understood, and one begins to discern the causes, effects and conditions. After establishing the knowledge of conditionality, it is through clear comprehension (*sampajañña*) that the meditator sees the three characteristics (*tilakkhaṇa*) and develops wisdom (*paññā*).[53]

'Having abandoned desires and discontent in regard to the world' (*vineyya loke abhijjhādomanassaṃ*)

Mindfulness (*sati*) is the quality of mind or mental concomitant (*cetasika*) that arises when there is no desire, craving, discontent or aversion towards any experience. In the *Satipaṭṭhānasutta*, the abandonment of desire and discontent is described in Pāli as *vineyya abhijjhādomanassaṃ*. This is usually translated as 'having put away or abandoned desire and discontent,' but this translation could be expanded to 'having recognised desire and discontent and then put them away.' If only abandoning was meant here, another Pāli word could have been used, such as *pajahati*, which means 'gives up, renounces, gets rid of.'[54] But here it is important to first see and recognise desire (*abhijjhā*) and discontent (*domanassa*) in order to understand how troublesome they can be; only then can one live in such a way that they cannot arise.[55] One can put something away or abandon it with aversion (*dosa*), because it is troublesome and unpleasant; for example, one may find certain people very taxing and difficult and consequently stays away from them. So simply putting things away due to aversion (*dosa*), however mild and subtle it may be, is not what the *Satipaṭṭhānasutta* means.

The term *abhijjhā*[56] refers to strong desire, greed or craving and *domanassa*[57] to disappointment, discontent or aversion in regard to experienced things. The main function of mindfulness (*sati*) in the *Satipaṭṭhānasutta* is to see desire (*abhijjhā*) and discontent (*domanassa*), to recognise our tendency to become attached or averse to objects and experiences. Having abandoned desire (*abhijjhā*) and discontent (*domanassa*), one perceives and knows the world with a free mind or, in other words, mindfully.

53. For a more detailed discussion on wisdom (*paññā*), see Chapter V.4. Seven factors of awakening, under the subheading 'Investigation-of-*dhammas* factor of awakening (*dhammavicayasambojjhaṅga*).'

54. See *pajahati* in PED (*s.v.*).

55. Here Pemasiri Thera seems to draw from his experience as a meditation teacher, pointing out how the idea of renunciation may be based on dislike, even a very subtle one, which seems to be a common issue among practitioners. Although I am unaware of such an explicit explanation of the phrase *vineyya abhijjhādomanassaṃ* in the Pāli canon or its commentaries, it is implicitly understood in the broader context of the Buddhist teachings, especially around the ideal of renunciation, which is always linked to wholesomeness. For example, it is said in the *Vibhaṅga* that 'all wholesome states are the element of renunciation' (Vibh 86: *Sabbe pi kusalā dhammā nekkhammadhātu*), thus implying the recognition and absence of aversion or dislike.

56. *Abhijjhā* is variously rendered into English: in DP (*s.v.*), PED (*s.v.*) and Ñāṇanamoli and Bodhi (1995, 145), it is translated as 'covetousness, longing for,' while in Anālayo (2003, 3) as 'desire.' In the Pāli canon and its commentaries, the term *abhijjhā* is frequently related to *lobha* 'greed,' *taṇhā* 'craving' (Nid I 9; Dhs 189) and *rāga* 'lust, desire' (Vibh 195). In the *Papañcasūdanī* commentary, *abhijjhā* is explained as *kāmacchanda* 'sense desire' (Ps I 244).

57. *Domanassa* is variously translated into English; in DP (*s.v.*) and PED (*s.v.*), it is translated as 'distress, dejectedness, unhappiness, melancholy, grief,' in Ñāṇanamoli and Bodhi (1995, 145) as 'grief' and in Anālayo (2003, 3) as 'discontent.' In the *Vibhaṅga*, the term *domanassa* is defined as uneasiness, suffering or painful feeling (Vibh 195: *yaṃ cetasikaṃ asātaṃ cetasikaṃ dukkhaṃ cetosamphassajaṃ asātaṃ dukkhaṃ vedayitaṃ cetosamphassajā asātā dukkhā vedanā: idaṃ vuccati 'domanassaṃ'*). In the *Papañcasūdanī* commentary, *domanassa* is linked to *vyāpāda* 'ill-will, anger' (Ps I 244: *domanassaggahaṇena vyāpādo saṅgahaṃ gacchati*).

Here the phrase 'in regard to the world' (*loke*) does not refer to the world around us in the sense of places, countries and so on; in meditation, such knowledge about the world around us is not useful. In the context of the *Satipaṭṭhānasutta,* the world (*loka*) means the world of the body (*kāya*), the world of feeling (*vedanā*), the world of the mind (*citta*) and the world of phenomena (*dhamma*). The world is subject to change, continuously breaking up and re-forming, as stated in the *Papañcasūdanī* commentary on the *Satipaṭṭhānasutta*:

> 'In the world' means in this body. Here the body is the world in the sense of breaking up and crumbling away (Ps I 244).[58]

The 'world' is interpreted in another way in the *Vibhaṅga*:

> This very body is the world, also the five aggregates of clinging are the world (Vibh 195).[59]

The world (*loka*) can thus be explained as the five aggregates (*khandha*), comprising:

1. materiality (*rūpa*)
2. feeling (*vedanā*)
3. perception (*saññā*)
4. mental formations (*saṅkhāra*)
5. consciousness (*viññāṇa*)

Alternatively, the world (*loka*) can refer to the four worlds—the world of the body (*kāya*), feeling (*vedanā*), the mind (*citta*) and phenomena (*dhamma*)—or in yet another way, to two worlds, namely, the world of the body and the world of the mind, or the world of mentality and materiality (*nāmarūpa*).

To summarise, to cultivate the four foundations of mindfulness (*cattāro satipaṭṭhānā*), the meditator should cultivate the qualities of being ardent (*ātāpī*), mindful (*satimā*) and clearly comprehending (*sampajāno*) while having abandoned desires and discontent in regard to the world (*vineyya loke abhijjhādomanassaṃ*).

58. Ps I 244: *loketi tasmiṃ yeva kāye. kāyo hi idha lujjanapalujjanaṭṭhena lokoti adhippeto.*

59. Vibh 195: *sveva kāyo loko, pañcapi upādānakkhandhā loko.*

— II —

Contemplation of the Body (*Kāyānupassanā*)

II 1 Mindfulness of breathing (*ānāpānasati*)[1]

Kathañca bhikkhave bhikkhu kāye ***kāyānupassī*** *viharati? Idha bhikkhave bhikkhu* ***araññagato*** *vā rukkhamūlagato vā suññāgāragato vā nisīdati* ***pallaṅkaṃ ābhujitvā*** *ujuṃ kāyaṃ paṇidhāya* ***pari-mukhaṃ*** *satim upaṭṭhapetvā. So sato va assasati sato passasati. Dīghaṃ vā assasanto dīghaṃ assasāmīti* ***pajānāti****, dīghaṃ vā passasanto dīghaṃ passasāmīti pajānāti; rassaṃ vā assasanto rassaṃ assasāmīti pajānāti, rassaṃ vā passasanto rassaṃ passasāmīti* ***pajānāti. Sabbakāyapaṭisaṃvedī*** *assasissāmīti* ***sikkhati****, sabbakāyapaṭisaṃvedī passasissāmīti sikkhati.* ***Passambhayaṃ kāyasaṅkhāraṃ*** *assasissāmīti sikkhati, passambhayaṃ kāyasaṅkhāraṃ passasissāmīti sikkhati. Seyyathāpi bhikkhave dakkho bhamakāro vā bhamakārantevāsī vā dīghaṃ vā añchanto dīghaṃ añchāmīti pajānāti, rassaṃ vā añchantorassaṃ añchāmīti pajānāti, evameva kho bhikkhave bhikkhu dīghaṃ vā assasanto: dīghaṃ assasāmīti pajānāti - pe - passambhayaṃ kāyasaṅkhāraṃ passasissāmīti sikkhati.*

'And how, monks, does a monk abide **contemplating the body** as a body? Here, monks, a monk, **gone into the forest,** or to the root of a tree, or to an empty hut, sits down **having folded his legs crosswise**, set his body erect and established mindfulness **in front**, mindful he breaths in, mindful he breathes out. Breathing in long, he **knows:** "I breathe in long"; or breathing out long, he knows: "I breathe out long." Breathing in short, he knows: "I breathe in short"; or breathing out short, he knows: "I breathe out short." He **trains** thus: "I shall breathe in **experiencing the whole body**"; he trains thus: "I shall breathe out experiencing the whole body." He trains thus: "I shall breathe in **calming the body formation**"; he trains thus: "I shall breathe out calming the body formation." Just as a skilled turner or his apprentice, when making a long turn, understands: "I make a long turn"; or, when making a short turn, understands: "I make a short turn"; so too, monks, breathing in long, a monk knows: "I breathe in long" ... [the paragraph above repeated] he trains thus: "I shall breathe out calming the body formation."'

Pemasiri Thera's commentary

'Contemplating the body' (*kāyānupassī*)

The contemplation of the body (*kāyānupassanā*) is one of the four foundations of mindfulness (*cattāro satipaṭṭhānā*). According to the *Satipaṭṭhānasutta,* it has fourteen aspects, which can be

1. Despite the frequent use of the recurring passage throughout the *sutta* (see the section 'Recurring passage indicating the ways to approach contemplation' below), which suggests some kind of notional divisions, indications of text divisions within the *sutta* are not found in the original Pāli version. The divisions, marked by the headings, are usually added by translators of the *Satipaṭṭhānasutta*, mostly based on the Pāli commentaries; this approach is also adopted in this book.

presented in six groups:

1. mindfulness of breathing
2. ways of movement (four postures of the body)
3. clear comprehension of bodily activities
4. reflection on the troublesomeness of the body (thirty-one parts of the body)
5. reflection on the four elements
6. nine cemetery contemplations (M I 56–59)

The contemplation of the body (*kāyānupassanā*) does not entail practising awareness of all these aspects of the body; it instead relates to mindfulness (*sati*) and clear comprehension (*sampajañña*) of the aggregates (*khandha*), elements (*dhātu*) and six sense spheres (*āyatana*) in relation to the body. The same also applies to the contemplation of feeling (*vedanānupassī*), the mind (*cittānupassī*) and phenomena (*dhammānupassī*).

Mindfulness of the body is also discussed in other *suttas* using the term *kāyagatāsati*, usually translated into English as 'mindfulness directed to the body,' which should be distinguished from the term 'contemplation of the body' (*kāyānupassanā*). *Kāyagatāsati* has a broader meaning, as explained in the *Kāyagatāsativagga* of the *Aṅguttaranikāya*; it encompasses all aspects of the cultivation of mindfulness (*sati*) related to the body through the cultivation of wholesome mental states:

> Monks, like one who encompasses within his mind the great ocean, which includes all the streams that run into the ocean, just so, monks, whoever develops and cultivates mindfulness directed to the body (*kāyagatāsati*) includes all wholesome states that are conducive to true knowledge. (A I 43)[2]

Further on, the *sutta* outlines how the cultivation of mindfulness directed to the body (*kāyagatāsati*) facilitates and is related to all aspects of the noble eightfold path. It facilitates the development of the tranquillity of the body and mind (*kāyo pi passambhati cittam pi passambhati*), clear comprehension and mindfulness (*satisampajañña*) and the arising of wholesome states (*kusalā dhammā*) and wisdom (*paññā*); it paves the way for the development of the four meditative absorptions (*jhānas*); and finally, it leads to the realisation of the fruit of knowledge and liberation (*vijjāvimuttiphala*) and to arahantship.[3]

The practice of mindfulness directed to the body (*kāyagatāsati*) is frequently interpreted as involving the contemplation of the thirty-one parts of the body.[4] The contemplation of the parts of the body as a reflection on the troublesomeness of the body (*paṭikkūlamanasikāra*) is outlined in the *Satipaṭṭhānasutta* in relation to the contemplation of the body (*kāyānupassanā*), whereas the term 'mindfulness directed to the body' (*kāyagatāsati*) more broadly refers to the cultivation of wholesome states in relation to the body. This means that all actions related to

2. A I 43: *Yassa kassaci bhikkhave mahāsamuddo cetasā phuṭo antogadhā tassa kunnadiyo yā kāci samuddaṅgamā, evameva kho bhikkhave yassa kassaci kāyagatāsati bhāvitā bahulīkatā antogadhā tassa kusalā dhammā ye keci vijjābhāgiyāti.*

3. A I 43–46.

4. Contemplation of the body (*kāyānupassanā*) is thus interpreted in the *Visuddhimagga* (Vism 240: *aṭikūlamanasikāravasena desitaṃ dvattiṃsākārakammaṭṭhānaṃ- idam idha kāyagatāsatī ti adhippetaṃ*). However, Pemasiri Thera argues for a broader understanding of the term; such an understanding is similarly indicated in the *Kāyagatāsatisutta*, where the ten benefits from the cultivation of mindfulness directed to the body (*kāyagatāsati*) listed in the *sutta* include the destruction of the taints (*āsava*), the deliverance of the mind (*cetovimutti*), and deliverance by wisdom (*paññāvimutti*) (M III 99).

the body should be done in a wholesome way. Or as stated in the *Avijjāsutta* (A V 115), through mindfulness and clear comprehension (*satisampajañña*), one cultivates the restraint of the senses (*indriyasaṃvara*) regarding the objects arising through any of the six sense doors, which in turn leads to the development of the four foundations of mindfulness (*cattāro satipaṭṭhānā*), the seven factors of awakening (*satta bojjhaṅgā*) and finally, true knowledge and liberation (*vijjāvimutti*). Thus, the terms *kāyānupassanā, kāyagatāsati*, and *satipaṭṭhāna* refer to three different, though related, conceptualisations.

'Gone to the forest' (*araññagato*)

At the beginning of the section on the contemplation of the body, a monk is instructed to go to a solitary place such as a forest (*arañña*), the root of a tree (*rukkhamūla*) or an empty hut (*suññāgāra*). This means that meditation practice is conducted away from others, in a natural environment, which can be an ideal place for developing strong effort and cultivation of the mind. The place should be sufficiently distant from towns or villages but close enough for monks to go for alms gathering (*piṇḍapāta*). The texts frequently mention that the Buddha and other monks would sit at the root of a tree in a forest, which was viewed as the most suitable place for meditation. For example, in the *Ariyapariyesanasutta*, the Buddha narrates how, before his awakening, he arrived at Uruvelā, at Senānigama:

> There I saw a delightful piece of ground, a pleasant grove and a clear flowing river with beautiful banks and close by a village for alms gathering (M I 167).[5]

He viewed this secluded place in nature as the most conducive environment for his strivings. It was here that he attained liberation (*nibbāna*). The *Satipaṭṭhānasutta* instructs that in such a place, the meditator should sit down (*nisīdati*) and begin the practice of mindfulness of breathing.

'Having folded his legs crosswise' (*pallaṅkaṃ ābhujitvā*)

According to the *sutta*, the practice should be conducted in the sitting posture; the meditator sits down (*nisīdati*) with the legs bent crosswise (*pallaṅkaṃ ābhujitvā*) and the body erect (*ujuṃ kāyaṃ paṇidhāya*). The *sutta* does not state whether the cross-legged position refers to the yogic lotus posture;[6] it may nevertheless be presumed that the posture should be stable, and the body kept upright to allow for long periods of sitting. Abiding in such a posture in a secluded and quiet environment, the meditator can naturally start observing in-breaths and out-breaths in a mindful manner (*so sato va assasati sato passasati*).

'In front' (*parimukham*)

Then the *sutta* says that mindfulness is to be established 'in front' (*parimukham*). The word *parimukham* is sometimes interpreted as 'having the attention fixed around the mouth (*mukha*),' but it rather means that one should bring mindfulness to the forefront.[7] Here the

---

5. M I 167: *Tatth' addasaṃ ramaṇīyaṃ bhūmibhāgaṃ pāsādikañ-ca vanasaṇḍaṃ, nadiñ-ca sandantiṃ setakaṃ sūpatitthaṃ ramaṇīyaṃ, samantā ca gocaragāmaṃ*.

6. The commentaries explain *pallaṅkaṃ ābhujitvā* as the yogic lotus posture. For example, in the *Papañcasūdanī* commentary on the *Satipaṭṭhānasutta*, it is said that having the legs bent crosswise (*pallaṅkaṃ ābhujitvā*) refers to a sitting posture with the thighs fully locked (Ps II 216: *pallaṅkanti samantato ūrubaddhāsanaṃ*). The same explanation is also provided in the commentary on the *Vibhaṅga*, the *Sammohavinodanī* (Vibh-a 368).

7. The Pāli word *mukha* has a range of diverse meanings such as 'mouth, face, front, top, cause, reason' (PED, *s.v.*), resulting in various interpretations of the term *parimukhaṃ* in the Pāli canon and its commentaries. For example, the *Papañcasūdanī* commentary interprets this phrase as 'having set up mindfulness towards

phrase *parimukham satim upaṭṭhapetvā* can be translated as 'bringing up mindfulness' or 'presenting mindfulness to oneself in the forefront.' The word *parimukham* can more broadly refer to an idea, thought or intention that is brought up in the mind. In the beginning of meditation practice, usually an initial object is chosen and brought to the mind, and then mindfulness (*sati*) may arise. Thus, the phrase *so sato parimukham* can refer to the meditator abiding in mindfulness (*sati*) after an object of meditation has been brought to mind.

But when the meditator is established in mindfulness (*sati*), no importance or special attention is given to any object that may arise, instead only very strong mindfulness (*sati*) is present at the forefront (*parimukham*). In other words, the phenomena are presented to the mind through mindfulness (*sati*), but the mind remains in a state of wakefulness without staying with any specific object of focus. We can say that when mindfulness (*sati*) is thus present at the forefront (*parimukha*), one remains in a state of mindful awareness without greed (*lobha*) or aversion (*dosa*). In such a state, one may spontaneously begin to notice the natural flow of the breath. Establishing 'mindfulness in the forefront' (*parimukham satim*) is a natural process or phenomenon, not something artificially created; the meditator sits with awareness, with her or his upper body erect, in a natural environment under a tree. There the mind reaches the state of *parimukham*, having set mindfulness (*sati*) 'in front,' without any clinging or greed (*lobha*) or aversion (*dosa*).

Some meditators cannot note the breath, but as soon as they sit down in meditation, their attention turns to the pain experienced in their body. In this case, feeling (*vedanā*) is 'at the front' (*parimukham*), and one becomes mindful of feeling, thus practising in the domain of the contemplation of feeling (*vedanānupassanā*). Sometimes a wandering mind with various thoughts arises at the forefront (*parimukham*); in this case, one is practising in the domain of the contemplation of the mind (*cittānupassanā*). When mindfulness (*sati*) is established at the forefront (*parimukham*), indeed any object may arise, such as thoughts, pain, breathing or any other phenomena within the four domains of mindfulness (*satipaṭṭhāna*), and the meditator is simply mindful of them. She or he does not choose an object within the body or mind since objects arise all the time and there is no need to search for them; they become apparent by themselves, all that is required is to be mindful of whatever arises. At the beginning, when one is still training, one may choose an initial object for the establishment of mindfulness (*sati*), but once one is well trained, there is no longer any need to choose an object, since everywhere and in every situation mindfulness (*sati*) can arise and be established at the forefront (*parimukham satim upaṭṭhapetvā*). If our entire life is dedicated to the practice of meditation, it can be said that awakening is at the forefront (*parimukham*).

Thus, when the meditator establishes mindfulness (*sati*) 'in front' (*parimukham*), she or he may naturally start observing the breath, as the *sutta* says: 'mindful he breathes in, mindful he breathes out' (*so sato va assasati, sato passasati*). Although it is not specifically mentioned in this passage of the *sutta*, it can be added that the meditator thus remains or abides (*viharati*) in this practice.

'He knows' (*pajānāti*)

The *sutta* then says that the meditator knows when she or he is breathing in and breathing out long (*dīghaṃ vā assasanto: dīghaṃ assasāmīti pajānāti, dīghaṃ vā passasanto: dīghaṃ passasāmīti pajānāti*) and when breathing in and breathing out short (*rassaṃ vā assasanto: rassaṃ assasāmīti*

the meditation object' (Ps II 216: *kammaṭṭhānābhimukhaṃ satiṃ ṭhapayitvā*). In the *Vibhaṅga*, the phrase *parimukhaṃ satiṃ upaṭṭhapetvā* is explained as referring to the establishment of mindfulness 'on the tip of the nose or upper lip' (Vibh 252: *sūpaṭṭhitā nāsikagge vā mukhanimitte vā*). See also Vibh-a 368.

pajānāti, rassaṃ vā passasanto: rassaṃ passasāmīti pajānāti). In the previous section, it was simply stated that the meditator is mindful as he breathes in and mindful as he breathes out (*so sato va assasati sato passasati*). As the word 'knows' (*pajānāti*) is introduced here for the first time in the *sutta*, we need to explore what it refers to.

The verb *jānāti* (i.e., without the prefix *pa-*) generally means 'knows,' whereas *pajānāti,* in the context of this *sutta,* could be rendered into English as 'knows well' or 'understands the object well.' Thus, in this *sutta, pajānāti* is not used in a general sense but appears specifically in relation to the meditator who knows the object of contemplation very well and clearly understands its nature without greed (*lobha*), aversion (*dosa*) or delusion (*moha*).[8] The term *pajānāti* 'knows' is related to the verb *viharati* 'abides,' explained earlier as referring to the meditator who dwells or abides with the object of contemplation. Comparing the two, *viharati* is a broader term, implying that the meditator knows the object of contemplation but not necessarily as well as in the case of *pajānāti,* which instead conveys a clear, in-depth understanding of the nature of the object.

As said in the *sutta*, the meditator knows when inhalation or exhalation is long (*dīghaṃ vā assasanto: dīghaṃ assasāmīti pajānāti, dīghaṃ vā passasanto: dīghaṃ passasāmīti pajānāti*), meaning that she or he can see and understand it as such. Some meditators experience the breath as if it is many meters long; this is an impression, the way it is experienced, seen without clinging or opposing. Or the meditator knows when the breathing is short (*rassaṃ vā assasanto: rassaṃ assasāmīti pajānāti, rassaṃ vā passasanto: rassaṃ passasāmīti pajānāti*). Sometimes, when the breath is experienced as very short and soft, the meditator wonders whether it is sufficient to stay alive; this experience actually indicates that the defilements (*kilesa*) (e.g., greed, aversion, delusion, conceit) have diminished. If the meditator does not like the subtleness of the breath, aversion (*dosa*) may arise, and she or he may think that the meditation was going very well up to that point, but now it has worsened. However, if the meditator clearly knows and understands (*pajānāti*) how greed (*lobha*) or aversion (*dosa*) arise, such thoughts that evaluate one's breathing as 'good' or 'not good' simply vanish. This explanation of *pajānāti* is not explicitly articulated in the *sutta*, although it is implied: when the meditator clearly knows (*pajānāti*) her or his breathing, the defilements (*kilesa*) fade away.

As humans, we are all born with greed (*lobha*), hatred (*dosa*) and delusion (*moha*), and so when we breathe in and out, our minds are influenced by them. But when the meditator knows and clearly understands (*pajānāti*) the nature of the mind, then these three unwholesome roots subside. It is the decrease in greed (*lobha*), hatred (*dosa*) and delusion (*moha*) that changes the perception of the breath from long to short; the breath gradually seems to fade along with the subsiding of defilements. In the early stages of practice, one often holds onto and notes the object of meditation with greed, thinking: 'I must maintain my mind on this object,' believing that this is the way to progress. When the meditator wants to maintain the mind in one place for a long time, it generates delusion (*moha*); however, in the initial stages of meditation, such an approach is more or less inevitable until one knows and clearly understands (*pajānāti*) the nature of the three unwholesome roots.

---

8. Generally, both verbs, *jānāti* and *pajānāti,* are rendered into English as 'knows, understands, recognises, distinguishes' (PED, *s.v.*). In this *sutta*, Pemasiri Thera associates *pajānāti* with the absence of greed (*lobha*), aversion (*dosa*) and delusion (*moha*). His interpretation can be linked to the explanation of *pajānāti* given in the *Atthasālinī*, where it is connected to (the etymologically related term) wisdom (*paññā*): 'Wisdom means that one knows. What does one know? The noble truths: this is suffering, etc.' (As 122: *Pajānātī ti paññā. Kiṃ pajānāti? Idaṃ dukkhan ti ādinā nayena ariyasaccāni*).

'Experiencing the whole body' (*sabbakāyapaṭisaṃvedī*)

After the instructions on knowing whether one is breathing long or short, the *sutta* continues: 'He trains thus: "I shall breathe in experiencing the whole body"; he trains thus: "I shall breathe out experiencing the whole body"' (*sabbakāyapaṭisaṃvedī assasissāmīti sikkhati, sabbakāyapaṭisaṃvedī passasissāmīti sikkhati*).

The canonical commentaries and many meditation teachers interpret 'experiencing the whole body' (*sabbakāyapaṭisaṃvedī*) in reference to the physical body[9] or, following the post-canonical commentaries, explain it as knowing the beginning, middle and end of the breath.[10] However, the term 'experiencing the whole body' (*sabbakāyapaṭisaṃvedī*) could be interpreted in a different way. Here the word 'body' (*kāya*) does not refer only to the physical body or the body of the whole breath but also to the 'mental body' (*nāmakāya*), that is, the body of mental concomitants (*cetasika*). As a result, the term *sabbakāyapaṭisaṃvedī* could be rendered as 'experiencing the whole mental body,' meaning the mental concomitants (*cetasika*).[11] This is the stage in meditation when unwholesome states (i.e., those that caused difficulties for the meditator in earlier stages) recede. When one is 'experiencing the whole mental body' (*sabbakāyapaṭisaṃvedī*), thoughts such as 'I have to pay attention to the breath in this way or I must calm myself' no longer occur, the breath is simply perceived as continuously flowing in and out and the mind starts to incline towards calm (*samatha*). Now the meditator can note the in-breaths and out-breaths without any problem, as the hindrances (*nīvaraṇa*) have subsided. The mind has become collected and tranquil, not only in regard to the breath but also when one eats, takes a bath or walks. The meditator has strong concentration (*samādhi*) based on the in-breaths and out-breaths with very few discursive thoughts, the five faculties (*pañc'indriyāni*) (i.e., trust, energy, mindfulness, concentration and wisdom) are well established and the mind has arrived at a stable level of calm (*samatha*). At this point, the meditator has a very free and easy state of mind and can sit in meditation for long periods of time, while some meditators may attain meditative absorption (*jhāna*).

When the meditator is at the stage of 'experiencing the whole body' (*sabbakāyapaṭisaṃvedī*), greed (*lobha*), hatred (*dosa*) and delusion (*moha*) are greatly diminished and cannot be seen;

---

9. This interpretation is given by some modern teachers of meditation such as Goenka (1999, 29) who connects 'experiencing the whole body' to experiencing bodily sensations.

10. This explanation is given, for example, in the *Visuddhimagga*, which interprets the phrase 'experiencing the whole body' (*sabbakāyapaṭisaṃvedī*) as: 'I shall breathe in making known, making clear, the beginning, middle and end of the whole body of breathing in' (Vism 273: *assāsakāyassa ādimajjhapariyosānaṃ viditaṃ karonto, pākaṭaṃ karonto assasissāmī ti sikkhati*). The text further explains that the meditator observes the beginning, middle and end of each in- and out-breath at one particular point using the metaphor of a person who sits at the foot of a swing, remaining still at one point while observing the middle of the swing plank and both its ends and knowing the movement of coming and going (Vism 280–281).

11. The Pāli word *kāya* has a broad spectrum of meanings such as 'heap, collection, aggregate, physical body, one of the senses, bodily action' (DP; PED, *s.v.*). Here Pemasiri Thera's interpretation of the term *kāya* has parallels with *Abhidhamma* texts; e.g., in the *Dhammasaṅgaṇi* (Dhs 14–16), *kāya* refers to the group of mental concomitants (*cetasika*) or, in other words, to the aggregates of feeling (*vedanā*), perception (*saññā*) and mental formations (*saṅkhāra*); the term is similarly interpreted in the *Abhidhammattha Saṅgaha* (Aung and Rhys Davids, 1910, 96; cf. Bodhi 1993, 87). Although the commentaries on the *Satipaṭṭhānasutta* do not interpret in this way, Pemasiri Thera's explanation seems reasonable: as the mindfulness of breathing progresses and concentration grows, the breath is increasingly perceived as shorter and subtler, while objects relating to the physical body occur less frequently or subside; at this point, mental concomitants such as peace and tranquillity may come to the forefront of the meditator's experience.

consequently, she or he may no longer perceive the breath as her or his own, but as something that seems external, just an air element, without being related to the other elements. Or, one can experience only the earth element without any connection to the other elements, or likewise the fire element.[12] This means that the elements are experienced as external phenomena, and the practice evolves into insight meditation (*vipassanā*). The realisation that there is no being called 'I' is particularly important since it represents the portal for the emergence of right view (*sammā diṭṭhi*).

'He trains' (*sikkhati*)

The *sutta* says that the meditator 'trains' (*sikkhati*) with each in- and out-breath 'experiencing the whole body' (*sabbakāyapaṭisaṃvedī assasissāmīti sikkhati, sabbakāyapaṭisaṃvedī passasissāmīti sikkhati*). When instructions are given about short and long breaths, the verb 'knows' (*pajānāti*) is used, whereas here the verb 'trains' (*sikkhati*) is introduced. In the section on the mindfulness of breathing (*ānāpānasati*), three different verbs are thus used: 'abides' (*viharati*), 'knows' (*pajānāti*) and 'trains' (*sikkhati*). The term 'abides' (*viharati*) has the broadest signification, referring to the entire training; its meaning encompasses the two other verbs: 'knows' (*pajānāti*) and 'trains' (*sikkhati*).

'Knows' (*pajānāti*) denotes the clear understanding of the object of meditation, whereas the word *sikkhati* signifies that 'one is disciplined or restrains oneself,'[13] meaning that one restrains oneself in relation to the object, which is the breath in this case. The term *sikkhati* could also be applied in other areas; for example, if used in relation to moral precepts (*sīla*), it would mean that one is restrained or well established in living according to the precepts, which become a natural way of life or second nature. When the *sutta* says that the meditator trains in experiencing the whole body while breathing, this means that she or he knows the whole body well and is restrained or established in that knowledge.[14]

In other words, when one lives or abides (*viharati*) with the object—here, the breath—this includes the understanding that the meditator restrains her or himself (*sikkhati*) in relation to the

12. In the *Satipaṭṭhānasutta*, the term *dhātu* occurs in the section on the contemplation of the body (*kāyānupassanā*) as the four basic qualities of materiality or elements (*dhātu*), namely, the earth element (*paṭhavīdhātu*), water element (*āpodhātu*), fire element (*tejodhātu*) and air element (*vāyodhātu*). For details, see Chapter II.5. Reflection on the four elements (*catudhātumanasikāra*) below.

13. The verb *sikkhati* is usually rendered as 'to train oneself, learn, attempt to overcome' (PED, *s.v.*), thus encompassing the meaning of 'restraint' to which Pemasiri Thera refers in his interpretation of this term.

14. Here Pemasiri Thera attempts to explore the different meanings of the two verbs (i.e., *sikkhati* and *pajānāti*) in this *sutta*. In the canonical Pāli texts and commentaries, the term *sikkhati* mainly appears in the context of the mindfulness of breathing (*ānāpānassati*) and only very occasionally when restraint in virtue (*sīla*) is discussed. By contrast, the term *pajānāti* has many attestations and occurs in all texts detailing the foundations of mindfulness (*satipaṭṭhāna*). It is worth noting that in the *Satipaṭṭhānasutta* (M I 55–63), the verb *sikkhati* is only used in the section on mindfulness of breathing (*ānāpānassati*), specifically in relation to experiencing and calming the whole body (M I 56: *Sabbakāyapaṭisaṃvedī assasissāmīti sikkhati, sabbakāyapaṭisaṃvedī passasissāmīti sikkhati. Passambhayaṃ kāyasaṅkhāraṃ assasissāmīti sikkhati, passambhayaṃ kāyasaṅkhāraṃ passasissāmīti sikkhati*). In all other sections of this *sutta*, the term *pajānāti* is used. Conversely, in the *Ānāpānasatisutta* (M III 78–99), the term *sikkhati* is used throughout the *sutta*, apart from the section on mindfulness of breathing (*ānāpānasati*) where the term *pajānāti* appears just four times in relation to the contemplation of short and long breaths (M III 82: *Dīghaṃ passasāmīti pajānāti; dīghaṃ vā passasanto: Dīghaṃ passasāmīti pajānāti; rassaṃ vā assasanto: Rassaṃ assasāmīti pajānāti; rassaṃ vā passasanto: Rassaṃ passasāmīti pajānāti*). This is one of the several indications that the two *suttas* may have originated from disparate sources or even schools and that the *Ānāpānasatisutta* may represent a separate (earlier?) layer of Buddhist transmissions.

object (i.e., the breath) and clearly knows (*pajānāti*) it with mindfulness (*sati*). The term *sikkhati* does not only apply to the breath but also to any other object or training towards *nibbāna*; it can also refer to monastic training or the cultivation of virtues. In this *sutta*, the term 'trains, restrains' (*sikkhati*) is used for the stage when the meditator has achieved a certain level of calmness, when the mental body (*nāmakāya*) (i.e., mental concomitants) has been tranquillised because of the restraint achieved through mindfulness (*sati*) and clear comprehension (*sampajañña*).[15]

'Calming the body formation' (*passambhayaṃ kāyasaṅkhāraṃ*)

In the next sentence, the *sutta* says that the meditator trains her or himself by breathing in and out, 'calming the body formation' (*passambhayaṃ kāyasaṅkhāraṃ*). However, in the expression 'body formation' (*kāyasaṅkhāraṃ*), the word *kāya* does not denote the physical body. At this stage, the meditator usually does not apprehend the breath at all, because she or he has reached a high level of tranquillity. The meditator sits in meditation for long periods of time, and the breath is so calm and subtle that it can no longer be noted. Because of the (temporary) absence of defilements, the breath is so refined that for the meditator, it seems to have completely stopped; she or he remains in this state of peacefulness and lightness with little or no awareness of the body. Previously, at the stage of 'experiencing the whole body' (*sabbakāyapaṭisaṃvedī*), the meditator could still perceive the breath, but when the stage of 'calming the body formation' (*passambhayaṃ kāyasaṅkhāraṃ*) is reached, she or he no longer feels it. Now the practice of calm (*samatha*) is well established, and the meditator may continue with it or turn to insight (*vipassanā*) meditation.[16]

When the meditator continues with insight (*vipassanā*) meditation, she or he may experience the body and breath as two different phenomena. This is not mentioned in the *Satipaṭṭhānasutta* but is included in another *sutta* on mindfulness of breathing, namely, the *Ānāpānasatisutta*:

> [He] trains thus: "I shall breathe in calming the body formation"; trains thus: "I shall breathe out calming the body formation." Monks, on that occasion, a monk abides contemplating the body as a body, ardent, clearly comprehending, mindful, having abandoned desires and discontent in regard to the world. I say, monks, that this is a certain body among the bodies, namely, in-breathing and out-breathing (M III 83).[17]

This means that breathing is perceived as a different, separate phenomenon or as a kind of body among the bodies, different from other phenomena or 'bodies' experienced in the practice. Such an understanding does not arise in every meditator but only in those who have profound insights into the nature of phenomena; this means that the body is contemplated

---

15. The *Visuddhimagga* interprets the term 'trains, restrains' (*sikkhati*) as training in higher virtue (*adhisīlasikkhā*), higher consciousness (*adhicittasikkhā*) and higher understanding (*adhipaññāsikkhā*) (Vism 274), while referring to the *Paṭisambhidāmagga* (Paṭis 184: *yo tattha saṃvaraṭṭho ayaṃ adhisīlasikkhā, yo tattha avikkhepaṭṭho ayaṃ adhicittasikkhā, yo tattha dassanaṭṭho ayaṃ adhipaññāsikkhā*).

16. Similarly, in a passage describing the stage of 'calming the body formation' (*passambhayaṃ kāyasaṅkhāraṃ*), the *Papañcasūdanī* (Ps I 248–249) comments that the breath becomes extremely subtle, complete calmness is achieved and the four absorptions (*jhāna*) arise. The text goes on to say how the practice then turns into insight (*vipassanā*) meditation, with the contemplation of the four elements (*cattāri mahābhūtāni*), mind and body (*nāmarūpa*) and dependent origination (*paṭiccasamuppāda*), with the development of insight into the three characteristics (*tilakkhaṇa*). Cf. Vism 274–276.

17. M III 83: *passambhayaṃ kāyasaṅkhāraṃ passasissāmī'ti sikkhati; kāye kāyānupassī, bhikkhave, tasmiṃ samaye bhikkhu viharati ātāpī sampajāno satimā vineyya loke abhijjhādomanassaṃ. kāyesu kāyaññatarāhaṃ, bhikkhave, evaṃ vadāmi yadidaṃ assāsapassāsaṃ.*

without an 'I,' without a sense of self (*anattā*).[18]

In the section on mindfulness of breathing (*ānāpānasati*), the word 'thus' (*iti*) is used with two verbs: 'thus he knows' (*iti pajānāti*) and 'thus he trains' (*iti sikkhati*). This word is used in Pāli to mark either direct and indirect speech or discursive thought (i.e., *iti* sets apart quotations from the surrounding text). Sometimes this use of 'thus' (*iti*) is interpreted by meditators as labelling or naming the object of contemplation; for example, the feeling of pain is labelled as 'pain, pain, pain' or the hearing of a sound is labelled as 'hearing, hearing, hearing.'[19] Such labelling may be helpful in the initial stages of meditation, but one should not continue labelling for too long, because one may cling to this practice as well as to the objects of mindfulness (*sati*). For example, when breathing in, one should simply know it without saying or verbalising it in the mind: 'breathing in, breathing in.' Instead, one should direct the mind to the inhalation and exhalation and then start abiding in this kind of contemplation. Or when one sees an object, it is enough to know that seeing takes place, or when hearing a sound to know that hearing takes place.

Table 2 Outline of the progressive stages in the cultivation of mindfulness of breathing (*ānāpānasati*).

1	Preliminary requirements	• gone to a secluded place (*araññagato vā rukkhamūlagato vā suññāgāragato vā nisīdati*) • sitting upright with folded legs (*pallaṅkaṃ ābhujitvā*) • having established mindfulness in front (*parimukhaṃ satim upaṭṭhapetvā*)
2	The meditator clearly knows (*pajānāti*)	• breathing in long, breathing out long (*dīghaṃ assasāmi, dīghaṃ passasāmi*) • breathing in short, breathing out short (*rassaṃ assasāmi, rassaṃ passasāmi*)
3	The meditator trains or is restrained (*sikkhati*) in relation to the breath	• experiencing the whole (mental) body (*sabbakāyapaṭisaṃvedī*)
4	The meditator trains or is restrained (*sikkhati*) in relation to the breath	• calming the body/mental formations (*passambhayaṃ kāyasaṅkhāra*)

To summarise, in the section on mindfulness of breathing (*ānāpānasati*), one is first instructed to be mindful as one breathes in and out (*so sato va assasati, sato passasati*), without attachment, craving or aversion. Then the meditator knows (*pajānāti*) whether she or he is breathing in and out long (*dīgham*) or short (*rassam*), this means that she or he knows the natural breath. The entire process of knowing occurs without any deliberation. As the practice continues, the breath is increasingly experienced as shorter and ever subtler, and the meditator experiences

18. Pemasiri Thera's interpretation of the term 'body among the bodies' is based on the experiences of some meditators at the stage when insight meditation (*vipassanā*) develops. However, the *Papañcasūdanī* commentary explains the term as referring to the air element (*vāyo*), thus signifying the body of breath, which is one of the four bodies, each corresponding respectively to one of the four elements (Ps IV 139–140: *Kāyaññataranti pathavīkāyādīsu catūsu kāyesu aññataraṁ vadāmi, vāyo kāyaṁ vadāmīti attho*).

19. Labelling or naming the physical or mental phenomena experienced in mindfulness training is a method that is recommended, especially for beginners, in the Mahāsi Sayadaw meditation tradition.

deep tranquillity. When the breath is experienced as rather gross and easily perceived, this is because it is connected with greed (*lobha*), aversion (*dosa*) and delusion (*moha*). As these three unwholesome roots become attenuated, the meditator stays more easily with the breath, reaching the stage of 'experiencing the whole body' (*sabbakāyapaṭisaṃvedī*). Here the process of breathing is experienced as if it continues on its own, without any relation to an 'I.' Although the breath is still experienced at this stage, the body is no longer felt, and thus the breath is experienced externally, sometimes as if situated in front of the meditator or to one side.

Later on, the breath becomes increasingly subtler, until the in-breaths and out-breaths seem to be no longer there; profound tranquillity is experienced. With this stage of 'calming the body formation' (*passambhayaṃ kāyasaṅkhāra*), the section on mindfulness of breathing (*ānāpānasati*) in the *Satipaṭṭhānasutta* ends.

Recurring passage indicating the ways to approach contemplation

The section on mindfulness of breathing (*ānāpānasati*), which is part of the chapter on the contemplation of the body (*kāyānupassanā*), is concluded by the following recurring passage, indicating ways to approach the practice(s) being presented:

> *Iti* ***ajjhattaṃ*** *vā kāye kāyānupassī viharati,* ***bahiddhā*** *vā kāye kāyānupassī viharati,* ***ajjhattabahiddhā*** *vā kāye kāyānupassī viharati.* ***Samudayadhammānupassī*** *vā kāyasmiṃ viharati,* ***vayadhammānupassī*** *vā kāyasmiṃ viharati,* ***samudayavayadhammānupassī*** *vā kāyasmiṃ viharati. Atthi kāyo ti vā panassa sati paccupaṭṭhitā hoti* ***yāvadeva*** *ñāṇamattāya patissatimattāya, anissito ca viharati na ca kiñci loke upādiyati. Evampi bhikkhave bhikkhu kāye kāyānupassī viharati.*
>
> 'Thus he abides contemplating the body as a body **internally**, or he abides contemplating the body as a body **externally**, or he abides contemplating the body as a body both **internally and externally**. He abides **contemplating the arising of phenomena** in the body, or he abides **contemplating the passing away of phenomena** in the body, or he abides **contemplating both the arising and passing away of phenomena** in the body. Or, mindfulness that "there is a body" is established in him **just to the extent necessary for knowledge and mindfulness**. And he abides without attachment, not clinging to anything in the world. Monks, thus a monk abides contemplating the body as a body.'

This and the subsequent sections of the *Satipaṭṭhānasutta* are always concluded by the same formulaic passage that summarises a range of specific ways to approach the practice. The passage follows every one of the four *satipaṭṭhanas*, i.e., the sections on the contemplation of the body (*kāyānupassanā*), the contemplation of feeling (*vedanānupassanā*), the contemplation of the mind (*cittānupassanā*), and the contemplation of phenomena (*dhammānupassanā*). In total, the recurring passage occurs twenty-one times in the *Satipaṭṭhānasutta*, indicating it to be exceptionally important or an essential aspect of the practice of the four *satipaṭṭhānas*. Furthermore, the formulaic passage indicates the end of a particular section or topic in the *sutta*, thus serving as a mark to separate the *sutta* into sections, as followed in this book (Table 3).[20]

20. I have added several tables and diagrams to the main body of the book to systematically present some of the main features of the comments made by Pemasiri Thera, who himself uses charts, tables and drawings in his talks. In addition, I would like to acknowledge that in Table 3 and some of the following ones, I have drawn inspiration from Anālayo (2003).

Table 3 Structure of the text with the recurring passage.

Contemplation of the body (*kāyānupassanā*)
1. Mindfulness of breathing (*ānāpānasati*)
   Recurring passage
2. Ways of movement (*iriyāpatha*)
   Recurring passage
3. Clear comprehension (*sampajañña*) of bodily activities
   Recurring passage
4. Reflection on the troublesomeness (*paṭikkūlamanasikāra*) of the body
   Recurring passage
5. Reflection on the four elements (*catudhātumanasikāra*)
   Recurring passage
6. Nine cemetary contemplations (*navasīvathikā*)
   Nine recurring passages (each cemetary contemplation followed by one)

Contemplation of feeling (*vedanānupassanā*)
   Recurring passage

Contemplation of the mind (*cittānupassanā*)
   Recurring passage

Contemplation of phenomena (*dhammānupassanā*)
1. Five hindrances (*pañca nīvaraṇāni*)
   Recurring passage
2. Five aggregates of clinging (*pañcas'upādānakkhandhā*)
   Recurring passage
3. Six sense spheres (*cha āyatanāni*)
   Recurring passage
4. Seven factors of awakening (*satta bojjhaṅgā*)
   Recurring passage
5. Four noble truths (*cattāri ariyasaccāni*)
   Recurring passage

Pemasiri Thera's commentary

'Internally' (*ajjhattam*), 'externally' (*bahiddhā*) and 'internally and externally' (*ajjhattabahiddhā*)

The recurring passage in the *sutta* states that the contemplation of the body (*kāyānupassanā*) can be practised in three different ways: internally (*ajjhattam*), externally (*bahiddhā*) or both internally and externally (*ajjhattabahiddhā*). The canonical Pāli commentaries as well as most modern meditation teachers interpret contemplation performed internally (*ajjhattam*) in reference to oneself, externally (*bahiddhā*) in reference to others, and internally and externally (*ajjhattabahiddhā*) in reference to both oneself and others.[21]

To exemplify this, when one begins cultivating mindfulness of breathing (*ānāpānasati*), the breath and any other objects are noted with the idea that there is someone called 'I' or 'myself,' that the breath is 'mine,' and that there is an 'I' who is mindful and observant of the breath and other phenomena experienced. This can be called the contemplation of breathing performed internally (*ajjhattam*). As the meditator progresses on the noble eightfold path and her or his practice evolves towards insight (*vipassanā*) meditation, an understanding gradually emerges that there is no 'I' but instead a flow of objects and processes. The meditator then starts contemplating the breathing process without the sense of 'I' and may experience it as though it were not taking place in its usual place but somewhere else, outside the body, or even in a body belonging to someone else. It sometimes seems to the meditator as if there were two people meditating. If the object of contemplation is the arising and falling of the abdomen, it may be perceived somewhere in front of the meditator, in space, without any connection to the physical abdomen. In walking meditation, the meditator may perceive as though somebody else's body is walking, or alternatively, she or he may experience it without any reference, as if there is no person walking but just the process of movement. Thus, the meditator starts to comprehend that there is just knowing and an object that is being known, but there is no 'I,' the knower. In this manner, the meditator can relate not only to the breath or bodily movements but also to feeling (*vedanā*) or any other object occurring in the four domains of mindfulness (i.e., the body, feeling, mind and phenomena). This way of experiencing breathing or any other process can be called contemplation carried out externally (*bahiddhā*).[22]

Or, if the object of contemplation is a pain in the knee, for example, initially it is noted as pain occurring in 'my' knee, thus being contemplated internally (*ajjhattam*). Later in meditation practice, the meditator may suddenly observe only pain, without connecting it to her or his knee, perceiving the pain as if it were not in the knee but somewhere else. Occasionally, the pain may be observed in the left knee but the noting of the pain is done in the right knee. In this case, the pain in the knee is experienced externally (*bahiddhā*). Thus, contemplation is carried out externally (*bahiddhā*) when the notion of 'I' no longer arises with experiences or, in other words, it means that the meditator relates to or perceives the objects of experi-

21. Buddhaghosa explains these three ways in the *Papañcasūdanī* and the other commentaries on the *Nikāyas* as follows: *ajjhattaṃ* refers to oneself (*attano*), *bahiddhā* to another (*parassa*) and *ajjhattabahiddhā* sometimes to oneself and sometimes to another (*kālena attano, kālena parassa*) (Ps I 249: *iti ajjhattaṃ vāti evaṃ attano vā assāsapassāsakāye kāyānupassī viharati. Bahiddhā vāti parassa vā assāsapassāsakāye. Ajjhattabahiddhā vāti kālena attano, kālena parassa assāsapassāsakāye*) (cf. Vism 450, 473; As 46, 325). This became the standard interpretation of the terms *ajjhattaṃ*, *bahiddhā* and *ajjhattabahiddhā* in the Theravāda tradition and has been followed by most modern interpreters and teachers of the practice of the *satipaṭṭhānas*. For an in-depth study of the three ways to approach contemplation, see Ditrich (2016b).

22. To my knowledge, only one passage in the *Tipiṭaka* gives a similar interpretation, namely, the *Satipaṭṭhānavibhaṅga*, which interprets the contemplation of the body 'internally and externally' (*ajjhattabahiddhā*) as experiencing the body as such, without any reference to 'oneself' or 'another' (Vibh 194: *ajjhattabahiddhā kāyaṃ ... paccavekkhati: atthi kāye*). This implies that such contemplation occurs while experiencing non-self (*anattā*); see Ditrich (2016b, 130–132).

ence without craving (*taṇhā*), conceit (*māna*) or views (*diṭṭhi*).[23] The interpretation of internally (*ajjhattam*) and externally (*bahiddhā*) contemplating as observing phenomena in oneself and others respectively seems to have been created only later in the post-canonical texts.[24]

'Contemplating the arising of phenomena (*samudayadhammānupassī*), 'contemplating the passing away of phenomena' (*vayadhammānupassī*) and 'contemplating the arising and passing away of phenomena' (*samudayavayadhammānupassī*)

The passage continues with the contemplation of the arising of phenomena (*samudayadhammānupassī*), the passing away of phenomena (*vayadhammānupassī*) and both the arising and passing away of phenomena (*samudayavayadhammānupassī*) in the body. The word *dhamma* has a wide range of meanings depending on the context.[25] In the broader sense of this word, all objects that are contemplated in the context of the four foundations of mindfulness (*satipaṭṭhāna*) could be called *dhamma*. When this *sutta* states that the meditator contemplates the arising and passing away of phenomena in the body (*samudayadhammānupassī vā kāyasmiṃ viharati, vayadhammānupassī vā kāyasmiṃ viharati, samudayavayadhammānupassī vā kāyasmiṃ viharati*),[26] the word *dhamma* refers to the phenomena of materiality (*rūpa*), the mind (*citta*) and mental concomitants (*cetasika*) that are arising (*samudaya*) and passing away (*vaya*) while the

23. As explained in the *Sāratthappakāsinī*, view(s) (*diṭṭhi*), craving (*taṇhā*) and conceit (*māna*) are linked to the three aspects of creating the self, namely, 'I am' (*aham asmi*) is linked to views (*diṭṭhi*), 'mine' (*mama*) to craving (*taṇhā*) and 'myself' (*me attā*) to conceit (*māna*) (Spk II 215: *ahaṅkāramamaṅkāramānānusayāti ahaṃkāradiṭṭhi ca mamaṃkārataṇhā ca mānānusayā ca*).

24. The *Suttapiṭaka* does not comment on the meaning of internally (*ajjhattam*) and externally (*bahiddhā*) or how such contemplations should be practised, save for one exception: in the *Janavasabhasutta*, *bahiddhā* is interpreted as referring to the body of another (*parakāye*), whereas *ajjhattaṃ* is not commented on (D II 216: ... *bahiddhā para-kāye ñāṇa-dassanaṃ abhinibbatteti*). The interpretation of *bahiddhā* as referring to another person occurs in some *Abhidhamma* texts and canonical commentaries (e.g., Dhs 187–188, 241–242; As 46; Vibh-a 219) (see Ditrich 2016b).

25. Like many other key Buddhist concepts, the term *dhamma* has no English equivalent. It signifies an ancient Indian concept that was adopted and, to a large extent, reinterpreted in Buddhism with a broad semantic spectrum. The term variously refers to the essential components of existence, natural law, the foundational constituent(s) of experience, Buddhist understanding and practice, religious teaching, theory, doctrine, etc. (see DP, *s.v.*). Here, I have opted for the more common English rendering of 'phenomenon,' since it is discussed in the context of the four foundations of mindfulness (*satipaṭṭhāna*), which largely revolve around the contemplation of the nature of experience at the level of ultimate reality (*paramattha*). According to the Theravāda *Abhidhamma*, the ultimate reality is comprised of four categories: i.e., the mind (*citta*), mental concomitants (*cetasika*), materiality (*rūpa*) and *nibbāna*. However, when the term refers to the Buddha's teachings as such, I adopt the commonly accepted, capitalised word Dhamma.

26. The translation of *samudayadhammānupassī vā kāyasmiṃ viharati* into English can be rendered in two ways depending on the parsing of the word *dhamma* in this compound: (1) if the word is read in the plural, it can be translated as 'he abides contemplating the arising phenomena (*dhammas*) in the body' (this interpretation is followed by Walshe 1995, 336); (2) if the word appearing at the end of the compound is read in the singular as 'having the nature of' (Warder 1971, 282–283), the phrase could be rendered: 'he abides contemplating the nature of the origination in the body' (thus interpreted by Bodhi 2000, 1659). Pemasiri Thera follows the first reading here. The second reading of *samudayadhammānupassī* is grammatically problematic, since as a *bahubbīhi* compound the phrase would primarily have an adjectival function. In translating this compound, I have opted for the first interpretation, which is also supported by commentaries such as the *Papañcasūdanī* (Ps I 249). By translating the three modes of contemplation as 'the arising of phenomena' (*samudayadhammānupassī*), 'the passing away of phenomena' (*vayadhammānupassī*) and both 'the arising and passing away of phenomena' (*samudayavayadhammānupassī*), I have stressed that the focus of this contemplation is on the impermanency of the process observed.

meditator contemplates the body (*kāya*).[27] For example, in the practice of walking meditation, the meditator experiences the arising and passing away of bodily materiality (*rūpa*) as well as the arising and passing away of the mind (*citta*) and its accompanying mental concomitants (*cetasika*) through which these changes are contemplated. The meditator may notice all three aspects equally (i.e., arising, passing away and both arising and passing away) or one aspect more strongly (i.e., passing away or arising of phenomena) or both arising and passing away equally. These three aspects are a vital part of the contemplation of any phenomena occurring in all four domains of mindfulness practice (*satipaṭṭhāna*), as they give rise to an insight into impermanence (*anicca*).

Changes over time like ageing and decay can be seen in the objects and processes around us, but what we see is only gross change (*vipariṇāma*), which occurs because of impermanence (*anicca*). This is why impermanence is often referred to as the first of the three characteristics of conditioned phenomena into which the meditator begins to gain insight. Initially, one can see change at the gross level (*vipariṇāma*) by observing the world around, seeing that everything that arises will eventually pass away and dissolve. People generally cannot see the more subtle impermanence (*anicca*) of the five aggregates (*khandha*) (i.e., materiality, feeling, perception, mental formations and consciousness) because of ignorance (*avijjā*), as stated in the *Khandhasaṃyutta*:

> [T]he uninstructed worldling ... does not understand ... [that] materiality is subject to arising and vanishing ... does not understand feeling ... perception ... mental formations ... [and] consciousness [are] subject to arising and vanishing. This is called ignorance, monks, and in this way, one is immersed in ignorance (S III 171).[28]

Only when mindfulness (*sati*) has evolved and the meditator contemplates phenomena (*dhammānupassī*) at the level of the aggregates (*khandha*), elements (*dhātu*) and sense spheres (*āyatana*) does a more refined perception of impermanence (*anicca*) emerge. For example, when raising the hand or looking at an object, the meditator may observe and comprehend this process as the arising (*samudaya*) and passing away (*vaya*) of the aggregate of materiality (*rūpa*) and understands impermanence (*anicca*) at a subtle level. When it is said in the *sutta* that the meditator 'abides contemplating the arising of phenomena in the body, or he abides contemplating the passing away of phenomena in the body, or he abides contemplating both the arising and passing away of phenomena in the body' (*samudayadhammānupassī vā kāyasmiṃ viharati, vayadhammānupassī vā kāyasmiṃ viharati, samudayavayadhammānupassī vā kāyasmiṃ viharati*), this does not only refer to the mindful observation of phenomena (*dhamma*) arising (*samudaya*) and passing away (*vaya*) in the body (*kāyasmiṃ*) but also to 'contemplating' (*anupassī*)[29] them, meaning that the phenomena are seen as the aggregates (*khandha*), elements (*dhātu*) and sense spheres (*āyatana*).

---

27. In other words, the practice takes place at the level of ultimate reality (*paramattha*) by contemplating the mind (*citta*), mental concomitants (*cetasika*) and materiality (*rūpa*).

28. S III 171: *assutavā puthujjano samudayadhammaṃ rūpaṃ 'samudayadhammaṃ rūpan'ti yathādhammaṃ na pajānāti; vayadhammaṃ rūpaṃ 'vayadhammam rūpan'ti yathābhūtaṃ na pajānāti; samudayavayadhammaṃ rupaṃ 'samudayavayadhammaṃ rūpan'ti yathābhūtaṃ na pajānāti. Samudayadhammaṃ vedanaṃ ... saññāṃ ... saṅkhāre ... viññāṇam na pajānāti. Ayaṃ vuccati bhikkhu avijjā.*

29. For the discussion on the term 'contemplation,' see Chapter I, under the subheading 'Contemplation (*anupassanā*).'

Although the meditator eventually develops insight into all three characteristics (*tilakkhaṇa*), the understanding of impermanence (*anicca*) usually comes first, especially in meditators with strong faith or trust (*saddhā*), whereas those with strong wisdom (*paññā*) tend to see non-self (*anattā*) and those with strong effort (*vāyāma*) perceive unsatisfactoriness (*dukkha*) more prominently. For most meditators, the insight into impermanence (*anicca*) indicates and initiates the development of wisdom (*paññā*) followed by the insight into unsatisfactoriness (*dukkha*) and non-self (*anattā*).

'To the extent necessary for knowledge and mindfulness' (*yāvadeva ñāṇamattāya patissatimattāya*)

Then the *sutta* states: 'mindfulness that "there is a body" is established in him just to the extent necessary for knowledge and mindfulness' (*yāvadeva ñāṇamattāya patissatimattāya*). The meditator who is well established in mindfulness, as the *sutta* continues, lives without attachment, without clinging to anything in the world (*anissito ca viharati na ca kiñci loke upādiyati*). Therefore, the meditator is simply mindful that 'there is a body' and lives contemplating in the knowledge that there is no 'I,' no self.[30] In the following sections, this recurring passage similarly indicates the ways to approach this contemplation in relation to feeling (*vedanā*), the mind (*citta*) and phenomena (*dhamma*).

The phrase 'just to the extent necessary for knowledge and mindfulness' (*yāvadeva ñāṇamattāya patissatimattāya*) means that mindfulness (*sati*) is established for the purpose of cultivating understanding and wisdom or, in other words, to the extent that the noble eightfold path (*ariyo aṭṭhaṅgiko maggo*) develops. Here the word *ñāṇa* refers to the knowledge or understanding of the noble eightfold path all the way up to path knowledge (*maggañāṇa*) and liberation (*nibbāna*).[31] Sometimes path knowledge (*maggañāṇa*) is also called *maggapaññā*, 'the path wisdom.'[32] Through wisdom (*paññā*), which is a perfected knowledge (*ñāṇa*), the hindrances are destroyed,[33] and the three characteristics (*tilakkhaṇa*) are understood. Thus, mindfulness (*sati*) is cultivated to the extent required for the meditator to gain insight into the three characteristics of all conditioned phenomena and attain path knowledge (*maggañāṇa*) and final liberation (*nibbāna*).

---

30. The *Papañcasūdanī* commentary similarly interprets this phrase: 'There is a body, but no being, no person, no woman, no man, no self, nothing related to self, no 'I,' nothing mine, no one, nothing belonging to anyone' (Ps I 249: *atthi kāyoti vā panassāti kāyova atthi, na satto, na puggalo, na itthī, na puriso, na attā, na attaniyaṃ, nāhaṃ, na mama, na koci, na kassacīti evamassa sati paccupaṭṭhitā hoti*).

31. The term *ñāṇa* has a wide spectrum of meanings such as 'knowledge, insight, understanding, reason' (DP; PED, *s.v.*). Pemasiri Thera's linking of knowledge (*ñāṇa*) to wisdom (*paññā*) and path knowledge (*maggañāṇa*) is found in the *Abhidhamma*, where knowledge (*ñāṇa*) of the four noble truths (*cattāri ariyasaccāni*) and dependent origination (*paṭiccasamuppāda*) is described as wisdom (*amoha*) (Dhs 189; Vibh 104), whereas the knowledge of the truths, path and fruition is linked to purity of view (*diṭṭhivisuddhi*) (Dhs 233: *Tattha katamā diṭṭhivisuddhi? Kammassa kataṃ ñāṇasaccānulomikaṃ ñāṇaṃ maggasa maṅgissa ñāṇaṃ phalasamaṅgissa ñāṇaṃ*). Path knowledge (*maggañāṇa*) refers to supramundane (*lokuttara*) knowledge, which arises separately in four instances (i.e., as knowledge of the path of stream-winner, once-returner, non-returner and arahant) by an insight into the four truths (Vibh-a 416: *maggañāṇaṃ catūsu saccesu ekapaṭivedhavasena catūsu ṭhānesu saṅgahitaṃ*).

32. The term *maggapaññā* is frequently found in the commentaries on the *Nikāyas* and *Abhidhamma* (e.g., Sv II 380; Ps II 51; Vibh-a 417–418).

33. For example, in the *Pattakammasutta*, the accomplishment of wisdom (*paññāsampadā*) is explained as the understanding and abandonment of the five hindrances, namely, sensory desire (*kāmacchanda*), ill-will (*vyāpāda*), sloth and torpor (*thīnamiddha*), restlessness and worry (*uddhaccakukkucca*) and doubt (*vicikicchā*) (A II 66–67).

In the *sutta*, it is said 'just to the extent,' meaning that the mindfulness practice is developed up to the level of path knowledge (*maggañāṇa*) and not any further, because it is through path knowledge (*maggañāṇa*) that the fetters (*saṃyojana*)[34] are destroyed and liberation from suffering (*dukkha*) is consequently achieved. This marks the end of the cultivation of mindfulness (*sati*), as it is not required beyond this point. Mindfulness (*sati*) and all the other components of the noble eightfold path (*ariyo aṭṭhaṅgiko maggo*) are like a raft used to cross a river; once the other shore is reached, the raft is no longer needed, as it is only necessary for the purpose of crossing the stream.[35] The qualities cultivated on the noble eightfold path resemble plants like the plantain, which die after producing fruit.[36] Thus, the entire noble eightfold path is only cultivated and maintained for the purpose of crossing over *saṃsāra*, the round of rebirths.

Table 4 Ways of conducting contemplation in the *Satipaṭṭhānasutta*.

• Internally (*ajjhattam*) • Externally (*bahiddhā*) • Internally and externally (*ajjhattabahiddhā*)	• Internally: from the perspective of self, with the notion of an 'I' or observer • Externally: from the perspective of non-self, there is just knowing and the object of knowing
• Contemplating the arising of phenomena (*samudayadhammānupassī*) • Contemplating the passing away of phenomena (*vayadhammānupassī*) • Contemplating both the arising and passing away of phenomena (*samudayavayadhammānupassī*)	Contemplation of impermanence: • Initial stage: observation of gross change (*vipariṇāma*) • Refined stage: perception of impermanence (*anicca*) of the aggregates (*khandha*), elements (*dhātu*) and sense spheres (*āyatana*)
• To the extent necessary for knowledge and mindfulness (*yāvadeva ñāṇamattāya patissatimattāya*)	Mindfulness practice is developed up to: • The level of path knowledges (*maggañāṇa*) when • The fetters (*saṃyojana*) are destroyed

II 2 Ways of movement (*iriyāpatha*)[37]

Puna ca paraṃ bhikkhave bhikkhu ***gacchanto*** *vā: gacchāmīti pajānāti,* ***ṭhito*** *vā ṭhitomhīti pajānāti,* ***nisinno*** *vā nisinnomhīti pajānāti,* ***sayāno*** *vā sayānomhīti pajānāti, yathā yathā vā panassa kāyo paṇihito hoti tathā tathā naṃ pajānāti.*

34. The Pāli canonical and post-canonical texts frequently list the following ten fetters (*saṃyojana*): (1) personality view (*sakkāyadiṭṭhi*), (2) doubt (*vicikicchā*), (3) attachment to rites and rituals (*sīlabbataparāmāsa*), (4) sense desire (*kāmacchanda*), (5) ill will (*vyāpāda*), (6) desire for material existence (*rūparāga*), (7) desire for immaterial existence (*arūparāga*), (8) conceit (*māna*), (9) restlessness (*uddhacca*) and (10) ignorance (*avijjā*). For details, see Chapter V.3, under the subheading 'Fetter (*saṃyojana*).'
35. The oft-cited raft parable appears, for example, in the *Alagaddūpamasutta* in the *Majjhimanikāya* (M I 134–135).
36. This parable is taken from the *Lābhasakkārasaṃyutta* (S II 241), where it is nevertheless used in a different context.
37. The chapters of the *Satipaṭṭhānasutta* in Pāli are not divided into sections; the headings are usually added by translators of the *sutta* into English, mostly based on the Pāli commentaries. The term *iriyāpatha* means ways of movement or posture; it is thus used in the *Papañcasūdanī* in the beginning (Ps I 250) and end of this section (Ps I 252).

'Again, monks, when **walking**, a monk knows: "I am walking"; when **standing**, he knows: "I am standing"; when **sitting**, he knows: "I am sitting"; when **lying down**, he knows: "I am lying down"; or he knows accordingly in whatever way his body is positioned.'

Recurring passage indicating the ways to approach the contemplation[38]

Iti ajjhattaṃ vā kāye kāyānupassī viharati, bahiddhā vā kāye kāyānupassī viharati, ajjhattabahiddhā vā kāye kāyānupassī viharati. Samudayadhammānupassī vā kāyasmiṃ viharati, vayadhammānupassī vā kāyasmiṃ viharati, samudayavayadhammānupassī vā kāyasmiṃ viharati. Atthi kāyo ti vā panassa sati paccupaṭṭhitā hoti yāvadeva ñāṇamattāya patissatimattāya, anissito ca viharati na ca kiñci loke upādiyati. Evampi bhikkhave bhikkhu kāye kāyānupassī viharati.

'Thus he abides contemplating the body as a body internally, or he abides contemplating the body as a body externally, or he abides contemplating the body as a body both internally and externally. He abides contemplating the arising of phenomena in the body, or he abides contemplating the passing away of phenomena in the body, or he abides contemplating both the arising and passing away of phenomena in the body. Or, mindfulness that "there is a body" is established in him just to the extent necessary for knowledge and mindfulness. And he abides without attachment, not clinging to anything in the world. Monks, thus a monk abides contemplating the body as a body.'

Pemasiri Thera's commentary

'Walking' (*gacchanto*), 'standing' (*ṭhito*), 'sitting' (*nisinno*) and 'lying down' (*sayāno*)

In the domain of the contemplation of the body (*kāyānupassanā*), mindfulness (*sati*) and clear comprehension (*sampajañña*) can be also established through the contemplation of the ways of movement (*iriyāpatha*), that is, the four postures: walking (*gacchanto*), standing (*ṭhito*), sitting (*nisinno*) and lying down (*sayāno*). The meditator should try to maintain mindfulness (*sati*) in these four postures without greed (*lobha*) or aversion (*dosa*). For example, if a monk goes on the alms round, he should keep walking as the object of concentration in his mind. While walking (*gacchanto*), his attention and concentration should be directed towards the two stages of walking—lifting and placing each foot. If the meditator walks at a slower pace, she or he may focus on three stages—lifting, moving forward and placing each foot—or even six stages—the intention to lift the foot, lifting, the intention to move it forward, moving it forward, the intention to place it down and placing it down. In this way, the meditator develops attention (*manasikāra*). Gradually through this training, mindfulness (*sati*) can emerge. If a monk practises in this manner, the alms round will take about two hours or more. Here the word 'knows' (*pajānāti*) is used again, meaning that the meditator knows well the nature of the meditation object without desire (*abhijjhā*) or discontent (*domanassa*)[39] and understands how the mind and body interrelate. Through this practice, the meditator starts comprehending impermanence (*anicca*) and non-self (*anattā*), namely, that there is no 'doer.'[40]

38. For comments on the recurring passage, see Chapter II.1, under the subheading 'Recurring passage indicating the ways to approach the contemplation.'

39. For example, in the *Mahāsuññatāsutta*, it is said that a monk who contemplates walking thus reflects: 'While I am walking in this way, no unwholesome states of desire or discontent will befall me' (M III 112–113: *evaṃ maṃ caṅkamantaṃ nābhijjhādomanassā pāpakā akusalā dhammā anvāssavissantīti*); then the *sutta* continues with the same statement in relation to the three other postures.

40. Pemasiri Thera again links the term 'clearly knows' (*pajānāti*) to wisdom (*paññā*), that is, the insight into the three characteristics (*tilakkhaṇa*). This is also highlighted in the *Atthasālinī*: 'Wisdom means that one clearly

The contemplation of the sitting posture is performed in two ways. While seated (*nisinno*), the meditation object can be either the touch points felt in the body or the breath (*ānāpānasati*). Especially for the meditator who cannot feel the breath, she or he may begin the contemplation of the sitting posture by focusing on various touch points felt in the body. Similarly, in the standing posture (*ṭhito*), the meditator can pay attention to two objects: either the touch felt on the soles of the feet or the breath. Very few meditators are taught mindfulness of breathing (*ānāpānasati*) in the standing posture, although it is a very valuable practice. In the prone or lying-down posture (*sayāno*), the touch points are the main object of attention for the establishment of mindfulness (*sati*). Sometimes mindfulness of breathing (*ānāpānasati*) is practised in the lying-down posture, but for this kind of practice, the meditator must already have strong mindfulness (*sati*).

In the *sutta*, it is said that the meditator 'knows' (*pajānāti*) a particular posture, which means that regardless of the bodily posture, she or he knows it clearly and understands it without greed (*lobha*), aversion (*dosa*) or delusion (*moha*). While engaged in the contemplation of the body (*kāyānupassanā*) that encompasses mindfulness of the four bodily postures, feeling (*vedanā*) can be observed, namely, pleasant (*sukham*), unpleasant (*dukkham*) or neither-pleasant-nor-unpleasant (*adukkhamasukham*).[41]

II 3 Clear comprehension (*sampajañña*) of bodily activities

Puna ca paraṃ bhikkhave bhikkhu abhikkante paṭikkante ***sampajānakārī*** *hoti, ālokite vilokite sampajānakārī hoti, samiñjite pasārite sampajānakārī hoti, saṅghāṭipattacīvaradhāraṇe sampajānakārī hoti, asite pīte khāyite sāyite sampajānakārī hoti, uccārapassāvakamme sampajānakārī hoti, gate ṭhite nisinne sutte jāgarite bhāsite tuṇhībhāve sampajānakārī hoti.*

'Again, monks, when going forward and returning, a monk **acts with clear comprehension**; when looking ahead and looking away, he acts with clear comprehension; when bending and stretching his limbs, he acts with clear comprehension; when wearing his robes, outer robe and bowl, he acts with clear comprehension; when eating, drinking, consuming food and tasting, he acts with clear comprehension; when defecating and urinating, he acts with clear comprehension; when walking, standing, sitting, falling asleep, waking up, talking and keeping silent, he acts with clear comprehension.'

Recurring passage indicating the ways to approach the contemplation[42]

Iti ajjhattaṃ vā kāye kāyānupassī viharati, bahiddhā vā kāye kāyānupassī viharati, ajjhattabahiddhā vā kāye kāyānupassī viharati. Samudayadhammānupassī vā kāyasmiṃ viharati, vayadhammānupassī vā kāyasmiṃ viharati, samudayavayadhammānupassī vā kāyasmiṃ viharati. Atthi kāyo ti vā panassa sati

---

knows. ... What makes it clearly know? Impermanence, unsatisfactoriness and non-self' (As 122: *Pajānātīti paññā. ... Kinti paññāpetīti? Aniccaṃ dukkhaṃ anattāti paññāpeti*). Similarly, the *Papañcasūdanī* commentary explains that the meditator explores the relationship between the four postures and the mind, aiming to gain insight into the absence of a being, a doer or a self (*anattā*). For example, when discussing walking, the commentary says: 'Who is walking? No living being or person is walking. Whose walking is it? The walking is not of any living being or person' (Ps I 251: *Tattha ko gacchatīti na koci satto vā puggalo vā gacchati. Kassa gamananti na kassaci sattassa vā puggalassa vā gamanaṃ*).

41. All types of feelings will be discussed in Chapter III.

42. For comments on the recurring passage, see Chapter II.1, under the subheading 'Recurring passage indicating the ways to approach the contemplation.'

paccupaṭṭhitā hoti yāvadeva ñāṇamattāya patissatimattāya, anissito ca viharati na ca kiñci loke upādiyati. Evampi bhikkhave bhikkhu kāye kāyānupassī viharati.

'Thus he abides contemplating the body as a body internally, or he abides contemplating the body as a body externally, or he abides contemplating the body as a body both internally and externally. He abides contemplating the arising of phenomena in the body, or he abides contemplating the passing away of phenomena in the body, or he abides contemplating both the arising and passing away of phenomena in the body. Or, mindfulness that "there is a body" is established in him just to the extent necessary for knowledge and mindfulness. And he abides without attachment, not clinging to anything in the world. Monks, thus a monk abides contemplating the body as a body.'

Pemasiri Thera's commentary

'Acts with clear comprehension' (*sampajānakārī*)

In this section, the meditator is instructed to act with clear comprehension (*sampajānakārī*) in every activity, focusing on whatever is happening at the present moment as an object of contemplation. There is no aspect of our daily activities that cannot be included in this section: talking or staying silent, eating or drinking, walking, falling asleep, going to the bathroom or dressing—everything becomes part of the practice of clear comprehension (*sampajañña*). As the meditator builds up mindfulness (*sati*) in all daily activities, without generating desire (*abhijjhā*) or discontent (*domanassa*) towards the experiences, clear comprehension (*sampajañña*) can emerge. Every bodily activity, even down to the very minutest action such as blinking the eyes, should be done knowingly with clear comprehension (*sampajañña*).

In the previous section on the ways of movement (*iriyāpatha*), it is said that a monk 'knows' (*pajānāti*) when walking, standing, sitting or lying down, which means that he knows the four postures comprehensively, with mindfulness (*sati*) at the forefront (*parimukham*). In this section, it is said that a monk acts with clear comprehension (*sampajānakārī*), positioning comprehension or understanding at the forefront (*parimukham*). In every action, even the most subtle, the meditator establishes an understanding, being aware not only of the actions performed but also of the intentions arising before the actions. It is very important to see and understand intentions in meditation practice. When the intentions and subsequent actions are clearly comprehended, the meditator understands the absence of a person, a self, involved in these processes, which arise and pass away.[43]

The term 'acting with clear comprehension' (*sampajānakārī*) is used only in this section of the *Satipaṭṭhānasutta*, while elsewhere the cultivation of mindfulness (*sati*) is at the forefront (*parimukham*). In the contemplation of daily activities, every small action should be observed

43. In the *Papañcasūdanī* commentary, a relatively long section is dedicated to the discussion of clear comprehension (*sampajañña*) and its four aspects: clear comprehension of purpose (*sātthakasampajañña*), clear comprehension of suitability (*sappāyasampajañña*), clear comprehension of resort (*gocarasampajañña*) and clear comprehension of non-delusion (*asammohasampajañña*) (Ps I 253: *tattha sātthakasampajaññaṃ sappāyasampajaññaṃ gocarasampajaññaṃ asammohasampajaññanti catubbidhaṃ sampajaññaṃ*). The first two aspects mean understanding the purpose and suitability of one's activities, that is, how appropriate they are for the life of a monk dedicated to the cultivation of virtue (*sīla*), meditation (*samādhi*) and wisdom (*paññā*). The third aspect means focusing on the meditation object (*kammaṭṭhāna*), i.e., always keeping the meditation object at the forefront and thus restraining the senses and protecting the mind. The fourth aspect is the comprehension of non-delusion (*asammoha*); this means understanding that there is no self, no person, who is involved in the activities but instead there are just interrelated impermanent processes and conditions, which are subject to suffering. The commentary particularly emphasises the importance of the insight into non-self (*anattā*), which is gained through the development of clear comprehension (*sampajañña*) (Ps I 253–261).

with understanding, thus acting with clear comprehension (*sampajānakārī*). For example, when blinking the eyes, the meditator cannot know that it is done without greed (*lobha*) or aversion (*dosa*) but can simply understand that blinking has occurred. Similarly, when moving the hand, the meditator knows that this movement has happened but cannot say that it is done without greed (*lobha*) or aversion (*dosa*), because it occurs too quickly; therefore, the meditator simply observes this process with clear understanding. Or when the meditator dresses, this process has nothing to do with wanting or aversion; it is rather an act comprised of innumerable changing processes that are performed out of necessity.

Similarly, in the process of eating, greed (*lobha*) or aversion (*dosa*) may arise just before one begins eating depending on whether the food is desirable or not, but in the process of eating itself there is only chewing, touching the food with the hand, lifting, seeing and so on. When seeing the food before eating, mindfulness (*sati*) alone should be at the forefront (*parimukham*), since this is the time when craving or aversion may arise. However, when bringing the food to the mouth, clear comprehension (*sampajañña*) is at the forefront (*parimukham*). Then, once the food touches the tongue and the meditator tastes it, a pleasant or unpleasant feeling (*vedanā*) may become prominent; herein the meditator enters the domain of the contemplation of feeling (*vedanānupassanā*). When eating, for a short period of time, greed (*lobha*) or aversion (*dosa*) may arise in regard to the taste of the food; mindfulness (*sati*) should once again be at the forefront (*parimukham*). But most of the time when eating, it is only necessary to have clear comprehension (*sampajañña*) to comprehend the ever-changing processes involved. In some meditation centres, very slow eating is practised, with the meditators perhaps taking two hours or more to finish their meal. This may be exaggerated; if eating is slowed down to such an extent, the meditator may lose both mindfulness (*sati*) and clear comprehension (*sampajañña*).

Performing daily activities with clear comprehension (*sampajānakārī*) is a very important aspect of meditation practice, and it is particularly helpful for the cultivation of mindfulness (*sati*) and wisdom (*paññā*). In the beginning, as a helpful tool to strengthen attention, meditators are sometimes asked to use words to label their daily activities. For example, the meditator labels the act of looking by the word 'looking,' or when stretching out the arm would label it 'stretching' and so on. However, labelling should only be performed in the initial stages of meditation practice and only in regard to the contemplation of bodily movements in daily activities. In all other domains of practice, it is sufficient to know (*pajānāti*) the arising of phenomena without labelling them. In other words, the most important thing is knowing and clearly understanding whatever one is doing.

To summarise, when mindfulness (*sati*) arises along with clear comprehension (*sampajañña*), the meditator can maintain mindfulness and stay in the state of wholesomeness for long periods. In daily activities, clear comprehension (*sampajañña*) is at the forefront (*parimukham*), while in other domains, it is mindfulness (*sati*). Clear comprehension (*sampajañña*) is an early stage in the development of wisdom (*paññā*),[44] which means understanding the three characteristics (*tilakkhaṇa*) of all phenomena and non-self (*anattā*). When mindfulness (*sati*) is established, the objects are seen without any aversion or craving, while clear comprehension (*sampajañña*) understands their impermanence, their arising and passing away.[45] In the contemplation of

44. As noted above, in the *Abhidhamma* texts, clear comprehension (*sampajañña*) is defined as the faculty of wisdom (*paññā*), which includes understanding, insight, analytical discrimination, wise reflection and so on (Dhs 16; Vibh 194).

45. This is described, for example, in the *Satipaṭṭhānasaṃyutta* (S V 180–181); for more details, see Chapter I, under

daily activities, the meditator sees in every movement the processes that rapidly change. This change is thus initially observed in bodily activities, but eventually it is comprehended in all phenomena arising at the six sense doors along with an insight into their conditionality and the three characteristics.

II 4 Reflection on the troublesomeness (*paṭikkūlamanasikāra*) of the body

Puna ca paraṃ bhikkhave bhikkhu imameva kāyaṃ uddhaṃ pādatalā adho kesamatthakā tacapariyantaṃ pūraṃ nānappakārassa asucino paccavekkhati: Atthi imasmiṃ kāye kesā lomā nakhā dantā taco maṃsaṃ nahāru aṭṭhī aṭṭhimiñjā vakkaṃ hadayaṃ yakanaṃ kilomakaṃ pihakaṃ papphāsaṃ antaṃ antaguṇaṃ udariyaṃ karīsaṃ, pittaṃ semhaṃ pubbo lohitaṃ sedo medo assu vasā kheḷo siṅghāṇikā lasikā muttanti. Seyyathā pi bhikkhave ubhato mukhā mutoḷī pūrā nānāvihitassa dhaññassa, seyyathīdaṃ: sālīnaṃ vīhīnaṃ muggānaṃ māsānaṃ tilānaṃ taṇḍulānaṃ, tamenaṃ cakkhumā puriso muñcitvā paccavekkheyya: ime sālī, ime vīhī, ime muggā, ime māsā ime tilā ime taṇḍulā ti, evameva kho bhikkhave bhikkhu imameva kāyaṃ uddhaṃ pādatalā adho kesamatthakā tacapariyantaṃ pūrannānappakārassa asucino paccavekkhati: Atthi imasmiṃ kāye kesā lomā nakhā dantā taco maṃsaṃ nahāru aṭṭhī aṭṭhimiñjā vakkaṃ hadayam yakanaṃ kilomakaṃ pihakaṃ papphāsaṃ antaṃ antaguṇaṃ udariyaṃ karīsaṃ, pittaṃ semhaṃ pubbo lohitaṃ sedo medo assu vasā kheḷo siṅghāṇikā lasikā muttanti.

'And again, monks, a monk reflects on this very body up from the soles of the feet and down from the top of the hair, bounded by skin, as full of many kinds of impurity: "In this body there are head-hairs, body-hairs, nails, teeth, skin, flesh, sinews, bones, bone-marrow, kidneys, heart, liver, diaphragm, spleen, lungs, intestines, mesentery, stomach contents, faeces, bile, phlegm, pus, blood, sweat, fat, tears, grease, spittle, snot, oil of the joints and urine." Just as if there were a bag with an opening at both ends, full of many sorts of grain such as hill rice, red rice, beans, peas, millet and white rice, and a man with good eyes were to open it and review it thus: "This is hill rice, this is red rice, these are beans, these are peas, this is millet, this is white rice"; so too, a monk reflects on this very body up from the soles of the feet and down from the top of the hair, bounded by skin, as full of many kinds of impurity thus: "In this body there are head-hairs, body-hairs, nails, teeth, skin, flesh, sinews, bones, bone-marrow, kidneys, heart, liver, diaphragm, spleen, lungs, intestines, mesentery, stomach contents, faeces, bile, phlegm, pus, blood, sweat, fat, tears, grease, spittle, snot, oil of the joints and urine."'

Recurring passage indicating the ways to approach the contemplation[46]

Iti ajjhattaṃ vā kāye kāyānupassī viharati, bahiddhā vā kāye kāyānupassī viharati, ajjhattabahiddhā vā kāye kāyānupassī viharati. Samudayadhammānupassī vā kāyasmiṃ viharati, vayadhammānupassī vā kāyasmiṃ viharati, samudayavayadhammānupassī vā kāyasmiṃ viharati. Atthi kāyo ti vā panassa sati paccupaṭṭhitā hoti yāvadeva ñāṇamattāya patissatimattāya, anissito ca viharati na ca kiñci loke upādiyati. Evampi bhikkhave bhikkhu kāye kāyānupassī viharati.

'Thus he abides contemplating the body as a body internally, or he abides contemplating the body as a body externally, or he abides contemplating the body as a body both internally and externally. He abides contemplating the arising of phenomena in the body, or he abides contemplating the passing away of phenomena in the body, or he abides contemplating both the arising and passing away of phenomena in the body. Or, mindfulness that "there is a body" is established in him just to the extent necessary for knowledge and mindfulness. And he abides without attachment, not clinging to anything in the world. Monks, thus a monk abides contemplating the body as a body.'

---

the subheading 'Clearly comprehending (*sampajāno*).'

46. For comments on the recurring passage, see Chapter II.1, under the subheading 'Recurring passage indicating the ways to approach the contemplation.'

Pemasiri Thera's commentary

'Troublesomeness' (*paṭikkūla*) of the body[47]

The section on the contemplation of the body (*kāyānupassanā*) also includes a reflection on the thirty-one parts of the body.[48] It is often called a reflection on the repulsiveness or impurity of the body (*paṭikkūlamanasikāra*), but in this context, the meaning of the term *paṭikkūla*[49] rather refers to the troublesome or disagreeable nature of the body. Any one of the body parts listed here, from the teeth and skin to the internal organs, can at some point cause many troubles, difficulties or pain in our lives and thus become a source of suffering. But we usually do not think about the body as being troublesome, rather the opposite; we are usually more attached to our body than to other things. But the reflection on the parts of the body does not mean that the meditator should generate bad feelings or disgust about her or his body, since this would give rise to aversion (*dosa*); properly cultivated contemplation should lead to understanding and tranquillity. If the meditator understands very well that any part of the body can become a source of trouble and suffering (*dukkha*), then there is nothing in the body to crave for or be angry about. When this is well understood, mindfulness (*sati*) and clear comprehension (*sampajañña*) can easily become established.

The contemplation of the parts of the body as the primary meditation object is usually recommended to meditators with a more clinging nature who are strongly attached to pleasures.[50] It can also be adopted as the meditation object for those who, for various reasons, cannot practise mindfulness of breathing (*ānāpānasati*), touching points or the four postures, however much they try. When teaching or practising meditation, it is important to be aware that one method is not suitable for everybody and that sometimes meditation objects have to be changed at various stages. Therefore, contemplation of the parts of the body may be the most suitable meditation object for some meditators but not for others. However, in the case of monks and nuns, this practice should be initially undertaken, as it is introduced at the ordination ceremony: when their hair is shaved off, the first five parts of the body from the list are given to novices for contemplation.

The contemplation of the thirty-one parts of the body is one of the most fruitful methods that allows mindfulness (*sati*) and clear comprehension (*sampajañña*) to arise. There are various ways to practise this contemplation, but the meditator most commonly begins with the parts of the body that can be seen from the outside, namely, the first five parts of the body

---

47. Pemasiri Thera here comments on the entire section without singling out any particular term attested in the *sutta* itself. I have added the subheading 'Troublesomeness (*paṭikkūla*) of the body,' since he comments mostly on this term. This section is introduced in the commentary *Papañcasūdanī* as 'reflection on troublesomeness' (Ps I 270: *idāni paṭikūlamanasikāravasena vibhajituṃ*). The reflection on the parts of the body is also known as *asubha bhāvanā*, often translated as the 'contemplation on the impurities of the body.' Similarly, this contemplation is called the 'perception of unattractiveness' (*asubhasaññā*) in the *Girimānandasutta* (A V 109).

48. The *Satipaṭṭhānasutta* lists thirty-one parts of the body. However, the *Papañcasūdanī* commentary speaks of thirty-two parts (Ps I 271). The *Visuddhimagga* explains that the additional part of the body is the brain (*matthalunga*), which is included in the *Satipaṭṭhānasutta* under bone marrow (*aṭṭhimiñjā*) (Vism 240: *matthalungaṃ aṭṭhimiñjena sangahetvā paṭikkūlamanasikāravasena desitaṃ dvattiṃskārakammaṭṭhānaṃ*).

49. The term *paṭikkūla* is usually translated as 'disagreeable, objectionable, loathsome, impurity' (see PED, *s.v.*).

50. Several instances in the canonical texts such as the *Udāyīsutta* (A III 323) recommend the contemplation of body parts as a method to abandon sense desire (*kāmarāgassa pahānāya*). A more detailed description of this contemplation is given in the *Visuddhimagga* (Vism 240–266), where it is presented as one of the recollection objects (*anussatikammaṭṭhāna*) of meditation.

listed in the *sutta*, as they can most easily be used as objects of attention:

1. head-hairs, body-hairs, nails, teeth and skin.

Then the other parts are contemplated in five separate groupings of five or six, arranged in the following manner:

2. flesh, sinews, bones, bone-marrow and kidneys;
3. heart, liver, diaphragm, spleen and lungs;
4. intestines, mesentery, stomach contents, faeces and bile;
5. phlegm, pus, blood, sweat and fat; and
6. tears, grease, spittle, snot, oil of the joints and urine.

The parts are first recited verbally and then repeated mentally. The first nineteen parts are related to the earth element and the last twelve to the water element; they are understood as being non-self.[51]

The meditator thus contemplates each group of five (or six) parts separately, starting with the first five listed. When the first five parts are contemplated, one of them will stand out more than the others. The meditator then contemplates the second group, and once again, one of the five parts will be perceived more prominently than the others. Thus, having contemplated all six groups in this manner, there will be six prominent parts in total, one from each of the six groups that will be contemplated again until one of those stands out, which will be selected as the main meditation object. This practice should be gradually undertaken in a systematic manner, slowly contemplating each part within each group, then the shortlisted parts and finally, the most prominent one.[52] While the meditator contemplates each part of the body, she or he pays attention to several aspects: its location in the body, its connection to the body and its colour, shape and smell.[53]

If the meditator contemplated all the parts of the body, the meditation object would be far too varied, making it difficult to develop sufficiently strong concentration.[54] Similarly, in the meditation on loving kindness (*mettābhāvanā*), one cannot build deep concentration if the object is too diversified; therefore, the meditator is often instructed to focus on just one person as the object of cultivation of loving kindness. Or, in recollection of the virtues of the Buddha (*buddhānussati*), the object is too complex, and therefore one cannot attain meditative

51. For example, this is also explained in the *Mahārāhulovādasutta*, which emphasises that the four elements should be understood with wisdom, seen as not being 'mine,' 'I' or 'myself' (M I 421–422: *Taṃ: n' etaṃ mama, n' eso hamasmi, na me so attā ti evam-etaṃ yathābhūtaṃ sammappaññāya daṭṭhabba*); this is similarly expressed in the *Dhātuvibhaṅgasutta* (M III 240–241).

52. The method of meditation on the parts of the body, which is described by several modern meditation teachers of the Theravāda tradition (e.g., Pa-Auk 2003, 67–72), draws largely from the *Visuddhimagga*, where it is said that the meditator, after thoroughly contemplating all the body parts, gives her or his entire attention only to the most prominent one (Vism 245: *... eko suṭṭhutaraṃ upaṭṭhāti, evaṃ upaṭṭhitaṃ pana tad eva punappunaṃ manasikarontena appanā uppādetabbā*).

53. Here Pemasiri Thera draws from the *Visuddhimagga*, where seven aspects of the contemplation of the body parts are listed: (1) verbal recitation of the parts, (2) mental recitation, (3) colour, (4) shape, (5) orientation in the body (above or below the navel), (6) location in the body and (7) delimitation in the body (juxtaposed to other parts) (Vism 241: *tattha vacasā, manasā, vaṇṇato, saṇṭhānato, disato, okāsato, paricchedato ti evaṃ sattadhā uggahakosallaṃ ācikkhitabbaṃ*).

54. As mentioned above, the *Visuddhimagga* recommends that the meditator should focus on only one body part to develop high concentration (Vism 245–246), and in this manner, she or he can reach absorption (*jhāna*) (Vism 265).

absorption(*jhāna*) but only access concentration (*upacāra samādhi*).[55] When applied and sustained thought (*vitakkavicāra*) are directed to and maintained on one object alone, other thoughts stop arising, and the mind remains with that object. The meditator can only then develop the four successive absorptions (*jhāna*). Applied thought (*vitakka*) and sustained thought (*vicāra*) are the first of the five components in the first absorption (*jhāna*); applied thought (*vitakka*) directs or applies attention to the meditation object, while sustained thought (*vicāra*) maintains or supports attention to remain on the object. The three other components are rapture or joy (*pīti*), happiness or contentment (*sukha*) and one-pointedness (*ekaggatā*) (Table 5)[56]

Table 5 Factors of absorptions (*jhāna*).

First absorption (*jhāna*)	**Second absorption (*jhāna*)**	**Third absorption (*jhāna*)**	**Fourth absorption (*jhāna*)**
applied thought (*vitakka*)			
sustained thought (*vicāra*)			
joy (*pīti*)	joy (*pīti*)		
happiness (*sukha*)	happiness (*sukha*)	happiness (*sukha*)	
one-pointedness (*ekaggatā*)	one-pointedness (*ekaggatā*)	one-pointedness (*ekaggatā*)	one-pointedness (*ekaggatā*)

In the case of insight (*vipassanā*) meditation, applied thought (*vitakka*) is directed towards an object such as the rising and falling process at the abdomen, while sustained thought (*vicāra*) maintains one's attention on the process. But the meditator must first understand what wise attention (*yoniso manasikāra*) is and what it is not, and what is the right and the wrong way of directing applied and sustained thought (*vitakkavicāra*) to the object. Applied and sustained thought (*vitakkavicāra*) are strongest when they arise together with mindfulness (*sati*) and clear comprehension (*sampajañña*). When they occur along with the understanding of the three characteristics (*tilakkhaṇa*), they are much stronger than in any other situation; therefore, the concentration (*samādhi*) that accompanies such insight is more powerful than in any other meditation practices. This is why at the end of the insight knowledges, just before reaching *nibbāna*, concentration (*samādhi*) is at its strongest, while applied and sustained thought (*vitakkavicāra*) dwell only on one of the three characteristics (*tilakkhaṇa*) without turning to another object.

Meditation on the body parts should be conducted gradually and slowly by initially concentrating on the name, shape and other characteristics of the body part until the meditator sees each part very clearly.[57] As the practice progresses, the troublesome and empty nature of the contemplated part becomes increasingly prominent. While focusing on a particular part of

55. Access concentration (*upacāra samādhi*) is a high level of concentration before absorption (*jhāna*); it is achieved when concentration (*samādhi*) on a chosen meditation object like the breath becomes strengthened, and the five hindrances (*nīvaraṇa*) are suspended. For details, see the *Visuddhimagga* (Vism 125–137).

56. A comprehensive presentation of the absorptions (*jhāna*) is given in the *Visuddhimagga* (Vism 122–169; 326–340).

57. In the *Visuddhimagga*, ten important aspects of the contemplation of the body parts are listed: (1) practising in the order listed, (2) not practising too quickly, (3) not practising too slowly, (4) warding off distractions, (5) overcoming concepts, (6) reducing the number of body parts to one, (7) developing high concentration, (8) equanimity, (9) coolness and (10) proficiency in the development of the factors of awakening (Vism 243: *evaṃ sattadhā uggahakosallaṃ ācikkhitvā anupubbato, nātisīghato, nātisaṇikato, vikkhepapaṭibāhanato, paṇṇattisamatikkamanato, anupubbamuñcanato, appanāto, tayo ca suttantā ti evaṃ dasadhā manasikārakosallaṃ ācikkhitabbaṃ*).

the body, the meditator becomes well concentrated and tranquil. In this practice, mindfulness (*sati*) and clear comprehension (*sampajañña*) can arise and especially an insight into non-self (*anattā*), an understanding that the body is not 'mine' and not 'myself,' that it does not behave in the way that I want it to, but that it is instead comprised of various parts and processes that can cause trouble and suffering (*dukkha*).[58] When the disagreeable and troublesome nature of the body is truly understood, the problems that arise from clinging to the body fall away.

II 5 Reflection on the four elements (*catudhātumanasikāra*)

Puna ca paraṃ bhikkhave bhikkhu imameva kāyaṃ yathāṭhitaṃ yathāpaṇihitaṃ dhātuso paccavekkhati: Atthi imasmiṃ kāye ***paṭhavīdhātu āpodhātu tejodhātu vāyodhātūti.*** *Seyyathā pi bhikkhave dakkho goghātako vā goghātakantevāsī vā gāviṃ vadhitvā cātummahāpathe bilaso paṭivibhajitvā nisinno assa, evameva kho bhikkhave bhikkhu imameva kāyaṃ yathāṭhitaṃ yathāpaṇihitaṃ dhātuso paccavekkhati: Atthi imasmiṃ kāye paṭhavīdhātu āpodhātu tejodhātu vāyodhātūti.*

'Again, monks, a monk reflects on this very body, however positioned and disposed, in terms of the elements thus: "In this body, there are **the earth element, the water element, the fire element and the air element**." Just as a skilled butcher or his apprentice, having killed a cow, were seated at a crossroads with the carcass cut up into pieces, so too a monk reflects on this very body, however positioned and disposed, in terms of the elements thus: "In this body, there are the earth element, the water element, the fire element and the air element."'

Recurring passage indicating the ways to approach the contemplation[59]

Iti ajjhattaṃ vā kāye kāyānupassī viharati, bahiddhā vā kāye kāyānupassī viharati, ajjhattabahiddhā vā kāye kāyānupassī viharati. Samudayadhammānupassī vā kāyasmiṃ viharati, vayadhammānupassī vā kāyasmiṃ viharati, samudayavayadhammānupassī vā kāyasmiṃ viharati. Atthi kāyo ti vā panassa sati paccupaṭṭhitā hoti yāvadeva ñāṇamattāya patissatimattāya, anissito ca viharati na ca kiñci loke upādiyati. Evampi bhikkhave bhikkhu kāye kāyānupassī viharati.

'Thus he abides contemplating the body as a body internally, or he abides contemplating the body as a body externally, or he abides contemplating the body as a body both internally and externally. He abides contemplating the arising of phenomena in the body, or he abides contemplating the passing away of phenomena in the body, or he abides contemplating both the arising and passing away of phenomena in the body. Or, mindfulness that "there is a body" is established in him just to the extent necessary for knowledge and mindfulness. And he abides without attachment, not clinging to anything in the world. Monks, thus a monk abides contemplating the body as a body.'

58. Pemasiri Thera comments that the contemplation of the body parts leads to the development of wisdom and liberation. This is also stated in the canonical texts; for example, in the *Therīgāthā*, a nun narrates how she became completely liberated after contemplating the parts of the body (Th 127: *uddhaṃ pādatalā amma adho ce kesamatthakā, paccavekkhassu 'maṃ kāyaṃ asuciṃ pūtigandhikaṃ. evaṃ viharamānāya sabbo rāgo samūhato, pariḷāho samucchinno sītibhūtamhi nibbutā*). This type of contemplation as the path to liberation is similarly described in the *Sampasādanīyasutta* (D III 104–105). The *Visuddhimagga* mentions that the benefits of the contemplation of the body parts (and other contemplations of the body) include incitement [towards liberation] (*saṃvega*), perfect peace (*yogakkhema*), mindfulness and clear comprehension (*satisampajañña*), attainment of insight knowledges (*ñaṇadassanapatilābha*), happy abiding in this world (*diṭṭhadhammasukhavihāra*) and attainment of the fruition of wisdom and liberation (*vijjāvimuttiphalasacchikiriya*) (Vism 239). By contrast, one of the most influential modern teachers of meditation, Mahāsi (2016, 255), states that the contemplation of the body parts cannot lead to insight and wisdom.

59. For comments on the recurring passage, see Chapter II.1, under the subheading 'Recurring passage indicating the ways to approach the contemplation.'

Pemasiri Thera's commentary

'Earth element' (*paṭhavīdhātu*), 'water element' (*āpodhātu*), 'fire element' (*tejodhātu*) and 'air element' (*vāyodhātu*)

When we investigate the body (*kāya*), we actually contemplate four aspects or modalities of materiality (*rūpa*), namely, the earth element (*paṭhavīdhātu*),[60] the water element (*āpodhātu*), the fire element (*tejodhātu*) and the air element (*vāyodhātu*).[61] These four elements comprise materiality (*rūpa*); there is nothing else in materiality but these elements combined. The four elements (*mahābhūta*)[62] always occur together in any type of materiality (*rūpa*); they are the ultimate components of materiality, present even in the minutest particles (*rūpakalāpa*).[63] For example, when the meditator contemplates a touch point or posture, she or he is mostly aware of the earth element (*paṭhavīdhātu*), meaning that she or he experiences heaviness, hardness and solidity. In the contemplation of the body, the fire element (*tejodhātu*) is experienced through temperature (heat or cold), the air element (*vayodhātu*) is especially apparent in breathing and movement and the water element (*āpodhātu*) provides coherence and fluidity.[64]

---

60. The Pāli word *dhātu* is usually translated into English as 'element,' although this translation significantly limits its broad semantic range, which includes 'natural condition, property, state, disposition, factor, item, principle, form, primary component' (DP, *s.v.*). The word *dhātu* is related to the word *dhamma*, which is another term with a very wide spectrum of meanings, including 'cosmic law, truth, Buddhist doctrine, condition, moral quality, righteousness, phenomenon, mental object, constituent, the fundamental unit of experience' (DP, *s.v.*). Here, I have retained the commonly accepted translation of *dhātu* as 'element,' but I would like to highlight that the word 'element' should not be exclusively associated with matter or linked to the concept of chemical elements as in modern Western science. Thus, as mentioned before, the word *dhātu* is explained in the *Bahudhātukasutta* (M III 61–63) in several ways as follows:

    1) eighteen components or elements of cognition: i.e., the five physical senses with their respective objects and consciousnesses and the mind element (*manodhātu*) with mental objects (*dhammadhātu*) and mind-consciousness (*manoviññāṇadhātu*);
    2) six elements or conditions: i.e., the elements of earth (*paṭhavīdhātu*), water (āpodhātu), air (*vāyodhātu*), fire (*tejodhātu*), space (*ākāsadhātu*) and consciousness (*viññāṇadhātu*);
    3) three elements or states: i.e., the sense sphere (*kāmadhātu*), fine material (*rūpadhātu*) and immaterial elements (*arūpadhātu*); or
    4) two elements or states: i.e., the conditioned (*saṅkhatā*) and unconditioned (*asaṅkhatā*) states.

    In the section on the contemplation of the body (*kāyānupassanā*) in the *Satipaṭṭhānasutta,* the term *dhātu* represents the basic aspects of materiality, namely, the earth element (*paṭhavīdhātu*), water element (āpodhātu), fire element (*tejodhātu*) and air element (*vāyodhātu*) (M I 157). For a more detailed analysis of the elements, see the *Vibhaṅga* (Vibh 82–98) and *Visuddhimagga* (Vism 484–490).

61. The four elements are discussed in several *suttas* such as the *Mahāhatthipadopamasutta* (M I 185–191) and, in greater detail, in post-canonical texts such as the *Visuddhimagga* (Vism 348–353; 364–371). For a comprehensive study of the Buddhist analysis of materiality, see Karunadasa (1967).

62. In the term 'great elements' (*mahābhūta*), the word *bhūta* refers to the four aspects of materiality; however, *bhūta* also has other meanings such as 'nature, world, truth, being' (DP, *s.v.*). In the *Papañcasūdanī*, it is explained as referring to the 'five aggregates, ghosts, elements, existence, those who are free from taints, all beings, plants and so on' (Ps I 31: *pañcakkhandhāmanussa-dhātu-vijjamāna-khīṇāsava-satta-rukkhādīsu dissati*).

63. The theory of minute particles (*rūpakalāpa*) is only recorded in commentarial Pāli literature from the *Visuddhimagga* onwards. For a detailed survey, see Karunadasa (1967, 142–163).

64. In the *Visuddhimagga* (Vism 365), the four elements are thus described:

    1) the earth element (*pathavīdhātu*) has the characteristic of hardness (*kakkhaḷattalakkhaṇā*), the function of supporting or grounding (*patiṭṭhānarasā*) and is manifested as acceptance or receiving (*sampaṭicchanapaccupaṭṭhānā*);
    2) the water element (*āpodhātu*) has the characteristic of trickling (*paggharaṇalakkhaṇā*), the function

Through the sense of touch (*phoṭṭhabba*), only three elements can be directly experienced—i.e., the earth element (*paṭhavīdhātu*), fire element (*tejodhātu*) and air element (*vāyodhātu*)—but not the water element (*āpodhātu*). For example, if a drop of water falls on the hand, one will feel the earth element (*paṭhavīdhātu*) through the heaviness of the falling drop, the fire element (*tejodhātu*) through the temperature of the water or the air element (*vāydhātu*) through the spreading quality of water. But the water element (*āpodhātu*) itself cannot be felt through the sense of touch (*phoṭṭhabba*); it can only be known by inference through the qualities of the three other elements, namely, solidity, temperature and spreading.[65] Water does not have a shape, colour, scent or taste; it cannot be known by the five bodily senses but only by the mind sense (*mano*), and hence it is experienced in the domain of mental objects (*dhammāyatana*). All the processes and changes in our bodies occur according to the functioning of the four elements. While all four elements (*mahābhūta*) are equally important, it is the fire element (*tejodhātu*) that plays a very prominent role in human life from birth to death; it strongly influences the processes of growing, ageing and dying. Thus, according to the Buddhist teachings, bodily changes such as greying hair, wrinkles and losing teeth are mainly influenced by the fire element (*tejodhātu*).

Materiality (*rūpa*) is considered to comprise twenty-seven material categories (*rūpadhamma*), which include the four great elements (*mahābhūta*) and twenty-three secondary or derived material categories (*upādāyarūpa*).[66] The *Satipaṭṭhānasutta* only discusses the four great elements (*mahābhūta*), which also comprise derived materiality (*upādāyarūpa*).[67] The space element (*ākāsadhātu*) is often mentioned along with the four great elements (*mahābhūta*);[68] it is

---

of increasing or intensifying (*brūhanarasā*) and is manifested as cohesion or holding together (*sangahapaccupaṭṭhānā*);

3) the fire element (*tejodhātu*) has the characteristic of heat (*uṇhattalakkhaṇā*), the function of ripening or maturing (*paripācanarasā*) and is manifested as providing softness (*maddavānuppadānapaccupaṭṭhānā*); and
4) the air element (*vayodhātu*) has the characteristic of supporting or distending (*vitthambhanalakkhaṇā*), the function of motion (*samudīraṇarasā*) and is manifested as directing or conveying (*abhinīhārapaccupaṭṭhānā*).

65. This is the Theravādin point of view; other early Buddhist schools propose that all four elements are tangible; for details, see Karunadasa (1967, 29–30).

66. The *Abhidhamma* texts contain several descriptions of the twenty-seven material elements (*rūpadhamma*) (e.g., Vibh 12–14; Dhs 124–179). In post-canonical texts such as the *Visuddhimagga,* twenty-eight material elements (*rūpadhamma*) are listed; the additional element is the heart base (*hadayavatthu*), viewed as a derived materiality (*upādārūpa*), which has the characteristic of being the foundation for the mind (*mano*) and mind-consciousness (*manoviññāna*) (Vism 447: *Manodhātumanoviññāṇadhatūnaṃ nissayalakkhaṇaṃ hadayavatthu*).

67. According to the *Visuddhimagga* (Vism 443–452), derived materiality (*upādāyarūpa*) includes:
1) five bodily sensitivities (*pasādarūpa*) and their objects (*gocararūpa*)
2) two gender faculties (*bhāvarūpa*)
3) life faculty (*jīvitarūpa*)
4) heart base (*hadayarūpa*)
5) nutriment (*āhārarūpa*)
6) space element (*ākāsadhātu*)
7) modes of communication (bodily and vocal) (*viññattirūpa*)
8) three modes of materiality (*vikārarūpa*)
9) four phases or characteristics of materiality (*lakkhaṇarūpa*)
For a detailed overview of derived materiality (*upādāyarūpa*), see Karunadasa (1967, 31–116).

68. The space element (*ākāsadhātu*) is usually listed along with the four great elements and consciousness; for example, in the *Dhātuvibhaṅgasutta*, it is said that a person consists of six elements: earth element (*paṭhavīdhātu*), water element (*āpodhātu*), fire element (*tejodhātu*), air element (*vāyodhātu*), space element, (*ākāsadhātu*) and consciousness element (*viññāṇadhātu*) (M III 237–247).

viewed as voidness, which allows for the separation or delimitation of material objects as well as for movement.[69] In the analysis of the four elements in the *Dhātuvibhaṅgasutta,* it is said that the cavities in the body such as the small spaces in the nose, ears, mouth and even skin are the element of space (*ākāsadhātu*):

> the holes of the ears, nose and mouth and the [space] where one swallows what is eaten, drunk, consumed and tasted, and where it is then eliminated below, or whatever else is internally separated space, spatial and clung to: this is called the internal space element. (M III 242)[70]

Thus, the parts of the body are not really connected to each other as we may think but are rather separated; there are minute spaces everywhere in the body, between minute particles of the body, which cannot be seen with the human eye. The element of space (*ākāsadhātu*) can be internal (*ajjhattika*)—within the body—or external (*bāhira*)—in the material world outside the body.[71] There are two types of spaces; the first is comprised of and depends on the four great elements (*mahābhūta*) and is therefore material, while the second is not conditioned by or dependent on material elements, is not produced by causes and is thus immaterial. In the world of our bodies (*kāyaloka*), both types of spaces are present.[72]

Materiality (*rūpa*) is conditioned (*saṅkhata*) and prompted by four causes: (1) *kamma,* (2) the mind (*citta*), (3) temperature (*utu*) and (4) nutriment (*āhāra*).[73] For example, when walking, as soon as the intention to lift the leg arises in the mind, the air element (*vayodhātu*) is activated and the leg is lifted. When the intention to put the leg down arises in the mind, the earth element (*paṭhavīdhātu*) is activated. As changes take place in the domain of one element, all the other elements likewise change and function accordingly. Thus, while walking, not only the air element (*vayodhātu*) but also other elements are part of this process: the earth element (*paṭhavīdhātu*) is experienced as hardness, heaviness and tightness; the water element (*āpodhātu*) can become prominent through the feeling of stickiness when the sole of the foot lifts off the ground; finally, the fire element (*tejodhātu*) is experienced as temperature—heat or coldness—when the foot touches the ground. Thus, all four elements are always present and active, even in the slightest movement of the body. Movements like walking are prompted

69. In the *Dhammasaṅgaṇi,* space is described as 'that which is space and belongs to space, is sky and belongs to sky, empty space and belongs to empty space and is not in contact with the four great elements' (Dhs 144: *yo ākāso ākāsaṅgataṃ aghaṃ aghagataṃ vivaro vivaragataṃ asamphuṭṭhaṃ catūhi mahābhūtehi—idan taṃ rūpaṃ ākāsadhātu*). According to the *Visuddhimagga,* its characteristic is to delimit materiality, its function is to show the boundaries of materiality, it manifests as untouchedness or confining materiality (i.e., in holes and gaps) and its proximate cause is delimited materiality (Vism 448: *Rūpaparicchedalakkhaṇā ākāsadhātu, rūpapariyantappakāsanarasā, rūpamariyādapaccupaṭṭhānā, asamphuṭṭhabhāvacchiddavivarabhāvapaccupaṭṭhānā vā paricchinnarūpapadaṭṭhānā*).

70. M III 242: *kaṇṇacchiddam nāsacchiddam mukhadvāraṃ, yena ca asitāpītakhāyitasāyitaṃ ajjhoharati, yattha ca asitapītakhāyitasāyitaṃ santiṭṭhati, yena ca asitapītakhāyitasāyitaṃ adhobhāgā nikkhamati; yaṃ vā pan'aññam pi kiñci ajjhattaṃ paccattaṃ ākāsaṃ ākāsagataṃ upādiṇṇaṃ; ayaṃ vuccati bhikkhu, ajjhattikā ākāsadhātu.*

71. This distinction is explained in several texts: for example, in the *Vibhaṅga,* the internal space element (*ajjhattikā ākāsadhātu*) is described as in the above quotation from the *Dhātuvibhaṅgasutta* (M III 242), whereas the external space element (*bāhirā ākāsadhātu*) is explained as 'what is external, space, spatial, open, openness, not in touch with the four elements, external, not clung to'(Vibh 84–85: *Yaṃ bāhiraṃ ākāso ākāsagataṃ aghaṃ aghagataṃ vivaro vivaragataṃ asamphuṭṭhaṃ catūhi mahābhūtehi bahiddhā anupādiṇṇam*).

72. These two types of spaces are distinguished and analysed mainly in post-canonical texts such as the *Milindapañha* and the commentaries on the *Abhidhamma* (Karunadasa 1967, 91–99).

73. A detailed classification of materiality (*rūpa*) and its conditions is presented in the *Dhammasaṅgaṇi* (Dhs 133–179); for an overview, see Bodhi (1993, 247–255).

by the mind (*cittasamuṭṭhāna*) as well as by the three other conditions: i.e., *kamma* (*kammasamuṭṭhāna*), temperature (*utusamuṭṭhāna*) and nutriment (*āhārasamuṭṭhāna*). Without the involvement of the mind, the four elements still function according to their own nature. When we think that we are doing what we want, the question arises as to whether it is the mind (*citta*) or materiality (*rūpa*) that prompts us to do so. The mind (*citta*) and materiality (*rūpa*) influence each other: when changes take place in the four elements, the mind also changes, and similarly when the mind changes, the four elements likewise change.

The four great elements (*mahābhūta*) also function in the body without being triggered by the mind (*cittasamuṭṭhāna*). For example, elimination (urinating, defecating), blinking the eyes and hunger are due to *kamma* (*kammasamuṭṭhāna*), whereas feeling hot or cold and sweating are due to climatic influences (*utusamuṭṭhāna*). Movements such as walking, picking up things and other intentional activities are triggered by the mind (*cittasamuṭṭhāna*). Heaviness or heat in the body can also be influenced by nutrients (*āhārasamuṭṭhāna*) as well as *kamma* (*kammasamuṭṭhāna*). Thus, materiality (*rūpa*) in living beings originates from these four causes. Conditioned by the materiality (*rūpa*) that arises from *kamma* (*kammasamuṭṭhāna rūpa*), ignorance (*avijjā*) and craving (*taṇhā*) can be generated; the materiality (*rūpa*) generated by nutrients (*āhārasamuṭṭhānarūpa*) then conditions the arising of *kamma* and the mind (*citta*), which, once again, condition the emergence of ignorance (*avijjā*) and craving (*taṇhā*), thus generating further arisings of the four elements (*mahābhūta*).

As mentioned in the previous section on the contemplation of the thirty-one body parts, the first nineteen parts relate to the earth element (*paṭhavīdhātu*) and the remainder to the water element (*āpodhātu*). However, the meditator should contemplate all four elements present in the body, including the air element (*vayodhātu*) and the fire element (*tejodhātu*).[74] When cultivating the four foundations of mindfulness (*satipaṭṭhāna*), the subtler manifestations of materiality (*rūpa*) can be observed. For example, one may feel a sense of lightness in the body, which is the lightness (*lahutā*), softness (*mudutā*) and adaptability (*kammaññatā*) of materiality.[75] The experience of these three qualities occurs when the mind is in a similar state of lightness, softness and adaptability. When the meditation practice deepens, all these aspects can be seen directly, well distinguished and understood. Furthermore, the meditator can also clearly perceive the four characteristics of materiality (*lakkhaṇarūpa*), namely, how things come into being (*upacaya*), their continuity (*santati*), decay (*jaratā*) and impermanence (*aniccatā*) when they finally break up and cease.[76] The breakup of materiality takes longer than the ceasing of

74. The four elements are presented in relation to the body parts in the *Mahāhatthipadopamasutta* (M I 185–191) in the following way:
 1) the first nineteen parts are listed under the earth element (*paṭhavīdhātu*);
 2) the next group of twelve parts are under the water element (*āpodhātu*);
 3) the body aspects relating to temperature, ageing and digestion are under the fire element (*tejodhātu*); and
 4) breathing and all movements in the body ('winds') are related to the air element (*vāyodhātu*).
 See also the *Mahārāhulavādasutta* (M I 420–426) and the *Dhātuvibhaṅgasutta* (M III 237–247).

75. The *Dhammasaṅgaṇi* presents the different types of materiality as follows: the lightness of materiality is the ability to easily change and the absence of sluggishness and stiffness; the softness of materiality is mildness, smoothness and non-rigidity; and the adaptability of materiality is wieldiness and malleability (Dhs 144: *Yā rūpassa lahutā lahupariṇāmatā adandhanatā avitthanatā. ... Yā rūpassa mudutā maddavatā akakkhaḷatā akathinatā ... Yā rūpassa kammaññatā kammaññattaṃ kammaññabhāvo*). See also the description in the *Visuddhimagga* (Vism 448–449).

76. According to the *Visuddhimagga*, the growth of materiality (*upacaya*) refers to the emergence or manifestation of materiality, continuity (*santati*) to its anchoring, decay (*jaratā*) to its maturing or ripening and impermanence

mind-moments; in the time that materiality arises, remains and passes away, the mind has already arisen and passed away seventeen times.[77]

In meditation practice, one can be mindful of all the processes related to the elements discussed here. In the initial stages of meditation, paying attention to the body and its elements (*dhātumanasikāra*) usually occupies a large part of the practice. It is important to understand that the cultivation of the foundations of mindfulness (*satipaṭṭhāna*) can begin from any of the four domains (i.e., the body, feeling, mind or phenomena), since paying attention to one or all of them has the same purpose, namely, the establishment of mindfulness (*sati*), clear comprehension (*sampajañña*) and other qualities required to achieve liberation from suffering. One single aspect or object of contemplation should not be overemphasised. According to the *Satipaṭṭhānasutta*, the areas of contemplation encompass the following:

- the contemplation of the body (*kāyānupassanā*) with fourteen objects
- the contemplation of feeling (*vedanānupassanā*) with nine objects
- the contemplation of the mind (*cittānupassanā*) with sixteen objects
- the contemplation of phenomena (*dhammānupassanā*) with five objects

In addition, each object has six aspects:

- contemplating internally
- contemplating externally
- contemplating both internally and externally
- contemplating the arising
- contemplating the passing away
- contemplating both the arising and passing away

In total, there are 264 ways in which the meditator can practise contemplation at different times.

As emerges from the Pāli texts, the Buddha's teaching methods varied greatly: sometimes he would teach using the metaphor of a leaf as in the *Khadirasutta* (S V 438–439) or the metaphor of a piece of cloth as described in the *Vatthūpamasutta* (M I 36–40). Some meditators can only see the arising process, others the ceasing process and some equally both. Some meditators may only see the internal aspect of their experience, others the external and some both.[78]

The contemplation of the parts of the body and the elements is an excellent practice for developing the understanding that in the world of the body (*kāyaloka*), there is no being, no person, no intrinsic self (*anattā*). Such an understanding arises with the cultivation of mindfulness (*sati*) and clear comprehension (*sampajañña*) through which an investigation of non-self

---

(*aniccatā*) to its complete breakdown (Vism 449–450). See also Dhs 14.

77. While materiality and mentality are both impermanent, material phenomena are viewed as having a longer duration than mental phenomena. According to the post-canonical commentaries, a material phenomenon lasts for seventeen mind-moments. Thus, it is said in the *Visuddhimagga*: 'The life-continuum mind arises and ceases sixteen times during one material moment. The moments of arising, presence and ceasing of the mind are equal; but in the case of materiality, the moments of arising and ceasing are as fast [as those of the mind], while the moment of its presence is long, as it lasts while sixteen minds arise and cease' (Vism 614: *Rūpe dharante yeva hi soḷasavāre bhavaṅgacittaṃ uppajjitvā nirujjhati. Cittassa uppādakkhaṇo pi ṭhitikkhaṇo pi bhaṅgakkhaṇo pi ekasadisā. Rūpassa pana uppādabhaṅgakkhaṇā yeva lahukā. Te hi sadisā, ṭhitikkhaṇo pana mahā; yāva soḷasacittāni uppajjitvā nirujjhanti, tāva vattati*). See also the *Sammohavinodanī* (Vibh-a 25–28).

78. For Pemasiri Thera's comments on contemplation approached internally or externally, see Chapter II.1, under the subheading 'Recurring passage indicating the ways to approach the contemplation.'

(*anattā*) takes place. This investigation focuses on whether consciousness belongs to or arises from any part of the body, and whether there is a part or aspect of the body that could be called an 'I.'[79] For example, if one believes that an 'I' exists in the body, then when part of the body is transplanted into another person's body (e.g., blood transfusion), the question thus arises as to whether this would mean that there are two entities in one body. According to the Buddhist teachings, there is no being or entity, neither in the body nor in the mind nor anywhere else. It is only when an 'I' or an individual is created in the mind that problems arise, which can lead to all kinds of conflicts, enmity between individuals or between countries. Jealousy, anger, craving and similar states are simply created by 'I'; these are phenomena that we mistakenly identify with, cling to and call 'I.' Even if one does not practise the foundations of mindfulness (*satipaṭṭhāna*), it may still be helpful to learn about them and intellectually understand the problems stemming from the creation of an 'I'. Thus, learning about mindfulness is always useful. But it is only through meditation practice that one gradually develops the profound insight and understanding that there is no 'I,' that there is nothing that can be called 'mine,' and that this idea of 'myself' is only created in our mind.[80]

II 6 Nine cemetery contemplations (*navasīvathikā*)

(1) *Puna ca paraṃ bhikkhave bhikkhu seyyathāpi passeyya sarīraṃ sīvathikāya chaḍḍitaṃ ekāhamataṃ vā dvīhamataṃ vā tīhamataṃ vā uddhumātakaṃ vinīlakaṃ vipubbakajātaṃ, so imameva kāyaṃ* ***upasaṃharati****: Ayampi kho kāyo evaṃdhammo evaṃbhāvī etaṃ anatīto ti.*

(Recurring passage)[81] *Iti ajjhattaṃ vā kāye kāyānupassī viharati, bahiddhā vā kāye kāyānupassī viharati, ajjhattabahiddhā vā kāye kāyānupassī viharati. Samudayadhammānupassī vā kāyasmiṃ viharati, vayadhammānupassī vā kāyasmiṃ viharati, samudayavayadhammānupassī vā kāyasmiṃ viharati. Atthi kāyo ti vā panassa sati paccupaṭṭhitā hoti yāvadeva ñāṇamattāya patissatimattāya, anissito ca viharati na ca kiñci loke upādiyati. Evampi kho bhikkhave bhikkhu kāye kāyānupassī viharati.*

'And again, monks, if a monk were to see a corpse discarded in a cemetery, one, two or three days dead, bloated, bluish and festering, he **approaches** this same body thus: "This body too is of the same nature, it will be like that, it is not exempt from that fate."'

(Recurring passage) 'Thus he abides contemplating the body as a body internally, or he abides contemplating the body as a body externally, or he abides contemplating the body as a body both internally and externally. He abides contemplating the arising of phenomena in the body, or he abides contemplating the passing away of phenomena in the body, or he abides contemplating both the arising and passing away of phenomena in the body. Or, mindfulness that "there is a body" is established in him just to the extent necessary for knowledge and mindfulness. And he abides without attachment, not clinging to anything in the world. Monks, thus a monk abides contemplating the body as a body.'[82]

79. Several *suttas* such as the *Mahāhatthipadopannasutta* (M I 185–191) highlight that the contemplation of the elements leads to an insight into non-self (*anattā*); this is also emphasised in post-canonical texts such as the *Papañcasūdanī* commentary (Ps I 271–272) and the *Visuddhimagga* (Vism 348).

80. These three aspects of non-self are mentioned in the *Dhātuvibhaṅgasutta*, for example, where for each of the four elements described, it is concluded: 'This is not mine, I am not this, this is not myself' (M III 240: *N' etaṃ mama, n' eso'ham asmi, na me so attā ti*).

81. For comments on the recurring passage, see Chapter II.1, under the subheading 'Recurring passage indicating the ways to approach the contemplation.'

82. Since this section is very repetitious, most editions of the Pāli text (e.g., M I 58–59) and English translations (e.g., Ñāṇanamoli and Bodhi 1995, 148–149) are heavily abbreviated, perhaps to the detriment of clarity.

(2) *Puna ca paraṃ bhikkhave bhikkhu seyyathāpi passeyya sarīraṃ sīvathikāya chaḍḍitaṃ kākehi vā khajjamānaṃ kulalehi vā khajjamānaṃ gijjhehi vā khajjamānaṃ supāṇehi vā khajjamānaṃ sigālehi vā khajjamānaṃ vividhehi vā pāṇakajātehi khajjamānaṃ, so imameva kāyaṃ* ***upasaṃharati:*** *Ayampi kho kāyo evaṃ dhammo evaṃbhāvī etaṃ anatīto ti.*

(Recurring passage) *Iti ajjhattaṃ vā kāye kāyānupassī viharati ... upādiyati. Evam-pi bhikkhave bhikkhu kāye kāyānupassī viharati.*

'And again, monks, if a monk were to see a corpse discarded in a cemetery, being devoured by crows, hawks, vultures, dogs, jackals or various kinds of worms, he **approaches** this same body thus: "This body too is of the same nature, it will be like that, it is not exempt from that fate."

(Recurring passage) 'Thus he abides contemplating the body as a body internally ... thus a monk abides contemplating the body as a body.'

(3) *Puna ca paraṃ bhikkhave bhikkhu seyyathāpi passeyya sarīraṃ sīvathikāya chaḍḍitaṃ, aṭṭhikasaṅkhalikaṃ samaṃsalohitaṃ nahārusambandhaṃ, so imameva kāyaṃ* ***upasaṃharati:*** *Ayampi kho kāyo evaṃ dhammo evaṃbhāvī etaṃ anatīto ti.*

(Recurring passage) *Iti ajjhattaṃ vā kāye kāyānupassī viharati ... upādiyati. Evam-pi bhikkhave bhikkhu kāye kāyānupassī viharati.*

'And again, monks, if a monk were to see a corpse discarded in a cemetery, a skeleton with flesh and blood, held together by sinews, he **approaches** this same body thus: "This body too is of the same nature, it will be like that, it is not exempt from that fate."

(Recurring passage) 'Thus he abides contemplating the body as a body internally ... thus a monk abides contemplating the body as a body.'

(4) *Puna ca paraṃ bhikkhave bhikkhu seyyathāpi passeyya sarīraṃ sīvathikāya chaḍḍitaṃ, aṭṭhikasaṅkhalikaṃ nimmaṃsalohitamakkhitaṃ nahārusambandhaṃ, so imameva kāyaṃ* ***upasaṃharati:*** *Ayampi kho kāyo evaṃ dhammo evaṃbhāvī etaṃ anatīto ti.*

(Recurring passage) *Iti ajjhattaṃ vā kāye kāyānupassī viharati ... upādiyati. Evam-pi bhikkhave bhikkhu kāye kāyānupassī viharati.*

'And again, monks, if a monk were to see a corpse discarded in a cemetery, a fleshless skeleton smeared with blood, held together by sinews, he **approaches** this same body thus: "This body too is of the same nature, it will be like that, it is not exempt from that fate."

(Recurring passage) 'Thus he abides contemplating the body as a body internally ... thus a monk abides contemplating the body as a body.'

(5) *Puna ca paraṃ bhikkhave bhikkhu seyyathāpi passeyya sarīraṃ sīvathikāya chaḍḍitaṃ, aṭṭhikasaṅkhalikaṃ apagatamaṃsalohitaṃ nahārusambandhaṃ, so imameva kāyaṃ* ***upasaṃharati:*** *Ayampi kho kāyo evaṃ dhammo evaṃbhāvī etaṃ anatīto ti.*

(Recurring passage) *Iti ajjhattaṃ vā kāye kāyānupassī viharati ... upādiyati. Evam-pi bhikkhave bhikkhu kāye kāyānupassī viharati.*

'And again, monks, if a monk were to see a corpse discarded in a cemetery, a skeleton without flesh and blood, held together by sinews, he **approaches** this same body thus: "This body too is of the same nature, it will be like that, it is not exempt from that fate."

(Recurring passage) 'Thus he abides contemplating the body as a body internally ... thus a monk abides contemplating the body as a body.'

Therefore, the Pāli text and its translation presented here retain the significant repetitions to a larger extent, and the numbers (1) to (9) are added to delineate each of the nine stages of bodily decomposition, each followed by the recurring passage.

(6) *Puna ca paraṃ bhikkhave bhikkhu seyyathāpi passeyya sarīraṃ sīvathikāya chaḍḍitaṃ, aṭṭhikāni apagatasambandhāni disāvidisā vikkhittāni, aññena hatthaṭṭhikaṃ aññena pādaṭṭhikaṃ aññena jaṅghaṭṭhikaṃ aññena ūraṭṭhikaṃ aññena kaṭaṭṭhikaṃ aññena piṭṭhikaṇṭakaṃ aññena sīsakaṭāhaṃ, so imameva kāyaṃ* ***upasaṃharati:*** *Ayampi kho kāyo evaṃ dhammo evaṃbhāvī etaṃ anatīto ti.*

(Recurring passage) *Iti ajjhattaṃ vā kāye kāyānupassī viharati ... upādiyati. Evam-pi bhikkhave bhikkhu kāye kāyānupassī viharati.*

And again, monks, if a monk were to see a corpse discarded in a cemetery, disconnected bones scattered in all directions—here a bone of the hand, there a bone of the foot, here a shin bone, there a thigh bone, here a hip bone, there a rib bone, here a skull—he **approaches** this same body thus: "This body too is of the same nature, it will be like that, it is not exempt from that fate."

(Recurring passage) 'Thus he abides contemplating the body as a body internally ... thus a monk abides contemplating the body as a body.'

(7) *Puna ca paraṃ bhikkhave bhikkhu seyyathāpi passeyya sarīraṃ sīvathikāya chaḍḍitaṃ, aṭṭhikāni setāni saṅkhavaṇṇūpanibhāni, so imameva kāyaṃ* ***upasaṃharati:*** *Ayampi kho kāyo evaṃ dhammo evaṃbhāvī etaṃ anatīto ti.*

(Recurring passage) *Iti ajjhattaṃ vā kāye kāyānupassī viharati ... upādiyati. Evam-pi bhikkhave bhikkhu kāye kāyānupassī viharati.*

'And again, monks, if a monk were to see a corpse discarded in a cemetery, bones bleached white, the colour of shells, he **approaches** this same body thus: "This body too is of the same nature, it will be like that, it is not exempt from that fate."

(Recurring passage) 'Thus he abides contemplating the body as a body internally ... thus a monk abides contemplating the body as a body.'

(8) *Puna ca paraṃ bhikkhave bhikkhu seyyathāpi passeyya sarīraṃ sīvathikāya chaḍḍitaṃ, aṭṭhikāni puñjakitāni terovassikāni, so imameva kāyaṃ* ***upasaṃharati:*** *Ayampi kho kāyo evaṃ dhammo evaṃbhāvī etaṃ anatīto ti.*

(Recurring passage) *Iti ajjhattaṃ vā kāye kāyānupassī viharati ... upādiyati. Evam-pi bhikkhave bhikkhu kāye kāyānupassī viharati.*

'And again, monks, if a monk were to see a corpse discarded in a cemetery, bones heaped up, more than a year old, he **approaches** this same body thus: "This body too is of the same nature, it will be like that, it is not exempt from that fate."

(Recurring passage) 'Thus he abides contemplating the body as a body internally ... thus a monk abides contemplating the body as a body.'

(9) *Puna ca paraṃ bhikkhave bhikkhu seyyathāpi passeyya sarīraṃ sīvathikāya chaḍḍitaṃ, aṭṭhikāni pūtīni cuṇṇakajātāni, so imameva kāyaṃ* ***upasaṃharati:*** *Ayampi kho kāyo evaṃdhammo evaṃbhāvī etaṃ anatīto ti.*

(Recurring passage) *Iti ajjhattaṃ vā kāye kāyānupassī viharati, bahiddhā vā kāye kāyānupassī viharati, ajjhattabahiddhā vā kāye kāyānupassī viharat. Samudayadhammānupassī vā kāyasmiṃ viharati, vaya-dhammānupassī vā kāyasmiṃ viharati, samudayavayadhammānupassī vā kāyasmiṃ viharati. Atthi kāyo ti vā panassa sati paccupaṭṭhitā hoti yāvadeva ñāṇamattāya patissatimattāya, anissito ca viharati na ca kiñci loke upādiyati. Evampi kho bhikkhave bhikkhu kāye kāyānupassī viharati.*

'And again, monks, if a monk were to see a corpse discarded in a cemetery, bones rotted and crumbled to dust, he **approaches** this same body thus: "This body too is of the same nature, it will be like that, it is not exempt from that fate."

(Recurring passage) 'Thus he abides contemplating the body as a body internally, or he abides contemplating the body as a body externally, or he abides contemplating the body as a body both internally and externally. He abides contemplating the arising of phenomena in the body, or he abides contemplating the passing away of phenomena in the body, or he abides contemplating both the arising and passing away of phenomena in the body. Or, mindfulness that "there is a body" is established in him just to the extent necessary for knowledge and mindfulness. And he abides without attachment, not clinging to anything in the world. Monks, thus a monk abides contemplating the body as a body.'

Pemasiri Thera's commentary

'Approaches' (*upasaṃharati*)

Nowadays, the cemetery contemplation is undertaken only very rarely, although a large part of the *Satipaṭṭhānasutta* is dedicated to it; it is also frequently mentioned in other *suttas* and commentaries.[83] The corpse at various stages of decay is considered to be a meditation object that can lead to arahantship.[84] The *Satipaṭṭhānasutta* says that one approaches (*upasaṃharati*) one's own body knowing that it has the same nature as the corpse, that it will also die and decay. In this context, the Pāli word *upasaṃharati*[85] is usually interpreted as 'to compare to or reflect on'; however, in this meditation, one does not actually compare one's body to a corpse but rather approaches it in a particular way, namely, with the knowledge that one's own body is also close to death and decay, although it is unknown when it will occur. The translation 'approaches' or 'gets close to' (*upasaṃharati*) does not actually mean being physically close to a corpse but rather approaching it mentally in one's mind. Without forgetting the object but instead being mindful of it, the meditator contemplates the fact that the state of the corpse will also transpire for her or his body.[86] Any one of the nine stages of decomposition can be chosen as the object of this contemplation. Some people are afraid of skeletons, but everybody always carries their own skeleton with them. Therefore, it is quite easy to bring it up in the mind, to approach it (*upasaṃharati*), as it is always there. One does not need to use this object of contemplation all the time, but just when one sits in meditation during certain training periods. If one continually repeats that 'I will die, I will die,' one can become quite mentally deranged or even think about committing suicide; this may also occur with the contemplation of the body parts. This is narrated in the *Vesālīsutta*, which describes how the monks contemplated the impurity (*asubha*) of the body in various ways (presumably meditating on the thirty-one parts of the

83. The contemplation of corpses is discussed or referred to in several canonical texts such as the *Kayāgatasatisutta* (M III 91–92), *Udāyīsutta* (S III 323–335), and *Theragāthā* (Th 37, 43, 62). There are also references to decomposing corpses in the context of overcoming attachment to sensual pleasures, for example, in the *Mahādukkhakkhandhasutta* (M I 88–89). In the post-canonical literature, the contemplation of corpses is examined in more detail, especially in the *Visuddhimagga* (Vism 178–198), where it is presented as a meditation on unattractiveness or impurity (*asubha*).

84. Several references in canonical and post-canonical texts explain that this object of contemplation can lead to arahantship: for example, in the story of Mahākāḷa who became an *arahant* when contemplating a corpse (Burlingame 1995, vol.1, 184–187) or Nāgasamāla in the *Theragāthā* (Th 33) who understood death after watching the live body of a dancer. However, according to the *Visuddhimagga*, only the first *jhāna* can be attained through this practice (Vism 194: *paṭhamajjhānam ev' ettha hoti, na dutiyādīni*).

85. The verb *upasaṃharati* has a wide range of meanings such as 'to bring together, collect, focus, concentrate, look after' (DP; PED, *s.v.*). English translations of this *sutta* often translate the verb as 'to compare' (e.g., Ñāṇanamoli and Bodhi, trans. 1995, 148–149).

86. This is also highlighted in the *Papañcasūdanī* commentary. The commentary then explains that one's body will be like a corpse when its three components—i.e., life (*āyu*), warmth (*usmā*) and consciousness (*viññāṇa*)—are separated (Ps I 273).

body and the nine cemetery contemplations) and became so disgusted by the repulsiveness of the body that several of them committed suicide. As a result, the Buddha recommended that they practise mindfulness of breathing (*ānāpānasati*) instead (S V 320–322).

The contemplation of the corpse at various stages of decay is practised in several ways.[87] Some meditators go to the cemetery and look at old decaying cadavers, staying near a corpse and gazing at it constantly. However, in these circumstances, it may be difficult to establish deep concentration since aversion towards the corpse may arise. In addition, such places can be infested with bacteria that can affect the meditator's health, especially at night or on rainy days when there is high humidity and when gases rising from the cemetery soil remain near the ground, potentially causing various ailments. Some people who stay there at night believe that they see ghosts, but these are merely visions caused by the mist and shiny fungi on the scattered wood in the cemetery. It is not an essential part of this practice to be physically close to dead bodies and look at them. Many doctors perform autopsies but do not develop any meditation sign (*nimitta*) despite working with corpses for long hours daily over many years.

For this contemplation, it is not necessary to stay in a cemetery, especially since even a small piece of bone from a skeleton is a suitable meditation object. It is enough to simply look at a corpse or piece of bone and then bring it up in one's mind. One then contemplates that one's own body has the same nature, that this fate awaits everyone. Indeed, every being that has ever lived in the world has ended up in this state. In such a contemplation, a mental image or sign (*nimitta*) may arise in the mind, which is a natural phenomenon that occurs when something makes a strong impression on us. The cemetery contemplation may be initially started externally after seeing a corpse or part of it and then internally when it is approached with the knowledge that 'this will also happen to me.' Later, the image or sign (*nimitta*) of the corpse can be contemplated internally or externally depending on how one's own body is perceived: internally if the meditator contemplates the corpse as her or his own body and externally if the corpse is perceived as the one originally seen.

The cemetery contemplation is different from thinking or talking about death, saying that someday we will all die. Even though people see a corpse, they usually do not think that they will also die; they only think about the person who has died. They talk about the qualities of the deceased, feel sad and cry, which is just an expression of craving (*abhijjhā*) or aversion (*domanassa*). However, if a thought about one's own death arises in the mind, then it may become a sign (*nimitta*) for contemplation. The cemetery contemplation is a very good meditation object. If the meditator has already cultivated mindfulness of breathing (*ānāpānasati*), then the contemplation of the corpse can evolve quite well, and mindfulness (*sati*) and clear comprehension (*sampajañña*) can be easily established. The aim of the cemetery contemplation is to establish mindfulness (*sati*) and recognise and clearly comprehend (*sampajañña*) desire (*abhijjhā*) and discontent (*domanassa*). Consequently, this will diminish or dispel clinging to one's body, family, material possessions and everything else, eventually leading to detachment and liberation.[88]

87. The *Satipaṭṭhānasutta* speaks of nine stages in the decomposition of the body, while the *Visuddhimagga* lists ten stages and provides a detailed descriptions of the practice (Vism 178–196).

88. The *Papañcasūdanī* commentary concludes this section (like the other sections of the *sutta*) by linking the cemetery contemplation to the insight into the four noble truths, leading to the final liberation, saying: 'Having thus strived by means of the four truths, one attains peace. For the monk who practises the nine cemetery contemplations, this is the entrance leading up to arahantship' (Ps I 274: *Evaṃ catusaccavaseneva ussakkitvā nibbutiṃ pāpuṇātī ti. Idaṃ navasivathikapariggāhakānaṃ bhikkhūnaṃ yāva arahattā niyyānamukhan ti*).

— III —

Contemplation of Feelings (*Vedanānupassanā*)

Kathañca bhikkhave bhikkhu vedanāsu vedanānupassī viharati? Idha bhikkhave bhikkhu ***sukhaṃ vedanaṃ*** *vediyamāno: sukhaṃ vedanaṃ vediyāmīti pajānāti,* ***dukkhaṃ vedanaṃ*** *vediyamāno: dukkhaṃ vedanaṃ vediyāmīti pajānāti,* ***adukkhamasukhaṃ vedanaṃ*** *vediyamāno: adukkhamasukhaṃ vedanaṃ vediyāmīti pajānāti,* ***sāmisaṃ*** *vā sukhaṃ vedanaṃ vediyamāno: sāmisaṃ sukhaṃ vedanaṃ vediyāmīti pajānāti,* ***nirāmisaṃ*** *vā sukhaṃ vedanaṃ vediyamāno: nirāmisaṃ vedanaṃ vediyāmīti pajānāti, sāmisaṃ vā dukkhaṃ vedanaṃ vediyamāno: sāmisaṃ vedanaṃ vediyāmīti pajānāti, nirāmisaṃ vā dukkhaṃ vedanaṃ vediyamāno: nirāmisaṃ vedanaṃ vediyāmīti pajānāti, sāmisaṃ vā adukkhamasukhaṃ vedanaṃ vediyamāno: sāmisaṃ adukkhamasukhaṃ vedanaṃ vediyāmīti, nirāmisaṃ vā adukkhamasukhaṃ vedanaṃ vediyamāno: nirāmisaṃ adukkhamasukhaṃ vedanaṃ vediyāmīti pajānāti.*

'And how, monks, does a monk abide contemplating feelings as feelings? Here, when feeling a **pleasant feeling**, a monk knows: "I feel a pleasant feeling"; when feeling an **unpleasant feeling**, he knows: "I feel an unpleasant feeling"; when feeling a **neither-unpleasant-nor-pleasant feeling**, he knows: "I feel a neither-unpleasant-nor-pleasant feeling." When feeling a **worldly** pleasant feeling, he knows: "I feel a worldly pleasant feeling"; when feeling an **unworldly** pleasant feeling, he knows: "I feel an unworldly pleasant feeling"; when feeling a worldly unpleasant feeling, he knows: "I feel a worldly unpleasant feeling"; when feeling an unworldly unpleasant feeling, he knows: "I feel an unworldly unpleasant feeling"; when feeling a worldly neither-unpleasant-nor-pleasant feeling, he knows: "I feel a worldly neither-unpleasant-nor-pleasant feeling"; when feeling an unworldly neither-unpleasant-nor-pleasant feeling, he knows: "I feel an unworldly neither-unpleasant-nor-pleasant feeling."'

Recurring passage indicating the ways to approach the contemplation[1]

Iti ajjhattaṃ vā vedanāsu vedanānupassī viharati, bahiddhā vā vedanāsu vedanānupassī viharati, ajjhattabahiddhā vā vedanāsu vedanānupassī viharati. Samudayadhammānupassī vā vedanāsu viharati, vayadhammānupassī vā vedanāsu viharati, samudayavayadhammānupassī vā vedanāsu viharati. Atthi vedanā ti vā panassa sati paccupaṭṭhitā hoti yāvadeva ñāṇamattāya patissatimattāya, anissito ca viharati na ca kiñci loke upādiyati. Evampi kho bhikkhave bhikkhu vedanāsu vedanānupassī viharati.

'Thus he abides contemplating feelings as feelings internally, or he abides contemplating feelings as feelings externally, or he abides contemplating feelings as feelings both internally and externally. He abides contemplating the arising of phenomena in feelings, or he abides contemplating the passing away of phenomena in feelings, or he abides contemplating both the arising and pass-

1. For comments on the recurring passage, see Chapter II.1, under the subheading 'Recurring passage indicating the ways to approach the contemplation.'

ing away of phenomena in feelings. Or, mindfulness that "there is feeling" is established in him just to the extent necessary for knowledge and mindfulness. And he abides without attachment, not clinging to anything in the world. Monks, thus a monk abides contemplating feelings as feelings.'

Pemasiri Thera's commentary

All four domains of contemplation (*anupassanā*)[2] are interrelated, although meditators usually begin their practice with the contemplation of the body (*kāyānupassanā*). For example, the meditator starts with mindfulness of breathing (*ānāpānasati*), but already during the initial stages, she or he may experience pain in the body, which gives rise to unpleasant feeling. If feeling is noted and comprehended as such, then she or he practises contemplation in the domain of feeling (*vedanānupassanā*), which is more subtle than the bodily domain and hence more challenging for many meditators. The contemplation of feeling (*vedanānupassanā*) takes place in a manner similar to the contemplation in the three other domains, namely, feeling is observed with mindfulness (*sati*) and clear comprehension (*sampajañña*) at the level of the aggregates (*khandha*), elements (*dhātu*) and sense spheres (*āyatana*), with an understanding of their impermanent nature.[3]

'Pleasant feeling' (*sukhavedanā*) and 'unpleasant feeling' (*dukkhavedanā*)

In the contemplation of feeling (*vedanānupassanā*), three kinds of feeling are distinguished: pleasant (*sukhavedanā*), unpleasant (*dukkhavedanā*) and neither-unpleasant-nor-pleasant (*adukkhamasukhavedanā*). To put it more precisely, it is the contemplation of objects that are experienced with feeling (*vedanā*). If the meditator is mindful and clearly comprehending, she or he may understand that the object and the feeling are two different things. Feeling (*vedanā*) is a mental factor or concomitant (*cetasika*), which is always present, in every moment of consciousness (*citta*);[4] only in *nibbāna* is there no feeling (*vedanā*). Even when the meditator reaches the fruition knowledges (*phalañāṇa*),[5] a particular kind of feeling is present, although it cannot be described or expressed in words. The feeling that appears in the four fruition knowledges does not condition another feeling, meaning that it cannot be an object of attention or thought.

Feeling (*vedanā*) can be related to the body (*kāya*) or the mind (*citta*); when related to the mind, it is experienced as pleasant (*somanassa*) or unpleasant (*domanassa*).[6] Our entire lives are

2. For a discussion on the meaning of the term 'contemplation,' see Chapter I, under the subheading 'Contemplation (*anupassanā*).'

3. The *Papañcasūdanī* commentary explains that the contemplation of the aggregates (*khandha*), elements (*dhātu*), sense spheres (*āyatana*), three characteristics (i.e., impermanence (*anicca*), unsatisfactoriness (*dukkha*) and non-self (*anattā*)), and foundations of mindfulness (*satipaṭṭhāna*) are the 'highest teaching' (*paramatthadesanā*) of the Buddha (Ps 137: *Aniccaṃ dukkhaṃ anattā, khandhā dhātū āyatanāni satipaṭṭhānā ti evarūpā paramatthadesanā*).

4. Feeling (*vedanā*) is one of the seven universal mental concomitants (*cetasika*), which appear in every mind (*citta*) moment; for a brief overview of the universal mental concomitants (*cetasika*), see Karunadasa (2014, 103–120) and Bodhi (1993, 78–81). See also Table 6.

5. The canonical and commentarial texts identify eight supramundane minds (*lokuttaracittāni*) that transcend the conditioned world through the attainment of *nibbāna*. They are linked to the four stages of liberation, with each stage comprising a path mind (*maggacitta*) followed by a fruition mind (*phalacitta*). For a more detailed description, see the *Dhammasaṅgaṇi* (Dhs 60–67) and *Visuddhimagga* (Vism 672–697).

6. In Pāli canonical sources, there are several ways to analyse feeling (*vedanā*). For example, in the *Bahuvedanīyasutta* (M I 397–398), feelings (*vedanā*) are presented in the following way:

   1) two kinds (bodily and mental)

built around the objects or modalities of feeling (*vedanā*), and by identifying with them, we create the illusion of an owner of feeling. This is because feeling (*vedanā*) generates craving (*taṇhā*); we crave to be in closer contact with pleasant objects and escape from unpleasant ones, thus entangling us in suffering (*dukkha*). However, feeling (*vedanā*) itself is just a mental concomitant (*cetasika*) that has no owner and should be noted and understood as such.[7] When none of the three feeling modalities is an object of attention, feeling (*vedanā*) still arises as one of the ever-present mental concomitants (*cetasika*). When the contemplation of feeling (*vedanānupassanā*) is practised, one of the feeling modalities is taken up as an object of attention, and the meditator knows (*pajānāti*) it well with mindfulness (*sati*) and clear comprehension (*sampajañña*), without any desire (*abhijjhā*) or discontent (*domanassa*) in relation to it.

Pleasantness or mental ease (*somanassa*) and unpleasantness or discontent (*domanassa*) are the qualities of the mind, which arise through contact (*phassa*) with an object; thus, they are also connected with the past and projected into the future. When an object arises through bodily contact, which is called touch (*phoṭṭhabba*), it is accompanied by one of the three modalities of feeling—i.e., pleasant (*sukhavedanā*), unpleasant (*dukkhavedanā*) or neither-unpleasant-nor-pleasant feeling (*adukkhamasukhavedanā*). In the context of the five aggregates (*khandha*), it may be said that bodily touch (*phoṭṭhabba*) is in the domain of the aggregate of materiality (*rūpakhandha*) and that feeling belongs to the aggregate of feeling (*vedanākhandha*). Meditators often think that they contemplate feeling (*vedanā*) in the body but what they really observe is bodily touch (*phoṭṭhabba*), or in other words, they experience materiality (*rūpa*). Thus, bodily pain and unpleasant feeling (*dukkhavedanā*) are different things.

Although people speak of feeling (*vedanā*) in relation to the body, it is rather a mental concomitant (*cetasika*) that arises with contact (*phassa*). In other words, contact with an object is required in order for feeling (*vedanā*) and perception (*saññā*) to arise.[8] The meditator should recognise and understand that contact (*phassa*) and feeling (*vedanā*) are two different things, which incessantly arise (*samudaya*) and pass away (*vaya*).

Only when feeling (*vedanā*) is understood in this manner can it be said that the meditator is engaged in the contemplation of feeling (*vedanānupassanā*). For example, the meditator

---

2) three kinds (pleasant, unpleasant and neither-unpleasant-nor-pleasant)
3) five kinds (pleasure, joy, pain, grief and equanimity)
4) six kinds (feelings generated by contact through the six senses)
5) eighteen kinds (joy, grief and equanimity, each generated by contact through one of the six senses)
6) thirty-six kinds (the previous eighteen kinds based on household life or renunciation)
7) one hundred and eight kinds (the previous thirty-six kinds, each referring to the past, present and future)

In addition to the three types of feelings presented in the *Satipaṭṭhānasutta*, feelings (*vedanā*) are also frequently classified into six kinds, i.e., each of the three feelings (i.e., pleasant, unpleasant and neither-unpleasant-nor-pleasant) is related to the body or mind. In the *Cūḷavedalasutta* (M I 302–303), feelings are grouped according to the six sense doors. The *Visuddhimagga* classifies feelings as fivefold: (bodily) pleasant (*sukha*), (bodily) unpleasant (*dukkha*), mental ease (*somanassa*), mental discontent (*domanassa*) and equanimity (*upekkhā*) (Vism 461: *Sā sabhāvabhedato pañcavidhā hoti; sukhaṃ, dukkhaṃ, somanassaṃ, domanassaṃ, upekkhā ti*).

7. The impersonal nature of feelings is discussed in many *suttas* such as the *Mahānidānasutta*, which repeatedly stresses that feeling is impermanent and not 'myself' (D II 66–67). This is similarly articulated in the *Papañcasūdanī* commentary, emphasising that there is no person or being who feels and that feeling has no owner (Ps I 275: *Tattha ko vedayatī ti? Na koci satto vā puggalo vā vedayati. Kassa vedanā ti? Na kassaci sattassa vā puggalassa vā vedanā*).

8. Pemasiri Thera refers here to the sixth and seventh components in the formula of dependent origination (*paṭiccasamuppāda*), where feeling (*vedanā*) is situated in the following way: (6) contact (*phassa*) (7) feeling (*vedanā*).

experiences pain in her or his leg, which arises because of an unsuitable contact in the body (*phoṭṭhabba*), meaning that the contact does not suit the materiality of the body. Consequently, this contact becomes the object, which triggers unpleasant feeling (*dukkhavedanā*). A thought may then arise in the meditator: 'I had a similar pain yesterday. I wonder whether it will also occur tomorrow.' This thought has now created the past and future.

Meditators can easily be deceived by feeling (*vedanā*): they become carried away by pleasant feeling (*sukhavedanā*), which is triggered by harmonious contact with the materiality of the body, and consequently, they do not note it but instead cling to it. By contrast, they attempt to note unpleasant feeling (*dukhavedanā*), because they hope that it will go away by simply noting it. However, it is important to note and clearly comprehend both pleasant and unpleasant touch (*phoṭṭhabba*) in the body as well as the contact (*phassa*) in the mind, which can generate mental ease (*somanassa*) or discontent (*domanassa*). This is why it is said in the *Ānāpānasatisutta* (M III 84), at the end of the section on the contemplation of feeling (*vedanānupassanā*), that the meditator should pay very close attention (*sādhukaṃ manasikāraṃ*) during her or his practice of mindfulness of breathing.[9]

To stress again, in the contemplation of feeling (*vedanānupassanā*), the meditator should not simply note unpleasant feeling (*dukkhavedanā*), hoping (however subtly) to make it go away. If the meditator has such an intention, mindfulness (*sati*) will not arise but instead a contact (*phassa*) will be triggered in the mind along with craving (*taṇhā*) for the pain to somehow disappear on account of noting it.[10] If this craving (*taṇhā*) is not noted by the meditator, it will evolve into clinging (*upādāna*), and consequently, mindfulness (*sati*) and clear comprehension (*sampajañña*) cannot be established. Clinging (*upādāna*) means trying to change whatever one is experiencing. The whole meditation should be practised in such a way that clinging (*upādāna*) does not appear; this means that the meditator should simply allow things to occur in the mind and to know them mindfully and with clear comprehension (*sampajañña*). Therefore, the practice of the four foundations of mindfulness (*satipaṭṭhāna*) is really the easiest thing in the world: it means just knowing things as they are (*yathābhūta*), without trying to change them. Remaining with things as they are creates a wonderful sense of freedom; however, for most people, it is too difficult to stay with or accept such freedom for long, because they are so used to living without it. Therefore, again and again, clinging (*upādāna*) arises, which prevents mindfulness (*sati*) from developing.

As discussed before, in the contemplation of feeling (*vedanānupassanā*), the meditator should clearly know (*pajānāti*) pain or pleasure without attachment and with the clear understanding that feeling (*vedanā*) has no owner, that it is empty, without being (*anattā*) or essence (*nisatta*).

---

9. Pemasiri Thera explains that in the *Ānāpānasatisutta*, the pivotal role played by the contemplation of feelings is emphasised by the phrase 'close attention' (*sādhukaṃ manasikāraṃ*); significantly, the text does not include the phrase 'close attention' (*sādhukaṃ manasikāraṃ*) at the end of the section on the contemplation of the body (*kāyānupassanā*) nor at the end of the section on the contemplation of the mind (*cittānupassanā*) (M III 83–85). However, this phrase does occur again at the end of the section on the contemplation of phenomena (*dhammānupassanā*), where it further underscores the importance of wisdom, careful attention and equanimity (M III 84–85: *So yaṃ taṃ abhijjhādomanassānaṃ pahānaṃ taṃ paññāya disvā sādhukaṃ ajjhupekkhitā hoti*).

10. In the *Cūḷavedalasutta*, it is mentioned that the tendency towards craving or lust (*rāgānusaya*) underlies pleasant feeling (*sukhavedanā*), the tendency towards aversion (*paṭighānusaya*) underlies unpleasant feeling (*dukkhavedanā*), and the tendency towards ignorance (*avijjānusaya*) underlies neither-unpleasant-nor-pleasant (*adukkhamasukhavedanā*) (M I 303: *Sukhāya kho āvuso Visākha vedanāya rāgānusayo anuseti, dukkhāya vedanāya paṭighānusayo anuseti, adukkhamasukhāya vedanāya avijjānusayo anusetīti*).

When clinging (*upādāna*) occurs and is attached to a feeling (*vedanā*), a being (*satta*) or an 'I' is created that sticks to the objects, and consequently, becoming (*bhāva*) arises.[11] So, understanding non-being or non-essence (*nissatta*) means non-attachment to objects, not being stuck to any objects. When the meditator lives without attachment, it means that her or his life energy (*jīvita*) does not evolve to the level of self or being (*satta*). In this way, the meditator realises that there are only phenomena that arise and pass away. Consequently, the meditator can regard the world (of the body and mind) as empty of self, as said in the *Suttanipāta*:

> Always mindful, Mogharāja, regard the world as empty; having removed the view of self, one may thus overcome death. (Sn 217)[12]

To summarise, the meditator will remain caught in different feelings until she or he understands that feeling (*vedanā*) has no owner, that all phenomena (*dhamma*) have no essence or living being (*nissattanijjīvata*).[13] This is an insight that can be reached through the contemplation of the body (*kāyānupassanā*), the contemplation of feeling (*vedanānupassanā*) or through the two other domains of contemplation. Feeling (*vedanā*) is one of the five aggregates (*khandha*), and since it is always present, it is impossible to make it go away.

If one of the feeling modalities is prominent during meditation, especially the unpleasant one, then it can be helpful for the meditator to take a different object of attention. For example, the meditator who cannot deal with a strong painful sensation should turn her or his attention to another object for some time and perhaps return to the primary object later. This is also mentioned in the *Vitakkasaṇṭānasutta*:

> When a monk focuses his attention on an object, which brings about bad unwholesome thoughts connected to desire, aversion and delusion, he should [instead] focus his attention on some other object connected with wholesomeness. Just as a skilled carpenter or his apprentice may remove, take out and get rid of a coarse peg by [driving through from the other side] a small peg, so too the monk ... should focus his attention on some other object connected with wholesomeness ... and thus his mind becomes steady, quiet, one-pointed and concentrated. (M I 119)[14]

It is similarly said in the *Bhikkhuṇīvāsakasutta* of the *Satipaṭṭhānasaṃyutta*:

> While contemplating the body in the body, there arises distress in the body or sluggishness in the mind or outward distraction. Then the monk should focus his mind on an inspiring object. (S V 156)[15]

11. Here Pemasiri Thera again refers to the following sequence of the elements of dependent origination (*paṭiccasamuppāda*): (7) feeling (*vedanā*) (8) craving (*taṅhā*) (9) clinging (*upādāna*) (10) becoming (*bhava*).

12. Sn 217: *'Suññato lokaṃ avekkhassu Mogharāja sadā sato attānudiṭṭhiṃ ūhacca, evaṃ maccutaro siyā: evaṃ lokaṃ avekkhantaṃ maccurājā na passatī' ti.*

13. The word *nissatta* means 'unsubstantial, lacking an essence,' while *nijjīvata* signifies 'lifeless' (see DP; PED, *s.v.*). The phrase 'no essence and no living being' (*nissattanijjīvata*), which refers to non-self, is only attested in post-canonical texts; for example, in the *Atthasālinī* (i.e., commentary on the *Dhammasaṅgani*), it is linked to the term *dhamma*: '*dhamma* implies no essence and no living being' (As 38–39: *... dhammesu dhammānupassī viharatī ti ādīsu nissattanijjīvatāyaṃ*).

14. M I 119: *Idha bhikkhave bhikkhuno yaṃ nimittaṃ āgamma yaṃ nimittaṃ manasikaroto uppajjanti pāpakā akusalā vitakkā chandūpasaṃhitā pi dosūpasaṃhitā pi mohūpasaṃhitā pi tena bhikkhave bhikkhunā tamhā nimittā aññaṃ nimittaṃ manasikātabbaṃ kusalūpasaṃhitaṃ. Seyyathā pi bhikkhave dakkho palagaṇḍo vā palagaṇḍantevāsī vā sukhumāya āṇiyā oḷārikaṃ āṇiṃ abhinīhaneyya abhinīhareyya abhinivajjeyya, evam-eva ... nimittā aññaṃ nimittaṃ manasikaroto kusalūpasaṃhitaṃ ... ajjhattam-eva cittaṃ santiṭṭhati sannisīdati ekodihoti samādhiyati.*

15. S V 156: *kāyārammano vā uppajjati kāyasmim pariḷāho cetaso vā līnattam bahiddhā vā cittaṃ vikkhipati. Tenānanda,*

Having thus settled the mind, the meditator can return to the primary object. The inspiring sign or object (*pasādaniya nimitta*) referred to in this *sutta* can be loving kindness (*mettā*), reflection on the qualities of the Buddha, or any object chosen for calm meditation (*samatha*) practice. It should be easy for the mind to stay with it and produce a peaceful state. Whenever the meditator encounters strong difficulties in the practice of mindfulness (*satipaṭṭhāna*), it is always very useful to focus on such an object until the mind calms down. It is interesting to note that in the *Bhikkhuṇīvāsakasutta*, it is said that mindful contemplation can be conducted with the mind focused on a meditation object, or alternatively, without being directed to a specific object;[16] this is the only *sutta* that specifically refers to these two different approaches.

As the practice of mindfulness (*sati*) evolves, pleasant feeling (*sukhavedanā*) usually becomes the prominent object of contemplation. In the *Ānāpānasatisutta* in the section on the cultivation of mindfulness of breathing (*ānāpānasati*), it is said that in the final stage of the contemplation of the body (*kāyānupassanā*), the meditator breathes in and out calming the body formation (*passambhayaṃ kāyasaṅkhāraṃ*).[17] Then, after calming the body formation (*kāyasaṅkhāra*), the *sutta* transitions to the contemplation of feeling (*vedanānupassanā*), saying that the meditator in the practice of mindfulness of breathing (*ānāpānasati*) experiences joy (*pīti*) and happiness (*sukha*):

> [The meditator] trains thus: "I shall breathe in experiencing joy, I shall breathe out experiencing joy; I shall breathe in experiencing happiness, I shall breathe out experiencing happiness."
> (M III 82–83)[18]

These experiences arise when applied thought (*vitakka*) and sustained thought (*vicāra*) are reduced to the extent that external objects rarely occur, and consequently, the feeling of joy (*pīti*) and peaceful happiness (*sukha*) become the predominant objects.[19] As the result of these peaceful and happy feelings, mental formations (*cittasaṅkhāra*) are reduced and calmed.[20] At these stages, the most prominent object observed is pleasant feeling (*sukhavedanā*), which can be experienced by the meditator as if joy (*pīti*) and happiness (*sukha*) are breathed in and out.

---

bhikkhunā kismiñcideva pasādaniye nimitte cittam paṇidahitabbam. tassa kismiñcideva pasādaniye nimitte cittaṃ paṇidahato pāmujjaṃ jāyati.

16. Both approaches are explained at the end of the *Bhikkhuṇīvāsakasutta*: 'Thus, Ānanda, I have taught meditation by directing [to an object] and I have taught meditation without directing' (S V 157: *Iti kho Ānanda desitā mayā paṇidhāya bhāvanā desitā apaṇidhāya bhāvanā*).

17. The *Ānāpānasatisutta* says: '[The meditator] trains thus: I shall breathe in calming the bodily formation; I shall breathe out calming the body formation' (M III 82: *Passambhayaṃ kāyasaṅkhāraṃ assasissāmīti sikkhati; passambhayaṃ kāyasaṅkhāraṃ passasissamīti sikkhati*).

18. M III 82–83: *Pītipaṭisaṃvedī assasissāmītī sikkhati; pītipaṭisaṃvedī passasissāmīti sikkhati; sukhapaṭisaṃvedī assasissāmīti sikkhati; sukhapaṭisaṃvedī passasissāmīti sikkhati.*

19. Applied thought (*vitakka*) and sustained thought (*vicāra*) are the first two of the five components of the first absorption (*jhāna*). The three other components are rapture or joy (*pīti*), happiness or contentment (*sukha*) and one-pointedness (*ekaggatā*); for a detailed description, see the *Visuddhimagga* (Vism 122–169; 326–340).

20. The section on the contemplation of feelings in the *Ānāpānasatisutta* describes these stages: '[The meditator] trains thus: I shall breathe in experiencing the mental formation, I shall breathe out experiencing the mental formation; I shall breathe in calming the mental formation; I shall breathe out calming the mental formation' (M III 83: *Cittasaṅkhārapaṭisaṃvedī assasissāmīti sikkhati; cittasaṅkhārapaṭisaṃvedī passasissāmīti sikkhati; passambhayaṃ cittasaṅkhāraṃ assasissāmīti sikkhati; passambhayaṃ cittasaṅkhāraṃ passasissāmīti sikkhati*).

Contemplation of Feelings (*Vedanānupassanā*)

Since the mind is now well established in wholesomeness—i.e., free from greed (*lobha*), hatred (*dosa*) and delusion (*moha*)—the meditator no longer experiences the breath going in and out. Instead, it seems as though the mind is going in and out, which means that the body is no longer experienced. Although the meditation started with observing and calming the body formations (*kāyasaṅkhāra*), it is now the mental formations (*cittasaṅkhāra*) that become the object of contemplation. The meditator experiences a peaceful mind along with pleasant feeling (*sukhavedanā*) and can stay in meditation for long periods without awareness of time passing. These states, which arise in insight meditation (*vipassanā*), are similar to meditative absorptions (*jhāna*); when joy (*pīti*) and happiness (*sukha*) are the prominent objects, this is like the first absorption (*jhāna*), whereas the stage of calming the mental formations would correspond to the fourth absorption (*jhāna*). In insight (*vipassanā*) meditation, if feeling (*vedanā*) accompanied by mental states such as joy (*pīti*) and happiness (*sukha*) is experienced as dominant, and its nature is clearly seen and understood by the meditator, then the meditation takes place in the domain of the contemplation of feeling (*vedanānupassanā*).[21] Later, when meditation reaches the level of calming the mental formations, it is difficult to differentiate between the contemplation of feeling (*vedanānupassanā*) and the contemplation of the mind (*cittānupassanā*). At this point, the practice changes from the contemplation of feeling (*vedanānupassanā*) to the contemplation of the mind (*cittānupassanā*). For example, the meditator may clearly see how a pleasant feeling (*sukhavedanā*) may arise as a dominant object, followed by the knowing mind (*citta*), which may arise with the desire (*sarāgacitta*) or without the desire (*vītarāgacitta*) to retain it.[22]

To summarise, if the practice of the four foundations of mindfulness begins with the contemplation of the body (*kāyānupassanā*), objects related to feeling (*vedanā*) will also frequently arise, because such is the nature of the body and mind. Some meditators begin their practice with the contemplation of feeling (*vedanānupassanā*), which becomes their main object of contemplation in sitting meditation. However, they still practise walking meditation and clear comprehension (*sampajañña*) of bodily activities, which are in the domain of the contemplation of the body (*kāyānupassanā*). Most commonly, meditators begin with the contemplation of the body (*kāyānupassanā*), and once mindfulness (*sati*) is established, pleasant feeling (*sukhavedanā*) may arise. If clear comprehension (*sampajañña*) has not yet evolved, the meditator may think: 'This pleasant feeling (*sukhavedanā*) is good, I hope that it remains for a long time.' This is how the hindrance of sense desire (*kāmachanda*) arises, because the meditator enjoys the pleasant feeling (*sukhavedanā*) and is deceived by desire. Any pleasant feeling (*sukhavedanā*) is bound to disappear, because it is impermanent (*anicca*); however, since clear comprehension (*sampajañña*) has not yet arisen or is not strong enough to lead to an understanding of impermanence

21. Similarly, the *Papañcasūdanī* commentary states that these feelings can be experienced in two ways—in the context of calm (*samatha*) or insight (*vipassanā*) meditation. When joy (*pīti*) is experienced as the predominant object, it can be viewed as an object of absorption in the first two *jhānas* or as non-delusion (*amoha*) when its characteristics of passing away (*khaya*) and decay (*vaya*) are clearly seen and understood (Ps IV 141: *Dvīhākārehi pīti paṭisaṃviditā hoti ārammaṇato ca asammohato ca. Kathaṃ ārammaṇato pīti paṭisaṃviditā hoti? Sappītike dve jhāne samāpajjati, tassa samāpattikkhaṇe jhānapaṭilābhena ārammaṇato pīti paṭisaṃviditā hoti ārammaṇassa paṭisaṃviditattā. Kathaṃ asammohato pīti paṭisaṃviditā hoti? Sappītike dve jhāne samāpajjitvā vuṭṭhāya jhānasampayuttaṃ pītiṃ khayato vayato sammasati, tassa vipassanākkhaṇe lakkhaṇapaṭivedhā asammohato pīti paṭisaṃviditā hoti*).

22. For the discussion on the contemplation of the mind with or without desire, see Chapter IV, under the subheading 'Mind with desire (*sarāgacitta*) and mind without desire (*vītarāgacitta*).'

(*anicca*), the meditator thinks: 'What a pity, I lost this pleasant feeling.' Consequently, the hindrance of ill will (*vyāpāda*) arises. This is how the hindrances (*nīvaraṇa*) function, and when they are activated, the contemplation of feeling (*vedanānupassanā*) cannot occur due to the lack of mindfulness (*sati*) and clear comprehension (*sampajañña*). Meditators are often misled and deluded by feelings (*vedanā*), which prevent them from grasping the three characteristics (*tilakkhaṇa*). They thus fail to understand impermanence (*anicca*), and suffering (*dukkha*) then ensues. Therefore, the contemplation of feeling (*vedanānupassanā*) with mindfulness (*sati*) and clear comprehension (*sampajañña*) of its nature (i.e., its three characteristics) is an essential component in the practice of the foundations of mindfulness (*satipaṭṭhāna*).[23]

'Neither-unpleasant-nor-pleasant feeling' (*adukkhamasukhavedanā*)

Apart from pleasant and unpleasant feeling, the *Satipaṭṭhānasutta* also mentions the third modality, namely, neither-unpleasant-nor-pleasant feeling (*adukkhamasukhavedanā*).[24] It is often interpreted as equanimity (*upekkhā*).[25] However, the two terms are different: why else would the *Satipaṭṭhānasutta* use the term neither-unpleasant-nor-pleasant feeling (*adukkhamasukhavedanā*) instead of simply referring to it as equanimity (*upekkhā*)? The difference between these two terms can be explained in the context of the two fundamental types of meditation, namely, the cultivation of the four foundations of mindfulness (*satipaṭṭhāna*) and calm meditation (*samatha*). When calm meditation (*samatha*) is practised and higher levels of absorption (*jhāna*) are reached, the meditator experiences equanimity (*upekkhā*).[26] However, this equanimity (*upekkhā*) has drawbacks, as described by the Buddha in the *Tapussasutta* in the context of the fourth absorption (*jhāna*):

> I entered and dwelt in the fourth *jhāna*. While I was dwelling in this state, perception and attention accompanied by equanimity occurred in me and I felt it as an affliction. (A IV 443)[27]

---

23. Similarly, the *Papañcasūdanī* commentary states that the contemplation of feeling and the four other aggregates leads to an insight into the three characteristics (Ps I 276: *suddhasaṅkhārapuñjamattamevāti sappaccayanāmarūpavasena tilakkhaṇaṃ āropetvā vipassanāpaṭipāṭiyā aniccaṃ dukkhaṃ anattā ti sammasanto vicarati*).

24. In the *Visuddhimagga*, *adukkhamasukhavedanā* is described as 'not pleasant (*sukha*), not unpleasant (*dukkha*), not mental ease (*somanassa*), not mental discontent (*domanassa*)' (Vism 167: *yaṃ neva sukhaṃ na dukkhaṃ na somanassaṃ na domanassaṃ, ayam adukkhamasukhā vedanā ti*).

25. For example, in the classification of feelings in the *Indriyasaṃyutta*, the faculty of equanimity (*upekkhindriya*) is presented as a feeling that is neither agreeable nor disagreeable (S V 209: *Yaṃ kho bhikkhave kāyikaṃ vā cetasikaṃ vā neva sātaṃ nāsātaṃ vedayitaṃ, idaṃ vuccati bhikkhave upekkhindriyaṃ*). In the *Visuddhimagga*, ten kinds of equanimity are listed in the section discussing the third *jhāna* (Vism 160–162); here the feeling of equanimity (*vedanupekkhā*) is related to neither pain nor pleasure (Vism 161: *yasmiṃ samaye kāmāvacaraṃ kusalaṃ cittaṃ uppannaṃ hoti upekkhāsahagatan ti evam āgatā adukkhamasukhasaññitā upekkhā – ayaṃ vedanupekkhā nāma*). Cf. Dhs 28–29. Later in the *Visuddhimagga*, in the section on the five aggregates, the fivefold classification of feelings (i.e., pleasant, unpleasant, mental ease, mental discontent and equanimity) does not include neither-unpleasant-nor-pleasant feeling (*adukkhamasukhavedanā*) but instead lists equanimity (*upekkhā*) as the fifth modality, which is described as having the characteristic of neutrality, the function of not intensifying, the manifestation of peacefulness and the proximate cause of a mind without joy (Vism 461: *Majjhattavedayitalakkhaṇā upekkhā, sampayuttānaṃ nāti upabrūhanamilāpanarasā, santabhāvapaccupaṭṭhānā, nippītikacittapadaṭṭhānāti*).

26. For example, in the *Visuddhimagga* section on the absorptions (*jhāna*), equanimity is equated with the third modality of feeling, namely, neither-unpleasant-nor-pleasant (Vism 167: *Tatiyavedanā nāma adukkhamasukhā, upekkhā ti pi vuccati*).

27. A IV 443: *catutthaṃ jhānaṃ upasampajja viharāmi. Tassa mayham Ānanda iminā vihārena viharato upekhāsahagatā saññāmanasikārā samudācaranti, svāssa me hoti ābādho.*

The state of equanimity (*upekkhā*) in calm (*samatha*) meditation indicates that the meditator has (temporarily) moved away from greed (*lobha*) or aversion (*dosa*), pleasure or pain, although it has occurred without wisdom (*paññā*), which means that the taints (*āsava*)[28] have not been eradicated. It is only with wisdom (*paññā*) that the taints (*āsava*) can be destroyed. The *Tapussa-sutta* thus continues:

> I entered and dwelt in the cessation of perception and feeling, and having seen with wisdom, my taints were utterly destroyed. (A IV 448)[29]

The difference between neither-unpleasant-nor-pleasant feeling (*adukkhamasukhavedanā*) and equanimity (*upekkhā*) can be explained by the following example. Equanimity (*upekkhā*) can be compared to the mental state of a student in a classroom who cannot understand the subject; she or he consequently enters into a kind of indifference or equanimity, arising out of foolishness or ignorance, simply because she or he has no other option. By way of contrast, a good student who grasps the subject very well may also appear quiet and equanimous; however, she or he is well concentrated and has a deep understanding of the subject: this could exemplify the neither-unpleasant-nor-pleasant feeling (*adukkhamasukhavedanā*) accompanying such a state.

For this reason, the section on the contemplation of feeling (*vedanā*) in the *Satipaṭṭhāna-sutta* does not mention equanimity (*upekkhā*) but instead speaks of the contemplation of neither-pleasant-nor-unpleasant (*adukkhamasukha*) feeling. Only those who lack wisdom (*paññā*) tend to develop equanimity (*upekkhā*) towards unpleasant feeling (*dukkhavedanā*), whereas meditators who have established clear comprehension (*sampajañña*) and freedom from desire and discontent (*vineyya abhijjhādomanassaṃ*) know the feeling as neither-unpleasant-nor-pleasant (*adukkhamasukhavedanā*).[30] If the meditator lacks sufficient mindfulness (*sati*) and clear

28. Taints (*āsava*) are the deeply ingrained tendencies or defilements that obstruct liberation and maintain further existence; the following four are usually listed: (1) sense desire (*kāma*), (2) becoming (*bhava*), (3) ignorance (*avijjā*) and (4) views (*diṭṭhi*) (see DP; PED, *s.v.*). The taints are discussed in Chapter V.3, under the subheading 'Fetter (*saṃyojana*).'

29. A IV 448: *sabbaso nevasaññānāsaññāyatanaṃ samatikkamma saññāvedayitanirodhaṃ upasampajja viharāmi, paññāya ca me disvā āsavā parikkhayaṃ agamaṃsu.*

30. I am not aware of any canonical or commentarial texts in which this distinction is articulated in the way that Pemasiri Thera interprets it here. However, this distinction is indicated by or can be deduced from several attestations of the term equanimity (*upekkhā*), which is usually discussed in the context of meditative absorptions (*jhāna*), particularly the fourth *jhāna* (e.g., D I 183; D III 270; A III 12; M II 227; M III 226). Equanimity (*upekkhā*) appears in both wholesome (*kusala*) mental states such as meditative absorptions (*jhāna*) (e.g., Dhs 28) and unwholesome states (*akusala*) (e.g., Dhs 81). The *Saḷāyatanavibhaṅgasutta* mentions that equanimity (*upekkhā*) can arise in a 'foolish ordinary person,' which is then called 'equanimity based on the household life' (M III 219: *upekkhā bālassa mūḷhassa puthujjanassa ... upekkhā gehasitā ti vuccati*), or equanimity can arise while seeing 'with wisdom that all phenomena are impermanent, non-satisfactory and subject to change,' which is called 'equanimity based on renunciation' (M III 219: *Pubbe c' eva dhammā etarahi ca sabbe te dhammā aniccā dukkha vipariṇāmadhammā ti evam etaṃ yathābhūtaṃ sammappaññāya passato uppajjati upekkhā ... sā upekkhā nekkhammasitā vuccati*). It may also be noted that the term 'neither-unpleasant-nor-pleasant feeling' (*adukkhamasukhavedanā*) is mainly attested in the context of the four foundations of mindfulness (*satipaṭṭhāna*) in relation to clear comprehension and understanding the impermanence of feelings (e.g., M I 252, 255, 500; M II 242–243; M III 274; S IV 19); in these instances, neither-unpleasant-nor-pleasant feeling (*adukkhamasukhavedanā*) is never equated with equanimity (*upekkhā*). However, quite a different approach is taken in the *Papañcasūdanī* commentary, which states that neither-unpleasant-nor-pleasant feeling (*adukkhamasukhavedanā*) is difficult to see and can only be known by the meditator through inference, by observing the absence of both pleasant and unpleasant feelings (Ps I 277).

comprehension (*sampajañña*) to remain with the feeling without craving (*taṇhā*) and clinging (*upādāna*) but instead identifies with it, then she or he will try to look at the feeling with indifference or equanimity (*upekkhā*). For example, the meditator may complain, 'my leg is hurting,' and may try to develop equanimity (*upekkhā*) towards this unpleasantness, because she or he has no wisdom (*paññā*) and thus no other way to approach it.

It is not easy to contemplate feeling (*vedanā*). Meditators do not usually distinguish feeling related to the body (*kāya*) from feeling related to the mind (*citta*), and because of this lack of understanding, they create an 'I' and believe that 'I am experiencing this feeling.' To understand the distinction between physical contact (*phoṭṭhabba*) and mental feeling (*vedanā*), clear comprehension (*sampajañña*) is required. Only when this difference is understood does the meditator start to practise insight meditation (*vipassanā*); she or he knows with clear comprehension (*sampajañña*) that a pleasant (*sukkha*) or unpleasant (*dukkha*) feeling may have arisen because of an inappropriate bodily contact (*phoṭṭhabba*), and thus, she or he understands how it triggers mental pleasure (*somanassa*) or aversion (*domanassa*). Thus, it is clear comprehension (*sampajañña*) that can observe and understand the physical contact (*phoṭṭhabba*), pain (*dukkha*) or happiness (*sukha*) as well as the pleasure (*somanassa*) or discontent (*domanassa*) that will arise in the mind. The meditator understands how suffering (*dukkha*) arises because of the body, how mental suffering is conditioned and how all these modalities and processes of feeling have the same nature (i.e., they are impermanent, subject to suffering and non-self).[31] When the meditator sees and understands all these aspects and modalities related to feeling with clear comprehension (*sampajañña*), it can be said that she or he contemplates neither-unpleasant-nor-pleasant feeling (*adukkhamasukhavedanā*). In other words, when the mind sees the true nature of the object with wisdom (*paññā*), the contemplation of feeling is in the domain of neither-unpleasant-nor-pleasant feeling (*adukkhamasukhavedanā*).

When the meditator can clearly distinguish between mentality (*nāma*) and materiality (*rūpa*), she or he begins to see cause and effect (*hetuphala*) and realises that the feeling (*vedanā*) is not 'mine,' that it has no owner.[32] At this point, the meditator attains the purification of view (*diṭṭhivisuddhi*);[33] she or he understands cause and effect, her or his practice becomes fairly stable and doubts surrounding the practice no longer arise. This is where insight meditation (*vipassanā*) begins. As insight meditation advances, the contemplation of feeling (*vedanā*) is no longer at the forefront. The meditator is no longer interested in investigating pleasant (*sukha*) and unpleasant (*dukkha*) feeling, as she or he no longer tries to determine or show an interest in any pleasurable or painful aspects of an object but rather turns all her or his attention, in conjunction with strong wisdom (*paññā*), to the contemplation and understanding of how the

---

31. The section on the contemplation of feelings in the *Papañcasūdanī* commentary concludes (as do other sections of the *Satipaṭṭhānasutta*) by linking the grasping of feeling to the truth of suffering: 'Indeed, mindfulness that takes up feeling is the truth of suffering. Thus, the way to deliverance for the monk who takes up [mindfulness of] feeling should be understood' (Ps I 279: *Kevalañhi idha vedanāpariggāhikā sati dukkhasaccan ti evaṃ yojanaṃ katvā vedanāpariggāhakassa bhikkhuno niyyānamukhaṃ veditabbaṃ*).

32. As mentioned before, the *Papañcasūdanī* commentary states that there is no person or being who feels and that feeling has no owner (Ps I 275: *Tattha ko vedayatī ti? Na koci satto vā puggalo vā vedayati. Kassa vedanā ti? Na kassaci sattassa vā puggalassa vā vedanā*).

33. Knowledge of the distinction between materiality and mentality (*nāmarūpaparicchedañāṇa*) is presented under purification of view (*diṭṭhivisuddhi*), which is the third of the seven stages of purification leading to final liberation; all the stages are described in the *Rathavinītasutta* (M I 145–151). For a detailed discussion on the purification of view (*diṭṭhivisuddhi*), see *Visuddhimagga* (Vism 587–597).

objects arise and pass away by focusing on their impermanence (as well as the two other characteristics, i.e., unsatisfactoriness and non-self). At this stage, the seven factors of awakening (*satta bojjhaṅgā*)[34] can evolve, and knowledge of equanimity about formations (*saṅkhārupekkhāñāṇa*)[35] is reached. Now, the contemplation of feeling (*vedanānupassanā*) is no longer at the forefront, but instead the contemplation of phenomena (*dhammānupassanā*) becomes the main domain of the meditation practice.

'Worldly' (*sāmisa*) and 'unworldly' (*nirāmisa*) feeling

The *Satipaṭṭhānasutta* distinguishes between 'worldly' (*sāmisa*) and 'unworldly' (*nirāmisa*) feeling. 'Worldly' (*sāmisa*) feeling arises in relation to the worldly experiences of pleasure or pain, connected with the worldly objects of the senses. By contrast, 'unworldly' (*nirāmisa*) feeling arises when the level of meditative absorptions (*jhāna*) is reached.[36] Unworldly feeling (*nirāmisa*) occurs both in the practice of calm (*samatha*) and insight (*vipassanā*) meditation when the meditator's hindrances (*nīvaraṇa*) have been (temporarily) removed. For example, joy (*pīti*) and happiness (*sukha*) are related to unworldly (*nirāmisa*) feelings that are prominent objects in calm (*samatha*) meditation, especially in the second and third absorptions (*jhāna*), respectively.[37]

Unworldly (*nirāmisa*) feeling is also experienced in insight (*vipassanā*) meditation when it arises in relation to meditation objects such as breathing and leads to high levels of concentration (*samādhi*). For example, the section on the contemplation of feeling (*vedanānupassanā*) in the *Ānāpānasatisutta* (M III 82–83) begins with the experience of joy (*pīti*) and happiness (*sukha*) during the practice of mindfulness of breathing (*ānāpānasati*). When the meditator reaches the level of absorption (*jhāna*), she or he experiences a kind of pleasant tranquillity (*sukha*) in the body and mind. The feeling of joy (*pīti*) or happiness (*sukha*) experienced in absorption (*jhāna*) dissolves when the meditator is no longer in that particular absorption (*jhāna*). For example, after experiencing absorption (*jhāna*), the meditator may have to collect alms (*piṇḍapāta*) by a very difficult route, sleep in an uncomfortable place or face various troubles related to the climate or insects; consequently, she or he may experience unpleasant feeling (*dukkhavedanā*). However, these are unworldly (*nirāmisa*) feelings because the hindrances (*nīvaraṇa*) are (temporarily) withdrawn. Many practitioners who develop absorption (*jhāna*), especially in

---

34. The seven factors of awakening (*satta bojjhaṅgā*) are as follows: (1) mindfulness (*sati*), (2) investigation of *dhammas* (*dhammavicaya*), (3) energy (*viriya*), (4) joy (*pīti*), (5) tranquillity (*passaddhi*), (6) concentration (*samādhi*) and (7) equanimity (*upekkhā*). For a detailed discussion, see Chapter V.4. Seven factors of awakening (*satta bojjhaṅgā*).

35. Knowledge of equanimity about formations (*saṅkhārupekkhāñāṇa*) is one of the most advanced stages in the development of the insight knowledges, which are described in detail in the *Visuddhimagga* (Vism 628–671). See also Mahāsi (2016, 303–466).

36. Similarly, the *Nirāmisasutta* links worldly (*sāmisa*) pleasant feeling related to joy (*pīti*), happiness (*sukha*) and equanimity (*upekkhā*) to the domain of sensual pleasures, whereas unworldly (*nirāmisa*) feeling is linked to the meditative absorptions (*jhāna*) and liberation (*vimokkha*) (S IV 235–237). According to the *Papañcasūdanī* commentary, worldly (*sāmisa*) pleasant feeling refers to the pleasures connected with worldly life (*gehasitasomanassavedanā*), whereas unworldly (*nirāmisa*) pleasant feeling refers to the pleasures related to renunciation (*nekkhammasitasomanassavedanā*) (Ps I 279).

37. The four absorptions (*jhāna*) in the realm of form (*rūpa*), the formless (*arūpa*) absorptions (*jhāna*) and their components are described in many canonical texts (e.g., M I 40–41; A IV 438–448; S IV 217; D I 73–74; Dhs 31–56). A comprehensive presentation of the absorptions (*jhāna*) is given in the *Visuddhimagga* (Vism 122–169; 326–340); for a shorter overview, see Bodhi (1993, 52–64).

remote hermitages, experience such an unworldly unpleasant feeling (*nirāmisadukkhavedanā*) before and after the absorptions (*jhāna*) when they face various challenges such as diseases or a lack of medicine, food or water. An experienced practitioner, without thinking too much about these inconveniences, simply continues with her or his practice.

To summarise, as described in the *Nirāmisasutta*, unworldly (*nirāmisa*) feeling may occur in the absorptions (*jhāna*), whereas even higher levels of unworldly feeling (*nirāmisatara*) may thus be experienced:

> When a monk, whose taints are eradicated, contemplates his mind liberated from desire, hatred and delusion, there arises deliverance. This is called deliverance that is more unworldly than the unworldly deliverance.[38] (S IV 237)[39]

Thus, a higher level of unworldly feeling (*nirāmisatara*) is experienced by meditators who have eradicated the defilements (*kilesa*), who are free from greed (*lobha*), aversion (*dosa*) and delusion (*moha*) and who have reached the state of deliverance.

38. In the *Paṭisambhidāmagga*, it is explained that the 'more unworldly than the unworldly deliverance' refers to the four paths and fruits as well as to *nibbāna* (Paṭis II 41: *Katamo nirāmisā nirāmisataro vimokkho? Cattāro ca ariyamaggā, cattāri ca sāmaññaphalāni, nibbānañca*).

39. S IV 237: *Yo kho bhikkhave khīṇāsavassa bhikkhuno rāgā cittaṃ vimuttam paccavekkhato / pe / mohā cittaṃ vimuttam paccavekkhato uppajjati vimokkho / pe / ayaṃ vuccati bhikkhave nirāmisā nirāmisataro vimokkho ti*.

— IV —

Contemplation of the Mind (*Cittānupassanā*)

*Kathañca bhikkhave bhikkhu **citte** cittānupassī viharati? Idha bhikkhave bhikkhu **sarāgaṃ** vā cittaṃ sarāgaṃ cittanti pajānāti, **vītarāgaṃ** vā cittaṃ vītarāgaṃ cittanti pajānāti, **sadosaṃ** vā cittaṃ sadosaṃ cittanti pajānāti, **vītadosaṃ** vā cittaṃ vītadosaṃ cittanti pajānāti, **samohaṃ** vā cittaṃ, samohaṃ cittanti pajānāti, **vītamohaṃ** vā cittaṃ vītamohaṃ cittanti pajānāti, **saṅkhittaṃ** vā cittaṃ saṅkhittaṃ cittanti pajānāti, **vikkhittaṃ** vā cittaṃ vikkhittaṃ cittanti pajānāti, **mahaggataṃ** vā cittaṃ mahaggataṃ cittanti pajānāti, **amahaggataṃ** vā cittaṃ amahaggataṃ cittanti pajānāti, **sa-uttaraṃ** vā cittaṃ sa-uttaraṃ cittanti pajānāti, **anuttaraṃ** vā cittaṃ anuttaraṃ cittanti pajānāti, **samāhitaṃ** vā cittaṃ samāhitaṃ cittanti pajānāti, **asamāhitaṃ** vā cittaṃ asamāhitaṃ cittanti pajānāti, **vimuttaṃ** vā cittaṃ vimuttaṃ cittanti pajānāti, **avimuttaṃ** vā cittaṃ avimuttaṃ cittanti pajānāti.*[1]

'And how, monks, does a monk abide contemplating the **mind** as the mind? Here, a monk knows a **mind with desire** as a desirous mind, a **mind without desire** as a mind without desire. He knows a **mind with aversion** as a mind with aversion, a **mind without aversion** as a mind without aversion. He knows a **mind with delusion** as a deluded mind, a **mind without delusion** as a mind without delusion. He knows a **contracted mind** as contracted, a **distracted mind** as distracted. He knows an **exalted mind** as exalted, an **unexalted mind** as unexalted. He knows a **surpassable mind** as surpassable, an **unsurpassable mind** as unsurpassable. He knows a **concentrated mind** as concentrated, an **unconcentrated mind** as unconcentrated. He knows a **liberated mind** as liberated, an **unliberated mind** as unliberated.'

Recurring passage indicating the ways to approach the contemplation[2]

Iti ajjhattaṃ vā citte cittānupassī viharati, bahiddhā vā citte cittānupassī viharati, ajjhattabahiddhā vā citte cittānupassī viharati. Samudayadhammānupassī vā cittasmiṃ viharati, vayadhammānupassī vā cittasmiṃ viharati, samudayavayadhammānupassī vā cittasmiṃ viharati. Atthi cittanti vā panassa sati paccupaṭṭhitā hoti yāvadeva ñāṇamattāya patissatimattāya, anissito ca viharati na ca kiñci loke upādiyati. Evam kho bhikkhave bhikkhu citte cittānupassī viharati.

'Thus he abides contemplating the mind as the mind internally, or he abides contemplating the mind as the mind externally, or he abides contemplating the mind as the mind both internally and externally. He abides contemplating the arising of phenomena in the mind, or he abides contemplating the passing away of phenomena in the mind, or he abides contemplating both the

1. Since this section is quite repetitious, the Pāli Text Society edition (M I 59–60) is heavily abbreviated, perhaps at the expense of clarity. Therefore, the Pāli text cited here retains the repetitions.

2. For comments on the recurring passage, see Chapter II.1, under the subheading 'Recurring passage indicating the ways to approach the contemplation.'

arising and passing away of phenomena in the mind. Or, mindfulness that "there is the mind" is established in him just to the extent necessary for knowledge and mindfulness. And he abides without attachment, not clinging to anything in the world. Monks, thus a monk abides contemplating the mind as the mind.'

Pemasiri Thera's commentary

The contemplation of the mind (*cittānupassanā*) is a very important component of meditation.[3] For its object, it takes thoughts, which are always linked to perceptions (*saññā*)[4] from the past. When various mental states that arise along with objects related to the past are noted, it can be said that the meditator practises the contemplation of the mind (*cittānupassanā*). However, if the meditator does not immediately note them but instead responds to them with a thought like 'Now, why is this thought coming up all the time? Perhaps I cannot practise meditation as I have too many thoughts,' then mindfulness (*sati*) is lost at that moment and hindrances (*nīvaraṇa*) such as restlessness and worry (*uddhaccakukkucca*) arise. In the contemplation of the mind (*cittānupassanā*), it is very common for past objects to arise with the hindrances of sense desire (*kāmacchanda*) or ill will (*vyāpāda*). The meditator should note either the thought that occurs with an object from the past or the hindrance (*nīvaraṇa*) that accompanies it. If the object is noted in this manner, the meditation practice is in the domain of insight meditation (*vipassanā*); otherwise, the thoughts begin to expand and proliferate, while mindfulness (*sati*) and clear comprehension (*sampajañña*) are absent.

Meditators usually do not have the necessary strength and quality of attention (*manasikāra*) or mindfulness (*sati*) to note perceptions (*saññā*), although they may note the feeling (*vedanā*) that arises along with perceptions (*saññā*) such as the pleasant and unpleasant feeling occurring with sense desire (*kāmacchanda*) and ill will (*vyāpāda*), respectively.[5] If this feeling (*vedanā*) is noted as it arises, the objects will pass away at the very moment of noting; in this case, the contemplation takes place in the domain of feeling (*vedanānupassanā*). If the feeling is not noted, then a thought will appear, and if noted immediately, the contemplation is in the domain of the mind (*cittānupassanā*). Sometimes the meditator cannot immediately stop the thought process by noting it but becomes aware of it only after the thought has already grown and expanded to some extent, and when recalling it, she or he thinks: 'I forgot to note this

3. In comparison with the three other sections in the *Satipaṭṭhānasutta*, the section on the contemplation of the mind (*cittānupassanā*) has received very little attention in the traditional commentaries (Ps I 279–280; Vibh-a 268–269) and the secondary literature (e.g., Mahāsi 2016, 206–208). For example, in the *Papañcasūdani* commentary, each of the sixteen states of the mind listed in the *sutta* is commented upon with just a few words, mainly focusing on the Abhidhammic taxonomy of the various types of the mind.

4. The term *saññā* is usually translated as 'perception, discernment, recognition' (PED, *s.v.*) in reference to the recognition of an object; for example, the recognition of colour in the case of a visual object (M I 293; S III 87). This term is further discussed in Chapter V.2. Five aggregates of clinging (*pañcas'upādānakkhandhā*), under the subheading 'Feeling (*vedanā*) and perception (*saññā*).'

5. When contact (*phassa*) with an object takes place in the process of cognition, feeling (*vedanā*) and perception (*saññā*) arise. Among the mental concomitants (*cetasika*) involved in this process, feeling (*vedanā*) dominates the experience of the object. This is also stated in the *Atthasālinī*: contact (*phassa*) merely 'touches' the object, perception (*saññā*) notes (or recognises) it, volition (*cetanā*) coordinates it and consciousness (*viññāṇa*) cognises it; but feeling (*vedanā*) alone is the chief component that experiences it, as it 'tastes' the object (As 109: *Phassassa hi phusanamattakam eva hoti, saññāya sañjānanamattakam eva, cetanāya cetanāmattakam eva, viññāṇassa vijānanamattakameva. Ekaṃsato pana issaravatāya vissavitāya sāmibhāvena vedanā va ārammaṇarasaṃ anubhavati*).

thought at the very start.' This means that the meditator only recalls it after mindfulness (*sati*) has been broken. Thinking about past objects serves no purpose, since all these objects are dead and empty and should be simply dropped.

The section on the contemplation of the mind (*cittānupassanā*) in the *Satipaṭṭhānasutta* lists sixteen states of mind. These are not qualities of the mind or mental concomitants (*cetasika*) but rather mind states that have *already* formed. This means that the processes involved in the formation of the mind states have already been completed, and the resulting mind state (*citta*) then becomes the object of contemplation. This is also stated at the beginning of the section on the contemplation of the mind (*cittānupassanā*) in the *Ānāpānasatisutta*:

> [The meditator] trains thus: "I shall breathe in experiencing the mind"; he trains thus: 'I shall breathe out experiencing the mind." (M III 83)[6]

When practising mindfulness of breathing (*ānāpānasati*), the meditator experiences the mind itself (*cittapaṭisaṃvedī*) as the predominant object; other aspects of cognition, namely, the mental concomitants (*cetasika*), are less prominent. If a certain mental concomitant (*cetasika*) is noted—for example, one of the five hindrances (*pañca nīvaraṇāni*)—then the meditator is practising mindfulness in the domain of the contemplation of phenomena (*dhammānupassanā*), but if the state of mind (*citta*) that arises with a hindrance is noted, then the practice is in the domain of the contemplation of the mind (*cittānupassanā*). Thus, in the context of the *Satipaṭṭhānasutta*, the contemplation of the mind (*cittānupassanā*) refers to mindfulness of the mind (*citta*) itself, whereas the contemplation of phenomena (*dhammānupassanā*) refers to mindfulness of mental concomitants (*cetasika*). In other words, the contemplation of phenomena (*dhammānupassanā*) involves the contemplation of mental formations (*saṅkhāra*), which comprise all the mental concomitants (*cetasika*) except for feeling (*vedanā*) and perception (*saññā*).[7]

To summarise, in the contemplation of the mind (*cittānupassanā*), the focus is on the thoughts that arise with perceptions (*saññā*) related to an object from the past, whereas in the contemplation of phenomena (*dhammānupassanā*), the focus is on the perception (*saññā*) itself. Thus, as the meditation moves from the contemplation of the body (*kāya*), to feeling (*vedanā*), to the mind (*citta*) and finally to phenomena (*dhamma*), the objects noted become increasingly refined, expanding from the gross objects of the body to the most subtle mental phenomena.

6. M III 83: *Cittapaṭisaṃvedī assasissāmīti sikkhati; cittapaṭisaṃvedī passasissāmīti sikkhati.*

7. Several models of cognitive processes involved in human experience are presented in the *Tipiṭaka*. One is the model of the five aggregates (*khandha*), comprising: (1) materiality (*rūpa*), (2) feeling (*vedanā*), (3) perception (*saññā*), (4) mental formations (*saṅkhāra*) and (5) consciousness (*viññāṇa*). Another model developed in the *Abhidhamma* literature presents the components of experiences (*dhammas*) through the following four categories: (1) the mind (*citta*) that knows or cognises, (2) mental concomitants (*cetasika*) that contribute specific aspects and functions to cognitive processes, (3) materiality (*rūpa*) that comprises various types of material phenomena and (4) *nibbāna*. The mental concomitants (*cetasika*) from the Abhidhammic model correspond to three of the components in the five aggregates' model: i.e., (2) feeling (*vedanā*), (3) perception (*saññā*) and (4) mental formations (*saṅkhāra*). This is similarly articulated in the *Visuddhimagga*: 'Feeling is associated with the feeling aggregate, perception with the perception aggregate, volition with the mental formation aggregate and the mind with the consciousness aggregate' (Vism 591–592: *taṃ-sampayuttā vedanā vedanākkhandho, saññā saññākkhandho, saddhiṃ phassena cetanā sankhārakkhandho, cittaṃ viññāṇakkhandho ti upaṭṭhāti*).

'Mind' (*citta*)[8]

In the section on the contemplation of the mind (*cittānupassanā*), the word *citta* is used, which is usually translated as 'mind.'[9] *Citta* is the component of the cognitive process that knows or cognises.[10] In the Theravāda *Abhidhamma* model, it arises in a series; one *citta* rapidly follows on from another in the process of cognition or knowing.[11] We can recognise or know that there is something called 'mind' (*citta*) only because of the activities of the mental concomitants (*cetasika*) that arise with it; otherwise, we would not be able to know that the mind exists. To reiterate, the ultimate components of experiences (*dhamma*) can be presented as four categories:

1) the mind (*citta*) that knows or cognises;
2) mental concomitants (*cetasika*) that determine *how* things are cognised;
3) materiality (*rūpa*) that comprises various types of material phenomena;
4) *nibbāna*.[12]

By nature, the mind (*citta*) is like pure clean water without form, colour, taste or smell. Whatever container the water is poured into, it will take that form; whatever colour is put into the water, it will turn that colour; and whatever fragrance is added to the water, it will have that smell.[13] Similarly, whatever mental concomitants (*cetasika*) such as anger, kindness or jealousy

8. In the section on the contemplation of the mind (*cittānupassanā*), Pemasiri Thera discusses the concept of the mind (*citta*) at length, unlike traditional and modern commentators who dedicate but scarce comments to this whole section. For example, the *Papañcasūdani* commentary does not address the concept of the mind (*citta*); instead, it only very briefly comments on the sixteen types of mind (Ps I 279–280). Similarly, modern commentators on the *Satipaṭṭhānasutta* and insight meditation like Mahāsi (2016, 206–208) provide limited comments on the contemplation of the mind.

9. The word *citta* is commonly rendered into English as 'mind' or 'consciousness' as well as 'thought, thinking, state of mind, a thought moment" (see DP, *s.v.*). *Citta*, which is one of the most fundamental terms of Pāli Buddhist philosophical and psychological vocabulary, has no equivalent concept or term in English or other European languages due to the considerable incommensurability between ancient Indian and modern Western discourses, particularly in the area of cognitive models. Here I follow the prevalent modern English renderings of the *Satipaṭṭhānasutta*, where *citta* is translated as 'mind' (see, for example, Anālayo 2006, 169–177; Bodhi 1995, 150–151). In the context of the Abhidhammic texts, *citta* is usually translated as 'consciousness' (e.g., Bodhi 1993) or 'thought' (e.g., Rhys Davids 2012), without any clear nuancing or detailed justifications for the choice of the English rendering. Although I do follow the generally established conventions of modern English translations when selecting equivalents for Pāli words, I consistently (and pointedly) include the Pāli terms (in parentheses) to avoid any unclarity or ambiguity about the Pāli term to which the English translation refers—my main aim is clarity in regard to the often subtle points presented in the Pāli texts and explanations.

10. This definition is given in the *Atthasālinī*, the commentary on the *Dhammasaṅgaṇi* (As 63: *Cittan ti ārammaṇaṃ cintetī ti cittaṃ vijānātīti attho*).

11. The *Atthasālinī* explains that '*citta* is common to all types of mind (i.e., worldly, wholesome, unwholesome, inoperative); in the process of cognition, it arranges itself in series' (As 63: *Yasmā vā cittan ti sabbacittasādhāraṇo esa saddo tasmā yad ettha lokiyakusalākusalakiriyacittaṃ taṃ javanavīthivasena attano santānaṃ cinotīti cittaṃ*).

12. For a comprehensive overview of this Abhidhammic model of cognition, see Bodhi (1993) and Karunadasa (2010).

13. The metaphor of water to represent the mind appears frequently in the Pāli literature; e.g., in the *Sīhanādasutta*, the Buddha says: 'I abide with a mind like water, great, exalted and boundless, without hostility and malevolence' (A IV 375: *āposamena cetasā vihārāmi vipulena mahaggatena appamāṇena averena avyāpajjhena*). Or in the *Saṅgāravasutta*, the Buddha explains the five hindrances using the metaphor of water: the mind obsessed with sense desire (*kāmacchanda*) is compared to water dyed with different colours; the mind with ill-will (*vyāpāda*) is like boiling water, the mind with sloth and torpor (*thīnamiddha*) like water covered with plants and algae, the mind with restlessness and worry (*uddhaccakukkucca*) like water stirred by the wind and the mind with doubt (*vicikicchā*) like muddy water (S V 121–124).

occur in the mind (*citta*), it will adopt their form. Shaped in this way, the mind (*citta*) arises and passes away, and as soon as one mind vanishes, another is immediately created. To reiterate, the mind (*citta*) depends on the mental concomitants (*cetasika*) that arise along with it: if the concomitants (*cetasika*) are wholesome, the mind (*citta*) will adopt a wholesome (*kusala*) shape, but if unwholesome, the mind (*citta*) will be unwholesome (*akusala*) (Table 6).[14]

Table 6 Mental concomitants (*cetasika*).

Ethically variable	**Ethically good**	**Ethically unwholesome**
Universal	***Universal***	***Universal***
1) Contact (*phassa*)	1) Trust (*saddhā*)	1) Delusion (*moha*)
2) Feeling (*vedanā*)	2) Mindfulness (*sati*)	2) Lack of restraint (*ahirika*)
3) Perception (*saññā*)	3) Restraint (*hiri*)	3) Disregard for misconduct (*anottappa*)
4) Volition (*cetanā*)	4) Regard for moral consequence (*ottappa*)	4) Restlessness (*uddhacca*)
5) One-pointedness (*ekaggatā*)	5) Lack of greed (*alobha*)	***Occasional***
6) Life faculty (*jīvitindriya*)	6) Lack of hatred (*adosa*)	5) Greed (*lobha*)
7) Attention (*manasikāra*)	7) Balance, neutrality of mind (*tatramajjhattatā*)	6) Wrong view (*diṭṭhi*)
Occasional	8) Tranquillity of mental body (*kāyapassaddhi*)	7) Conceit (*māna*)
8) Applied thought (*vitakka*)	9) Tranquillity of consciousness (*cittapassaddhi*)	8) Hatred (*dosa*)
9) Sustained thought (*vicāra*)	10) Lightness of mental body (*kāyalahutā*)	9) Envy (*issā*)
10) Intention (*adhimokkha*)	11) Lightness of consciousness (*cittalahutā*)	10) Miserliness (*macchariya*)
11) Energy (*viriya*)	12) Softness/malleability of mental body (*kāyamudutā*)	11) Worry/regret (*kukkucca*)
12) Rapture (*pīti*)	13) Softness/malleability of consciousness (*cittamudutā*)	12) Sloth (*thīna*)
13) Will (to act) (*chanda*)	14) Readiness/wieldiness of mental body (*kāyakammaññatā*)	13) Torpor (*middha*)
	15) Readiness/wieldiness of consciousness (*cittakammaññatā*)	14) Doubt/confusion (*vicikicchā*)
	16) Proficiency of mental body (*kāyapāguññatā*)	
	17) Proficiency of consciousness (*cittapāguññatā*)	
	18) Straightness/rectitude of mental body (*kāyujjukatā*)	
	19) Straightness/rectitude of consciousness (*cittujjukatā*)	
	Occasional	
	20) Right speech (*sammāvācā*)	
	21) Right action (*sammākammanta*)	
	22) Right livelihood (*sammā-ājīva*)	
	23) Compassion (*karuṇā*)	
	24) Sympathetic joy (*muditā*)	
	25) Wisdom (*paññā*)	

14. This is a slightly amended table from Bodhi (1993, 79), with the Pāli terms added in parentheses.

If good or wholesome mental concomitants (*sobhana cetasika*) such as trust (*saddhā*), energy (*viriya*), mindfulness (*sati*), one-pointedness (*ekaggatā*) and wisdom (*amoha*) arise along with the mind (*citta*), then the meditation practice can advance. Concentration (*samādhi*) cannot be listed here as one of the concomitants (*cetasika*); even though it is an important quality to be cultivated by meditators, it is not a mental concomitant (*cetasika*) but rather a combination of several of them. If the mind (*citta*) is enmeshed with hindrances or unwholesome mental concomitants (*cetasika*) such as greed (*lobha*), aversion (*dosa*), delusion (*moha*), sloth and torpor (*thīnamiddha*), restlessness and worry (*uddhaccakukkucca*) and doubt (*vicikicchā*), an array of problems will ensue.[15] Using the metaphor of pure water for the mind (*citta*), it means that when unwholesome (*akusala*) mind states arise, it is as if many colours are added to the water, making it muddy; in such mind states, thoughts expand, confusion sets in, and consequently, suffering (*dukkha*) is created. But since the mind (*citta*) is by nature very pure, bright, colourless, simple and innocent, we can live in great freedom as long as various colours are not added to it. The problem is that most people identify with the mind (*citta*), believing that it is their 'own' or indeed their 'self.' When they refer to the mind as an 'I,' mental proliferation (*papañca*)[16] is triggered, obstacles and defilements expand, and a wide range of troubles ensue. One might ignorantly think that 'I know this much' or 'I am like this or that,' which produces all kinds of issues that emerge in the mind and are followed by verbal and bodily actions, generating conflicts and various problems in relation to other people.

As meditation practice becomes increasingly refined, the meditator develops an understanding that the mind (*citta*) is pure and luminous by nature.[17] At that point, the meditator can also see that the contemplating mind is different from the mind that is the object of contemplation. In such refined states, the meditator may even feel as though there is no mind (*citta*) at all, because the mental concomitants (*cetasika*) operate at a very minimal level. This may occur in the meditative absorptions (*jhāna*); the higher the level of an absorption, the more subtle and limited the mental concomitants (*cetasika*) become. In the formless (*arūpa*) absorptions, mental concomitants (*cetasika*) are even further refined until only perception (*saññā*) and feeling (*vedanā*) are experienced, although sometimes they too seem to be absent. However, it is because of perception (*saññā*) and feeling (*vedanā*) that the meditator knows that there is something called the 'mind' (*citta*). At the most refined stage of formless absorption (*arūpajhāna*), the so-called state of 'neither-perception-nor-non-perception' (*nevasaññāsaññāyatana*), perception is intermittently not observed.[18] Only in the four fruitions (*phalacitta*) does perception (*saññā*)

15. All mental concomitants (*cetasika*) that comprise wholesome and unwholesome mind states (*citta*) are systematically presented in the *Dhammasaṅgaṇi* (Dhs 9–87); they are also discussed in Bodhi (1993, 76–113) and Karunadasa (2010, 103–144).

16. The word *papañca* is usually translated as 'proliferation, expansion, impediment, illusion, obsession' (see PED, *s.v.*). In the *Madhupiṇḍikasutta*, several causes and conditions for perceptual notions born from proliferation (*papañcasaññāsaṅkhā*) are listed, namely, the underlying latent tendencies (*anusaya*) of desire (*rāga*), anger (*paṭigha*), views (*diṭṭhi*), doubt (*vicikicchā*), conceit (*māna*), desire for being (*bhavarāga*) and ignorance (*avijjā*) (M I 109–110).

17. Buddhist texts often speak of the luminosity of the mind; for example, it is said in the *Pabhassarasutta*: 'Monks, this mind is luminous and free from adventitious defilements. The learned noble disciple understands this as it really is. Hence, I say that for the learned noble disciple, there is the cultivation of the mind' (A I 10: *Pabhassaram idaṃ bhikkhave cittaṃ tañ ca kho āgantukehi upakkilesehi vippamuttaṃ. Taṃ sutavā ariyasāvako yathābhūtaṃ pajānāti. Tasmā sutavato ariyasāvakassa cittabhāvanā atthī ti vadāmī ti*).

18. Many canonical and post-canonical texts (e.g., M I 40-41; A IV 438–448; S IV 217; D I 73–74; Dhs 31–56; Vism

not occur; however, feeling (*vedanā*) is still present, although due to the absence of perception, the meditator does not know what is being experienced and cannot think or talk about it. In cessation (*nirodha*)—i.e., the four path minds (*maggacitta*)—feeling (*vedanā*) is also absent; in other words, it is only in *nibbāna* that nothing is conditioned, and therefore it is called 'unconditioned' or 'unconstructed' (*asaṅkhata*), without cause and effect, free from all fetters (*saṃyojana*).[19] In all other mind states (*citta*), at least a very subtle level of feeling (*vedanā*) is present.

Apart from *citta*, there are two Pāli words that are usually translated as 'consciousness' or 'mind,' namely, *mano* and *viññāṇa*. Although the three terms—*citta*, *mano* and *viññāṇa*—are often regarded as mere synonyms, they differ according to the way they relate to an object and the way in which the mental concomitants (*cetasika*) are combined and operate together. For example, when the term *viññāṇa* is used, the mental concomitants (*cetasika*) with the greatest impact on the mind are feeling (*vedanā*) and perception (*saññā*). Therefore, when the texts mention path (*magga*), the term *citta* is used for the path mind (*maggacitta*) instead of *viññāṇa* or *mano*, because there is no feeling (*vedanā*) or perception (*saññā*) in the path mind (*maggacitta*).[20] Similarly, the term *citta* is also used in relation to the absorptions (*jhāna*) but not *mano* or *viññāṇa*, because feeling (*vedanā*) and perception (*saññā*), though present, do not have the greatest impact in the *jhānic* mind states.

The term *viññāṇa*, which is usually translated as 'consciousness,' is frequently used when the mind arises or becomes focused on a new object. Consciousness (*viññāṇa*) arises depending on one of the six senses and their corresponding object,[21] and conditions contact (*phassa*), feeling (*vedanā*) and perception (*saññā*), which can be followed by thoughts (*vitakka*). Consequently, mental proliferation (*papañca*) may ensue, an 'I' is created, and the past, present and future are constructed. This is described in the *Madhupiṇḍikasutta*, beginning with the example of the eye sense sphere:

> Eye-consciousness arises dependent on the eye and visible form. The meeting of the three is contact and contact conditions feeling. What one feels, one perceives. What one perceives, one

137–169, 326–340) provide a detailed description of the four (or five) absorptions (*jhāna*) in the realm of form (*rūpa*) in addition to the formless (*arūpa*) absorptions (*jhāna*) and their components. Several descriptions of the formless absorptions and voidness (*suññatā*) can be found in the *Suññatavagga* section of the *Majjhimanikāya* (M III 104–178). For a comprehensive discussion on the absorptions (*jhāna*), see the *Visuddhimagga* (Vism 122–169; 326–340); a brief overview is given in Bodhi (1993, 52–64).

19. The canonical and commentarial texts identify eight supramundane minds (*lokuttaracitta*) that transcend the conditioned world through the attainment of *nibbāna*. They are presented in the context of the four stages of liberation; each stage comprises a path mind (*maggacitta*) and a fruition mind (*phalacitta*):
    1) path of stream-entry (*sotāpattimaggacitta*) and fruition of stream-entry (*sotāpattiphalacitta*)
    2) path of once-returning (*sakadāgāmimaggacitta*) and fruition of once-returning (*sakadāgāmiphalacitta*)
    3) path of non-returning (*anāgāmimaggacitta*) and fruition of non-returning (*anāgāmiphalacitta*)
    4) path of arahantship (*arahattamaggacitta*) and fruition of arahantship (*arahattaphalacitta*)

    At each of the four stages, the fetters (*saṃyojana*) are attenuated or eliminated. For detailed descriptions, see the *Dhammasaṅgaṇi* (Dhs 60–75) and *Visuddhimagga* (Vism 672–697).

20. For example, in the *Kevaddhasutta* (D I 223), liberation is described as the 'cessation of consciousness' (*viññāṇassa nirodho*) or 'consciousness that is non-manifested' (*viññāṇaṃ anidassanaṃ*).

21. Depending on the senses and their respective objects, six kinds of consciousness (*viññāṇa*) are listed in the Pāli canon and its commentaries: (1) eye-consciousness (*cakkhuviññāṇa*), (2) ear-consciousness (*sotaviññāṇa*), (3) nose-consciousness (*ghānaviññāṇa*), (4) tongue-consciousness (*jivhāviññāṇa*), (5) body-consciousness (*kāyaviññāṇa*) and (6) mind-consciousness (*manoviññāṇa*). The six sense spheres are discussed in the collection of *suttas* in the *Saḷāyatanasaṃyutta* (S IV 1–261).

> thinks about. What one thinks about, one mentally proliferates. With what one mentally proliferates as the source, through that a person is assailed by perceptions and notions in relation to past, future and present visible forms that are cognised though the eye. (M I 111–112)[22]

While the term *viññāṇa* is frequently used in the context of the six sense spheres (*āyatana*), the term *mano*, which is usually translated as 'mind,' is often used in reference to the 'door for thinking activity' (*manokammadvāra*)[23] from which speech and actions ensue. It is presented as the chief and forerunner of arising phenomena, as it is said, for example, in the famous first two verses of the *Dhammapada*:

> Phenomena are preceded by the mind, ruled by the mind and made of the mind.
> If one speaks or acts with an impure mind, suffering follows like the wheel follows the hoof of the ox.
> Phenomena are preceded by the mind, ruled by the mind and made of the mind.
> If one speaks or acts with a pure mind, happiness follows like a shadow that never leaves. (Dhp 1)[24]

The word *mano* is also used for one of the sense spheres, namely, the mind-sphere (*manāyatana*) through which mind-consciousness (*manoviññāṇa*) arises with a new object.[25] After one mental object passes away but before another arises, the mind is in the state of *bhavaṅga*, a passive state, sometimes called 'life continuum' or 'subliminal consciousness.'[26] The *bhavaṅga* mind occurs when no outside phenomena are perceived, and the person is not aware of anything. This happens in deep sleep without dreams, in a state of coma, and between active mind-moments. It starts operating from the very first moment of life at conception, immediately following the rebirth-linking mind (*paṭisandhicitta*), and continues until the last mind-moment

22. M I 111–112: *Cakkhuñc'āvuso paṭicca rūpe ca uppajjati cakkhuviññāṇaṃ, tiṇṇaṃ saṅgati phasso, phassapaccayā vedanā, yaṃ vedeti taṃ sañjānāti, yaṃ sañjānāti taṃ vitakketi, yaṃ vitakketi taṃ papañceti, yaṃ papañceti tatonidānaṃ purisaṃ papañcasaññāsaṅkhā samudācaranti atītānāgatapaccuppannesu cakkhuviññeyyesu rūpesu.*

23. Activities or actions (*kamma*) are presented in three groups activated through (1) the body (*kāyakamma*), (2) speech (*vacīkamma*) or (3) the mind (*manokamma*) (cf. M I 372–373; S IV 132–133; As 88). According to the *Atthasālinī*, the mind (*mano*) is viewed as the door for thinking activities (As 88: *mano manokammadvāraṃ nāma*), whereas the act of thinking is presented as volition (*cetanā*), which is executed through this door (As 88: *yā pana tasmiṃ manodvāre siddhā cetanā ... idaṃ manokammaṃ nāma*).

24. Dhp 1: *Manopubbaṅgamā dhammā manoseṭṭhā manomayā, manasā ce paduṭṭhena bhāsatī vā karoti vā, tato naṃ dukkham anveti cakkaṃ va vahato padaṃ. Manopubbaṅgamā dhammā manoseṭṭhā manomayā, manasā ce pasannena bhāsatī vā karoti vā tato naṃ sukham anveti chāyā va anapāyinī.* It is similarly said in the *Upālisutta* that of the three kinds of actions (through the body, speech and mind), mental action is the primary one (M I 373: ... *tiṇṇaṃ kammānaṃ evaṃ paṭivibhattānaṃ evaṃ paṭivisiṭṭhānaṃ manokammaṃ mahāsāvajjataraṃ paññāpemi pāpassa kammassa kiriyāya pāpassa kammassa pavattiyā, no tathā kāyakammaṃ no tathā vacīkammanti*).

25. *Mano* is usually listed as an internal sense sphere (i.e., *manāyatana*), with mental phenomena (*dhamma*) as its objects (e.g., S IV 1–261; Vibh 70–73). One of the functions of the mind-door (*manodvāra*) is integrating the experiences gained through the five bodily senses; for example, in the *Mahāvedallasutta*, it is said that the five sense faculties (*indriya*)—i.e., the faculties of the eyes, ears, tongue, nose and the body—each have their own objects and domains and cannot experience other objects and domains, whereas the mind (*mano*) experiences all objects and domains (M I 295: *Imesaṃ kho āvuso pañcannaṃ indriyānaṃ nānāvisayānaṃ nānāgocarānaṃ na aññamaññassa gocaravisayaṃ paccanubhontānaṃ mano paṭisaraṇaṃ, mano ca nesaṃ gocaravisayaṃ paccanubhoti*).

26. The term *bhavaṅga* (literally 'a component or limb of becoming') was initially recorded in the *Abhidhamma Piṭaka* (i.e., in the *Paṭṭhāna*) and then expanded in the commentarial literature. It is presented as a resultant passive mind (*citta*) that has the same object throughout an entire lifetime and is identical to the last mind-moment from the previous existence. It arises whenever no active cognitive process takes place. For a discussion on the role of the *bhavaṅga* in cognitive processes, see Bodhi (1993, 130, 149–184), Karunadasa (2010, 145–158), and Gethin (2012).

at death, which is followed by the death mind (*cuticitta*).[27] The *bhavaṅga* of which we are not aware always arises with the same object, namely, that experienced in the last moment of the previous existence. Because the mind mostly stays in the state of *bhavaṅga,* we tend to forget many things in life and generally remember only those experiences that are accompanied by sufficiently strong feeling (*vedanā*); otherwise, the mind (*citta*) remains in a state of half-sleep, a state of unawareness. The ending of the *bhavaṅga* state is what we call the experience of the present moment; this is when a new object comes up and mind-consciousness (*manoviññāṇa*) arises, only to be followed by the *bhavaṅga* again. Throughout our lives, there is a continuous flow of active cognitive mind-moments alternating with the *bhavaṅga.*[28] This continuous stream of minds (*citta*), which alternate between cognitive moments and dormant states (*bhavaṅga*), is interrupted or cut out only when the path (*magga*) is reached.

The word *bhavaṅga* itself appears in the *Abhidhamma* and the commentaries, whereas in the *Suttapiṭaka*, the concept of the *bhavaṅga* can be linked to the term *anusaya,* translated as 'underlying, latent tendencies,' in reference not only to unwholesome but also to wholesome dormant tendencies in the mind.[29] In the context of dependant origination (*paṭiccasamuppāda*), the concept *bhavaṅga* is related to the term 'becoming' (*bhava*),[30] which can also refer to wholesome or unwholesome occurrences that happen in the present based on past habits. To take a rebirth, the latent tendencies (*anusaya*) have to be present; for example, if one meditates in this life, these habits could emerge in the next life when one would be drawn to meditation irrespective of the circumstances. Thus, becoming (*bhava*) is based on latent tendencies (*anusaya*) or past habits, which will arise at some point in life. Among the latent tendencies, the problematic ones are the dormant defilements, the unwholesome dormant tendencies,

27. For further discussion on the rebirth mind (*paṭisandhicitta*), the death mind (*cuticitta*) and *bhavaṅga,* see Bodhi (1993, 185–233) and Wijeratne and Gethin (2007, 159–214).

28. These comments by Pemasiri Thera reflect the presentation of the cognitive process in the Theravāda *Abhidhamma* texts and commentaries, which describe experiences as a series of moments of the mind (*citta*), rapidly arising and passing away. Active mind-moments (*vīthicitta*) in the cognitive processes are followed by passive mind-moments (*bhavaṅga*), thus allowing for their continuity, arising and passing away throughout one's life. See Gethin (2012) and Karunadasa (2010, 145–147).

29. The term *anusaya* usually refers to unwholesome latent dispositions or tendencies; for example, in the *Khandhasaṃyutta* (S III 131), it is linked to the underlying conceit 'I am' (*asmīti māno*) and the underlying desire 'I am' (*asmīti chando*). In the *Vibhaṅga* (Vibh 340), *anusaya* is defined as the latent tendency of lust (*kāmarāgānusayo*), ill-will (*paṭighānusayo*), conceit (*mānānusayo*), wrong view (*diṭṭhānusayo*), doubt (*vicikicchānusayo*), desire for existence (*bhavarāgānusayo*) and ignorance (*avijjānusayo*). By contrast, Pemasiri Thera states that *anusaya* may also refer to wholesome underlying or dormant tendencies. Although I am not aware of direct support for this view in the *Tipiṭaka*, it may be implied in several passages; for example, in the *Cetanāsutta*, it is said that the basis for maintaining consciousness (*viññāṇa*) includes what one intends (*ceteti*) and plans (*pakappeti*) and what lies latent (*anuseti*) (S II 65: *Yañca kho bhikkhave ceteti yañ ca pakappeti yañca anuseti, ārammaṇam etaṃ hoti viññāṇassa ṭhitiyā*). In this case, the latent tendencies may not only be unwholesome, even though the commentators interpret them in this manner. Similarly, in the *Aññatarabhikkhusutta*, the word *anuseti* could refer to any dormant tendencies: 'When one has an underlying tendency towards something, one is defined by it' (S III 35: *Yaṃ kho bhikkhu anuseti tena saṅkhaṃ gacchati*).

30. 'Becoming' (*bhava*) is the tenth link in the formula of dependent origination (*paṭiccasamuppāda*), which refers to the occurrences of phenomena based on the past habitual tendencies founded on ignorance. Becoming represents the condition for birth: (1) ignorance (*avijjā*) (2) mental formations (*saṅkhāra*) (3) consciousness (*viññāṇa*) (4) mentality and materiality (*nāmarūpa*) (5) sense bases (*saḷāyatana*) (6) contact (*phassa*) (7) feelings (*vedanā*) (8) craving (*taṅhā*) (9) clinging (*upādāna*) (10) becoming (*bhava*) (11) birth (*jāti*) (12) ageing, death, suffering, lamentation, pain, displeasure and despair (*jarāmaraṇaṃ soka-parideva-dukkhadomanassupāyāsā*) (S II 1). For a detailed description of this process, see the *Visuddhimagga* (Vism 517–577).

whereas the wholesome ones simply dissolve when one is liberated from ignorance (*avijjā*). Wholesome actions (i.e., bodily, verbal, and mental) must be learned and cultivated, whereas unwholesome ones occur on their own.

We spend most of the time in this dormant state (*bhavaṅga*) without any awareness. Only rare meditators, known as 'the vigilant ones' (*jāgariya*),[31] can maintain mindfulness while in *bhavaṅga*; such meditators are (temporarily) free from the hindrances (*nīvaraṇa*) or have already attained the path and fruition (*maggaphala*). The mind (*citta*) always arises from causes and conditions, and when it passes away, it gives rise to new causes and conditions, to new perceptions (*saññā*) and feelings (*vedanā*). If the meditator cultivates mindfulness (*sati*) and clear comprehension (*sampajañña*), the mind does not tend to create new causes and conditions. But most people live in the past or future, showing greed (*lobha*) and aversion (*dosa*) towards things that they have created and that do not actually exist in the present. Thus, it is said in the *Bhārasutta*, that people carry the burden of the five aggregates of clinging (*pañcupādānakkhandhā*), which are based on:

> the craving that leads to renewed existence, accompanied by pleasure and lust, finding enjoyment here and there. This is craving for sensual pleasures, craving for existence and craving for non-existence. (S III 26)[32]

This burden can be set aside and relinquished only through wisdom (*paññā*), which arises with the cultivation of mindfulness (*sati*) and clear comprehension (*sampajañña*).

It is through the mind door (*manodvāra*) that mental processes operate, thoughts proliferate, an 'I' is constructed and the past, present and future are created.[33] For example, an object that is experienced through one of the five physical sense doors is immediately followed by a thought emerging through the mind door (*manodvāra*). This thought could be about the future, expecting or planning that the object will be experienced in the same way again tomorrow. But when this does not happen in the desired way, we are disappointed and angry. Except for *arahants*, we are all under the sway of these processes, influenced by conditions, causes and effects; there is nothing in life beyond that. Our lives are therefore like a strange comedy but no one can understand this, because it is hidden and concealed by a complex web of entanglements. Only in deep contemplation, in seclusion, can one begin to understand these mental processes as they really are.

However, we usually approach meditation with a thought about the future, expecting that our meditation practice will be 'successful.' Through such projections and expectations, an 'I' is constructed, the 'meditation' is created and a future 'progress' in meditation is envisaged, thus reflecting how the mind (*citta*) is under the power of cause and effect. The meditator imagines that there is a person, an 'I,' who must be liberated, hence making it necessary to act in some way. Until we clearly understand that in this process of cause and effect, there is no being, no person or anyone to be liberated, we still have to do something. Thus, we undertake

31. In the *Sekkhasutta* (M I 355), a vigilant (*jāgariya*) meditator is described as someone who purifies the mind (*cittam parisodheti*) of obstructive states both day and night.

32. S III 26: *Yāyam taṇhā ponobhavikā nandirāgasahagatā tatra tatrābhinandinī. Seyyathīdaṃ kāmataṇhā bhavataṇhā vibhavataṇhā. Idaṃ vuccati bhikkhave bhārādānaṃ.*

33. The mental processes that arise through the mind door (*manodvāra*) can appear as a response to cognition arising through any of the five physical sense doors or they may occur without any contact with the five physical senses, which is the case with memory, reflection, and conceptual thinking. This is described, for example, in the *Atthasālinī* (As 72–74).

meditation practice. The very idea that there is someone, a person to be liberated, is actually an object of the mind (*dhammārammana*). Therefore, both the mind (*citta*), which arises with this thought, and the thought itself are 'ultimate phenomena' (*paramatthadhamma*)[34] that must be noted as such. Only then can one understand that there is no being and that thought itself is influenced by ignorance (*avijjā*).

The section in the *Satipaṭṭhānasutta* on the contemplation of the mind (*cittānupassanā*) lists sixteen states of mind to be observed with mindfulness (*sati*) and clear comprehension (*sampajañña*). The first eight are mental states (*citta*) in which the presence or absence of desire (*rāga*), aversion (*dosa*) and delusion (*moha*) (i.e., three unwholesome roots) are contemplated; the last eight are meditative states related to the absorptions (*jhāna*) and liberation (*vimutti*) (Table 7).

Table 7 Sixteen states of mind (*citta*) contemplated in the *Satipaṭṭhānasutta*.

(1) Mind with desire (*sarāgacitta*)	(2) Mind without desire (*vītarāgacitta*)
(3) Mind with aversion (*sadosacitta*)	(4) Mind without aversion (*vītadosacitta*)
(5) Mind with delusion (*samohacitta*)	(6) Mind without delusion (*vītamohacitta*)
(7) Contracted mind (*saṅkhittacitta*)	(8) Distracted mind (*vikkhittacitta*)
(9) Exalted mind (*mahaggatacitta*)	(10) Unexalted mind (*amahaggatacitta*)
(11) Surpassable mind (*sa-uttaracitta*)	(12) Unsurpassable mind (*anuttaracitta*)
(13) Concentrated mind (*samāhitacitta*)	(14) Unconcentrated mind (*asamāhitacitta*)
(15) Liberated mind (*vimuttacitta*)	(16) Unliberated mind (*avimuttacitta*)

'Mind with desire' (*sarāgacitta*) and 'mind without desire' (*vītarāgacitta*)

In the contemplation of the mind (*cittānupassanā*), the *Satipaṭṭhānasutta* states that a monk knows (*pajānāti*) the mind with desire (*sarāga*) or the mind without desire (*vītarāga*). When it is said 'mind with desire' (*sarāga*), this means that the mind (*citta*) arises with a desired object from the past, although desire (*kāma*) for this object has not yet emerged at the moment of noting it.[35] The mind with desire (*sarāga*) should be contemplated as it occurs in conjunction with a perception (*saññā*) from the past before attachment to the object emerges. However, if the meditator does not note such a mind state (*citta*) with mindfulness (*sati*) and clear comprehension (*sampajañña*) as it arises, she or he will gradually start liking or enjoying the object, and mental proliferation (*papañca*) will then occur while mindfulness (*sati*) will be lost.

34. In the *Abhidhamma*, two realities are distinguished: (1) conventional reality (*sammuti*) comprising concepts (*paññatti*) and conventional ways of expression (*vohāra*); and (2) ultimate (*paramattha*) reality comprising four categories—i.e., the mind (*citta*), mental concomitants (*cetasika*), materiality (*rūpa*) and *nibbāna* (Bodhi 1993, 25–27).

35. In the *Papañcasūdani* commentary, the mind with desire (*sarāga*) is briefly described as 'the eight types of mind that arise along with greed' (Ps I 279: *Tattha sarāgan ti aṭṭhavidhalobhasahagataṃ*). These eight types are rooted in greed (*lobha*) and arise along with: (1) contentment (*somanassasahagata*) and wrong view (*diṭṭhigatasampayutta*), (2) contentment (*somanassasahagata*) and dissociation from wrong view (*diṭṭhigatavipayutta*), (3) equanimity (*upekkhāsahagata*) and wrong view (*diṭṭhigatasampayutta*) and (4) equanimity (*upekkhāsahagata*) and dissociation from wrong view (*diṭṭhigatavipayutta*). Each of these four types can be either prompted (*saṅkhārika*) or unprompted (*asaṅkhārika*), resulting in a total of eight types. An identical description is given in the commentary on the *Vibhaṅga*, the *Sammohavinodanī* (Vibh-a 268). The *Dhammasaṅgaṇi* provides a comprehensive presentation of different classifications of wholesome, unwholesome and indeterminate minds (Dhs 9–124); for a short overview, see Karunadasa 2010, 89–102.

The mind without desire (*vītarāga*) refers to a state of mind that is pure and wholesome.[36] Within the framework of the *Satipaṭṭhānasutta*, the mind without desire (*vītarāga*) does not denote the mind of an *arahant*, as claimed by some interpreters, since this *sutta* focuses on the cultivation of mindfulness (*sati*) and does not seek to describe the mind of an *arahant*.[37] The mind without desire (*vītarāga*) refers to the state of mind that is not accompanied by liking (*vītarāga*) when a thought arises along with a perception (*saññā*) from the past. Since there is no attachment at all, the state of mind without desire (*vītarāga*) is sometimes experienced as a kind of blank mental space that emerges with a great sense of freedom, and as a result, the meditator may imagine that she or he has reached path knowledge (*maggañāṇa*) or meditative absorption (*jhāna*), although this may not be the case. The state of mind without desire (*vītarāga*) can sometimes arise because the meditator has been thinking about the Buddhist teachings during meditation or about what she or he has learned or heard about the Dhamma such as the five aggregates (*khandha*) or dependent origination (*paṭiccasamuppāda*). When the mind is without desire (*vītarāga*), the meditation is very comfortable, and the meditator (temporarily) cannot see any defilements (*kilesa*). As long as the meditator understands or knows (*pajānāti*) such states of mind (*citta*) as they arise, her or his practice remains in the domain of the contemplation of the mind (*cittānupassanā*).

'Mind with aversion' (*sadosacitta*) and 'mind without aversion' (*vītadosacitta*)

When the mind is with aversion or anger (*sadosacitta*), it occurs with an object from the past, which is perceived with aversion and should be noted as such.[38] Again, if the meditator does not note and understand (*pajānāti*) this state of the mind when it arises, proliferation (*papañca*) of thinking will follow.

In the case of the mind without aversion (*vītadosacitta*), the perception (*saññā*) of an object from the past triggers a thought without any aversion (*dosa*).[39] Although such an object from the past would normally arouse dislike, displeasure or anger, now it can appear in meditation without aversion (*vītadosacitta*), without any trace of discontentment or dislike towards the thought. Such a mind (*citta*) is very calm and pure, (temporarily) without any defilements (*kilesa*). The mind free from aversion (*vītadosacitta*) appears only when the cultivation of the four foundations of mindfulness (*satipaṭṭhāna*) is firmly grounded; the meditator can then note any past objects as they arise and clearly knows and understands (*pajānāti*) them as they are.

36. In the *Papañcasūdani* commentary, the mind without desire (*vītarāga*) is described as the 'wholesome and indeterminate mundane mind' (Ps I 279: *Vītarāgan ti lokiyakusalāvyākataṃ*). For a comprehensive description of wholesome and indeterminate states, see the *Dhammasaṅgaṇi* (Dhs 9–75).

37. There are many instances in the *Tipiṭaka* (e.g., S I 220) in which *arahants* as well as the Buddha are described as free from greed (*lobha*), aversion (*dosa*) and delusion (*moha*). However, in the context of the *Satipaṭṭhānasutta*, the mind without desire (*vītarāga*) would more likely refer to temporary freedom from the unwholesome roots as opposed to their complete eradication. Similarly, the *Papañcasūdani* commentary states that only mundane phenomena are dealt with in this section of the *Satipaṭṭhānasutta* (Ps I 279: *idha ekapade pi lokuttaraṃ na labhati*).

38. In the *Papañcasūdani* commentary, the mind with aversion (*sadosacitta*) is said to refer to two types of mind states, which arise along with discontent or displeasure (Ps I 279–280: *sadosan ti duvidhaṃ domanassasahagataṃ*): (1) mind states that arise with displeasure (*domanassasahagata*) and are prompted (*sasaṅkhārika*) and (2) those that arise with displeasure (*domanassasahagata*) and are unprompted (*asaṅkhārika*). This is similarly described in the *Sammohavinodanī* (Vibh-a 268).

39. The mind without aversion (*vītadosacitta*) is described in the same way as the mind without desire (*vītarāga*), namely, as a mundane wholesome and indeterminate mind (Ps I 280; Vibh-a 268: *vītadosan ti lokiyakusalābyākataṃ*).

'Mind with delusion' (*samohacitta*) and 'mind without delusion' (*vītamohacitta*)

During meditation, the mind may be deluded (*samohacitta*)[40] in relation to an object arising from the past or it may be without delusion (*vītamohacitta*).[41] Both states of mind should be noted as soon as they emerge provided that mindfulness (*sati*) and clear comprehension (*sampajañña*) are present. For example, the meditator can be mindful during chanting; she or he can understand the meaning of the words and be aware of any bodily sensation and phenomena such as mosquito bites or outside sounds. In the midst of all these phenomena of which the meditator is mindful, she or he may fall asleep while the chanting continues—in this case, the moments of sleep are the mind with delusion (*samohacitta*), which would usually be noted after the meditator awakens and realises that she or he has fallen asleep. Delusion (*moha*) also arises frequently in the mind during the waking state; for example, when the meditator has very weak clear comprehension (*sampajañña*) and mindfulness (*sati*), thoughts arise with delusion (*moha*), which she or he only notes after some delay. Delusion (*moha*) is also present in the states of mind with desire (*sarāga*) or aversion (*sadosacitta*); this happens when the meditator either likes or dislikes an object and tends to remain in that state for some time.[42]

Conversely, the states of mind without delusion (*vītamohacitta*) only occur when the meditation practice is well established. Then the meditator is continuously in a very awakened state, can see every mind-moment very clearly and lucidly and remains mindful and clearly comprehending without being carried away or deceived by any phenomena.

'Contracted mind' (*saṅkhittacitta*) and 'distracted mind' (*vikkhittacitta*)

When the mind is contracted (*saṅkhittacitta*),[43] contact (*phassa*) with the object is weak and unclear, and consequently, the feeling (*vedanā*) and perception (*saññā*) that arise with the object cannot be seen. Therefore, volition (*cetanā*)[44] is very weak, and wrong view (*diṭṭhi*) can

40. Two types of mind with delusion (*samohacitta*) are presented in the *Papañcasūdani* commentary: (1) unwholesome mind linked to doubt (*vicikicchāsahagata*) and (2) unwholesome mind linked to agitation (*uddhaccasahagatacitta*) (Ps I 280; Vibh-a 268: *Samohan ti vicikicchāsahagatañ c'eva uddhaccasahagatañ cā ti duvidhaṃ*).

41. The mind without delusion (*vītamohacitta*) is described in the same way as the mind without desire (*vītarāga*) or without aversion (*vītadosacitta*): i.e., as a mundane wholesome and indeterminate mind (*lokiyakusalāvyākatacitta*) (Ps I 280; Vibh-a 268: *Vītamohan ti lokiyakusalābyākataṃ*).

42. The *Papañcasūdani* commentary similarly mentions that because delusion (*moha*) occurs in all unwholesome (*akusala*) states, the other unwholesome states should be added to the two aforementioned types (i.e., the mind linked to doubt and that linked to agitation). Thus, the mind with delusion (*samohacitta*) should include all twelve unwholesome mental states (Ps I 280; Vibh-a 268: *Yasmā pana moho sabbākusalesu uppajjati, tasmā sesāni pi idha vaṭṭanti yeva. Imasmiṃ yeva hi duke dvādasākusalacittāni pariyādiṇṇānī ti*). The twelve unwholesome states mentioned here are the eight rooted in greed (*lobha*), two in hatred (*dosa*) and two in delusion (*moha*). They are described in the *Dhammasaṅgaṇi* (Dhs 75–87) as well as briefly in Bodhi (1993, 32–40) and Karunadasa (2010, 89–91).

43. According to the *Papañcasūdanī* commentary, the contracted mind (*saṅkhittacitta*) is a shrunken mind (*saṅkuṭitacitta*) affected by sloth and torpor (*thinamiddhānupatita*) (Ps I 280, Vibh-a 269: *saṃkhittan ti thinamiddhānupatitaṃ. Etaṃ hi saṅkuṭitacittaṃ nāma*). The same explanation is given in the *Visuddhimagga* (Vism 410: *Thīnamiddhānugataṃ pana saṅkhittaṃ*). The word *saṅkhitta* has other significations such as 'concentrated, attentive, concise, thin, slender' (PED, *s.v.*).

44. Volition (*cetanā*) is one of the universal mental concomitants (*cetasika*) arising with every mind state (see Table 6), whether wholesome (*kusalacitta*), unwholesome (*akusalacitta*), resultant (*vipākacitta*) or functional (*kiriyacitta*). Volition (*cetanā*) is the motivating aspect of cognition, defined in the *Dhammasaṅgaṇi* as 'volition, intention, intendedness, arising from contact with the suitable element of mind-consciousness' (Dhs 5: *Yā tasmiṃ samaye tajjā manoviññāṇadhātusamphassajā cetanā sañcetanā cetayitattaṃ — ayaṃ tasmiṃ samaye cetanā*

ensue. The contracted mind is affected by sloth and torpor (*thīnamiddha*); sloth (*thīna*) is a dull state of mind (*citta*), whereas torpor (*middha*) is an unyielding mental concomitant (*cetasika*).[45] When the mental concomitants (*cetasika*) are contracted, the mind (*citta*) also becomes contracted and vice versa. If the contracted mind (*saṅkhittacitta*) is not noted with clear understanding as it arises, the contraction increases and further unwholesome states ensue such as laziness, lethargy or drowsiness.

By contrast, the distracted mind (*vikkhittacitta*)[46] is accompanied by restlessness (*uddhacca*) and is experienced as a scattered, confused and non-unified state of mind.[47] Restlessness (*uddhacca*) is one of the mental concomitants (*cetasika*) that occurs in all unwholesome states. Like other mental states observed in the contemplation of the mind (*cittānupassanā*), the distracted mind (*vikkhittacitta*) should be understood and noted as it arises, otherwise the meditator cannot develop wise attention (*yoniso manasikāra*), mindfulness (*sati*) and clear comprehension (*sampajañña*).[48]

'Exalted mind' (*mahaggatacitta*) and 'unexalted mind' (*amahaggatacitta*)

The 'exalted mind' (*mahaggatacitta*) literally means a 'state of mind that has become great.' It refers to the state of mind in meditative absorption (*jhāna*).[49] When the state of absorption arises in the practice of the four foundations of mindfulness (*satipaṭṭhāna*), the meditator should note it with mindfulness (*sati*) and clear comprehension (*sampajañña*), just as any other object of meditation should be noted, without any wish or hope of remaining in it. If mindfulness (*sati*) is well established, no clinging or attachment to meditative absorption (*jhāna*) will occur, and consequently, the practice of mindfulness (*satipaṭṭhāna*) will turn into insight meditation (*vipassanā*). The state of absorption (*jhāna*) that is reached through the practice of the four foundations of mindfulness (*satipaṭṭhāna*) can be called 'right concentration' (*sammā samādhi*); it can reach the level of the fourth absorption (*jhāna*) or continue even further to the four formless absorptions (*arūpajhāna*).[50] When any one of these absorptions (*jhāna*) arises and is recognised as such and noted by the meditator, it can be said that this state of mind, known as the 'exalted mind' (*mahaggatacitta*), is the object of contemplation.

---

hoti). Volition (*cetanā*) is also described in the *Visuddhimagga*: 'Its meaning is that it assembles, its characteristic is the state of volition, its function is endeavour and it is manifested as coordination.' (Vism 463: *Abhisandahatī ti attho. Sā cetanābhāvalakkhaṇā, āyūhanarasā, saṃvidahanapaccupaṭṭhānā*).

45. For a discussion on sloth and torpor, see Chapter V.1, under the subheading 'Sloth and torpor (*thīnamiddha*).'

46. According to the *Papañcasūdanī* commentary, the distracted mind (*vikkhittacitta*) is dissipated and accompanied by restlessness (*uddhaccasahagata*) (Ps I 280, Vibh-a 269: *Vikkhittan ti uddhaccasahagataṃ. Etaṃ hi pasaṭacittaṃ nāma*). The same explanation is given in the *Visuddhimagga* (Vism 410: *uddhaccānugataṃ vikkhittaṃ*).

47. For a discussion on restlessness, see Chapter V.1, under the subheading 'Restlessness and worry (*uddhaccakukkucca*).'

48. It is similarly stated in the *Tayodhammasutta* that with a distracted mind, one cannot abandon unwise attention or mental dullness and cannot stop following the wrong path (A V 147: *So vikkhittacitto samāno abhabbo ayonisomanasikāraṃ pahātuṃ kummaggasevanaṃ pahātuṃ cetaso līnattaṃ pahātuṃ*).

49. The *Papañcasūdanī* commentary explains that the exalted mind (*mahaggatacitta*) is the mind of absorptions in the realms of form and formlessness (Ps I: *Mahaggatan ti rūpārūpāvacaraṃ*). A comprehensive presentation of the absorptions (*jhāna*) is given in the *Visuddhimagga* (Vism 122–169; 326–340).

50. The four formless absorptions (*arūpajhāna*) comprise: (1) the sphere of infinite space (*ākāsānañcāyatana*), (2) the sphere of infinite consciousness (*viññāṇañcāyatana*), (3) the sphere of nothingness (*ākiñcaññāyatana*) and (4) the sphere of neither-perception-nor-non-perception (*nevasaññāsaññāyatana*).

The states of mind (*citta*) prior to absorption (*jhāna*) as well as those that follow absorption (*jhāna*) are called the 'unexalted mind' (*amahaggatacitta*), signifying that the mind has not grown great. The unexalted mind occurs in the sense sphere (*kāmāvacara*), while the exalted mind (*mahaggata*) arises in the fine material (*rūpāvacara*) or immaterial (*arūpāvacara*) spheres (Table 8).[51]

Table 8 Absorptions (*jhāna*) developed in calm (*samatha*) meditation and the three realms.

Realm of sense desire (*kāmāvacara*)	**Realm of pure form (*rūpāvacara*)**	**Formless realm (*arūpāvacara*)**
Access concentration (*upacārasamādhi*)	First absorption (*jhāna*)	Sphere of infinite space (*ākāsānañcāyatana*)
	Second absorption (*jhāna*)	Sphere of infinite consciousness (*viññāṇañcāyatana*)
	Third absorption (*jhāna*)	Sphere of nothingness (*ākiñcaññāyatana*)
	Fourth absorption (*jhāna*)	Sphere of neither-perception-nor-non perception (*nevasaññāsaññāyatana*)

Absorption (*jhāna*) lasts one or two moments of the exalted mind (*mahaggata*), whereas the unexalted (*amahaggatacitta*) mind-moments that precede and follow the absorption are the mind states of access concentration (*upacārasamādhi*), which belongs to the world of the sense sphere (*kāmāvacara*).[52] The access concentration (*upacārasamādhi*) after absorption (*jhāna*) is more advanced than that preceding it; however, both occur in the sense sphere (*kāmāvacara*). A meditator who is well grounded in the practice of insight meditation (*vipassanā*) is mindful and clearly knows (*pajānāti*) these states, while having no inclination or desire to remain in the absorption (*jhāna*).

'Surpassable mind' (*sa-uttaracitta*) and 'unsurpassable mind' (*anuttaracitta*)

The 'surpassable mind' (*sa-uttaracitta*) belongs to the sense sphere (*kāmāvacara*): it is neither absorption (*jhāna*) nor the path (*magga*) but a very fine and pure state of mind without any hindrances (*nīvaraṇa*).[53] By contrast, the 'unsurpassable mind' (*anuttaracitta*) is very close to the path mind (*maggacitta*);[54] it refers to the two most advanced states of mind (*citta*)—i.e., the mind-moments known as 'conformity' (*anuloma*) and 'change-of-lineage' (*gotrabhū*)[55]—which are then

51. This is similarly explained in the *Papañcasūdani* commentary, which states that the unexalted mind occurs in the sense realm (*amahaggatacitta*) (Ps I 280: *Mahaggatan ti rūpārūpāvacaraṃ. Amahaggatanti kāmāvacaraṃ*).

52. Access concentration (*upacāra samādhi*) is a very high level of concentration, which is at the point of access to absorption (*jhāna*). For further details, see the *Visuddhimagga* (Vism 125–137).

53. The *Papañcasūdanī* and *Sammohavinodanī* commentaries briefly state that the surpassable (*sa-uttara*) mind belongs to the sense sphere (*kāmāvacara*) and the fine material sphere (*rūpāvacara*) (Ps I 280; Vibh-a 269: *Sa-uttaran ti kāmāvacaraṃ, ... Tatrāpi sa-uttaraṃ rūpāvacaraṃ*).

54. The *Papañcasūdanī* and *Sammohavinodanī* commentaries position the unsurpassable (*anuttara*) mind in the fine material (*rūpāvacara*) and immaterial (*arūpāvacara*) spheres (Ps I 280; Vibh-a 269: *Anuttaran ti rūpāvacaraṃ. ... Anuttaram arūpāvacaram eva*).

55. The term *gotrabhū*, usually translated as 'change-of-lineage,' refers to the mind-moment (*citta*) that precedes

followed by the path mind (*maggacitta*).[56] Thus, the unsurpassable (*anuttara*) mind arises after the highest level of insight knowledges, namely, after reaching the knowledge of the equanimity of formations (*saṅkhār'upekkhāñāṇa*); it occurs just before the path mind (*maggacitta*).[57] At that point, all three characteristics (*tilakkhaṇa*) of phenomena—i.e., impermanence (*anicca*), unsatisfactoriness (*dukkha*) and non-self (*anattā*)—can be very clearly observed, and at the moment of conformity (*anuloma*), one of them is seen more prominently than the other two. The conformity mind (*anulomacitta*) is followed by the change-of-lineage mind (*gotrabhūcitta*), which is neither a worldly (*lokiya*) nor an unworldly (*lokuttara*) state; it is always followed by the path mind (*maggacitta*). In this case, the conformity (*anuloma*) and change-of-lineage (*gotrabhū*) mind states are unsurpassable (*anuttara*) in relation to the mind states experienced in the equanimity of formations (*saṅkhār'upekkhā*), which are surpassable (*sa-uttara*). However, the meditator may reach the conformity (*anuloma*) stage but not make the leap to the change-of-lineage (*gotrabhū*) and path (*magga*). Instead, the meditator returns to the knowledge of the equanimity of formations (*saṅkhār'upekkhāñāṇa*), again contemplating surpassable (*sa-uttara*) states of mind.

'Concentrated mind' (*samāhitacitta*) and 'unconcentrated mind' (*asamāhitacitta*)

The 'concentrated mind' (*samāhitacitta*) refers to the state of absorption (*jhāna*) and the 'unconcentrated mind' (*asamāhitacitta*) to the mind without absorption.[58] For example, if the

the supramundane path (*magga*) and fruition (*phala*); it is the transition from the worldly (*putthujana*) to the noble (*ariya*) state or lineage (*gotra*); this interpretation of *gotrabhū* is mostly found in commentarial texts such as the *Visuddhimagga* (Vism 672–675). For the description of the role of conformity mind (*anulomacitta*) and change-of-lineage mind (*gotrabhūcitta*) in the process leading to the path mind (*maggacitta*), see the *Atthasālinī* (As 310–319) and *Visuddhimagga* (Vism 669–675). For a brief description, see Mahāsi (2016, 408–411).

56. Most traditional and modern commentators (e.g., Mahāsi 2016, 207) follow the *Papañcasūdanī* commentary (As I 280), which relates the unsurpassable (*anuttara*) mind to the fine material (*rūpāvacara*) and immaterial (*arūpāvacara*) spheres experienced in the absorptions (*jhāna*). However, Pemasiri Thera links the unsurpassable (*anuttara*) mind to the mind-moments that occur just before the path mind (*maggacitta*). This interpretation can be linked to the passage in the commentary on the *Ñāṇavibhaṅga*, which states that the unsurpassable (*anuttara*) mind is even further advanced, as it is considered to be supramundane (Vibh-a 417: *Ayaṃ pana viseso: idha anuttaraṃ vā cittaṃ, vimuttaṃ vā cittan ti ettha lokuttaram pi labbhati*). In addition, the term *anuttara* is frequently used as an epithet for *nibbāna*. For example, in the *Mūlapariyāyasutta*, the term occurs in the phrase 'supreme peace' of *nibbāna* (M I 167: *anuttaraṃ yogakkhemaṃ*) and in the *Mahāparinibbānasutta*, it is used as an attribute to describe full awakening (D II 83: *anuttaraṃ sammāsambodhiṃ*).

57. The progress of the insight knowledges from the stage of the knowledge of equanimity of formations (*saṅkhār'upekkhāñāṇa*) up to path knowledge (*maggañāṇa*) is described in the *Visuddhimagga* (Vism 669–675); see also Mahāsi (2016, 396–413).

58. The *Papañcasūdanī* and *Sammohavinodanī* commentaries also state that the concentrated mind (*samāhitacitta*) refers to the absorption concentration or access concentration and the unconcentrated mind (*asamāhitacitta*) to the mental states without these two (As I 280 and Vibh-a 269: *Samāhitan ti yassa appanāsamādhi upacārasamādhi vā atthi. Asamāhitan ti ubhayasamādhivirahitaṃ*). The word *samāhitacitta* is frequently used in a more general sense, simply referring to the concentrated mind; for example, in the *Dvedhāvitakkasutta*, the Buddha describes how he meditated before attaining awakening and how his mind was 'concentrated and unified' (e.g., M I 117: *samāhitaṃ cittaṃ ekaggaṃ*). The term is often used in the description of the concentrated mind (*samāhitacitta*) in access concentration, as stated in the *Visuddhimagga* (Vism 126, 286: *upacārasamādhinā cittaṃ samāhitam*). The concentrated mind (*samādahacitta*) is also listed as one of the four meditation objects under the contemplation of the mind (*cittānupassanā*) in the *Ānāpānasatisutta* (M III 83). Here the term for concentrated mind is *samādahacitta*, which occurs rather infrequently in the Pāli canon and its commentaries, almost exclusively in the context of mindfulness of breathing (*ānāpānasati*) (e.g., S V 324, 339; A V 112; Paṭis I 176). Conversely, the term *samāhitacitta* is attested in a range of different contexts, mostly in relation to the practice of the four foundations of mindfulness (*satipaṭṭhāna*).

meditator has entered the first two absorptions (*jhāna*) of the immaterial sphere (*arūpāvacara*)—i.e., the sphere of infinite space (*ākāsānañcāyatana*) and the sphere of infinite consciousness (*viññāṇañcāyatana*)[59]—the mind state of these two absorptions is called the 'concentrated mind' (*samāhitacitta*), which should be noted during the contemplation of the mind (*cittānupassanā*). As the meditator moves from one absorption (*jhāna*) to another, i.e., from the absorption (*jhāna*) in the sphere of infinite space (*ākāsānañcāyatana*) towards the next absorption in the sphere of infinite consciousness (*viññāṇañcāyatana*), unconcentrated mind (*asamāhitacitta*) may occur for a few moments. This unconcentrated mind (*asamāhitacitta*), which may belong to the fine material sphere (*rūpāvacara*), arises along with the basic object of concentration such as the visual object (*kaṣina*), which was initially used as a starting point for the development of the state of infinite space. Some very experienced meditators may not experience this gap between two absorptions but instead move directly from one absorption (*jhāna*) to another. However, if the meditator, after staying in one absorption (*jhāna*) for some time, engages in an activity or a thought arises, then the state of mind is unconcentrated (*asamāhitacitta*).

The concentrated mind (*samāhitacitta*) can also refer to the state of mind with superior knowledge (*abhiññā*), that is, special abilities or powers (*iddhī*) that can emerge when concentration is at the strength of the fourth absorption (*jhāna*).[60] The moments before or after the superior knowledges (*abhiññā*), when the meditator has a thought about the object of superior knowledge (*abhiññā*), for example, can be called the state of unconcentrated mind (*asamāhitacitta*).

The meditator must spend much time practising meditation to achieve the absorptions (*jhāna*) and must also be able to move from one to another. For this training, a peaceful secluded environment without distractions such as a forest or jungle is very conducive. Monks and nuns trained in the Buddha's time would go to the forest to meditate and then come back to the Buddha to report about their meditation. Mental states related to meditative absorption (*jhāna*) can arise when practising the four foundations of mindfulness (*satipaṭṭhāna*); in this case, the meditator should clearly see them with mindfulness (*sati*) and clear comprehension (*sampajañña*) as they arise and then let go of them. The concentrated mind (*samāhitacitta*) can be experienced as the predominant object in the absorptions (*jhānas*); in insight (*vipassanā*) meditation, concentration is experienced as a momentary one-pointedness that arises along with clear understanding of the three characteristics.[61] Thus, when the meditator practises the contemplation of the mind (*cittānupassanā*), it means that she or he should note and clearly understand the concentrated mind (*samāhitacitta*) as it occurs from moment to moment.

59. For a comprehensive description of the absorptions (*jhāna*), see the *Visuddhimagga* (Vism 122–69; 326–340). In addition, many *suttas* and commentaries discuss the absorptions (*jhāna*) such as the *Sallekhasutta* (M I 40-41) and the *Sāmaññaphalasutta* (D I 73–75); see also A IV 438–448; S IV 217; Dhs 31–56.

60. There are several descriptions of such superior knowledges (*abhiññā*) in the *Tipiṭaka*; for example, the *Dasuttarasutta* (D III 281) lists six: (1) the ability to become many, (2) divine ear, (3) knowledge of the minds of other beings, (4) knowledge of past lives, (5) divine eye and (6) certainty of attaining liberation. In the *Visuddhimagga* (Vism 373–435), a large section is dedicated to the description of superior knowledges (*abhiññā*).

61. This is similarly explained in the *Visuddhimagga*, where the experience of the concentrated mind is commented on in the context of calm (*samatha*) and insight (*vipassanā*) meditation. For example, in the section on absorptions (*jhāna*), it is said that after entering and then emerging from the absorptions, the meditator 'comprehends with insight the mind associated with the *jhāna* as liable to passing away and decay, and then at the time of insight, momentary one-pointedness arises through the insight into the [three] characteristics' (Vism 289: *jhānasampayuttaṃ cittaṃ khayato vayato sampassato vipassanākkhaṇe lakkhaṇapaṭivedhena uppajjati khaṇikacitt' ekaggatā*).

'Liberated mind' (*vimuttacitta*) and 'unliberated mind' (*avimuttacitta*)

The liberated mind (*vimuttacitta*) refers to the path and fruition knowledge (*maggaphalañāṇa*), and the subsequent reviewing knowledge (*paccavekkhaṇañāṇa*).[62] The unliberated mind (*avimuttacitta*) signifies all other states of mind apart from these three. In addition, the liberated mind (*vimuttacitta*) sometimes refers to the fruition mind (*phalacitta*) of an *arahant*;[63] like other fruition minds, it arises without any perception (*saññā*). More generally, the liberated mind (*vimuttacitta*) is frequently understood as the mind that is temporarily free from defilements (*kilesa*) or separated from and free from hindrances (*nīvaraṇa*).[64] The liberated mind is also listed as the last of the four meditation objects under the contemplation of the mind (*cittānupassanā*) in the *Ānāpānasatisutta*:

> He trains thus: "I shall breathe in liberating the mind"; he trains thus: "I shall breathe out liberating the mind." (M III 83)[65]

Here the liberating mind refers to the mind free from hindrances (*nīvaraṇa*).[66] If the meditator clearly sees and understands the three characteristics (*tilakkhaṇa*) of the liberated mind (*vimuttacitta*) as well as the unliberated mind (*avimuttacitta*) as they arise, the practice is in the domain of insight meditation (*vipassanā*).[67] Contemplation of the liberated mind (*vimuttacitta*) and unliberated mind (*avimuttacitta*) can be viewed as the last stage in the domain of the contemplation of the mind (*cittānupassanā*).

To reiterate, in the contemplation of the mind (*cittānupassanā*), a mental state that is already fully formed, resulting from the perception (*saññā*) of a past object, becomes the object of contemplation. To make clear the distinction, in the contemplation of phenomena (*dhammānupassanā*), the meditator sees and notes the activity of the mental components or concomitants (*cetasika*) before the mental state is fully formed.

---

62. Both path and fruition knowledge (*maggaphalañāṇa*) as well as reviewing knowledge (*paccavekkhaṇañāṇa*) are described in the *Visuddhimagga* in the section on purification by knowledge and vision (*ñāṇadassanavisuddhinidesa*) (Vism 672–710). See also Mahāsi (2016, 411–466).

63. There are many instances in the *Tipiṭaka* where the mind of an *arahant* is described as liberated (*vimutta*). For example, in the *Mahānidānasutta*, it is said that the monk has a liberated mind (*vimuttacitta*) when he knows that 'birth is over, the holy life has been fulfilled, what had to be done has been completed and there is nothing more' (D II 67: *Khīṇā jāti, vusitaṃ brahmacariyaṃ, kataṃ karaṇīyaṃ, nāparaṃ itthattāyāti pajānāti. Evaṃ-vimutta-cittaṃ*).

64. It is thus interpreted in the *Papañcasūdani* and *Sammohavinodanī* commentaries: '*Vimuttacitta* is the mind liberated through the suppression [of defilements]' (Ps I 280; Vibh-a 269: *vimuttan ti tadaṅgavikkhambhanavimuttīhi vimuttaṃ*), as would happen in the absorptions (*jhāna*). The unliberated mind (*avimuttacitta*) is then interpreted as the mind without the aforementioned liberation (Ps I 280: *avimuttan ti ubhayavimuttivirahitaṃ*).

65. M III 83: *vimocayaṃ cittaṃ assasissāmīti sikkhati; vimocayaṃ cittaṃ passasissāmīti sikkhati.*

66. It is thus explained in the *Visuddhimagga* that the liberating mind refers to freedom from hindrances (*nīvaraṇa*) in the first absorption (*jhāna*) (Vism 289: *Vimocayaṃ cittan ti paṭhamajjhānena nīvaraṇehi cittaṃ mocento vimocento*).

67. According to the *Visuddhimagga*, in insight meditation (*vipassanā*), the meditator is liberated from the perception of permanence through the contemplation of impermanence (*anicca*), from the perception of pleasure through the contemplation of unsatisfactoriness (*dukkha*), from the perception of self through the contemplation of non-self (*anattā*), from enjoyment through the contemplation of disenchantment (*nibbidā*), from desire through the contemplation of dispassion (*virāga*), from arising through the contemplation of cessation (*nirodha*) and from grasping though the contemplation of abandonment (*paṭinissagga*) (Vism 289: *So vipassanākkhaṇe aniccānupassanāya niccasaññato cittaṃ mocento vimocento, dukkhānupassanāya sukhasaññato, anattānupassanāya attasaññato, nibbidānupassanāya nandito, virāgānupassanāya rāgato, nirodhānupassanāya samudayato, paṭinissaggānupassanāya ādānato cittaṃ mocento vimocento*).

— V —

Contemplation of Phenomena (*Dhammānupassanā*)

V 1 Five hindrances (*pañca nīvaraṇāni*)

Kathañca bhikkhave bhikkhu dhammesu ***dhammānupassī*** *viharati? Idha bhikkhave bhikkhu dhammesu dhammānupassī viharati pañcasu nīvaraṇesu. Kathañca bhikkhave bhikkhu dhammesu dhammānupassī viharati pañcasu nīvaraṇesu? Idha bhikkhave bhikkhu santaṃ vā ajjhattaṃ* ***kāmacchandaṃ****: atthi me ajjhattaṃ kāmacchando ti pajānāti, asantaṃ vā ajjhattaṃ kāmacchandaṃ: natthi me ajjhattaṃ kāmacchando ti pajānāti, yathā ca anuppannassa kāmacchandassa uppādo hoti tañca pajānāti, yathā ca uppannassa kāmacchandassa pahānaṃ hoti tañca pajānāti, yathā ca pahīnassa kāmacchandassa āyatiṃ anuppādo hoti tañca pajānāti. Santaṃ vā ajjhattaṃ* ***vyāpādaṃ****: atthi me ajjhattaṃ byāpādo ti ... pajānāti. Santaṃ vā ajjhattaṃ* ***thīnamiddhaṃ****: atthi me ajjhattaṃ thīnamiddhanti ... pajānāti. Santaṃ vā ajjhattaṃ* ***uddhaccakukkuccaṃ****: atthi me ajjhattaṃ uddhaccakukkuccanti ... pajānāti. Santaṃ vā ajjhattaṃ* ***vicikicchaṃ****: atthi me ajjhattaṃ vicikicchā ti pajānāti, asantaṃ vā ajjhattaṃ vicikicchaṃ: natthi me ajjhattaṃ vicikicchā ti pajānāti, yathā ca anuppannāya vicikicchāya uppādo hoti tañca pajānāti, yathā ca uppannāya vicikicchāya pahānaṃ hoti tañca pajānāti, yathā ca pahīnāya vicikicchāya āyatiṃ anuppādo hoti tañca pajānāti.*

'And how, monks, does a monk abide **contemplating phenomena** as phenomena? Here, a monk abides contemplating phenomena as phenomena in regard to the five hindrances. And how does a monk abide contemplating phenomena as phenomena in regard to the five hindrances? Here, when **sense desire** is present in him, a monk knows: "There is sense desire present in me"; or when no sense desire is present in him, he knows: "There is no sense desire present in me"; and he also knows how the arising of unarisen sense desire comes to be, and how the abandoning of arisen sense desire comes to be, and how the future non-arising of abandoned sense desire comes to be. When **ill will** is present in him ... When **sloth and torpor** is present in him ... When **restlessness and worry** is present in him ... When **doubt** is present in him, a monk knows: "There is doubt present in me"; or there being no doubt present in him, he knows: "There is no doubt present in me"; and he knows how the arising of unarisen doubt comes to be, and how the abandoning of arisen doubt comes to be, and how the future non-arising of abandoned doubt comes to be.'

Recurring passage indicating the ways to approach the contemplation[1]

Iti ajjhattaṃ vā dhammesu dhammānupassī viharati, bahiddhā vā dhammesu dhammānupassī viharati, ajjhattabahiddhā vā dhammesu dhammānupassī viharati. Samudayadhammānupassī vā dhammesu viharati, vayadhammānupassī vā dhammesu viharati, samudayavayadhammānupassī vā dhammesu

1. For comments on the recurring passage, see Chapter II.1, under the subheading 'Recurring passage indicating the ways to approach the contemplation.'

viharati. Atthi dhammā ti vā panassa sati paccupaṭṭhitā hoti yāvadeva ñāṇamattāya patissatimattāya, anissito ca viharati na ca kiñci loke upādiyati. Evam kho bhikkhave bhikkhu dhammesu dhammānupassī viharati pañcasu nīvaraṇesu.

'Thus he abides contemplating phenomena as phenomena internally, or he abides contemplating phenomena as phenomena externally, or he abides contemplating phenomena as phenomena both internally and externally. He abides contemplating the arising of phenomena in phenomena, or he abides contemplating the passing away of phenomena in phenomena, or he abides contemplating both the arising and passing away of phenomena in phenomena. Or, mindfulness that "there are phenomena" is established in him just to the extent necessary for knowledge and mindfulness. And he abides without attachment, not clinging to anything in the world. Monks, thus a monk abides contemplating phenomena as phenomena in regard to the five hindrances.'

Pemasiri Thera's commentary

'Contemplating phenomena' (*dhammānupassī*)

In the practice of the four foundations of mindfulness (*satipaṭṭhāna*), the contemplation of phenomena (*dhammānupassanā*) cannot be separated from the three other domains—i.e., the contemplation of the body (*kāyānupassanā*), feeling (*vedanānupassanā*) and the mind (*cittānupassanā*). This is because the cultivation of mindfulness (*satipaṭṭhāna*) always encompasses the contemplation of the five aggregates (*khandha*), which are comprised of materiality (*rūpa*), feeling (*vedanā*), perception (*saññā*), mental formations (*saṅkhāra*) and consciousness (*viññāṇa*). The aggregates (*khandha*) are contemplated in the four domains of the foundations of mindfulness (*satipaṭṭhāna*): materiality (*rūpa*) in the contemplation of the body (*kāyānupassanā*), feeling (*vedanā*) in the contemplation of feeling (*vedanānupassanā*), perception (*saññā*) and mental formations (*saṅkhāra*) in the contemplation of phenomena (*dhammānupassanā*) and consciousness (*viññāṇa*) in the contemplation of the mind (*cittānupassanā*) (Table 9).[2]

Table 9 Five aggregates (*khandha*) in relation to the four domains of contemplation (*anupassanā*).

Five aggregates (*khandha*)	**Four domains of contemplation (*anupassanā*)**
(1) Materiality (*rūpa*)	(1) Contemplation of the body (*kāyānupassanā*)
(2) Feeling (*vedanā*)	(2) Contemplation of feeling (*vedanānupassanā*)
(3) Perception (*saññā*)	(4) Contemplation of phenomena (*dhammānupassanā*)
(4) Mental formations (*saṅkhāra*)	
(5) Consciousness (*viññāṇa*)	(3) Contemplation of the mind (*cittānupassanā*)

2. This is similarly explained in the *Papañcasūdani* commentary at the start of the section on the contemplation of phenomena (*dhammānupassanā*): 'For the contemplation of the body, the aggregate of materiality was expounded [by the Blessed One]; for the contemplation of feeling, the aggregate of feeling was expounded; for the contemplation of the mind, the aggregate of consciousness was expounded; and now are the aggregates of perception and mental formations' (Ps 281: *kāyānupassanāya vā rūpakkhandhapariggaho kathito, vedanānupassanāya vedanākkhandhapariggaho va, cittānupassanāya viññāṇakkhandhapariggaho va. Idāni saññāsaṅkhārakkhandhapariggaham pi kathetuṃ*).

However, all five aggregates (*khandha*) can also be contemplated at a deeper and more refined level in the domain of the contemplation of phenomena (*dhammānupassanā*). For example, in the contemplation of the body (*kāyānupassanā*), the meditator may note the arising of feeling (*vedanā*), perception (*saññā*), mental formations (*saṅkhāra*) and consciousness (*viññāṇa*); if she or he clearly comprehends (*pajānāti*) how the five aggregates (*khandha*) arise and how they function (e.g., their impermanence), this understanding itself forms part of the contemplation of phenomena (*dhammānupassanā*). Or when the meditator knows how feeling (*vedanā*) arises, how it is impermanent (*anicca*) and how it cannot be controlled, this understanding of feeling (*vedanā*) occurs in the domain of the contemplation of phenomena (*dhammānupassanā*).

Similarly, if the meditator can clearly see how materiality (*rūpa*) arises and passes away in the contemplation of the body (*kāyānupassanā*), this very understanding of impermanence is part of the contemplation of phenomena (*dhammānupassanā*); in other words, this contemplation involves both materiality (*rūpa*) and mentality (*nāma*). Or to take another example, the act of seeing involves knowing that there is seeing (*cakkhuviññāṇa*), the object of seeing (*rūpa*) and the eye that sees (*cakkhu*). When the meditator observes and comprehends these three components involved in the sense experience of seeing and how defilements may arise or pass away in this process, the practice is in the domain of the contemplation of phenomena (*dhammānupassanā*). Furthermore, when the meditator clearly observes and comprehends (*pajānāti*) from which states of mind the defilements grow and from which they do not, she or he is practising the contemplation of phenomena (*dhammānupassanā*). Hence, the contemplation of phenomena (*dhammānupassanā*) is more profound, refined and deeper than the contemplation in the three other domains.

The contemplation of phenomena (*dhammānupassanā*) also takes place in regard to the mind (*citta*) when it wanders to objects from the past, often with desire (*kāmachanda*) or aversion (*vyāpāda*). Here the meditator begins to see how the mind (*citta*) arises and passes away, and as soon as it is gone, a new mind arises; she or he then understands that the newly arisen mind has no connection whatsoever to the mind that has passed away. After seeing the successive arising and passing away of minds, a thought (*vitakka*) may arise in the meditator, wondering what is going on, since she or he can see that the noting mind differs from the mind that has passed away. The meditator then understands that the thought (*vitakka*), consciousness (*viññāṇa*) and the noting mind (*citta*) are three different things. It thus seems to the meditator that she or he observes several different parts of the mind, as if one part of the mind is watching another. This means that the meditator can now note the mind (*citta*) as well as the mental concomitants (*cetasika*); thus, she or he understands that the object of thought (*vitakka*) is consciousness (*viññāṇa*), and because of consciousness (*viññāṇa*) itself, another thought (*vitakka*) arises. When this understanding matures, right thought (*sammā saṅkappa*)[3] emerges with great clarity; the thoughts become very lucid, without any confusion, and the meditator understands clearly that she or he can let go of objects, as the mind no longer clings to anything. At this stage, the meditator observes and understands with great ease and lucidity what renunciation (*nekkhamma*)[4]

3. In the *Vibhaṅga*, right thought (*sammā saṅkappa*) is presented as the thought associated with renunciation along with an absence of ill will and cruelty (Vibh 104: *katamo sammāsaṅkappo? nekkhammasaṅkappo, avyāpādasaṅkappo, avihiṃsāsaṅkappo*).

4. The term *nekkhamma* is usually translated as 'giving up or emancipation from worldliness, dispassionateness' (DP; PED, *s.v.*); most frequently, it refers to the renunciation of worldly life or to freedom from desires and aversions. In the *Vibhaṅga*, it is said that 'all wholesome states are the component of renunciation' (Vibh 86: *Sabbe pi kusalā dhammā nekkhammadhātu*).

in the mind is. This is a very purified state of mind in which right thoughts (*sammā saṅkappa*) arise. There is no attachment to any of the states or qualities of the mind, and consequently, right mindfulness (*sammā sati*) is well established. Now, the meditator sometimes wants to note an object, but by the time it is noted, it has already passed away. The meditator understands that the noted object is always a dead object that has already ceased to exist. This means that only the effect is noted, not the cause; what is observed is just an activity without any person or being behind the processes. In this manner, the noble eightfold path (*ariyo aṭṭhaṅgiko maggo*) is developed in the domain of the contemplation of phenomena (*dhammānupassanā*).

To summarise, the contemplation of phenomena (*dhammānupassanā*) contains all the other domains of the foundations of mindfulness (*satipaṭṭhāna*). Therefore, the meditator can make mindfulness (*sati*) and wisdom (*paññā*) evolve all the way up to path knowledge (*maggañāṇa*) through walking meditation or any other mindful daily activities such as eating. Many stories in the *Tipiṭaka* narrate how people would listen to the Buddha's talks about the Dhamma and then attain path knowledge (*maggañāṇa*).[5] Sitting practice is not necessarily the most essential component of meditation. The most important aspect of the meditation path is the cultivation of mindfulness (*sati*) and clear comprehension (*sampajañña*) in all circumstances.

In the contemplation of phenomena (*dhammānupassanā*), the meditator recognises and notes mental concomitants (*cetasika*), which are involved in the process of forming a certain state of mind (*citta*). However, as mentioned before, if mental concomitants (*cetasika*) are noted only after the mental state is completely formed, then the meditator is practising the contemplation of the mind (*cittānupassanā*). In the contemplation of phenomena (*dhammānupassanā*), the meditator is able to discern mental concomitants (*cetasika*), including perception (*saññā*), as they arise. For example, the meditator notes hearing a sound as it arises together with a feeling (*vedanā*); in this case, if the feeling (*vedanā*) is immediately noted as such, then the noting is in the domain of the contemplation of phenomena (*dhammānupassanā*). All objects of the other senses are similarly noted. For example, in seeing, there is only seeing; it is noted and finished. This is narrated in the *Udāna* in which the Buddha gave the following instructions to the ascetic Bāhiya:

> When for you, Bāhiya, in the seen there will be only the seen, in the heard only the heard, in the sensed only the sensed, in the cognised only the cognised, then, Bāhiya, there is no you there. When there is no you with that, Bāhiya, there is no you therein. When there is no you therein, you are neither here nor there nor in between. This, indeed, is the end of suffering. (Ud 8)[6]

Immediately after hearing these words of the Buddha, Bāhiya attained arahantship.

The first section in the contemplation of phenomena (*dhammānupassanā*) in the *Satipaṭṭhāna-sutta* focuses on the five hindrances (*pañca nīvaraṇāni*):

1. sense desire (*kāmacchanda*)
2. ill will (*vyāpāda*)
3. sloth and torpor (*thīnamiddha*)
4. restlessness and worry (*uddhaccakukkucca*)
5. doubt (*vicikicchā*)

5. There are many instances in Pāli canonical and post-canonical texts describing the instant attainment of path knowledge after listening to the Buddha's teachings (e.g., Ud 8; S V 420–424; S III 66–67).

6. Ud 8: *yato kho te Bāhiya diṭṭhe diṭṭhamattaṃ bhavissati, sute sutamattaṃ bhavissati, mute mutamattaṃ bhavissati, viññāte viññātamattaṃ bhavissati, tato tvaṃ Bāhiya na tattha, yato tvaṃ Bāhiya nev 'attha, tato tvaṃ Bāhiya nev' idha na huraṃ na ubhayamantarena, es'ev'anto dukkhassā'ti.*

It is said that if a hindrance (*nīvaraṇa*) occurs, the meditator should note it, but if it is absent, the meditator should know that it is not present. Then the *sutta* continues by saying that the meditator should not only observe and understand the presence or absence of hindrances but also know how they arise and how they can be abandoned or prevented. The condition that gives rise to hindrances is found in the present object, not in a past or future object; if the object emerging through one of the six senses is immediately noted as it arises, the hindrances (*nīvaraṇa*) do not occur. In other words, in the contemplation of phenomena (*dhammānupassanā*), the meditator sees materiality (*rūpa*) and mentality (*nāma*) very clearly and understands the causes and conditions of phenomena as they emerge. For example, the meditator understands that because she or he did not note an object as it arose at one of the six sense doors, a certain thought was triggered—failing to note the object as it arises is the cause, while the emergence of the hindrance (*nīvaraṇa*) is the effect.

The cause of not noting or clearly understanding the object is ignorance (*avijjā*), while the hindrance (*nīvaraṇa*) that subsequently occurs is the effect. A meditator who practises well sees causes and effects in everything, in every sense experience, and understands that because of knowing and noting them, desire (*lobha*) or aversion (*dosa*) do not arise in relation to the object. At this point, the five faculties (*pañc'indriyāni*) are strengthened, the hindrances are reduced and the contemplation of phenomena (*dhammānupassanā*) is very lucid and balanced.

Although it is often said that mindfulness (*sati*) and clear comprehension (*sampajañña*) should be established in relation to the present object, one should not only let go of the past and future but also of the present, as frequently stated in the texts.[7] According to Theravāda Buddhist teachings, there is actually no present, and no time exists by itself.[8] The term used for the present is *paccuppanna*,[9] which refers to that which has arisen (*uppajjati*) due to causes and conditions. When the meditator understands with perfect clarity that what is called the 'present' is just a process of causes and effects, then she or he has reached the end of her or his practice. Thus, in the contemplation of phenomena (*dhammānupassanā*), the meditator should not be attached to nor stuck on any object, instead simply contemplating the *processes* involved in what we call 'experience,' realising that in these processes, there is neither 'I' nor 'other.' Only then can the meditator understand that there is no past, no future and no present, and therefore there is nothing that she or he should think about.

To recapitulate, consciousness (*viññāṇa*) is neither a person nor an 'I' that remains for life; it is not located in a particular place, and it does not belong to objects. However, people are unable to see or accept that consciousness (*viññāṇa*) cannot be found, and hence they keep searching for it. Meditators frequently want to rediscover a consciousness (*viññāṇa*) that was experienced in the past, and therefore they trigger a thought (*vitakka*) about a past mental state and maintain it, thus allowing greed (*lobha*) and aversion (*dosa*) to arise. But if the meditator clearly understands that there is no past, present or future, craving and aversion cannot

7. For example, the *Dhammapada* (verse 348) states: 'Let go of the past, the future, the present. Having gone beyond existence, with a liberated mind, you will no longer undergo birth and decay' (Dhp 98: *muñca pure muñca pacchato majjhe muñca bhavassa pāragū, sabbattha vimuttamānaso na punañ jātijaraṃ upehisi*).

8. For example, the *Atthasālinī* explains that time is only a concept or designation that is derived along with certain phenomena; it does not exist of its own accord (As 58–59: *Taṃ taṃ upādāya paññatto, kālo vohāramattako, puñjo phassādidhammānaṃ, samūhoti vibhāvito. Evaṃ taṃ taṃ upādāya paññatto kālo nāma. So panesa sabhāvato avijjamānattā paññattimattako evāti veditabbo*).

9. The word *paccuppanna* means 'what has arisen [just now], present, existing' (PED. *s.v.*); it usually occurs in opposition to the past (*atīta*) and future (*anāgata*).

arise; only then will right mindfulness (*sammā sati*) emerge. At that stage, the meditator no longer has a stable object to note, as everything is passing away momentarily, and there is nothing to be noted; then she or he understands the unsatisfactoriness (*dukkha*) and emptiness (*anattā*) of all phenomena. When the meditator contemplates the various aspects of the three characteristics (*tilakkhaṇa*), yearning for existence (*bhava*) or the round of rebirths (*saṃsāra*) ceases, while the contemplation of phenomena (*dhammānupassanā*) comes to an end.

'Sense desire' (*kāmacchanda*)

The hindrance 'sense desire' (*kāmacchanda*) refers to the desire for a pleasurable object.[10] The term *chanda* refers to one of the mental concomitants (*cetasika*) that can occur in unwholesome or wholesome mental states.[11] It is frequently translated as 'desire'; however, this rendering is more appropriate in relation to unwholesome objects, as in the case of sense desire (*kāmacchanda*). When *chanda* appears with wholesome states without craving or aversion, it would be better translated as 'will,' especially in connection with right effort (*sammā vāyāma*), which is the quality of mind that maintains the drive towards wholesomeness or, in other words, an inclination to continue cultivating virtue (*sīla*) and meditation (*bhāvanā*).[12]

The meaning of sense desire (*kāmacchanda*) is often misunderstood by meditators. Sometimes monks avoid washing their robes, cleaning their lodgings, offering flowers or even eating tasty food, because they believe that these activities relate to sense desire (*kāmacchanda*). However, this would only be the case if such activities were accompanied by indulgence or craving for sensuality. For example, if the meditator has only a few pieces of clothing, which are kept very clean, neat and tidy without seeking beautification or attraction, no sense desire (*kāmacchanda*) is present. But if one wears clothes with the aim to look good, beautiful and attractive, then it is sense desire (*kāmacchanda*). Some people dislike sense desire (*kāmacchanda*); in this case, they can develop ill will (*vyāpāda*) towards it, as they seek to uproot desire with anger instead of simply letting it go. Such anger, if prolonged, can even evolve into a kind of mental illness, such is the nature of ill will (*vyāpāda*).

---

10. In the *Dhammasaṅgaṇi*, the hindrance of sense desire (*kāmacchanda*) is described as 'sensual passion, delight, craving, desire, fever, infatuation, greed' (Dhs 204: *yo kāmesu kāmacchando kāmarāgo kāmanandī kāmataṇhā kāmasineho kāmapariḷāho kāmamucchā kāmajjhosānaṃ*). In the *Papañcasūdani* commentary, the condition for the arising of sense desire (*kāmacchanda*) is identified as the lack of wise attention (*ayoniso manasikāra*) towards a pleasant sense object (*subhanimitta*); because of this unwise attention, one views 'the impermanent as permanent, or the unpleasant as pleasant, or non-self as self, or the unwholesome as wholesome' (Ps 281: *anicce aniccan ti vā, dukkhe sukhan ti vā, anattani attā ti vā, asubhe subhan ti vā*). Similarly, the *Bojjhaṅgasaṃyutta* states: 'The sign of an attractive or pleasurable object to which unwise attention is repeatedly given is the nutriment for the arising of unarisen sense desire and for the expansion of the arisen sense desire' (S V 64: *Atthi bhikkhave subhanimittam. Tattha ayonisomanasikārabahulīkāro ayam āhāro anuppannassa vā kāmacchandassa uppādāya uppannassa vā kamacchandassa bhiyyobhāvāya vepullāya*).

11. The term *chanda* has a range of meanings such as 'impulse, intention, resolution, desire, will, striving, zeal, eagerness' (DP; PED, *s.v.*). In the *Atthasālinī*, *chanda* is defined as the 'will to act, its characteristic is the will to act, its function is the search for an object, its manifestation is the need for an object, its proximate cause is the object of desire' (As 132–33: *chando ti kattukamyatāy'etaṃ adhivacanaṃ. Tasmā so kattukamyatālakkhaṇo chando, ārammaṇapariyesanaraso, ārammaṇena atthikatāpaccupaṭṭhāno tad ev'assa padaṭṭhānaṃ*). In the *Abhidhamma* texts, *chanda* is regarded as one of the mental concomitants (*cetasika*) that can arise along with other wholesome or unwholesome concomitants.

12. *Chanda* in the sense of the will to develop wholesomeness (*kusala*) is comprehensively discussed in the *Sammappadhānavibhaṅga* (Vibh 208–215).

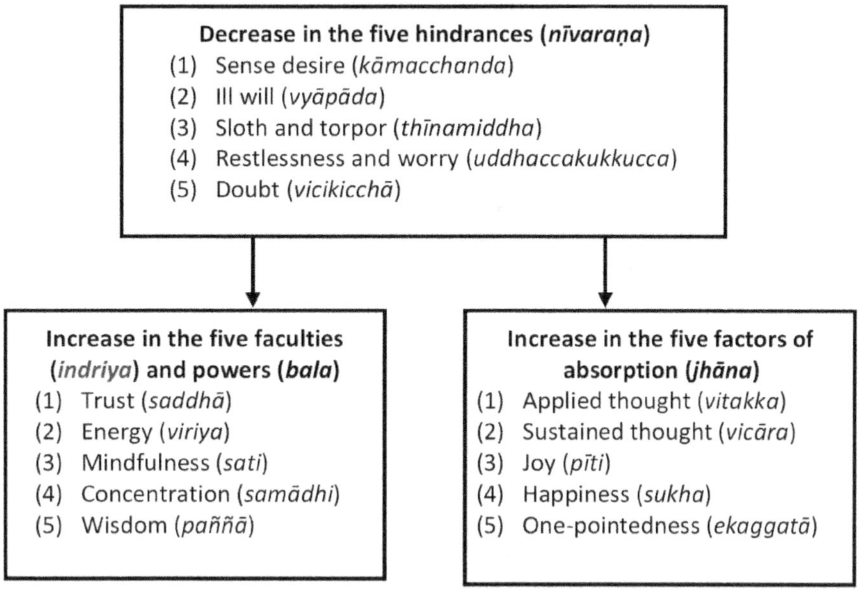

Figure 2 Relationships between the hindrances, faculties, powers and factors of absorption.

If sense desire (*kāmacchanda*) is reduced or (temporarily) abolished, the four other hindrances (*nīvaraṇa*) are diminished or removed to the same extent. When cultivating concentration for meditative absorption (*jhāna*), all five hindrances (*nīvaraṇa*) should be equally diminished, not just one or two. At the same time, the five faculties (*indriya*) or five powers (*bala*) as well as the five factors of absorption (*jhāna*) must grow and be maintained at an equal level (Figure 2). When the hindrances (*nīvaraṇa*) are (temporarily) removed, the five faculties (*indriya*) and the five factors of absorption (*jhāna*) should be noted with mindfulness (*sati*) and clear comprehension (*sampajañña*).

The hindrances of sense desire (*kāmacchanda*) and ill will (*vyāpāda*) often arise in relation to past objects. When they are recognised as they arise and understood with mindfulness (*sati*) and clear comprehension (*sampajañña*), the necessary space for wisdom (*paññā*) to arise is created, and the nature of the hindrances (*nīvaraṇa*) (i.e., impermanence, unsatisfactoriness and non-self) is then understood.[13] The ten defilements (*kilesa*)[14] no longer appear even when one fails to note the arising of an object; this indicates that the meditation practice is well established in the domain of the contemplation of phenomena (*dhammānupassanā*).

13. The *Papañcasūdani* commentary (Ps 281) explains that sense desire (*kāmacchanda*) can be removed through wise attention (*yoniso manasikāra*) directed towards a non-attractive object and an understanding of the three characteristics—i.e., impermanence (*anicca*), unsatisfactoriness (*dukkha*) and non-self (*anattā*). To abandon sense desire (*kāmacchanda*), the commentary recommends six practices: (1) using unattractive objects (of contemplation), (2) practising the contemplation of unattractiveness, (3) guarding the senses, (4) being moderate with food, (5) noble friendship and (6) suitable conversations (Ps 281–282: *Api ca cha dhammā kāmacchandassa pahānāya saṃvattanti: asubhanimittassa uggaho, asubhabhāvanānuyogo, indriyesu guttadvāratā, bhojane mattaññutā, kalyāṇamittatā, sappāyakathā ti*).

14. The ten defilements (*kilesa*) commonly include: (1) greed (*lobha*), (2) aversion (*dosa*), (3) delusion (*moha*), (4) conceit (*māna*), (5) views (*diṭṭhi*), (6) doubt (*vicikicchā*), (7) sloth (*thīna*), (8) restlessness (*uddhacca*), (9) shamelessness (*ahirika*) and (10) disregard for consequence (*anottappa*) (Dhs 257; Vibh 341).

'Ill will' (*vyāpāda*)

The term *vyāpāda* refers to ill will, anger, dislike or aversion.[15] It is a very dangerous hindrance; if the meditator does not recognise it, ill will can gradually increase and intensify into enmity, which wants to destroy the object of the ill will.[16]

Ill will (*vyāpāda*) has a wide range of intensities. A very strong form of ill will is called *upanāha*;[17] this is anger that completely engulfs a person so that she or he seems perpetually on fire, at the point of exploding and unable to engage in any positive communication. This occurs because strong clinging (*upādāna*) to anger has increased to such an extent that it becomes a kind of mental illness. Such people have very unfavourable rebirths, as their anger continues into the next life. Another very strong and intense form of anger is known as hostility (*baddhavera*); it can extend over many lifetimes, unlike ill will (*vyāpāda*) that can end within a single lifetime. Sometimes a display of anger such as telling people off, if conducted *without* aversion or dislike in the mind, may be a kind of skilful means that aims to reduce or prevent the damage or problems that some people may create by harming themselves or others.

Generally, society is not favourable towards ill will (*vyāpāda*); people do not like encountering it, as they find it unacceptable. However, people usually like and embrace sense desire (*kāmacchanda*); they enjoy seeing or participating in dancing, drinking and all kinds of indulgent and pleasurable activities. Thus, sense desire (*kāmacchanda*) is almost universally accepted in society, whereas ill will (*vyāpāda*) is not, even though both are linked to unwholesome mental states and lead to unwholesome rebirths. Sense desire (*kāmacchanda*) and ill will (*vyāpāda*) are both present whenever attachment arises in the mind. In meditation, both need to be reduced and eventually eliminated, as stated in the beginning of this *sutta*: the four foundations of mindfulness (*satipaṭṭhāna*) must be practised by the meditator only after she or he has 'abandoned desires and discontent in regard to the world' (*vineyya loke abhijjhādomanassaṃ*). This means that desires and discontent are clearly understood and abandoned; they cannot be said to be eradicated, because if the meditator tries to destroy them, she or he will fall into the trap of showing anger and aversion in regard to them. It is only through clear understanding and wisdom (*paññā*) that the meditator can be liberated from them.

---

15. In the *Dhammasaṅgaṇi*, the hindrance of ill will (*vyāpāda*) is described as 'resentment, malevolence, ill-temper, harmfulness, anger, hatred, hostility, irritation, etc.' (Dhs 204: *cittassa āghāto paṭighāto paṭighaṃ virodho kopo pakopo sampakopo doso padoso sampadoso cittassa vyāpatti manopadoso kodho kujjhanā kujjhitattaṃ doso dussanā dussitattaṃ vyāpatti vyāpajjanā vyāpajjitattaṃ virodho paṭivirodho caṇḍikkaṃ asuropo anattamanatā cittassa, idaṃ vuccati vyāpādanīvaraṇaṃ*). According to the *Papañcasūdani* commentary, the condition for the arising of ill will (*vyāpāda*) is unwise attention (*ayoniso manasikāra*) towards an object of aversion or anger (*paṭighanimitta*) (Ps 282: *paṭighanimitte ayonisomanasikārena pana vyāpādassa uppādo hoti*).

16. The *Bojjhaṅgasaṃyutta* states that ill will (*vyāpāda*) can be prevented from arising or diminished if already arisen through the practice of wise attention (*yoniso manasikāra*), which focuses on the cultivation of friendliness (*mettā*) (S V 105: *Atthi bhikkhave mettācetovimutti. Tattha yonisomanasikārabahulīkāro ayam anāhāro anuppannassa vā vyāpādassa uppādāya uppannassa vā vyāpādassa bhiyyobhāvāya vepullāya*). The *Papañcasūdani* commentary lists six things to remove ill will (*vyāpāda*): (1) knowledge about the contemplation on friendliness, (2) practice of the friendliness/loving kindness meditation (*mettā*), (3) reflection on one's actions, (4) abundant wise reflections, (5) noble friendship and (6) suitable conversations (Ps 282–283: *Apica cha dhammā vyāpādassa pahānāya saṃvattanti: mettānimittassa uggaho mettābhāvanānuyogo kammassakatāpaccavekkhaṇā paṭisaṅkhānabahutā kalyāṇamittatā sappāyakathāti*).

17. The word *upanāha* is translated as 'grudge, enmity' (DP; PED, *s.v.*). In the *Khuddakavatthuvibhaṅga*, it is said that what is initially anger (*kodha*) can develop into enmity (*upanāha*) (Vibh 357: *pubbakāle kodho, aparakāle upanāho*).

'Sloth and torpor' (*thīnamiddha*)

Sloth and torpor (*thīnamiddha*) refer to a kind of withdrawn state of mind that emerges when energy (*viriya*) is diminished or disappears. This occurs when the mind withdraws from the object and the meditator turns away from practice, being disinclined to cultivate wholesomeness and instead dwelling in unwholesome states. For example, imagine that a meditator on a meditation retreat has to leave the meditation centre for a day. If she or he spends the day without any unwholesome (*akusala*) states occurring and then, after returning to the centre, feels tired and goes to sleep, the energy (*viriya*) for meditation still remains, and sloth and torpor (*thīnamiddha*) have not arisen. However, if the meditator spends the day involved in unwholesome states with desire (*lobha*) or aversion (*dosa*), energy (*viriya*) would be lost, leading to sloth and torpor (*thīnamiddha*). Or, for example, when the meditator falls asleep in meditation, this can happen due to physical tiredness, but since her or his aim is to meditate and cultivate wholesome states, it means that sloth and torpor (*thīnamiddha*) are not present. However, some meditators fall asleep because of a distaste for meditation; in this case, the mind does not cultivate wholesome mental states, and hence sloth and torpor (*thīnamiddha*) arise. Sloth and torpor (*thīnamiddha*) on the one hand and physical tiredness and exhaustion on the other hand are two different things; just because the body is tired does not mean that the unwholesome state of sloth and torpor (*thīnamiddha*) is present. Physical tiredness also appears in *arahants* who are free from sloth and torpor (*thīnamiddha*), and according to the Buddhist texts, even the Buddha used to feel tired and suffer from backache and had to rest or lie down.[18]

Sloth (*thīna*)[19] is a contracted and dull state of mind (*citta*), whereas torpor (*middha*)[20] is a stiff and unwieldy mental concomitant (*cetasika*). The two occur simultaneously; when the mental concomitants (*cetasika*) are contracted, the mind (*citta*) also becomes contracted and vice versa.[21]

---

18. For example, the *Sekhasutta* (M I 354) narrates how the Buddha had a sore back and asked Ānanda to give the teachings in his place while he lay down. The *Sakalikasutta* (S I 27–29) describes how the Buddha had experienced severe pains, and while lying down, approached them with mindfulness (*sati*) and clear comprehension (*sampajañña*).

19. The word *thīna* is translated as 'stiffness, stolidity, lethargy, sloth, immobility' (DP; PED, *s.v.*). In the *Dhammasaṅgaṇi*, sloth (*thīna*) is presented as 'disinclination, unwieldiness, stickiness, stolidity, clinging, adhering, cleaving to, sloth, stiffness, rigidity of the mind' (Dhs 204–205: *Tattha katamaṃ thīnaṃ? Yā cittassa akalyatā akammaññatā olīyanā sallīyanā līnaṃ līyanā līyitattaṃ thīnaṃ thyanā thīyitattaṃ cittassa*). The *Vibhaṅga* links *thīna* to the 'sluggishness' (*līnatta*) and 'lethargy' (*akammaññatā*) of the mind (Vibh 352: *Yā cittassa akalyatā akammaññatā olīyanā sallīyanā līnaṃ līyanā līyitattaṃ thīnaṃ thīyanā thīyitattaṃ cittassa idaṃ vuccati cetaso līnattaṃ*).

20. The word *middha* is translated as 'torpor, stupidity, sluggishness' (DP; PED, *s.v.*). In the *Dhammasaṅgaṇi*, torpor (*middha*) is described as 'disinclination, unwieldiness, covering up, enveloping, barricading within, torpor, sleepiness, nodding off, somnolence and slumber of mental concomitants' (Dhs 205: *Tattha katamaṃ middhaṃ? Yā kāyassa akalyatā akammaññatā onāho pariyonāho anto samorodho middhaṃ soppaṃ pacalāyikā soppaṃ supanā supitattaṃ*).

21. In commentaries like the *Papañcasūdani* and *Sumaṅgalavilāsinī*, sloth (*thīna*) is described as a sickness of the mind (*citta*) and torpor (*middha*) as a sickness of the mental concomitants (Ps II 217 and Sv I 212: *thīnaṃ cittagelaññaṃ. middhaṃ cetasikagelaññaṃ*). The *Visuddhimagga* further explains: 'The characteristic of sloth is the lack of endeavour, its function is removing energy and its manifestation is subsiding. The characteristic of torpor (*middha*) is unwieldiness, its function is shrouding and its manifestation is sluggishness or dozing and sleep. The proximate cause of both sloth and torpor is unwise attention (*ayoniso manasikāra*) in relation to boredom, drowsiness etc.' (Vism 469: *Tattha thīnaṃ anussāhalakkhaṇam, viriyāvinodanarasaṃ, saṃsīdanapaccupaṭṭhānaṃ, middhaṃ akammaññatālakkhaṇam, onahanarasaṃ, līnatāpaccupaṭṭhānaṃ pacalāyikāniddāpaccupaṭṭhānaṃ vā; ubhayam pi arativijambhikādisu ayonisomanasikārapadaṭṭhānaṃ*).

In such a sluggish and contracted mental state, contact (*phassa*)[22] with objects is not clear. For example, in a comatose state, the mental concomitants (*cetasika*) are not experienced since the contact is not felt. Because of the unclear contact, the feeling (*vedanā*) and perception (*saññā*) that arise with the object cannot be seen. Therefore, volition (*cetanā*) is very weak, and wrong view (*diṭṭhi*) ensues. In other words, the mind with sloth and torpor (*thīnamiddha*) arises with unwholesome states, which appear in conjunction with delusion (*moha*) and restlessness (*uddhacca*); they can also arise along with greed (*lobha*) or aversion (*dosa*), thus leading to unwholesome deeds. If the meditator observes and clearly understands sloth and torpor (*thīnamiddha*) as phenomena (*dhamma*) arising and passing away, she or he practises mindfulness (*sati*) in the domain of the contemplation of phenomena (*dhammānupassanā*) and is not troubled by them. If any of these hindrances (*nīvaraṇa*) occur along with thoughts, then meditation takes place in the domain of the contemplation of the mind (*cittānupassanā*).

Because of unwise attention (*ayoniso manasikāra*), the mind becomes contracted through sloth and torpor (*thīnamiddha*). The meditator cannot see her or his boredom (*arati*) or dislike for the cultivation of wholesomeness. When sloth and torpor (*thīnamiddha*) grow, they develop into distaste or languor (*tandī*) and then into stronger unwholesomeness, experienced as laziness, stretching and yawning (*vijambhikā*), drowsiness after a meal (*bhattasammada*) and general mental lethargy (*cetaso līnattaṃ*).[23] The person may fall asleep or, if awake, her or his mind cannot approach the wholesome mental states because of a lack of energy (*viriya*), mindfulness (*sati*) and clear comprehension (*sampajañña*).[24]

Mental states with sloth and torpor (*thīnamiddha*) always arise in conjunction with delusion (*moha*).[25] Delusion (*moha*) is different from ignorance (*avijjā*):[26] it is always unwholesome,

22. Contact (*phassa*) is explained in the Abhidhammic texts as one of the seven universal mental concomitants (*cetasika*) that are present in every mind (*citta*) moment; for an overview of the universal mental concomitants (*cetasika*), see Karunadasa (2014, 103–120).

23. This description of sloth and torpor (*thīnamiddha*) can be found in the *Sammohavinodanī* and *Papañcasūdani* commentaries (Vibh-a 272; Ps I 283: *Arati nāma ukkaṇṭhitatā. Tandī nāma kāyālasiyatā. Vijambhikā nāma kāyavināmanā. Bhattasammado nāma bhattamucchā bhattapariḷāho. Cetaso līnattaṃ nāma cittassa līnākāro. Imesu arati ādīsu ayoniso manasikāraṃ bahulaṃ pavattayato thīnamiddhaṃ uppajjati*). Cf. S V 103.

24. The *Papañcasūdani* commentary lists six things that can remove sloth and torpor (*thīnamiddha*): (1) eating less, (2) changing meditation posture, (3) perceiving light, (4) staying in the open air, (5) noble friendship and (6) suitable conversations (Ps 284: *apica cha dhammā thīnamiddhassa pahānāya saṃvattanti: atibhojane nimittaggāho, iriyāpathasamparivattanatā, ālokasaññāmanasikāro, abbhokāsavāso, kalyāṇamittatā, sappāyakathā ti*).

25. The term *moha* is usually translated as 'delusion, stupidity, dullness' (PED, *s.v.*). The *Vibhaṅga* and *Atthasālinī* define delusion (*moha*) as the absence of knowledge about the four truths, causality and dependent origination (Vibh 362; As 254: *Dukkhe aññāṇaṃ dukkhasamudaye aññāṇaṃ dukkhanirodhe aññāṇaṃ dukkhanirodhagāminiyā paṭipadāya annāṇaṃ; pubbante aññāṇaṃ aparante aññāṇaṃ pubbantāparante aññāṇaṃ idappaccayatāpaṭiccasamuppannesu dhammesu aññāṇaṃ, yaṃ evarūpaṃ aññāṇaṃ adassanaṃ ... avijjālaṅgī moho akusalamūlaṃ: ayaṃ vuccati moho*). The *Visuddhimagga* describes delusion (*moha*) as follows: 'Its characteristic is blindness or not knowing, its function is concealing the true nature of an object, its manifestation is the absence of right conduct or dullness, darkness, and its proximate cause is unwise attention. It is the root of all that is unwholesome.' (Vism 468: *Moho cittassa andhabhāvalakkhaṇo, aññāṇalakkhaṇo vā; asampaṭivedharaso, ārammaṇasabhāvacchādanaraso vā; asammāpaṭipattipaccupaṭṭhāno, andhakārapaccupaṭṭhāno vā; ayonisomanasikārapadaṭṭhāno, sabbākusalānaṃ mūlan ti*).

26. Ignorance (*avijjā*) is often defined in similar terms to delusion (*moha*) (e.g., Vibh 166). In the context of dependent origination (*paṭiccasamuppāda*), it is presented as the initial link, namely, the root condition for continuous rebirth; thus, it is not limited to unwholesome states alone. It is also described as a taint (*avijjāsava*) (Dhs 195), a fetter (*avijjāsaṃyojana*) (Dhs 199) and a hindrance (*avijjānīvaraṇa*) (Dhs 206–207).

as it arises with all unwholesome states of mind (*citta*) and completely blocks any wholesomeness, whereas ignorance (*avijjā*) can be present in both wholesome and unwholesome mental states. Delusion (*moha*) is one of the mental concomitants (*cetasika*) that is always unwholesome, whereas ignorance (*avijjā*) is not a mental concomitant (*cetasika*) but rather a combination of several of them. Even the most wholesome activities can be done with ignorance (*avijjā*) but not necessarily with delusion (*moha*). If a person is reborn under the influence of delusion (*moha*), the rebirth will always take place in one of the lower realms, whereas a rebirth under the influence of ignorance (*avijjā*) can be on a higher plane.[27] In order for rebirth to take place, ignorance (*avijjā*) must be present; hence, only the mind of an *arahant* is free from ignorance (*avijjā*).

Even in the most refined stage of formless (*arūpa*) absorption (*jhāna*), the so-called 'neither-perception-nor-non-perception' (*nevasaññāsaññāyatana*),[28] which is the highest level of wholesomeness, there is ignorance (*avijjā*). However, because the hindrances (*nīvaraṇa*) are totally hidden, it is not possible to see ignorance (*avijjā*) nor understand how it functions. In such refined mental states, ignorance (*avijjā*) operates together with delight for life (*jīvitanikanti*), a joy in being alive, which is maintained by feeling (*vedanā*) and perception (*saññā*). Despite being of utmost wholesomeness, this is still a worldly state that leads to becoming (*bhava*) and rebirth (*punabbhava*). In the absorptions (*jhāna*) arising in the realm of form (*rūpāvacara*), mental formations (*saṅkhāra*) are more active, since they are connected with happiness or pleasure, whereas the formless (*arūpa*) absorptions occur with equanimity (*upekkhā*), and thus mental formations (*saṅkhāra*) are very weak. In all absorptions (*jhāna*), ignorance (*avijjā*) is concealed; it cannot be seen by the meditator, since the objects of the sense sphere do not occur. However, the temporarily suppressed mental concomitants (*cetasika*) related to the sense sphere are liable to arise again. Insight meditation (*vipassanā*) is also conducted in the world of the senses; it is only in the mind-moments of change-of-lineage (*gotrabhū*),[29] path (*magga*) and fruition (*phala*) that the mind functions without ignorance (*avijjā*).

Thus, in the absorptions (*jhāna*), ignorance (*avijjā*) is present, especially when the meditator is enjoying the absorptions and does not endeavour to strive towards the higher wholesome states by cultivating mindfulness (*sati*) and clear comprehension (*sampajañña*). Consequently, sloth and torpor (*thīnamiddha*) may ensue at a very slight, almost imperceptible level, and a sort of grossness or roughness (*thambha*)[30] may arise in the mind, often accompanied by pride or confusion. Only *arahants* have completely eradicated this roughness (*thambha*). Whoever

27. According to early Buddhist cosmology as presented in the Pāli canon, there are different realms of rebirth: the lower realms include the animal kingdom (*tiracchānayoni*), ghosts (*peta*) and hells (*niraya*), whereas the higher realms are those of humans (*manussa*), gods (*deva*) and titans (*asura*). In addition, the higher realms include the refined sphere of pure form (*rūpāvacara*) and the most refined formless sphere (*arūpāvacara*), which is purely mental without any material form.

28. For a comprehensive presentation of the absorptions (*jhāna*), see the *Visuddhimagga* (Vism 122–169; 326–340); a shorter overview is given in Bodhi (1993, 52–64) and Bucknell (1993).

29. The term *gotrabhū*, usually translated as 'change-of-lineage,' refers to the mind-moment (*citta*) that precedes the supramundane path (*magga*) and fruition (*phala*); it is the transition from the worldly (*putthujana*) to the noble (*ariya*) state or lineage (*gotra*); this explanation of *gotrabhū* is mostly found in commentarial texts such as the *Visuddhimagga* (Vism 672–675).

30. The term *thambha* can be rendered into English as 'rigidity, hardness, roughness' (DP; PED, *s.v.*); it is defined in the *Vibhaṅga* as 'that which is roughness, a rough state, hardness, harshness, unwieldiness of the mind, non-pliancy' (Vibh 350: *yo thambho thambhanā thambhitattaṃ kakkhaḷiyaṃ phārusiyaṃ ujucittatā amudutā: ayaṃ vuccati thambho*).

gives up grossness or roughness of the mind lives with lightness, as depicted in the *Mettāsutta* (Sn 25–26); she or he is soft (*mudu*), upright (*uju*), gentle in speech (*suvaco*), content (*santussako*), easily satisfied (*sallahukavutti*) and free from torpor (*vigatamiddho*). In the first line of this *sutta (karaṇīyam atthakusalena)*, the word *atthakusala* refers to the utter wholesomeness cultivated by the meditator. The cultivation of friendliness or loving kindness (*mettā*) is an excellent way for meditators to diminish and relinquish sloth and torpor (*thīnamiddha*) as well as the other hindrances.

Through training in virtue (*sīla*), one can (temporarily) put aside delusion (*moha*), although ignorance (*avijjā*) continues to influence the mental states. Ignorance (*avijjā*) arises due to various conditions, and as stated in the *Avijjāsutta*:

> The nutriment (*āhāra*) for ignorance (*avijjā*) is the five hindrances (*nīvaraṇa*); the nutriment for the five hindrances is the three kinds of misconduct (*tīṇi duccaritāni*); the nutriment for the three kinds of misconduct is the non-restraint of the sense faculties (*indriyāsaṃvara*); the nutriment for the non-restraint of the sense faculties is the lack of mindfulness (*sati*) and clear comprehension (*sampajañña*); the nutriment for the lack of mindfulness and clear comprehension is unwise attention (*ayoniso manasikāra*); the nutriment for unwise attention is the lack of trust (*assaddhiya*); the nutriment for the lack of trust is not hearing the good Dhamma (*asaddhammasavana*); the nutriment for not hearing the good Dhamma is not associating with good people (*asappurisasaṃseva*). (A V 113)[31]

If the five hindrances (*nīvaraṇa*) are absent, ignorance (*avijjā*) does not arise. However, only *arahants* are completely free from the hindrances, whereas some of them are always present in others, unless their mind arises with both mindfulness (*sati*) and wisdom (*paññā*). As said in the *Satipaṭṭhānasutta*, this occurs when the meditator has clearly comprehended desires and discontent and abandoned them (*vineyya loke abhijjhādomanassaṃ*). This does not mean that the meditator is free from the arising of desires (*abhijjhā*) and discontent (*domanassa*) but rather that she or he can recognise them, understand their nature and let go of them.

In every wholesome mental state, there is some degree of mindfulness (*sati*), which appears in conjunction with the other mental concomitants (*cetasika*).[32] However, it is rare for mindfulness (*sati*) to be the most prominent mental concomitant (*cetasika*). Normally, the meditator starts with the contemplation of an object such as breathing (*ānāpānasati*), which is one of the specific meditation practices known as the 'recollections' (*anussati*),[33] and only later on and

31. A V 113: *Ko cāhāro avijjāya? Pañca nīvaraṇā ti'ssa vacanīyaṃ. Pañca p'ahaṃ bhikkhave nīvaraṇe sāhāre vadāmi, no anāhāre. Ko cāhāro pañcannaṃ nīvaraṇānaṃ? Tīṇi duccaritāni ti'ssa vacanīyaṃ. Tīṇi p'ahaṃ bhikkhave duccaritāni sāhārāni vadāmi, no anāhārāni. Ko cāhāro tiṇṇaṃ duccaritānaṃ? Indriyāsaṃvaro ti'ssa vacanīyaṃ. Indriyāsaṃvaram p'ahaṃ bhikkhave sāhāraṃ vadāmi, no anāhāraṃ. Ko cāhāro indriyāsaṃvarassa? Asatāsampajaññan ti 'ssa vacanīyaṃ. Asatāsampajaññam p'ahaṃ bhikkhave sāhāraṃ vadāmi, no anāhāraṃ. Ko cāhāro asatāsampajaññassa? Ayonisomanasikāro ti'ssa vacanīyaṃ. Ayonisomanasikāram p'ahaṃ bhikkhave sāhāraṃ vadāmi, no anāhāraṃ. Ko cāhāro ayoniso manasikārassa? Assaddhiyan ti'ssa vacanīyaṃ. Assaddhiyam p'ahaṃ bhikkhave sāhāraṃ vadāmi, no anāhāraṃ. Ko cāhāro assaddhiyassa? Asaddhammasavanan ti'ssa vacanīyaṃ. Asaddhammasavanam p'ahaṃ bhikkhave sāhāraṃ vadāmi, no anāhāraṃ. Ko cāhāro asaddhammasavanassa? Asappurisasaṃsevo ti'ssa vacanīyaṃ.*

32. According to the Theravāda tradition, mindfulness (*sati*) arises only with the wholesome mental concomitants (*cetasika*), which occur in all wholesome mental states (Dhs 9); see Bodhi (1993, 85–90).

33. Usually, six subjects of recollection or remembering (*anussati*) can be the focus of meditation: (1) the Buddha, (2) the Dhamma, (3) the Saṅgha, (4) virtues, (5) generosity and (6) divine beings (e.g., D III 280: *Cha anussatiṭṭhānāni: buddhānussati, dhammānussati, saṅghānussati, sīlānussati, cāgānussati, devatānussati. Ime cha dhammā bhāvetabbā*). Sometimes the list is expanded with four additional objects: (7) mindfulness of breathing, (8) mindfulness of death, (9) mindfulness directed to the body and (10) recollection of peace (e.g., A I 30:

very gradually, does true mindfulness (*sati*) emerge without a chosen object. If the meditator can stay with mindfulness (*sati*) without any greed (*lobha*) or aversion (*dosa*), this could provide a foundation for wisdom (*paññā*); only then is ignorance (*avijjā*) absent.

'Restlessness and worry' (*uddhaccakukkucca*)

Restlessness (*uddhacca*) refers to a disturbed, non-unified state of mind, while worry (*kukkucca*) stands for remorse or regret about things that were neglected or not done.[34] The two often occur together: the presence of restlessness (*uddhacca*) may prompt the arising of worry (*kukkucca*), whereas worry (*kukkucca*) is always accompanied by restlessness (*uddhacca*).[35] Generally, younger people experience more restlessness (*uddhacca*) and older people more remorse (*kukkucca*). In old age, people tend to think about the things that they should have done in their youth or they regret what they did in the past.

In addition, restlessness (*uddhacca*) alone is listed both as one of the fetters (*saṃyojana*)[36] and one of the defilements (*kilesa*). It is also one of the mental concomitants (*cetasika*) that accompany all unwholesome mental states, which means that restlessness (*uddhacca*), in conjunction with delusion (*moha*), lack of restraint (*ahirika*) and disregard for consequence (*anottappa*), is always present when the other hindrances arise.[37] When worry (*kukkucca*) appears along with restlessness (*uddhacca*), they are taken together as one of the hindrances (*nīvaraṇa*), which can give rise to doubt (*vicikiccha*). Until the meditator reaches the stage of *arahant*, restlessness (*uddhacca*) can arise on its own as a fetter (*saṃyojana*), whereas worry (*kukkucca*) is overcome at the stage of non-returners (*anāgāmin*).

ānāpānasati ... maraṇasati ... kāyagatāsati ... upasamānussati). For a detailed description of the ten recollections (*anussati*), see the *Visuddhimagga* (Vism 197–294).

34. Restlessness (*uddhacca*) is presented is the *Dhammasaṅgaṇi* and *Vibhaṅga* as 'agitation, disturbance, turmoil of the mind' (Dhs 205; Vibh 255: *avūpasamo cetaso vikkhepo bhantattaṃ cittassa*), and worry (*kukkucca*) as perplexity about 'what is appropriate in the inappropriate, what is inappropriate in the appropriate, immoral in the moral, moral in the immoral—this is worry, remorse, remorsefulness, regretfulness of the mind' (Dhs 205; Vibh 255: *akappiye kappiyasaññitā, kappiye akappiyasaññitā, avajje vajjasaññitā, vajje avajjasaññitā. yaṃ evarūpaṃ kukkuccaṃ kukkuccāyanā kukkuccāyitattaṃ cetaso vippaṭisāro manovilekho*).

35. The *Papañcasūdani* commentary states that restlessness (*uddhacca*) and worry (*kukkucca*) arise because of unwise attention (*ayoniso manasikāra*) (Ps 284: *ayoniso manasikārena uddhaccakukkuccassa uppādo hoti*); (cf. S V 103). The commentary also lists six things that can remove restlessness and worry: (1) knowledge, (2) questioning, (3) knowing the monastic rules, (4) association with elders, (5) noble friendship and (6) suitable talk (Ps 285: *Api ca cha dhammā uddhaccakukkuccassa pahānāya saṃvattanti: bahussutatā, paripucchakatā, vinaye pakataññutā, vuddhasevitā, kalyāṇamittatā, sappāyakathāti*).

36. The most common list of fetters comprises the following ten: (1) personality or identity view (*sakkāyadiṭṭhi*), (2) doubt (*vicikicchā*), (3) attachment to rites and rituals (*sīlabbataparāmāsa*), (4) sense desire (*kāmacchanda*), (5) ill will (*vyāpāda*), (6) desire for material existence (*rūparāga*), (7) desire for immaterial existence (*arūparāga*), (8) conceit (*māna*), (9) restlessness (*uddhacca*) and (10) ignorance (*avijjā*); see the *Oghasutta* (S V 61) or *Sammappadhānasaṃyutta* (S V 247–248).

37. In the Theravāda Abhidhammic texts, restlessness (*uddhacca*) and remorse/worry (*kukkucca*) are both listed as unwholesome mental concomitants (*akusalacetasika*): restlessness (*uddhacca*) is associated with all unwholesome mental states, whereas worry (*kukkucca*) can occasionally join unwholesome states. The texts identify the following fourteen unwholesome mental concomitants (*akusalacetasika*): (1) delusion (*moha*), (2) lack of restraint (*ahirika*), (3) disregard for consequence (*anottappa*), (4) restlessness (*uddhacca*), (5) greed (*lobha*); (6) views (*diṭṭhi*), (7) conceit (*māna*), (8) hatred (*dosa*), (9) envy (*issā*), (10) miserliness (*macchariya*), (11) worry/regret (*kukkucca*), (12) sloth (*thīna*), (13) torpor (*middha*) and (14) doubt/confusion (*vicikicchā*). The first four are universally present in all unwholesome states, whereas the others occur occasionally in varying combinations (Table 6). See also Dhs 75–87; Bodhi (1993, 83–84) and Karunadasa (2010, 121–131).

'Doubt' (*vicikicchā*)

Doubt or uncertainty (*vicikicchā*)[38] is a hindrance that is similar to worry (*kukkucca*), though more subtle and complex. Doubt (*vicikicchā*) does not refer to the various uncertainties that we encounter in ordinary daily life. In the context of the Buddhist teachings, doubt (*vicikiccha*) is outlined in regard to the following:

1. the Buddha or the master (*satthar*)
2. the Dhamma (*dhamma*)
3. the Saṅgha (*saṅgha*)
4. three trainings (*sikkhā*)
5. past, future and both past and future (*pubbanta, aparanta, pubbantāparanta*)
6. causality and conditionality (*idappaccayatā paṭiccasamuppannesu dhammesu*)[39]

Doubt (*vicikicchā*) about the Buddha or the master (*satthar*) involves uncertainty about who he was, what he knew, what kind of qualities he had and whether he was omniscient.[40] One has such doubts about the Buddha (*satthari kaṅkhati*) due to confusion about what he represents, because the causes and conditions for the Buddha's existence or for his reaching *nibbāna* are unknown. In other words, this uncertainty is not about a particular person called the Buddha; instead it relates to a lack of understanding about what the Buddha represents.

Doubt about the Dhamma is uncertainty or a lack of understanding about the Buddhist teachings. Some people think that this relates to doubt about what is said in the *Tipiṭaka* or uncertainty as to whether the canonical texts include the actual words of the Buddha or whether the *Vinayapiṭaka* is earlier than the *Suttapiṭaka* or *Abhidhammapiṭaka*. However, such questions are not really doubts about the Dhamma. One is uncertain about the Dhamma (*dhamme kaṅkhati*) when one wonders whether the cultivation of virtue (*sīla*), meditation (*samādhi*) and wisdom (*paññā*) will lead to liberation, *nibbāna*.[41] This uncertainty occurs, because the Dhamma cannot

38. Doubt (*vicikicchā*) is frequently described as puzzlement and uncertainty of the mind (Vibh 364; Dhs 221: *thambhitattaṃ cittassa manovilekho*). The *Papañcasūdani* commentary explains that the expansion of doubt (*vicikicchā*) is due to unwise attention (Ps I 285: *ayonisomanasikārena vicikicchāya uppādo hoti*) and then lists six things that can remove doubt: (1) knowledge, (2) inquiry, (3) knowing the monastic rules, (4) firm resolve (or reliance on the teachings), (5) noble friendship and (6) suitable talk (Ps I 286: *Api ca cha dhammā vicikicchāya pahānāya saṃvattanti: bahussutatā, paripucchakatā, vinaye pakataññutā, adhimokkhabahulatā, kalyāṇamittatā, sappāyakathāti*). This list is very similar to that summarised above for the removal of restlessness and worry (*uddhaccakukkucca*).

39. Doubt (*vicikicchā*) in relation to these six items is similarly described in the *Khuddakavatthūnivibhaṅga* and *Dhammasaṅgaṇi* (Vibh 364–365; Dhs 183: *Satthari kaṅkhati vicikicchati—dhamme kaṅkhati vicikicchati—saṅghe kaṅkhati vicikicchati—sikkhāya kaṅkhati vicikicchati—pubbante kaṅkhati vicikicchati—aparante kaṅkhati vicikicchati—pubbantāparante kaṅkhati vicikicchati idappaccayatā paṭiccasamuppannesu dhammesu kaṅkhati vicikicchati*). A different presentation is given in the *Cetikhilasutta* in which doubt is associated with the following: (1) the Buddha, (2) the Dhamma, (3) the Saṅgha, (4) training and (5) resentfulness towards one's companions (M I 101: *Satthari kaṅkhati vicikicchati ... dhamme kaṅkhati vicikicchati ... saṅghe kaṅkhati vicikicchati ... sikkhāya kaṅkhati vicikicchati ... sabrahmacārisu kupito hoti anattamano āhatacitto khilajāto*).

40. Doubt about the Buddha is similarly described in the *Atthasālinī*, which also includes uncertainty about his body (i.e., thirty-two characteristics), his qualities and his omniscience and ability to know the past, present and future (*sabbaññutaññāṇa*) (As 354: *Satthari kaṅkhatī ti satthu sarīre vā tassa guṇe vā ubhayattha vā kaṅkhati ... atītānāgatapaccuppannajānanasamatthaṃ sabbaññutañāṇaṃ atthi nu kho n'atthī'ti kaṅkhati*).

41. The *Atthasālinī* comments that doubt (*vicikicchā*) about the Dhamma corresponds to uncertainty about the four noble paths (*magga*) and fruits (*phala*), the great deathless *nibbāna* and the liberation from the cycle of rebirths (As 354: *Cattāro ariyamaggā paṭippassaddhakilesāni cattāri sāmaññaphalāni. Maggaphalānaṃ*

be comprehended from the outside, from debates or from reading. It has to be seen and understood within oneself, uncovered by oneself—and it was through such deep insight into the Dhamma that the Buddha's mind was liberated.

The Dhamma is essentially timeless (*akālika*). Human understanding of life is normally limited in time, as people speak of tomorrow or the next birth, or plan meditation retreats and try to find a suitable place for meditation. Although it is necessary to go in search of liberation, the problem with this endeavour is that it always occurs within a certain timeframe instead of the here-and-now. The meditator may be sitting in meditation, putting in great effort in search of deeper concentration (*samādhi*) or path (*magga*) knowledge that may be achieved in the future. In this manner, the meditator limits her or his knowledge or wisdom to a specific time and place, seeking happiness in a certain future, instead of understanding the present moment in which this very seeking is taking place. Inevitably, most meditators are searching for peace and liberation in the future; however, what they really need to do is quite simple—just to know where their mind is at that very moment. This is why the Buddha taught people to let go of time, to let go of the past, the present and the future.[42] Since the Dhamma is timeless (*akālika*), it is within oneself and cannot be found elsewhere. While it is useful to understand the external world, to understand the Dhamma in its timelessness one needs direct experience or insight—only then will doubt or uncertainty (*vicikicchā*) about the Dhamma disappear.

Doubt (*vicikicchā*) about the Saṅgha does not relate to the *bhikkhus* and *bhikkhunīs* in general, but about the noble disciples of the Buddha who reached the path (*magga*) and fruition (*phala*) knowledges or approached those.[43] In other words, it is uncertainty about the existence of people who diminished or destroyed the defilements (*kilesa*) such as greed (*lobha*), aversion (*dosa*), delusion (*moha*), conceit (*māna*) and views (*diṭṭhi*). However, as the meditator's practice evolves, this doubt (*vicikicchā*) about whether people walked the entire path diminishes.

Another kind of doubt or uncertainty (*vicikicchā*) relates to the three trainings (*sikkhā*), namely, virtue (*sīla*), meditation (*samādhi*) and wisdom (*paññā*).[44] Training in virtue (*sīla*) means maintaining one's monastic discipline or upholding the five or eight precepts[45] that are used

---

ārammaṇapaccayabhūtaṃ amatamahānibbānaṃ nāma atthi nu kho n'atthī ti kaṅkhanto pi ayaṃ dhammo niyyāniko nu kho aniyyāniko ti kaṅkhanto pi dhamme kaṅkhati nāma).

42. For example, in the *Dhammapada* (Dhp 98).

43. The *Atthasālinī* explains doubt (*vicikicchā*) in regard to the Saṅgha as the uncertainty about whether those who achieved the four paths (*magga*) and fruits (*phala*) really existed or not, whether they had good conduct or not and whether any result can be obtained from supporting them (As 355: *Cattāro maggaṭṭhakā cattāro phalaṭṭhakāti idaṃ saṅgharatanaṃ. Atthi nu kho natthī'ti kaṅkhanto pi 'ayaṃ saṅgho suppaṭipanno nu kho duppaṭipanno' ti kaṅkhanto pi, 'etasmiṃ saṅgharatane dinnassa vipākaphalaṃ atthi nu kho n'atthī'ti kaṅkhanto pi saṅghe kaṅkhati nāma*).

44. The three trainings (*sikkhā*) are similarly explained in several texts such as the *Sikkhāsutta*, which states that they comprise 'the training in higher virtue, the training in higher mind and the training in higher wisdom' (A I 235: *Tisso imā bhikkhave sikkhā. Katamā tisso? Adhisīlasikkhā, adhicittasikkhā, adhipaññāsikkhā*). The *Visuddhimagga* comments that the three trainings are to be repeatedly practised by means of mindfulness and attention (Vism 274: *imā tisso sikkhāyo tasmiṃ ārammaṇe, tāya satiyā, tena manasikārena sikkhati, āsevati, bhāveti, bahulīkarotī ti*).

45. Monastics are guided by a lengthy set of guidelines, whereas for lay individuals the five precepts are the moral guidelines or trainings to abstain from: (1) killing, (2) stealing, (3) sensual misconduct, (4) lying and (5) intoxication. Three further precepts can be added for special observances: (6) abstaining from eating after noon, (7) beautification and participation in entertainment and (8) using luxurious beds. For a short survey of the precepts, see Harvey (2013, 268–278).

to control or discipline one's speech and body. Virtue (*sīla*) is different from the rules of law within a particular society or country; if the law is broken, a person can be punished, whereas in the case of virtue (*sīla*), the precepts are adopted by a person only for her or his own betterment or improvement. The practice of virtue (*sīla*) is developed with the aim to change one's own lifestyle for the better; it is not enforced by anybody. The second component of the three trainings (*sikkhā*) is meditation (*samādhi*). Many people think that this means sitting steadily for long periods of time like a rock. Sitting meditation is certainly useful, since the meditator is at least not creating any problems, as she or he is not speaking or doing anything else. But it is not necessary to allocate a certain time—say one hour—to sitting meditation. The meditator should just sit without a time limit or any goal, otherwise they will start clinging (*upādāna*) to the meditation object and the whole meditation practice. The most important aspect of meditation is maintaining wholesome (*kusala*) mental states without greed (*lobha*) or aversion (*dosa*) in order for mindfulness (*sati*) and clear comprehension (*sampajañña*) to arise. The training in meditation (*samādhi*) means the cultivation of a concentrated and tranquil mind,[46] which sees, cognises and clearly understands objects as they arise. The third component of the trainings is wisdom (*paññā*); before it can arise, the meditator has to develop knowledge or understanding about how to improve one's virtue (*sīla*) and conduct and how to live in a way that enhances wholesomeness. Through meditation practice, especially the cultivation of mindfulness (*sati*) and clear comprehension (*sampajañña*), one gradually increases knowledge and understanding and creates the foundation for wisdom (*paññā*)—i.e., direct insight into the three characteristics of all phenomena and the four noble truths.[47] Uncertainty or doubt (*vicikicchā*) about wisdom (*paññā*) can only be overcome through the cultivation of virtue (*sīla*) and meditation (*samādhi*), which provide the foundation for wisdom (*paññā*) to emerge.

Doubts about the past, present and future primarily relate to the uncertainty as to whether somebody whom I call 'I' or 'myself' existed in the past, exists in the present and will continue to exist in the future.[48] In other words, if there was an 'I' in the past, what part of this 'I' still exists in the present and what part will continue into the future? Did a being that I call 'myself' exist in the past and will this being continue to exist in the future?[49] People have troubled themselves with these questions since even before the Buddha's time and have continued to do so up until the present day. This very questioning and uncertainty has given rise to religions. Often people undertake meditation with the aim to identify an 'I,' a 'self,' or alternatively to remove a 'self' or shift this 'self' to another place or some other sphere of existence such as the realm of the gods and seek liberation for this 'self.' In this process, they fear that this 'self' or 'I' will end

46. In texts such as the *Sikkhātayasutta*, training (*sikkhā*) in meditation (*samādhi*) is often presented as the cultivation of wholesome mental states that lead to the meditative absorptions (*jhāna*) (A I 235: *Idha bhikkhave bhikkhu vivicc' eva kāmehi. catutthajjhānaṃ upasampajja viharati. Ayaṃ vuccati bhikkhave adhicittasikkhā*).

47. In texts such as the *Sikkhātayasutta*, training in wisdom (*paññā*) is often explained as understanding reality in terms of the four noble truths (A I 235: *Idha bhikkhave bhikkhu idaṃ dukkhan ti yathābhūtaṃ pajānāti ... ayaṃ dukkhanirodhagāminī paṭipadā ti yathābhūtaṃ pajānāti. Ayaṃ vuccati bhikkhave adhipaññāsikkhā*).

48. Such speculations and questions are described, for example, in the *Sabbāsavasutta* (M I 8), *Mahātaṇhāsaṅkhayasutta* (M I 265) and *Saṅgitisutta* (D III 217).

49. In the *Sammohavinodanī* (Vibh-a 496), doubt about the past (*atītaṃ addhānaṃ ārabbha kaṅkhati*) is described as wondering what kind of a person one was in the past (e.g., social class, appearance), will be in the future (*anāgataṃ addhānaṃ ārabbha kaṅkhati*) and is in the present (*paccuppannaṃ addhānaṃ ārabbha kaṅkhati*). Doubt about the present also includes uncertainty about whether one is materiality, feeling, perception, mental formation or consciousness (Vibh-a 496: *kiṃ vā ahaṃ rūpaṃ udāhu vedanā saññā saṅkhārā viññāṇan'ti kaṅkhanto*).

up in a realm of suffering like the hell. Other people think that there is no suffering realm such as hell and that there is only this life, so there is no need for meditation or even any religion; this view is referred to as *ucchedavāda*.[50] Some people who do not believe in any existence after death still perform many wholesome and meritorious acts in their lives, although they may have doubts about causality (*kammaphala*) and dependent origination (*paṭiccasamuppada*).[51] Following any particular religion can be seen as an attempt to create a model of liberation for the 'self.' Whenever an idea or view (*diṭṭhi*) about oneself or reality is created in the mind, uncertainties about that view will ensue. Thus, only the mind that is empty of any ideas or views (*diṭṭhi*) is free from doubts or uncertainties (*vicikicchā*).

V 2 Five aggregates of clinging (*pañcas'upādānakkhandhā*)

Puna ca paraṃ bhikkhave bhikkhu dhammesu dhammānupassī viharati ***pañcas'upādānakkhandhesu.*** *Kathañca bhikkhave bhikkhu dhammesu dhammānupassī viharati pañcas'upādānakkhandesu? Idha bhikkhave bhikkhu: iti* ***rūpaṃ,*** *iti rūpassa samudayo, iti rūpassa atthagamo; iti* ***vedanā,*** *iti vedanāya samudayo, iti vedanāya atthagamo; iti* ***saññā,*** *iti saññāya samudayo, iti saññāya atthagamo; iti* ***saṅkhārā,*** *iti saṅkhārānaṃ samudayo, iti saṅkhārānaṃ atthagamo; iti* ***viññāṇaṃ,*** *iti viññāṇassa samudayo, iti viññāṇassa atthagamo ti.*

'And again, monks, a monk abides contemplating phenomena as phenomena in regard to **the five aggregates of clinging.** And how does a monk abide contemplating phenomena as phenomena in regard to the five aggregates of clinging? Here, monks, a monk (knows): "Such is **materiality**, such is its arising, such is its passing away; such is **feeling**, such is its arising, such is its passing away; such is **perception**, such is its arising, such is its passing away; such are **mental formations**, such are their arising, such are their passing away; such is **consciousness**, such is its arising, such is its passing away."'

Recurring passage indicating the ways to approach the contemplation[52]

Iti ajjhattaṃ vā dhammesu dhammānupassī viharati, bahiddhā vā dhammesu dhammānupassī viharati, ajjhattabahiddhā vā dhammesu dhammānupassī viharati. Samudayadhammānupassī vā dhammesu viharati, vayadhammānupassī vā dhammesu viharati, samudayavayadhammānupassī vā dhammesu viharati. Atthi dhammā ti vā panassa sati paccupaṭṭhitā hoti yāvadeva ñāṇamattāya patissatimattāya, anissito ca viharati na ca kiñci loke upādiyati. Evam kho bhikkhave bhikkhu dhammesu dhammānupassī viharati pañcasu upādānakkhandhesu.

'Thus he abides contemplating phenomena as phenomena internally, or he abides contemplating phenomena as phenomena externally, or he abides contemplating phenomena as phenomena both internally and externally. He abides contemplating the arising of phenomena in phenomena, or he abides contemplating the passing away of phenomena in phenomena, or

50. *Ucchedavāda* was a school of thought in ancient India that professed the doctrine of annihilation and did not accept rebirth or the law of *kamma*. The Buddhist texts label *ucchedavāda* as a 'wrong view'; see, for example, the *Brahmajālasutta* (D I 34; 55). In the *Verañjāsutta*, the annihilationist view is given a new interpretation by the Buddha who speaks about 'the annihilation of lust, hatred, delusion and numerous unwholesome qualities' (A IV 174: *Ahaṃ hi brāhmaṇa ucchedaṃ vadāmi rāgassa dosassa mohassa, anekavihitānaṃ pāpakānaṃ akusalānaṃ dhammānaṃ ucchedaṃ vadāmi*).

51. Doubt about the twelve links of dependent origination is also mentioned in the *Atthasālinī* as one aspect of the hindrance of doubt (*vicikicchā*) (As 355: *Dvādasapadikaṃ paccayavaṭṭaṃ atthi nu kho n'atthī'ti kaṅkhanto idappaccayatāpaṭiccasamuppannesu dhammesu kaṅkhati nāma*).

52. For comments on the recurring passage, see Chapter II.1, under the subheading 'Recurring passage indicating the ways to approach the contemplation.'

he abides contemplating both the arising and passing away of phenomena in phenomena. Or, mindfulness that "there are phenomena" is established in him just to the extent necessary for knowledge and mindfulness. And he abides without attachment, not clinging to anything in the world. Monks, thus a monk abides contemplating phenomena as phenomena in regard to the five aggregates of clinging.'

Pemasiri Thera's commentary

'Five aggregates' (*pañca khandhā*) and 'five aggregates of clinging' (*pañca upādānakkhandhā*)

The cultivation of mindfulness (*satipaṭṭhāna*) is always related to the five aggregates (*khandha*), namely:

1. materiality (*rūpa*)
2. feeling (*vedanā*)
3. perception (*saññā*)
4. mental formations (*saṅkhāra*)
5. consciousness (*viññāṇa*)

It is important to clearly distinguish between the five aggregates (*khandha*) and the five aggregates of clinging (*upādānakkhandha*). When contemplating the five aggregates (*khandha*), the meditator should clearly see and understand materiality (*rūpa*) and feeling (*vedanā*), how they are grasped by perception (*saññā*), how various intentions (*cetanā*) and other mental formations (*saṅkhāra*) arise and connect with feeling (*vedanā*) and perception (*saññā*), how consciousness (*viññāṇa*) emerges and how the whole group of aggregates immediately ceases, only to be instantly followed by another set of aggregates (*khandha*). If the meditator understands the five aggregates (*khandha*) as such and comprehends how they arise and pass away, then this contemplation takes place in the domain of phenomena (*dhammānupassanā*).

Instead, we usually cling to the five aggregates (*upādānakkhandha*), which allows the defilements (*kilesa*) and fetters (*saṃyojana*) to arise and proliferate. For example, the meditator looks at her or his leg; if there is any idea of an 'I,' then the leg becomes 'my' leg, which is perceived as an object of craving (*taṇhā*)[53] and clinging (*upādāna*), while this perception (*saññā*) itself takes place within 'myself.' The same applies to feeling (*vedanā*), perception (*saññā*), mental formations (*saṅkhāra*) and consciousness (*viññāṇa*); within the domain of the five aggregates (*khandha*), the internal 'I' and 'my' can arise in relation to any of them. This is how we tend to spend our lives without realising that through clinging (*upādāna*) to the five aggregates (*khandha*), we continuously create an 'I' (*aham*), 'mine' (*mama*) and 'myself' (*me attā*). To give another example, when clinging (*upādāna*) to an object like a book, the associated feeling (*vedanā*), perception (*saññā*) and mental formations (*saṅkhāra*) create the idea of 'my book.' The idea of my book does not arise in the book itself but within myself; in other words, feeling (*vedanā*), perception (*saññā*) and mental formations (*saṅkhāra*) trigger the arising of consciousness (*viññāṇa*) with the idea of 'my book.' Thus, consciousness (*viññāṇa*) is not something that was previously there; there is always a new occurrence of it that arises due to the four other aggregates. If there is nothing that is called an 'I,' how can there be an external object called 'my?' If there is nothing called 'I,' how could a feeling (*vedanā*) remain 'mine'? Only through

53. Pāli texts often link the idea 'mine' (*mama*) to craving (*taṇhā*); for example, see the *Sāratthappakāsinī* (Spk II 215)

clear comprehension (*sampajañña*) can the meditator perceive an object without an 'I' (*aham*), 'mine' (*mama*) and 'myself' (*me attā*), and it is then viewed as neither internal nor external.

The meditator contemplates the five aggregates of clinging (*upādānakkhandha*) by clearly comprehending (*pajānāti*) how the aggregates (*khandha*) arise, how each of them functions and how they are by nature impermanent (*anicca*), unsatisfactory (*dukkha*) and without self (*anattā*). The impermanence (*anicca*) of the five aggregates (*khandha*) is frequently emphasised in the *suttas*, especially in the *Khandhasaṃyutta* (S III 1–188). The texts often begin with the Buddha asking his audience whether the aggregates (*khandha*) are permanent or not;[54] when the audience replies that they are impermanent (*anicca*), he outlines their nature as having three characteristics (*tilakkhaṇa*).[55] The Pāli texts frequently highlight that by seeing impermanence (*anicca*), the meditator also sees the two other characteristics (*lakkhaṇa*).[56] When the meditator gains an initial insight into the impermanence (*anicca*) of the five aggregates (*khandha*), she or he understands that the belief in permanence always entails suffering (*dukkha*). With such an insight, the meditator begins to comprehend the selfless nature (*anattā*) of all five aggregates (*khandha*).

People who do not meditate can observe only the more obvious, evident or apparent changes (*vipariṇāma*)[57] in themselves and their environment. Such apparent changes (*vipariṇāma*) occur due to the impermanence (*anicca*) of the five aggregates; this is why impermanence (*anicca*) is listed as the first of the three characteristics (*tilakkhaṇa*) to be observed by the meditator. Yet observing apparent changes (*vipariṇāma*) and contemplating impermanence (*anicca*) are two different things. One can begin by seeing apparent changes (*vipariṇāma*) in the surrounding world, but it is only by cultivating the four foundations of mindfulness (*satipaṭṭhāna*) that an insight into the more subtle impermanence (*anicca*) of the five aggregates (*khandha*) can arise. This insight brings about an understanding that we actually create or condition the five aggre-

54. See, for example, the *Soṇasutta* (S III 49) and *Piṇḍolyasutta* (S III 94).

55. Impermanence (*anicca*) is listed in many *suttas* as the first of the three characteristics (*tilakkhaṇa*) of the five aggregates (*khandha*); for example, in the *Aniccavagga* of the *Khandhasaṃyutta* (S III 21–25), it is said that understanding the impermanence (*anicca*) of the five aggregates leads to weariness and dispassion towards them and (consequently) to liberation (S III 21: *Rūpam bhikkhave aniccaṃ. Vedanā aniccā. Saññā aniccā. Saṅkhārā aniccā. Viññāṇaṃ aniccaṃ. Evam passam bhikkhave sutavā ariyasāvako rūpasmim pi nibbindati. Vedanāya pi nibbindati. Saññāya pi nibbindati. Saṅkhāresu pi nibbindati. Viññāṇasmim pi nibbindati. Nibbindaṃ virajjati virāgā vimuccati vimuttasmiṃ vimuttam iti ñāṇaṃ hoti. Khīṇā jāti vusitaṃ brahmacariyaṃ kataṃ karaṇīyaṃ nāparam itthattāyāti pajānātīti*). The *sutta* then continues with the same presentation for the understanding of suffering (*dukkha*) and non-self (*anattā*). See also S III 94; S III 104.

56. For example, in the *Aniccatāsutta* of the *Attadīpavagga*, each aggregate is said to be impermanent (*anicca*), and what is impermanent is unsatisfactory (*dukkha*) and what is unsatisfactory is non-self (*anattā*) (S III 44–45: *Rūpam bhikkhave aniccam, yad aniccaṃ taṃ dukkhaṃ, yaṃ dukkhaṃ tad anattā*). See also S III 88; S III 180–181.

57. The term *vipariṇāma* is presented in the *Sammohavinodanī* as one of the four facets in the contemplation of impermanence (*anicca*), because of: (1) arising and passing away (*uppādavaya*), (2) change (*vipariṇāma*), (3) temporariness (*tāvakālika*) and (4) absence of permanence (*niccapaṭikkhepa*) (Vibh-a 48: *Aparehipi catūhi kāraṇehi aniccaṃ—uppādavayavantato, vipariṇāmato, tāvakālikato, niccapaṭikkhepatoti*). In the *Visuddhimagga*, the term *vipariṇāma* is one of the aspects of 'passing away' (*vaya*), which encompasses the characteristics of change (*vipariṇāmalakkhaṇa*), decay (*khaya*) and dissolution (*bhaṅga*) (Vism 360: *nibbattilakkhaṇaṃ jātiṃ uppādaṃ abhinavākāraṃ udayo ti: vipariṇāmalakkhaṇaṃ khayaṃ bhaṅgaṃ vayo ti samanupassati*). *Vipariṇāma* is also often linked to suffering (*dukkha*); thus, for example, in the *Saṅgītisutta*, it is listed as one of the three kinds of suffering: (1) suffering in relation to change (*vipariṇāmadukkhatā*), (2) suffering in relation to pain (*dukkhadukkhatā*) and (3) suffering in relation to mental formations (*saṅkhāradukkhatā*) (D III 216: *Tisso dukkhatā. Dukkhadukkhatā, saṅkhāradukkhatā, vipariṇāmadukkhatā*). Cf Vibh-a 93; Vism 499.

gates (*khandha*) throughout our lives and then complain about the ensuing suffering (*dukkha*). When suffering (*dukkha*) is experienced as in the case of a minor illness, we want to be well again, because we cling to the five aggregates (*khandha*). But if the suffering is really great, when we are severely sick, for example, we may want to die, to be rid of the five aggregates (*khandha*). Some people even commit suicide. In the Buddhist texts, there are accounts of monks killing themselves,[58] but in this case, rebirth would ensue and suffering (*dukkha*) would not cease. Both approaches, namely, clinging (*upādāna*) and aversion (*dosa*) to the five aggregates (*khandha*), are due to a lack of understanding and wisdom (*paññā*). The five aggregates are produced by ignorance (*avijjā*) and cannot be maintained in the way that we want, as there is no intrinsic self that can control them. Therefore, liberation from suffering results from an understanding of non-self (*anattā*), which arises through wisdom (*paññā*) by clearly comprehending the three characteristics (*tilakkhaṇa*) of all phenomena (*dhamma*).

'Materiality' (*rūpa*)[59]

The term 'materiality' (*rūpa*)[60] refers to the four elements and their various combinations. The materiality aggregate (*rūpakkhandha*) consists of twenty-seven material categories or phenomena (*rūpadhamma*), which include the four great elements (*mahādhātu*) and twenty-three secondary or derived material categories (*upādāyarūpa*).[61] Materiality (*rūpa*) occurs due to four conditions, namely, *kamma*, the mind (*citta*), temperature (*utu*) and nutriment (*āhāra*).[62] It conditions and is conditioned by ignorance (*avijjā*) and craving (*taṇhā*). Materiality (*rūpa*) conditions the arising of *kamma* and the mind (*citta*), which in turn condition, yet again, the emergence of ignorance (*avijjā*) and craving (*taṇhā*) and generate further arisings of the four elements (*mahādhātu*). Thus, these processes involving ignorance (*avijjā*), craving (*taṇhā*), *kamma* and materiality (*rūpa*) go on and on.[63]

If the meditator clearly observes and comprehends how materiality (*rūpa*) arises (*samudaya*) and passes away (*atthagama*), her or his meditation is in the domain of the contemplation of the materiality aggregate (*rūpakkhandha*). Even in the contemplation of the body (*kāyānupassanā*), the aim is not to know the various aspects of the body as such but to cultivate mindfulness (*sati*) and clear comprehension (*sampajañña*) and see the impermanence (*anicca*) of phenomena such as the five aggregates (*khandha*), elements (*dhātu*) and sense spheres (*āyatana*).

58. See, for example, the *Vesālīsutta* (S V 320–322).

59. Materiality or matter (*rūpa*) is discussed in relation to the four elements in Chapter II.5. Reflection on the four elements (*catudhātumanasikāra*) above; for a comprehensive study of the Theravāda analysis of materiality, see Karunadasa (1967).

60. The term *rūpa* can refer to any kind of materiality (e.g., S II 252, IV 382), including the physical body. It is thus defined in the *Visuddhimagga*: 'Materiality comprises the four great elements and the materiality derived from clinging to the four great elements' (Vism 558: *Rūpan ti cattāri mahābhūtāni catunnañ ca mahābhūtānaṃ upādāya rūpaṃ*).

61. The four great elements (*mahādhātu*) are the earth element (*paṭhavīdhātu*), water element (*āpodhātu*), fire element (*tejodhātu*) and air element (*vāyodhātu*). The Theravāda *Abhidhamma* texts classify twenty-seven material phenomena (*rūpadhamma*) (Vibh 12–14; Dhs 124–179), whereas post-canonical texts speak of twenty-eight, adding the heart base (*hadayavatthu*) as another derived materiality. For a comprehensive survey of materiality, see the *Visuddhimagga* (Vism 443–452).

62. See Chapter II.5. Reflection on the four elements (*catudhātumanasikāra*) above.

63. Here Pemasiri Thera refers to dependent origination (*paṭiccasamuppāda*) while highlighting the following components: (1) ignorance (*avijjā*) (2) mental formations (*saṅkhāra*) (3) consciousness (*viññāṇa*) (4) mentality and materiality (*nāmarūpa*) (8) craving (*taṅhā*). (S II 1).

If the meditator does not experience phenomena (*dhamma*) in this manner but is instead only aware of the various material processes, it may be said that she or he 'abides in the body' (*kāyasmiṃ viharati*) but does not abide contemplating (*anupassī*) the body. The contemplation of materiality (*rūpa*) in its impermanence (*anicca*) generates the insight that there is no intrinsic self (*anattā*) in the world of materiality (including the body).

'Feeling' (*vedanā*) and 'perception' (*saññā*)

The *sutta* then says that the meditator knows feeling (*vedanā*)[64] and perception (*saññā*)[65] as well as their arising (*samudaya*) and passing away (*atthagama*). Although the five aggregates (*khandha*) are active throughout our lives, when we are born, feeling (*vedanā*) is the most prominent and only later, perhaps after a week or so, does perception (*saññā*) become stronger. At this early stage, feeling (*vedanā*) and perception (*saññā*) are not greatly linked to objects in the infant's environment, and thus the defilements (*kilesa*) are not very active. As the child grows older, however, feeling (*vedanā*) and perception (*saññā*) expand and mental formations (*saṅkhāra*) increase; consequently, memory strengthens. This is why we forget the earliest period of our lives—because at that stage, the mental formations (*saṅkhāra*), which arise based on feeling (*vedanā*) and perception (*saññā*), are very weak. Even though we think that memory is something from the past, it always arises in the present with the perception (*saññā*) of an object. Thus, the experience of remembering starts with a present perception (*saññā*) linked to a past feeling (*vedanā*). In fact, most people live with perceptions (*saññā*) based on feelings (*vedanā*) that have already died, and consequently, they do not know the nature of the mind.

In meditation practice such as the cultivation of mindfulness of breathing (*ānāpānasati*), the meditator does not train to relate or react to various objects arising with feeling (*vedanā*) and perception (*saññā*). When the absorption (*jhāna*) is reached, the meditator is free from connecting with or reacting to objects; at this point, she or he may remember her or his very early childhood or even past lives. In worldly life, it is very difficult for such memories to emerge, because we are continuously associating with all kinds of useless objects, which

64. In the *Mahāvedallasutta*, the term *vedanā* is explained as 'feeling that feels [itself],' indicating that there is no person who feels (M I 293: *Kittāvatā nu kho āvuso vedanā ti vuccatīti? Vedeti vedetīti kho āvuso*). The *sutta* then points out the three types of feeling: pleasant, unpleasant and neither-pleasant-nor-unpleasant (M I 293: *kiñca vedeti: sukham'pi vedeti, dukkham'pi vedeti, adukkhamasukham'pi vedeti*). There are several classifications of feeling (*vedanā*) in the Pāli sources, grouped into two, three, five, six, thirteen, eighty-six or one hundred and eight modalities (see the *Bahuvedanīyasutta*, M I 398; Vibh 15–28; S IV 224). Most commonly, apart from the three types defined in the *Satipaṭṭhānasutta*, feeling (*vedanā*) is classified into six types: pleasant, unpleasant and neither-pleasant-nor-unpleasant in relation to the body or mind (e.g., *Cūḷavedalasutta*, M I 302–303). Six types of feeling are also linked to the six sense doors (e.g., the *Chachakkasutta*, M III 281).

65. The term *saññā* is usually translated as 'perception, discernment, recognition' (PED, *s.v.*) in reference to the recognition of an object; for example, in the case of a visual object, the recognition of colour (M I 293; S III 87). Perception is often classified as sixfold in relation to the six sense doors (*āyatana*) through which the contact is made with objects, resulting in the creation of common designations or conceptual expressions (A III 413: *Katamo ca bhikkhave saññānaṃ vipāko? Vohāravepakkāhaṃ bhikkhave saññā vadāmi; yathā yathā naṃ sañjānāti, tathā tathā voharati 'evaṃ saññī ahosin' ti*). In the *Abhidhamma* texts, perception (*saññā*) is presented as one of the universal mental concomitants (*cetasika*), which is classified in several modalities. For example, in the *Vibhaṅga*, it is presented as:
1) singlefold through its association with contact (*ekavidhena saññākkhandho: phassasampayutto*);
2) threefold (*tividhena saññākkhandha*) as wholesome (*kusala*), unwholesome (*akusala*) or neither (*avyākata*);
3) fivefold (*pañcavidhena saññākkhandha*) in relation to physical pleasure (*sukhindriyasampayutta*), physical pain (*dukkhindriyasampayutta*), mental pleasure (*somanassindriyasampayutta*), mental pain (*domanassindriyasampayutta*) or equanimity (*upekkhindriyasampayutta*) (Vibh 28).

prevents us from grasping the potential of the mind. When experiencing an object through contact (*phassa*), feeling (*vedanā*) and perception (*saññā*), it manifests in such a wide variety of ways because of the mental formations (*saṅkhāra*). In meditation, feeling (*vedanā*) and perception (*saññā*) should ideally trigger fewer and fewer thoughts. Only then do mental formations (*saṅkhāra*) diminish, thus allowing the meditator to do away with old habits, which are actually various groupings of mental formations (*saṅkhāra*). When the meditator is in the absorptions (*jhāna*), old habits can temporarily be forgotten. However, only at path knowledge (*maggañāṇa*) are they completely broken up. Or more precisely, in the first three path knowledges (*maggañāṇa*), some mental formations (*saṅkhāra*) are completely destroyed, while others are simply weakened. At the stage of arahantship, all mental formations (*saṅkhāra*) are completely extinguished except for those that serve as the basis for the continuation of living. Nevertheless, new mental formations (*saṅkhāra*) are no longer formed.[66]

Feeling (*vedanā*) and perception (*saññā*) are mental concomitants (*cetasika*) that are always present. Therefore, it is impossible to make them go away by simply noting them. When the impermanent nature of feeling (*vedanā*) and perception (*saññā*) is clearly seen and comprehended, the two are contemplated at the level of phenomena (*dhammānupassanā*). For example, the meditator notes a sound as it occurs along with a feeling (*vedanā*); if the feeling (*vedanā*) is noted as it emerges and ceases, this means that the meditator knows how the feeling (*vedanā*) arises (*samudaya*) and passes away (*atthagama*), that it is impermanent (*anicca*) and cannot be controlled. It is important not to be deceived by feeling (*vedanā*) and perception (*saññā*), which arise along with objects all the time—when sitting, walking, breathing, eating and in any other situation. This means that the meditator should not latch onto objects, which inevitably keep arising and are cognised along with feeling (*vedanā*) and perception (*saññā*). When feeling (*vedanā*) and perception (*saññā*) function in a pure way, without being clung to and without strongly linking them to mental formations (*saṅkhāra*)—as during insight meditation (*vipassanā*)—clear comprehension (*sampajañña*) and wisdom (*paññā*) can emerge; this is why many *suttas* narrate how the Buddha uttered just a few words or gave very brief instructions, with some listeners immediately grasping his teachings.[67]

When there is clinging to feeling (*vedanā*) and perception (*saññā*), mental formations (*saṅkhāra*) are formed in a great variety of ways. Such formations are related to *kamma*, a kind of energetic impulse, triggered by feeling (*vedanā*) and perception (*saññā*).[68] *Kamma* is like the

---

66. Here Pemasiri Thera refers to dependent origination (*paṭiccasamuppāda*), which lies at the core of the Buddhist teachings (e.g., as explained in the *Mahāhatthipadopamasutta*, M I 190–191). Only after attaining arahantship does one become free from the initial link in the formula of dependent origination (*paṭiccasamuppāda*), namely, ignorance (*avijjā*), which conditions the arising of mental formations (*saṅkhāra*). For further details, see the *Nidānasaṃyutta* (S II 1–131).

67. There are many such accounts in the *suttas*. Apart from the abovementioned story of the ascetic Bāhiya (Ud 8), the *Dhammacakkapavattanasutta* (S V 420–424), *Anattalakkhaṇasutta* (S III 66–67) and many other texts describe how some (or all) of the listeners achieved arahantship or at least one of the stages of awakening at the end of the Buddha's discourse.

68. *Kamma* is explained in the *Mahāvagga* as volition or intention (*cetanā*) on which one acts with the body, speech or mind (A III 415: *Cetanāhaṃ bhikkhave kammaṃ vadāmi; cetayitvā kammaṃ karoti kāyena vācāya manasā*). The *Saḷāyatanasaṃyutta* explains that the six senses result from previous *kamma* generated by volition (S IV 132: *abhisaṅkhato abhisañcetayito*), while new *kamma* relates to present actions with the body, speech or mind (S IV 132: *Yaṃ kho bhikkhave etarahi kammaṃ karoti kāyena vācāya manasā idam vuccati bhikkhave navakammaṃ*). Thus, *kamma* is usually presented as one of the causes that leads beings to have different births in different realms or different circumstances, since past actions are believed to condition future results. For a discourse

remote control of a television: when the right conditions come together, one can watch things on the screen; but without a television, there is no opportunity to watch the programme. In other words, to activate *kamma,* several causes and conditions have to be present. In the practice of insight meditation (*vipassanā*), when the meditator sees and clearly comprehends causes and effects, *kamma* cannot connect with the arising phenomena, and consequently, no future *kamma* is generated. This does not mean that the meditator has destroyed the past *kamma* but only that no new *kamma* is created.

There is no mental state (apart from *nibbāna*) without feeling (*vedanā*) and perception (*saññā*); they are present at every moment and cannot be removed from any experience. Normally, throughout our lives, we link feeling (*vedanā*) to aversion (*dosa*) or greed (*lobha*), believing that feeling (*vedanā*) is a 'self' or that 'I am feeling.' This is where the problems stem from: our sadness, sorrow or suffering (*dukkha*) arise, because we mentally hold onto feeling (*vedanā*). But there is really no 'self' or 'I' in the process of feeling and perceiving; there is nothing that is 'mine' or belongs to 'me.' If the meditator can become free from this idea of 'I am feeling this feeling,' then she or he will no longer feel aversion (*dosa*) towards an unpleasant feeling or crave for a pleasant feeling.

'Mental formations' (*saṅkhāra*) and 'consciousness' (*viññāṇa*)

The last two aggregates (*khandha*) in this section of the *Satipaṭṭhānasutta* are mental formations (*saṅkhāra*)[69] and consciousness (*viññāṇa*).[70] The meditator is instructed to know them and

on the functioning of *kamma* and rebirth, see, for example, the *Cūḷakammavibhaṅgasutta* (M III 203–206) or *Mahākammavibhaṅgasutta* (M III 207–215).

69. The term *saṅkhāra* has a wide range of meanings and occurs in many contexts, which makes its translation into English particularly problematic. Here the commonly accepted rendering into modern English as 'mental formation(s)' is followed, although it should be stressed that any English equivalent is inadequate for expressing the wide semantic range of this key Pāli word. In the *Khajjanīyasutta* of the *Khandhasaṃyutta*, it is said that mental formations (*saṅkhāra*) generate what is conditioned or compounded (*saṅkhata*) (S III 87: *Saṅkhataṃ abhisaṅkharontīti tasmā saṅkhārā ti vuccanti*), which is comprised of the five aggregates (S III 87); thus, *saṅkhāras* generate or produce conditioned phenomena. According to the formula of dependent origination (*paṭiccasamuppāda*), mental formations (*saṅkhāra*) are positioned as the second link between ignorance (*avijjā*) and consciousness (*viññāṇa*): (1) ignorance (*avijjā*) (2) mental formations (*saṅkhāra*) (3) consciousness (*viññāṇa*) (S II 1). *Saṅkhāra* is often defined as volition (*cetanā*). For example, the *Vibhaṅga* states that *saṅkhāra* is 'volition, being volitional or in a volitional state' (Vibh 173:*Tattha katamo saṅkhāro? Yā cetanā sañcetanā sañcetayitattaṃ: ayaṃ vuccati saṅkhāro*). It can be classified in several ways. For example, in the *Vibhaṅga* it is presented as:
(1) singlefold through its association with the mind (Vibh 72: *Ekavidhena saṅkhārakkhandho: cittasampayutto*); or
(2) threefold by being wholesome, unwholesome or neither (Vibh 72: *Tividhena saṅkhārakkhandho: atthi kusalo, atthi akusalo, atthi avyākato*).

70. The term *viññāṇa* is usually translated as 'consciousness' (PED, *s.v.*). In addition to referring to one of the five aggregates (*khandha*), it is frequently used in relation to the six spheres (*āyatana*), which represent the component of cognition that cognises the sense object arising at a particular sense door (as explained in the *Mahāhatthipadopamasutta* (M I 190)). According to the formula of dependent origination (*paṭiccasamuppāda*), it is positioned as the third link between mental formations (*saṅkhāra*) and mentality-materiality (*nāmarūpa*) (S II 1). It is said that consciousness (*viññāṇa*) conditions mentality-materiality (*nāmarūpa*) and is also conditioned by them (S II 113: *nāmarūpaṃ apica viññāṇapaccayā nāmarūpanti ... viññāṇam api ca nāmarūpapaccayā viññāṇanti*).
In the *Abhidhamma* texts, it is classified in several ways. For example, the *Vibhaṅga* defines it as:
1) singlefold through its association with contact (*phassasampayutto*);
2) threefold by being wholesome (*kusala*), unwholesome (*akusala*) or neither (*avyākata*); and
3) fivefold when associated with physical pleasure (*sukhindriyasampayutta*), physical pain (*dukkhindriya-*

understand their arising (*samudaya*) and passing away (*atthagama*), or in other words, to contemplate their impermanence (*anicca*). Mental formations (*saṅkhāra*) are related to *kamma*. We cannot say where *kamma* is nor what it is nor how it works; it is neither a state of mind (*citta*) nor materiality (*rūpa*) nor a mental concomitant (*cetasika*),[71] but it is a kind of impulse that arises, triggered by these three categories. It is like lightening, a burst of energy that we see as light when the explosion takes place; the light reaches us even before we know what has really happened. There is no entity called 'lightening,' although we see its results, as it can kill someone or destroy a building. We cannot experience or see how the light is conditioned by the explosion of energy nor how the resultant damage is related to that energy: we only see the light and the ensuing damage. This is how *kamma* works: for example, at the moment when something occurs, the cognition of it is comparable to the light at the time of the explosion of energy—we recognise it when it has already been generated. Only when all the necessary conditions are present can old or resultant *kamma* manifest; otherwise, it cannot be said that old *kamma* exists in the mind or anywhere else.

People often say that whatever happens to them, especially when it is unpleasant, is the result of past *kamma*. However, not everything that happens to us can be put down to *kamma* and its results (*vipāka*). The *Sīvakasutta* (S IV 230–231) narrates how the Buddha opposes the view that all experiences are caused by what was done in the past (*pubbbakatahetuvāda*) and explains that *kamma* is only one of the following eight explanations for the unpleasant things experienced by people:

1. bile disorders
2. phlegm disorders
3. wind disorders
4. imbalance [of the three]
5. change of climate
6. careless behaviour
7. assault
8. the result of *kamma*[72]

Kamma cannot be eradicated as indicated in the *Devadahasutta* (M II 214–228), where the Buddha disputes the Jain view that all past *kamma* can be exhausted. According to the Buddhist teachings, *kamma* can be prevented from arising through the attainment of path knowledge (*maggañāṇa*). When the meditator realises *nibbāna*, her or his *kamma* cannot be activated, since craving (*taṅhā*), conceit (*māna*) or views (*diṭṭhi*) are absent; in other words, there are no conditions for the arising of *kamma*. The results of *kamma* (*vipāka*) only appear when craving (*taṅhā*), conceit (*māna*) or views (*diṭṭhi*) are present; what we call the result of past *kamma* is actually the present situation that involves these three unwholesome states.

sampayutta), mental pleasure (*somanassindriyasampayutta*), mental pain (*domanassindriyasampayutta*) or equanimity (*upekkhindriyasampayutta*) (Vibh 53–54).

71. In other words, in the *Abhidhamma* literature, *kamma* is not given as one of the components of experiences (*dhammas*) that represent ultimate reality (*paramattha*)—i.e., the mind (*citta*), mental concomitants (*cetasika*), materiality (*rūpa*) and *nibbāna*—nor is it one of the five aggregates (*khandha*).

72. S IV 230–231: *Pittasamuṭṭhānāni pi kho Sīvaka idhekaccāni vedayitāni uppajjanti ... Semhasamuṭṭhānāni ... Vātasamuṭṭhānāni ... Sannipātikāni ... Utupariṇāmajāni ... Visamaparihārajāni ... Opakkamikāni ... Kammavipākajāni pi kho Sīvaka idhekaccāni vedayitāni uppajjanti.*

The concept of *kamma* is related to volition (*cetanā*), perception (*saññā*) and feeling (*vedanā*). Every action (i.e., mental, verbal or bodily) involves volition (*cetanā*), which is a mental concomitant (*cetasika*) that arises at various strengths with every mind-moment (*citta*). *Kamma* does not occur with every volition (*cetanā*) but only when perception (*saññā*) and feeling (*vedanā*) are sufficiently strong to constitute mental formations (*saṅkhāra*) in conjunction with other mental concomitants (*cetasika*). For example, if volition (*cetanā*) arises along with greed (*lobha*), aversion (*dosa*) or delusion (*moha*), then this group of mental concomitants (*cetasika*) is called a mental formation (*saṅkhāra*). In this case, we could say that *kamma* was created.[73] Thus, *kamma*, whether wholesome or unwholesome, only arises under certain conditions. For example, we can combine certain chemicals and create a toxic substance, but if the same chemicals were combined in a different manner and proportion, a good substance such as medicine could be created.

To restate this, depending on the intensity of action (*kamma*), mental formations (*saṅkhāra*) are formed; if volition (*cetanā*) is strong, it produces mental formations (*saṅkhāra*). But if volition (*cetanā*) is weak, it does not create any action (*kamma*), or in other words, it does not build up to a sufficient intensity to generate mental formations (*saṅkhāra*); otherwise, it would be impossible to live if every volition (*cetanā*) produced *kamma*. Volition (*cetanā*), present in every mind-moment (*citta*), is not very strong by itself, but if it becomes stronger due to the strength of feeling (*vedanā*) and perception (*saññā*), it may result in *kamma*, thus creating mental formations (*saṅkhāra*), which are comprised of various groups of mental concomitants (*cetasikas*). Only in the *arahant*'s mind are mental formations (*saṅkhāra*) not created, and thus no results ensue; this is why her or his mind is called 'indeterminate' (*avyākata*).

A mental formation (*saṅkhāra*) is neither a state of mind (*citta*) nor a mental concomitant (*cetasika*)—just as ignorance (*avijjā*) is neither. However, it is a condition for the arising of mental states. Mental formation (*saṅkhāra*) generally means any kind of assembled formation,[74] but in the context of dependent origination (*paṭiccasamuppāda*), it specifically refers to volition (*cetanā*). Because of ignorance (*avijjā*), various wholesome (*kusala*) or unwholesome (*akusala*) mental concomitants (*cetasikas*) occur. When these mental concomitants (*cetasika*) arise along with an intention or volition (*cetanā*) to act (through the body, speech or mind) in a wholesome or unwholesome manner, this group of concomitants is called a mental formation (*saṅkhāra*). When the mental formation (*saṅkhāra*) arises, it is always accompanied by feeling (*vedanā*) and perception (*saññā*), since both are universal concomitants, present in every mind-moment (*citta*).[75]

73. As explained in the *Kammasutta*, there are four kinds of *kamma*: 'Monks, there is dark *kamma* with dark results, bright *kamma* with bright results, dark-and-bright *kamma* with dark-and-bright results (*kaṇhasukkavipāka*) and neither-dark-nor-bright *kamma* with neither-dark-nor-bright results (*akaṇha-asukkavipāka*), [with the last one] leading to the destruction of *kamma*' (A II 230: *Atthi bhikkhave kammaṃ kaṇhaṃ kaṇhavipākaṃ, atthi bhikkhave kammaṃ sukkaṃ sukkavipākaṃ, atthi bhikkhave kammaṃ kaṇhasukkaṃ kaṇhasukkavipākaṃ, atthi bhikkhave kammaṃ akaṇhamasukkaṃ akaṇha-asukkavipākaṃ kammaṃ kammakkhayāya saṃvattati*.)

74. The aggregate of mental formations (*saṅkhārakkhandha*) is presented in the *Visuddhimagga* thus: 'Whatever has the characteristic of forming, all taken together' (Vism 462: *yaṃ kiñci abhisankharaṇalakkhaṇaṃ sabban taṃ ekato katvā sankhārakkhandho*).

75. Here Pemasiri Thera correlates two prevalent models of cognitive processes presented in the Pāli canon: on the one hand, the five aggregates (*khandha*)—i.e., materiality (*rūpa*), feeling (*vedanā*), perception (*saññā*), mental formations (*saṅkhāra*) and consciousness (*viññāṇa*)—and on the other, the Abhidhammic model of the four categories of *dhammas*—i.e., the mind (*citta*), mental concomitants (*cetasika*), materiality (*rūpa*) and *nibbāna*. The fifty-two mental concomitants (*cetasika*) from the Abhidhammic model correspond to the three components of the five aggregates model, namely, feeling (*vedanā*), perception (*saññā*) and mental formations

In the formula of dependent origination (*paṭiccasamuppāda*), mental formations (*saṅkhāra*) condition consciousness (*viññāṇa*). Consciousness (*viññāṇa*) is thus the result of preceding causes and conditions, which in turn further conditions the arising of other phenomena. Consciousness (*viññāṇa*) is not stable, lasting or permanent; as soon as it arises, it ceases, not lasting for even a fraction of a second. It is not a person, an 'I' that would remain there for life. It cannot be located in any place, and it does not belong to any object that it cognises.

Consciousness (*viññāṇa*) is like a seed that falls off a stalk. At first, the fallen seed is the cause of something new: it sprouts roots, shoots and then leaves. For its growth, it requires many conditions such as soil, water, sunlight and the work of the farmer. Then the plant produces new seeds but as long as they are still on the plant, they are still connected to the cause. Only when the seed falls to the ground does it become a result (*phala*). In the same way, consciousness (*viññāṇa*) is a result or effect of the preceding causes and conditions. Causes and conditions are two different things; for example, the cause of a person is her or his mother—the person was born thanks to the mother—but in order to grow up, numerous conditions are necessary. Similarly, the root cause of consciousness is volition (*cetanā*). This is expressed in the formula of dependent origination (*paṭiccasamuppāda*) in the following way:

> (1) ignorance (*avijjā*)→(2) mental formations (*saṅkhāra*)→(3) consciousness (*viññāṇa*)→(4) mentality and materiality (*nāmarūpa*)→(5) sense bases (*saḷāyatana*)→(6) contact (*phassa*)→(7) feeling (*vedanā*)→(8) craving (*taṅhā*)→(9) clinging (*upādāna*)→(10) becoming (*bhava*)→(11) birth (*jāti*)→(12) ageing, death, suffering, lamentation, pain, displeasure and despair (*jarāmaraṇaṃ sokaparidevadukkhadomanassupāyāsā*).[76]

Thus, consciousness (*viññāṇa*) is the condition for the arising of mentality and materiality (*nāmarūpa*), but to maintain mentality and materiality (*nāmarūpa*), consciousness (*viññāṇa*) also has to be their cause. Consciousness (*viññāṇa*) has both functions, but at the same time, it is not something that is really anywhere, since it arises and ceases instantly; after arising, it has to cease immediately in order for the other four aggregates to arise again. As consciousness (*viññāṇa*) instantly breaks off, how do we remember things from the past? How does memory function? On what is it based? As said before, mental formations (*saṅkhāra*) are the condition for consciousness (*viññāṇa*); therefore, mental formations (*saṅkhāra*) allow or make it possible for memory to occur. For example, an object with which one makes contact (*phassa*) in the present moment causes consciousness (*viññāṇa*) to arise in relation to something that no longer exists. The condition here is the past object or experience. However, when we say that we remember, this memory is actually the ceasing moment of consciousness (*viññāṇa*) in the present moment. Modern science says that memory is located in a certain area of the brain, but from the Buddhist perspective, there is no place where memory is stored.[77] When conditions and causes come together in the present moment, an experience can occur that we link to the past. If contact (*phassa*) with a certain object does not provide this impulse, it is not possible for a past experience to appear, which means that it is simply not there. Only because of the contact (*phassa*) with an object in the present, which arises along with feeling (*vedanā*),

(*saṅkhāra*). Thus, a total of fifty mental concomitants (*cetasika*) can be situated within the aggregate of mental formation (*saṅkhārakhandha*), whereas the mental concomitants of feeling (*vedanā*) and perception (*saññā*) correspond to the aggregate of feeling (*vedanākhandha*) and the aggregate of perception (*saññākhandha*), respectively.

76. For details on dependent origination (*paṭiccasamuppāda*), see the *Nidānasaṃyutta* (S II 1–131).

77. For an overview of the Buddhist perspective of memory and mindfulness, see Gyatso (1992).

perception (*saññā*) and volition (*cetanā*), do we think and talk about memory—although there is nothing there in reality that could be called consciousness (*viññāṇa*) or mental formation (*saṅkhāra*) or memory.[78]

As long as ignorance (*avijjā*) is present, mental formations (*saṅkhāra*) and consciousness (*viññāṇa*) can arise and becoming (*bhava*) (i.e., the tenth link of dependent origination) may ensue. Becoming (*bhava*) refers to the process by which things continue to happen again and again, in this life as well as from one life to another. People assume that there is an entity or a soul that goes from this life to another, because they believe that consciousness (*viññāṇa*) endures—this is called personality view (*sakkāyadiṭṭhi*).[79] If the idea of an entity called 'I' is created and one holds onto it, then questions and doubts about past, present and future births are generated. Because of the idea of an 'I,' people meditate: they aim to eradicate this 'I.' But since there is no 'I' or 'self' in the first place, who then is this 'I' that the meditator is trying to extinguish?

For the idea of an 'I' to occur, the so-called 'taints' (*āsava*)[80] must be present, comprising:

1. taint of sense desire (*kāmāsava*)
2. taint of becoming (*bhavāsava*)
3. taint of views (*diṭṭhāsava*)
4. taint of ignorance (*avijjāsava*)[81]

The taints (*āsava*) condition ignorance (*avijjā*), belief in future lives, becoming (*bhava*) and re-becoming (*punarbhava*). Notwithstanding the speculations about the future or the past, the sense of 'I' continues to arise now, in the present life, from moment to moment; therefore, if one pays full attention to this and sees what is truly happening in the present moment, then questions about past or future lives will not occur at all.

V 3 Six sense spheres (*cha āyatanāni*)

Puna ca paraṃ bhikkhave bhikkhu dhammesu dhammānupassī viharati chasu ajjhattikabāhiresu ***āyatanesu.*** *Kathañca bhikkhave bhikkhu dhammesu dhammānupassī viharati chasu ajjhattikabāhiresu āyatanesu? Idha bhikkhave bhikkhu cakkhuñca pajānāti rūpe ca pajānāti, yañca tadubhayaṃ paṭicca uppajjati* ***saṃyojanaṃ*** *tañca pajānāti, yathā ca anuppannassa saṃyojanassa uppādo hoti tañca pajānāti,*

78. Here Pemasiri Thera discusses the process of memory in relation to consciousness (*viññāṇa*) and mental formations (*saṅkhāra*) from the perspective of non-self (*anattā*): it is only after gaining deep insight into the empty nature of the five aggregates (*khandha*), their impermanence and non-substantiality that the meditator can see consciousness (*viññāṇa*) as a series of fleeting moments that are intrinsically empty. Consequently, she or he clearly comprehends that there is no time—no past, no future and also no present—and thus, there is intrinsically no consciousness (*viññāṇa*) or mental formation (*saṅkhāra*). It may be argued that the Buddhist teachings, especially the *Abhidhamma* texts, are primarily founded on and presented from the perspective of non-self (*anattā*). Therefore, what is ordinarily called 'memory' is ultimately viewed as nothing but phenomena occurring along with the fleeting moments of cognition.
79. *Sakkāyadiṭṭhi* is a belief that the five aggregates (*khandha*) constitute a 'self,' that there is a permanent entity or individuality that continues to be reborn; for example, the view that any of the five aggregates (*khandha*) is a 'self' is expounded in the *Cūḷavellasutta* (M I 300) and *Upādāparitassanāsutta* (S III 16).
80. The term 'taint' (*āsava*) refers to the predispositions that obstruct liberation and prompt further existence (see DP; PED, *s.v.*). According to the *Atthasālinī*, the term *āsava* refers to deeply rooted corruptions, defilements or 'intoxicants' that flow from the senses and the mind (As 48: *Āsavagocchake āsavantī ti āsavā. Cakkhuto pi...pe... manato pi sandanti pavattantī ti vuttaṃ hoti*). In the *Sammādiṭṭhisutta*, it is said that ignorance (*avijjā*) arises with the arising of the taints (*āsava*) (M I 54: *āsavasamudayā avijjāsamudayo*).
81. These four taints (*āsava*) are listed in many instances in the *Tipiṭaka*; for example, in the *Mahāparinibbānasutta* (D II 81) and *Dhammasaṅgaṇi* (Dhs 195).

yathā ca uppannassa saṃyojanassa pahānaṃ hoti tañca pajānāti, yathā ca pahīnassa saṃyojanassa āyatiṃ anuppādo hoti tañca pajānāti; sotañca pajānāti sadde ca pajānāti ... ghānañca pajānāti gandhe ca pajānāti ... jivhañca pajānāti rase ca pajānāti ... kāyañca pajānāti phoṭṭhabbe ca pajānāti ... manañca pajānāti dhamme ca pajānāti, yañca tadubhayaṃ paṭicca uppajjati saṃyojanaṃ tañca pajānāti, yathā ca anuppannassa saṃyojanassa uppādo hoti tañca pajānāti, yathā ca uppannassa saṃyojanassa pahānaṃ hoti tañca pajānāti, yathā ca pahīnassa saṃyojanassa āyatiṃ anuppādo hoti tañca pajānāti.

'And again, monks, a monk abides contemplating phenomena as phenomena in regard to the six internal and external **sense spheres**. And how does a monk abide contemplating phenomena as phenomena in regard to the six internal and external sense spheres? Here, monks, a monk knows the eye, he knows forms and he knows the **fetter** that arises dependent on both; and he also knows how there comes to be the arising of the unarisen fetter, and how there comes to be the abandoning of the arisen fetter, and how there comes to be the future non-arising of the abandoned fetter. He knows the ear, he knows sounds ... He knows the nose, he knows odours ... He knows the tongue, he knows flavours ... He knows the body, he knows tangibles ... He knows the mind, he knows mental phenomena and he knows the fetter that arises dependent on both; and he also knows how there comes to be the arising of the unarisen fetter, and how there comes to be the abandoning of the arisen fetter, and how there comes to be the future non-arising of the abandoned fetter.'

Recurring passage indicating the ways to approach the contemplation[82]

Iti ajjhattaṃ vā dhammesu dhammānupassī viharati, bahiddhā vā dhammesu dhammānupassī viharati, ajjhattabahiddhā vā dhammesu dhammānupassī viharati. Samudayadhammānupassī vā dhammesu viharati, vayadhammānupassī vā dhammesu viharati, samudayavayadhammānupassī vā dhammesu viharati. Atthi dhammā ti vā panassa sati paccupaṭṭhitā hoti yāvadeva ñāṇamattāya patissatimattāya, anissito ca viharati na ca kiñci loke upādiyati. Evam kho bhikkhave bhikkhu dhammesu dhammānupassī viharati chasu ajjhattikabāhiresu āyatanesu.

'Thus he abides contemplating phenomena as phenomena internally, or he abides contemplating phenomena as phenomena externally, or he abides contemplating phenomena as phenomena both internally and externally. He abides contemplating the arising of phenomena in phenomena, or he abides contemplating the passing away of phenomena in phenomena, or he abides contemplating both the arising and passing away of phenomena in phenomena. Or, mindfulness that "there are phenomena" is established in him just to the extent necessary for knowledge and mindfulness. And he abides without attachment, not clinging to anything in the world. Monks, thus a monk abides contemplating phenomena as phenomena in regard to the six internal and external sense spheres. Monks, thus a monk abides contemplating phenomena as phenomena in regard to the six internal and external sense spheres.'

Pemasiri Thera's commentary

'Sense spheres' (*āyatana*)

According to the *Satipaṭṭhānasutta*, the next domain for the contemplation of phenomena (*dhammānupassanā*) is 'in regard to the six internal and external sense spheres' (*chasu ajjhattikabāhiresu āyatanesu*). Even for an experienced meditator, it is extremely difficult to clearly understand what a sense sphere (*āyatana*) is. The term *āyatana* generally refers to a place where

82. For comments on the recurring passage, see Chapter II.1, under the subheading 'Recurring passage indicating the ways to approach the contemplation.'

something is produced, developed or increased.[83] When the term is used in the sense of 'sense sphere,' it signifies the place where the fetters (*saṃyojana*) are produced. When we say that we are living, it actually means that we are continuously producing fetters (*saṃyojana*), which keep arising through the sense spheres (*āyatana*).[84] The sense spheres (*āyatana*) comprise the six sense organs and their respective objects: (1) eye (*cakkhu*) and visible form (*rūpa*), (2) ear (*sota*) and sounds (*saddā*), (3) nose (*ghāna*) and smell (*gandhā*), (4) tongue (*jivhā*) and taste (*rasā*), (5) the body (*kāya*) and tangible objects (*phoṭṭhabba*) and (6) the mind (*mano*) and mental phenomena (*dhamma*).[85] In other words, the sense sphere (*āyatana*) is where the sense organ, the sense object and the corresponding consciousness come together (Table 10).

Table 10 Six sense spheres (*saḷāyatana*).

Internal sense spheres (*ajjhattikāni āyatanāni*)	**External sense spheres** (*bāhirāni āyatanāni*)	**Corresponding consciousnesses** (*viññāṇa*)
Eye (*cakkhu*)	Visible form (*rūpa*)	Eye-consciousness (*cakkhuviññāṇa*)
Ear (*sota*)	Sound (*sadda*)	Ear-consciousness (*sotaviññāṇa*)
Nose (*ghāna*)	Smell (*gandhā*)	Nose-consciousness (*ghānaviññāṇa*)
Tongue (*jivhā*)	Taste (*rasā*)	Tongue-consciousness (*jivhāviññāṇa*)
Body (*kāya*)	Tangible object (*phoṭṭhabba*)	Body-consciousness (*kāyaviññāṇa*)
Mind (*mano*)	Mental phenomena (*dhamma*)	Mind-consciousness (*manoviññāṇa*)

When the sense organ, the object and the corresponding consciousness join together, various mental states are produced, which can be wholesome or unwholesome. For example, the eye (*cakkhu*) is the internal base, and because it comes into contact with an external form (*rūpa*), which can be a visual object or even part of the body, consciousness (*viññāṇa*) arises, which then conditions feeling (*vedanā*), craving (*taṅhā*), clinging (*upādāna*) and becoming (*bhava*), as framed in the formula of dependent origination (*paṭiccasamuppāda*):

> (3) consciousness (*viññāṇa*) (4) mentality and materiality (*nāmarūpa*) (5) sense bases (*saḷāyatana*) (6) contact (*phassa*) (7) feeling (*vedanā*) (8) craving (*taṅhā*) (9) clinging (*upādāna*) (10) becoming (*bhava*). (S II 1)

Again, when the ear (*sota*) is in contact with a sound (*sadda*), various wholesome or unwholesome states are produced depending on whether the sound is perceived as pleasant or irritating. The same applies in the case of contact between the nose (*ghāna*) and smell (*gandha*) as well as the tongue (*jivhā*) and taste (*rasa*). It is slightly different in the case of the body (*kāya*) and tangible objects (*phoṭṭhabba*) because the organ of touch is present everywhere in the physical

83. The term *āyatana* has a range of meanings such as 'place, region, sphere, plane, working, production, performance, sphere of perception, sense organ and its object' (DP; PED, *s.v.*). The *Atthasālinī* states that the word *āyatana* refers to 'abode, ground, coming together, origin and cause' (As 140–141: *Tattha nivāsaṭhānaṭṭhena ākaraṭṭhena samosaraṇaṭhānaṭṭhena sañjātidesaṭṭhena kāraṇaṭṭhena ca āyatanaṃ veditabbaṃ*). See also the *Sumaṅgalavilāsinī* (Sv I 124) and *Visuddhimagga* (Vism 481–484).

84. It is similarly said in the *Visuddhimagga* that the sense bases (*āyatana*) produce phenomena that continue to arise throughout many lives along with the suffering of the cycle of rebirths (Vism 481: *Idañ ca anamatagge saṃsāre pavattam atīva āyataṃ saṃsāradukkhaṃ yāva na nivattati tāva nayante va pavattayanti*).

85. The six internal and external sense spheres (*āyatana*) are listed in many Pāli texts such as the *Papañcasūdani* commentary (Ps I 287) and discussed at length in the *Saḷāyatanavagga* (S IV 1–203).

body,[86] while contact with the materiality of the body can be either harmonious and conducive to the body or disharmonious.

The result of the contact between the sense organ and the sense object is the arising of consciousness (*viññāṇa*). Consequently, a great deal of mental proliferation (*papañca*) may emerge. For example, for seeing to take place, there has to be sentient materiality (*pasāda*)[87] in the eye (*cakkhu*), light and visual materiality (*rūpa*). Due to this contact (*phassa*), various mental formations (*saṅkhāra*)—i.e., groups of mental concomitants (*cetasika*) such as greed or aversion—occur, often related to past experiences of a similar object; based on these mental formations, eye consciousness (*cakkhuviññāṇa*) then emerges. In meditation, consciousness (*viññāṇa*) is experienced as the dissolution or breaking up of mental formations (*saṅkhāra*), making it seem to the meditator as though something is disintegrating or is just not there. In each of the six sense bases (*āyatana*), a respective type of consciousness (*viññāṇa*) emerges; there are thus six types of consciousness: eye-consciousness (*cakkuviññāṇa*), ear-consciousness (*sotaviññāṇa*), nose-consciousness (*ghānaviññāṇa*), tongue-consciousness (*jivhāviññāṇa*), body-consciousness (*kāyaviññāṇa*) and mind-consciousness (*manoviññāṇa*).

Eye-consciousness (*cakkuviññāṇa*) and ear-consciousness (*sotaviññāṇa*) appear more frequently than nose-consciousness (*ghānaviññāṇa*) and tongue-consciousness (*jivhācakkuviññāṇa*), because the eye and ear can be in contact with both nearby and distant objects, whereas smell and taste are usually restricted to proximate objects. However, mind-consciousness (*manoviññāṇa*), which is a component of the mental sense sphere (*manāyatana*), arises the most frequently.[88] In the mental sense sphere (*manāyatana*), the mental sense is the mind (*mano*), and the mental sense objects are phenomena (*dhamma*); when the two are in contact, mind-consciousness (*manoviññāṇa*) emerges. For example, after learning that a friend is going to travel, a related thought may arise, which means that the mental sense sphere (*manāyatana*) is activated, and consequently, other thoughts about the friend may follow. In other words, numerous mental concomitants (*cetasika*) emerge, and the mental sense sphere (*manāyatana*) and mental sense objects (*dhammāyatana*) are continuously formed, thus conditioning the occurrence of new mental formations (*saṅkhāra*) and the arising of consciousness (*viññāṇa*). When new thoughts keep appearing again and again, they create successive mental sense spheres (*manāyatana*) with their sense objects (*dhammāyatana*), which are followed by the arising of consciousness (*viññāṇa*); these ongoing processes lead to mental proliferation (*papañca*).

When mindfulness (*sati*) and clear comprehension (*sampajañña*) are well established, the

86. For example, the *Atthasālinī* states that 'in the body, wherever the materiality is grasped, everywhere is the bodily sense base' (As 311: *Yāvatā pana imasmiṃ kāye upādiṇṇakarūpaṃ nāma atthi, sabbattha kāyāyatanaṃ*).

87. In the Abhidhammic texts, each sense is described as made of a compound organ (*sasambhāra*), which is the physical base for the more subtle sentient organ (*pasāda*). For a more detailed description, see the *Atthasālinī* (As 306–307) and *Visuddhimagga* (Vism 445–446).

88. *Mano* is usually listed as an internal sense sphere (i.e., *manāyatana*) with mental phenomena (*dhamma*) as its objects. The mental processes arising through the mind door (*manodvāra*) can be a response to cognition arising through any of the five physical sense doors, or they can occur without contact with the five physical senses, as in the case of memory, reflection, conceptual thinking and so on; this is well described in the *Atthasālinī* (As 74). It is similarly stated in the *Mahāvedallasutta* that the five bodily senses each have 'a separate field, a separate domain, and they do not experience each other's field and domain, but they have the mind as their resort and the mind experiences their fields and domains' (M I 295: *Imesaṃ kho āvuso pañcannaṃ indriyānaṃ nānāvisayānaṃ nānāgocarānaṃ na aññamaññassa gocaravisayaṃ paccanubhontānaṃ mano paṭisaraṇaṃ, mano ca nesaṃ gocaravisayaṃ paccanubhotīti*). For a brief description of the mind-door processes, see Bodhi (1993, 163–166) and Karunadasa (2000, 157–158).

meditator can distinguish between the three components of the sense spheres—i.e., object, sense and consciousness (*viññāṇa*). For example, the meditator can clearly see that the sound, ear, and hearing are three different things or otherwise, she or he can distinguish between the visual object, eye and seeing. The meditator also comprehends that the noting mind and the state of mind that is its object are two separate phenomena. If the meditator contemplates the mental sense sphere (*manāyatana*) and mental sense objects (*dhammāyatana*), her or his meditation is in the domain of phenomena (*dhammānupassanā*), whereas if the consciousness (*viññāṇa*) itself is contemplated, then the contemplation is in the domain of the mind (*cittānupassanā*).

The problem is that we relate to all sense objects that arise through the six senses with craving (*taṇhā*); we are continuously stirred or agitated by the sense objects. As the *Ejāsutta* in the *Saḷāyatanasaṃyutta* repeatedly says:

> Monks, being stirred is a disease, being stirred is a boil, being stirred is a dart. ... Therefore, if a monk wishes to dwell unstirred, without the dart, he should not consider the eye, he should not consider in the eye, he should not consider from the eye, he should not consider 'the eye is mine.' ... He should not consider all, he should not consider in all, he should not consider from all, he should not consider 'all is mine.' Since he does not consider anything thus, he does not cling to anything in the world. Not clinging, he is not agitated; being unagitated, he attains *nibbāna*. (S IV 64–65)[89]

The meditator should not consider the six sense spheres as 'mine,' which means that she or he should not identify with them—this is actually the essence of meditation. To put it simply, meditation is training in how not to relate to sense objects with craving (*taṇhā*), which means not considering the sense spheres as 'mine' (*mama*), 'I am' (*aham asmi*), or 'myself' (*me attā*).'

'Fetter' (*saṃyojana*)

Fetters (*saṃyojana*) are produced at the sense spheres (*āyatana*); when a sense sphere (*āyatana*) has arisen, this means that fetters (*saṃyojana*) can occur. Most commonly, Buddhist texts list the following ten fetters (*saṃyojana*):

1. personality or identity view (*sakkāyadiṭṭhi*)
2. doubt (*vicikicchā*)
3. attachment to rites and rituals (*sīlabbataparāmāsa*)
4. sense desire (*kāmacchanda*)
5. ill will (*vyāpāda*)
6. desire for material existence (*rūparāga*)
7. desire for immaterial existence (*arūparāga*)
8. conceit (*māna*)
9. restlessness (*uddhacca*)
10. ignorance (*avijjā*)[90]

---

89. S IV 64–65: *Ejā bhikkhave rogo ejā gaṇḍo ejā sallaṃ ... Tasmā ti ha bhikkhave bhikkhu ce pi ākaṅkheyya anejo vihareyya vītasalloti ... Cakkhuṃ na maññeyya, cakkhusmiṃ na maññeyya, cakkhuto na maññeyya, cakkhu me ti na maññeyya. Rūpe na maññeyya, rūpesu na maññeyya, rūpato na maññeyya, rūpā me ati na maññeyya. Cakkhuviññāṇaṃ na maññeyya, cakkhuviññāṇasmiṃ na maññeyya, cakkhuviññāṇato na maññeyya, cakkhuviññāṇam me ti na maññeyya. ... Sabbaṃ na maññeyya, sabbasmiṃ na maññeyya, sabbato na maññeyya, sabbam me ti na maññeyya. So evam amaññamāno na kiñci pi loke upādiyati, anupādiyaṃ na paritassati, aparitassaṃ paccattaññeva parinibbāyati.*

90. This list of fetters (*saṃyojana*) is given, for example, in the *Oghasutta* of the *Maggasaṃyutta* (S V 61) in which the first five are called 'lower fetters' (*orambhāgiyāni saṃyojanāni*) and the last five 'higher fetters'

The term *saṃyojana* signifies something that binds or compounds; in the context of the *Satipaṭṭhānasutta*, it refers to binding oneself to continuous becoming (*bhava*).[91] In the *Saṃyojanasutta* of the *Cittasaṃyutta* (S IV 281–283), a metaphor is used to describe fetters (*saṃyojana*): when a black ox and a white ox are bound together by a single yoke, it is not the black ox that binds the white one or vice versa but it is the yoke that binds them. Similarly, this *sutta* continues:

> Neither the sense [such as] the eye (*cakkhu*) nor the sense object [such as] the visual object (*rūpa*) are fetters (*saṃyojana*) but the lustful desire (*chandarāga*) that arises dependent on both. (S IV 283)[92]

Thus, lustful desire (*chandarāga*) acts like the yoke that binds the oxen. As long as there is lustful desire (*chandarāga*), the fetters (*saṃyojana*) occur.[93]

The hindrances (*nīvaraṇa*)[94] are different from the fetters (*saṃyojana*). The five hindrances (*nīvaraṇa*) are often suppressed during meditation, but the fetters (*saṃyojana*) remain. If the meditator reduces or is free from the fetters (*saṃyojana*), then the five hindrances (*nīvaraṇa*) will be reduced proportionally. For example, if the fetter of doubt (*vicikicchā*) is removed, then the hindrance of doubt (*vicikicchā*) will no longer arise but not vice versa: the removal of the hindrances (*nīvaraṇa*) does not necessarily affect the fetters (*saṃyojana*). The hindrances (*nīvaraṇa*) may be subdued or suppressed through calm (*samatha*) meditation, but the fetters (*saṃyojana*) can only be broken by wisdom (*paññā*), that is, an insight into the three characteristics (*tilakkhaṇa*) of all phenomena. The hindrances (*nīvaraṇa*) can be suppressed in calm (*samatha*) meditation but not destroyed, since this type of practice does not deal with the fetters (*saṃyojana*).

A person who is skilled in calm (*samatha*) meditation and can remain in wholesome states because of the subdued hindrances (*nīvaraṇa*) would usually be very reluctant to start practising the four foundations of mindfulness (*satipaṭṭhāna*) and insight meditation (*vipassanā*), because the state of blissful peace achieved in the absorptions (*jhāna*) is too great. If the desire

(*uddhambhāgiyāni saṃyojanāni*). In the *Papañcasūdani* commentary (Ps I 287) and *Dhammasaṅgaṇi* (Dhs 197), a different list of ten fetters (*saṃyojana*) is given: (1) sensual lust (*kāmarāga*), (2) anger (*paṭigha*), (3) conceit (*māna*), (4) views (*diṭṭhi*), (5) doubt (*vicikicchā*), (6) attachment to rites and rituals (*sīlabbataparāmāsa*), (7) desire for existence (*bhavarāga*), (8) jealousy (*issā*), (9) avarice (*macchariya*) and (10) ignorance (*avijjā*). In other texts, fetters (*saṃyojana*) are grouped in a different way. For example, the *Potaliyasutta* (M I 360–361) lists eight fetters: (1) destroying life (*pāṇātipāta*), (2) stealing (*adinnādāna*), (3) false speech (*musāvāda*), (4) malicious speech (*pisunā*), (5) covetousness and greed (*giddhilobha*), (6) blame and scolding (*nindārosa*), (7) anger and malice (*kodhūpāyāsa*) and (8) conceit (*atimāna*).

91. Here Pemasiri Thera explains the term 'becoming' (*bhava*) as the processes that repeatedly occur in this life as well as the continuous cycle of rebirths. In both cases, becoming (*bhava*) takes place because of the fetters (*saṃyojana*) that arise in the sense spheres (*saḷāyatana*). In terms of dependent origination (*paṭiccasamuppāda*), he refers to the following links: (6) sense spheres (*saḷāyatana*) (8) craving (*taṅhā*) (9) clinging (*upādāna*) (10) becoming (*bhava*).

92. S IV 283: *na cakkhu rūpānaṃ saṃyojanaṃ na rūpā cakkhussa saṃyojanaṃ, yañca tattha tadubhayaṃ paṭicca uppajjati chandarāgo taṃ tattha saṃyojanaṃ*. The fetters (*saṃyojana*) are similarly described in the *Koṭṭhitasutta* (S IV 163).

93. It is difficult to render the term *chandarāga* into English; it is often translated as 'exciting desire' (DP; PED, *s.v.*) or 'lustful desire.' In the *Mahānidānasutta* (D II 58), it is said that *chandarāga* is conditioned by craving (*taṅhā*) and leads to a range of unskilful states. The *Mahāhatthipadopannasutta* emphasises that removing lustful desire (*chandarāga*) for the five aggregates of clinging (*upādānakkhandha*) leads to the cessation of suffering (*dukkhanirodha*) (M I 191: *yo imesu pañcas'upādānakkhandhesu chandarāgavinayo chandarāgappahānaṃ so dukkhanirodho*).

94. For a discussion on hindrances, see Chapter V.1. Five hindrances.

for fine material (*rūparāga*) and immaterial (*arūparāga*) absorptions arise in calm (*samatha*) meditation, the meditator will stop there and may cling to these states, thus creating fetters (*saṃyojana*). To break down the fetters (*saṃyojana*), it is necessary to practise insight meditation (*vipassanā*); in this practice, the meditator will not cling to absorptions but instead see and understand their nature, causes, conditions and characteristics (i.e., impermanence, unsatisfactoriness and non-self), thus approaching them in the same manner as any other object that arises.

The meditator, who is not fooled by the fetters (*saṃyojana*), will progress very rapidly and incline towards *nibbāna* in the same way as a log carried along by the current of the Ganges will reach the ocean if not obstructed. This metaphor is given in the *Paṭhamadārukkhandhopamasutta*:

> If the log does not collide with the near or far shore, does not sink in the middle, is not cast up onto high ground, is not taken by humans or non-humans, is not caught up in a whirlpool or does not become rotten inside, then it will slant, slope and incline towards the ocean. ... The near shore refers to the six internal sense spheres, the far shore to the six external sense spheres, the sinking in mid-stream to pleasure and lust, being cast up on high ground to the conceit 'I am.' Being taken by humans means that one lives in association with lay people ... and is involved in their affairs. Being taken by non-humans means that one lives the holy life with the aim of being [reborn] among certain deities ... Being caught up in a whirlpool refers to the five strands of sensual pleasure and rotting inside means that one is immoral. (S IV 179–180)[95]

Thus, if not stuck or obstructed by various defilements (*kilesa*) and fetters (*saṃyojana*), the meditator will naturally incline towards liberation or *nibbāna*.

However, the fetters (*saṃyojana*) are difficult to see. Throughout life, they continuously keep arising, one after the other, and consequently, mental proliferation (*papañca*) abounds. For example, it is described in the *Madhupiṇḍikasutta*:

> Dependent on the eye and form, eye-consciousness arises, and the meeting of the three of them is contact, which conditions feeling. What one feels, one perceives, and what one perceives, one thinks about. And what one thinks about, one mentally proliferates. (M I 111–112)[96]

Thus, when the fetters (*saṃyojana*) arise and proliferate, distortions occur in the mind, and an 'I' is repeatedly created. In other words, living with the fetters (*saṃyojana*) means continuously living with craving (*taṇhā*), conceit (*māna*) and views (*diṭṭhi*). Fetters (*saṃyojana*) are not with us all the time; a fetter (*saṃyojana*) only arises when the sense sphere (*āyatana*) is created through contact with an object. Fetters (*saṃyojana*) occur in the mind because we hold onto objects; they arise in relation to objects from the past and trigger thinking about the future. Thus, it is due to craving (*taṇhā*) that the past and the future are created.

95. S IV 179: *Sace kho bhikkhave dārukkhandho na orimantīraṃ upagacchati na pārimantīram upagacchati, na majjhe saṃsīdissati, na thale ussīdissati, na manussagāho bhavissati, na amanussagāho bhavissati, na āvaṭṭagāho bhavissati, na antopūti bhavissati, evaṃ hi so bhikkhave dārukkhandho samuddaninno bhavissati samuddapoṇo samuddapabbhāro ... Orimantīran ti kho bhikkhu channetam ajjhattikānam āyatanānam adhivacanaṃ. Pārimantīran ti kho bhikkhu channaṃ bāhirānam āyatanānam adhivacanaṃ. Majjhe saṃsīdo ti kho bhikkhu nandirāgassetam adhivacanaṃ. Thale ussādo ti kho bhikkhu asmimānassetam adhivacanaṃ. Katamo ca bhikkhu manussagāho? Idha bhikkhu gihī saṃsaṭṭho viharati ... uppannesu kiccakaraṇīyesu attanā tesu yogam āpajjati. Katamo ca bhikkhu amanussagāho? Idha bhikkhu ekacco ekacco aññataraṃ devanikāyam paṇidhāya brahmacariyaṃ carati ... Āvaṭṭagāho ti kho bhikkhu pañcannetam kāmaguṇānam adhivacanaṃ. Katamo ca bhikkhu antopūtibhāvo? Idha bhikkhu ekacco dussīlo hoti.*

96. M I 111–112: *Cakkhuñ-c'āvuso paṭicca rūpe ca uppajjati cakkhuviññāṇaṃ, tiṇṇaṃ saṅgati phasso, phassapaccayā vedanā, yaṃ vedeti taṃ sañjānāti, yaṃ sañjānāti taṃ vitakketi, yaṃ vitakketi taṃ papañceti.*

It is very difficult to understand the processes occurring at the sense spheres (*āyatana*), since the meditator must very clearly see and comprehend what arises in the mind from moment to moment and recognise the fetter (*saṃyojana*) right when it arises. If the meditator notes the fetter (*saṃyojana*) without reacting to it, it will not immediately be followed by another; in this way, the meditator can clearly understand both the arising and the non-occurrence of the fetter (*saṃyojana*). This section of the *Satipaṭṭhānasutta* also states that the meditator knows the 'non-arising of the abandoned fetter' (*pahīnassa saṃyojanassa āyatiṃ*); this happens only after the meditator has reached one of the path knowledges (*maggañāṇa*) and thus abandoned certain fetters (*saṃyojana*); only then does she or he know that they can no longer arise. The first three fetters are abandoned by the stream-winner (*sotāpanna*) and the first five by the non-returner (*anāgāmin*) (Table 11).[97]

Table 11 Correspondence between the eradicated fetters (*saṃyojana*) and the four path knowledges.

<table>
<tr><th></th><th colspan="4">Four path knowledges</th></tr>
<tr><th rowspan="12">Eradicated fetters (saṃyojana)</th><th>Stream entry (sotāpatti)</th><th>Once-returning (sakadāgāmi)</th><th>Non-returning (anāgāmi)</th><th>Arahantship (arahatta)</th></tr>
<tr><td colspan="4">Personality view (sakkāyadiṭṭhi)</td></tr>
<tr><td colspan="4">Doubt (vicikicchā)</td></tr>
<tr><td colspan="4">Attachment to rites and rituals (sīlabbataparāmāsa)</td></tr>
<tr><td rowspan="8"></td><td rowspan="8"></td><td colspan="2">Sense desire (kāmacchanda)</td></tr>
<tr><td colspan="2">Ill will (vyāpāda)</td></tr>
<tr><td rowspan="5"></td><td>Desire for material existence (rūparāga)</td></tr>
<tr><td>Desire for immaterial existence (arūparāga)</td></tr>
<tr><td>Conceit (māna)</td></tr>
<tr><td>Restlessness (uddhacca)</td></tr>
<tr><td>Ignorance (avijjā)</td></tr>
</table>

There is an essential difference between recognising a fetter (*saṃyojana*) and being under its influence: the meditator recognises the fetter (*saṃyojana*) through mindfulness (*sati*) and wisdom (*paññā*), but in their absence, fetters (*saṃyojana*) become active and take over. In other words, the meditator follows the noble eightfold path (*aṭṭhaṅgika magga*) only when she or he experiences a sense object without relating to it with views (*diṭṭhi*)—i.e., with an 'I' or 'mine'—which means without any craving (*taṇhā*). As soon as the meditator is (temporarily) free from fetters (*saṃyojana*), the factors of awakening (*bojjhaṅga*) begin to evolve.

Living for extended periods with the fetters (*saṃyojana*) leads to the development of taints (*āsava*). The term taint (*āsava*) refers to something that has been around for a long time; it is like fermented apples that produce alcohol or vinegar.[98] As mentioned before, the Pāli texts usually list the four following taints (*āsava*): sense desire (*kāmāsava*), becoming (*bhavāsava*), views (*diṭṭhāsava*) and ignorance (*avijjāsava*) (D II 81; Dhs 195). The taint of views (*diṭṭhāsava*) is

97. A similar explanation is found in the *Papañcasūdani* commentary (Ps I 288) in which the fetters are abandoned at each of the four stages of awakening. However, the *Papañcasūdani* lists a somewhat different set of ten fetters (Ps I 287).

98. Likewise, in the *Atthasālinī* (As 48), the taints (*āsava*) are compared to intoxicating drinks obtained after the prolonged fermentation of various fruit juices.

linked to the first three fetters (*saṃyojana*)—i.e., personality view (*sakkāyadiṭṭhi*), doubt (*vicikicchā*) and attachment to rites and rituals (*sīlabbataparāmāsa*). The taint of sense desire (*kāmāsava*) corresponds to the next two fetters—i.e., sense desire (*kāmacchanda*) and ill will (*vyāpāda*). Finally, the taint of becoming (*bhavāsava*) is connected to all ten fetters (*saṃyojana*) (Table 12).

Table 12 Correspondences between the four taints (*āsava*) and the ten fetters (*saṃyojana*).

	Four taints (*āsava*)			
Ten fetters (*saṃyojana*)	**Sense desire** (*kāmāsava*)	**Becoming** (*bhavāsava*)	**Views** (*diṭṭhāsava*)	**Ignorance** (*avijjāsava*)
		Personality view (*sakkāyadiṭṭhi*)	Personality view (*sakkāyadiṭṭhi*)	
		Doubt (*vicikicchā*)	Doubt (*vicikicchā*)	
		Attachment to rites and rituals (*sīlabbataparāmāsa*)	Attachment to rites and rituals (*sīlabbataparāmāsa*)	
	Sense desire (*kāmacchanda*)	Sense desire (*kāmacchanda*)		
	Ill will (*vyāpāda*)	Ill will (*vyāpāda*)		
		Desire for material existence (*rūparāga*)		
		Desire for immaterial existence (*arūparāga*)		
		Conceit (*māna*)		
		Restlessness (*uddhacca*)		
		Ignorance (*avijjā*)		Ignorance (*avijjā*)

Ignorance (*avijjā*) is both a taint (*āsava*) and a fetter (*saṃyojana*); it is always present, usually in every moment of our lives. If there were no taint of ignorance (*avijjāsava*), contact with an object would not take place.[99] Even when we listen to or read the Dhamma with the aim to overcome ignorance (*avijjā*), we position ourselves at another level of ignorance (*avijjā*). There may be instances when ignorance (*avijjā*) is absent for brief moments; this happens, for example, at the fleeting moment when the eye makes contact with a visual object or the ear with a sound. However, if, at that moment, the meditator does not clearly see the process of cause (*hetu*) and effect (*phala*), then ignorance (*avijjā*) arises, which is immediately followed by craving (*taṇhā*) and then the thoughts 'I have seen' or 'I am listening to this sound,' a 'person' or an 'I' is born. Thus, based on ignorance (*avijjā*) and craving (*taṇhā*), we live in a continuous process of becoming (*bhava*).[100] Only when cause (*hetu*) and effect (*phala*) are seen and comprehended at the very moment of contact between the senses and their objects, is there no opportunity for ignorance (*avijjā*) to arise and therefore no space for craving (*taṇhā*) and the creation of an 'I' to occur.

99. Here Pemasiri Thera links the first and sixth components of dependent origination (*paṭiccasamuppāda*): (1) (*avijjā*) (6) contact (*phassa*).

100. Pemasiri Thera yet again refers to dependent origination (*paṭiccasamuppāda*), connecting the first, eighth, and tenth links: (1) ignorance (*avijjā*) (8) craving (*taṅhā*) (10) becoming (*bhava*) (S II 1).

Ten fetters (*saṃyojana*)

Among the ten fetters (*saṃyojana*), the first five—i.e., personality or identity view (*sakkāya-diṭṭhi*), doubt (*vicikicchā*), attachment to rites and rituals (*sīlabbataparāmāsa*), sense desire (*kāma-cchanda*) and ill will (*vyāpāda*)—are known as the 'lower fetters' (*orambhāgiyāni saṃyojanāni*).[101]

The first fetter (*saṃyojana*) of personality view (*sakkāyadiṭṭhi*)[102] can arise in various ways. It is very difficult to be rid of it; we may think that we no longer have this fetter (*saṃyojana*), but it is still present. Personality view (*sakkāyadiṭṭhi*) is related to the notion of an 'I' and 'mine'; it arises through clinging (*upādāna*) to an object of experience approached with craving (*taṅhā*)[103] and is linked to conceit (*māna*) and views (*diṭṭhi*). If clinging (*upādāna*) towards a certain object has arisen, the meditator should examine whether it is connected with views (*diṭṭhi*). The aim of meditation is to minimise and eventually eradicate craving (*taṇhā*), views (*diṭṭhi*) and conceit (*māna*) by clearly seeing them as they arise without clinging (*upādāna*).

The fetter (*saṃyojana*) of doubt (*vicikicchā*)[104] that arises along with the personality view (*sakkāyadiṭṭhi*) is always connected to clinging (*upādāna*). It can emerge from the fear of losing one's personality, from uncertainty about how to liberate oneself[105] or from doubts about the Buddhist teachings, the Buddha or the Saṅgha.[106]

The fetters of personality view (*sakkāyadiṭṭhi*) and doubt (*vicikicchā*) are closely related to the third fetter, namely, attachment to rites and rituals (*sīlabbataparāmāsa*) that occurs in many

101. The first five fetters (*saṃyojana*) are eradicated by a non-returner (*anāgāmin*) and only the last five by an *arahant* (Table 11).

102. Personality view (*sakkāyadiṭṭhi*) is discussed in many Pāli texts. For example, in the *Cūḷavedallasutta* and *Dhammasaṅgaṇi*, it is explained as viewing each of the five aggregates 'as self, or self as having the particular aggregate, or the aggregate [existing] in self, or self [existing] in the aggregate (M I 299; Dhs 182–183: *rūpaṃ attato samanupassati, rūpavantaṃ vā attānaṃ, attani vā rūpaṃ, rūpasmiṃ vā attānaṃ; vedanaṃ attato ... viññāṇaṃ attato samanupassati, viññāṇavantaṃ vā attānaṃ, attani vā viññāṇaṃ, viññāṇasmiṃ vā attānaṃ*). The *Papañcasūdani* commentary explains that the fetter of views (*diṭṭhisaṃyojana*) means (wrongly) grasping objects like visual form as permanent and solid (Ps I 288: *etaṃ rūpārammaṇaṃ niccaṃ dhuvan'ti gaṇhato diṭṭhisaṃyojanaṃ uppajjati*).

103. According to the doctrine of dependent origination, craving (*taṅhā*) is the eighth link that conditions the following link of clinging (*upādāna*). The *Cūḷavedallasutta* elaborates this by saying that clinging (*upādāna*) means that there is lustful desire (*chandarāga*) in relation to the five aggregates of clinging (M I 300: *Yo kho āvuso Visākha pañcas'upādānakkhandhesu chandarāgo taṃ tattha upādānanti*). The problem of clinging (*upādāna*) is also underscored in the *Anāthapiṇḍikovādasutta*, which narrates how the dying householder Anāthapiṇḍika is advised to avoid clinging (*upādāna*) to the sense spheres (*āyatana*), aggregates (*khandha*) or anything else in this world and beyond (M II 259–263).

104. The word *vicikicchā* is usually translated as 'doubt, perplexity, uncertainty' (PED. s.v.). It is so described in the *Vibhaṅga* and *Dhammasaṅgaṇi* as 'puzzlement and uncertainty of the mind' (Vibh 364; Dhs 221: *thambhitattaṃ cittassa manovilekho*). According to the *Papañcasūdani* commentary (Ps I 286), doubt (*vicikiccha*) arises due to unwise attention (*ayoniso manasikāra*). For more details, see Chapter V.1, under the subheading 'Doubt (*vicikiccha*).'

105. For example, doubts about the path to liberation are discussed in the *Tissasutta* (S III 108–109), where the Buddha compares doubt (*vicikiccha*) to a forked road (S III 108: *dvidhāpatho ti vicikicchāyetam adhivacanaṃ*) and explains that the person who is not skilled in the path is a worldling, whereas the skilled person is the Tathāgata, *arahant*, the perfectly enlightened one (S III 108: *puriso amaggakusalo ti kho Tissa puthujjanassetaṃ adhivacanaṃ. Puriso maggakusalo ti kho Tissā Tathāgatass'etam adhivacanam arahato sammāsambuddhassa*).

106. The importance of removing doubt (*vicikicchā*) and personality view (*sakkāyadiṭṭhi*) through perfect confidence or trust (*aveccapasāda*) in the Buddha, Dhamma and Saṅgha is narrated in many *suttas* such as the *Gilānasutta* (S IV 302–304).

contexts.[107] For example, if a person recites lay or monastic moral precepts (*sīla*) but does not practise the noble eightfold path (*ariyo aṭṭhaṅgiko maggo*), means that she or he is attached to mere rites and rituals (*sīlabbataparāmāsa*). Moral precepts (*sīla*) are like a fence erected around a newly planted tree to protect it. If people only look after the fence, while forgetting to cultivate the seedling in the middle, it will eventually die. Moral precepts (*sīla*) are required as a sort of protection for the cultivation of meditation (*samādhi*) and wisdom (*paññā*), but if they are just recited in rituals while right speech (*sammāvācā*), right action (*sammākammanta*) and right livelihood (*sammāājīva*) are not cultivated, those precepts become the fetter of attachment to rites and rituals (*sīlabbataparāmāsa*) and the noble eightfold path (*ariyo aṭṭhaṅgiko maggo*) cannot develop. Only at the stage of the stream-winner (*sotāpanna*) is the meditator free from the fetters of personality view (*sakkāyadiṭṭhi*), doubt (*vicikicchā*) and attachment to rites and rituals (*sīlabbataparāmāsa*). This means that she or he no longer has any speculations or thoughts such as, 'Now I am really free from wrong view or doubts,' since there is simply no need to examine oneself in this manner.

The next two fetters (*saṃyojana*) are sense desire (*kāmacchanda*) and ill will (*vyāpāda*);[108] they are very dangerous and extremely difficult to extinguish. Let us say that the meditator has cultivated her or his mind to such an extent that the first three fetters—i.e., personality view, doubt and attachment to rites and rituals—have been eradicated, which means that they no longer create the new becoming (*bhava*) that stems from them. However, becoming (*bhava*) that stems from sense desire (*kāmacchanda*) or ill will (*vyāpāda*) will still continue. Sense desire (*kāmacchanda*) denotes the liking for sensuality or the desire for a pleasurable object.[109] It is always connected with ill will (*vyāpāda*), which is presented as hostility, anger or irritation towards a sense object.[110] Both sense desire (*kāmacchanda*) and ill will (*vyāpāda*) commonly appear in conjunction with the first three fetters (*saṃyojana*), although they keep arising even after the first three have been overcome and are only eradicated by non-returner (*anāgāmin*).

The last five fetters (*saṃyojana*) are known as the 'higher fetters' (*uddhambhāgiyāni saṃyojanāni*) and include desire for material existence (*rūparāga*), desire for immaterial existence (*arūparāga*), conceit (*māna*), restlessness (*uddhacca*) and ignorance (*avijjā*) (S V 61). Desire for material existence (*rūparāga*) and desire for immaterial existence (*arūparāga*) are always linked to the meditative absorptions (*jhāna*); at that stage, all the fetters (*saṃyojana*) arise in relation to non-material objects, because sensuality and aversion are greatly reduced. Desire for material existence (*rūparāga*) and desire for immaterial existence (*arūparāga*) are very difficult to eradicate, because the meditator likes to stay in the states of high meditative absorptions (*jhāna*)—i.e., in the realm of pure form (*rūpāvacara*) or the formless realm (*arūpāvacara*)—which are beyond

107. The *Papañcasūdani* commentary explains that attachment to rites and rituals (*sīlabbataparāmāsa*) arises in someone who thinks that they will be able to obtain an object (e.g., visual object) in the future by performing certain rites and rituals (Ps I 288: *Āyatim pi evarūpaṃ sīlabbataṃ samādiyitvā sakkā laddhun ti sīlabbataṃ samādiyantassa sīlabbataparāmāsasaṃyojanaṃ uppajjati*).

108. Sense desire (*kāmacchanda*) and ill will (*vyāpāda*) are discussed in Chapter V.1. Five hindrances.

109. The *Bojjhaṅgasaṃyutta* (S V 6) explains that the nutriment for sense desire (*kāmacchanda*) is an attractive or pleasurable object (*subhanimitta*). The *Papañcasūdani* commentary (Ps I 281) states that sense desire (*kāmacchanda*) arises because of unwise attention (*ayoniso manasikāra*) and that the condition for the arising of sense desire (*kāmacchanda*) is the lack of wise attention (*ayoniso manasikāra*) towards a pleasant sense object (*subhanimitta*).

110. According to the *Papañcasūdani* commentary, the condition for the arising of ill will (*vyāpāda*), similarly to sense desire (*kāmacchanda*), is unwise attention (*ayoniso manasikāra*) towards an object of aversion or anger (*paṭighanimitta*) (Ps 282: *paṭighanimitte ayonisomanasikārena pana vyāpādassa uppādo hoti*).

sensuality (*kāmāvacara*). Only when the meditator develops a high level of mindfulness (*sati*) and wisdom (*paññā*) can she or he recognise these two fetters, and consequently, no longer desires or clings to the states of high concentration. If mindfulness (*sati*) and wisdom (*paññā*) are not strong enough to see these two fetters, this does not mean that the meditator is in unwholesome states but rather the opposite: she or he is at the highest level of wholesomeness related to the meditative absorptions (*jhāna*) but cannot recognise the desire for material (*rūparāga*) and immaterial existence (*arūparāga*) and therefore cannot go beyond them.

The last three fetters (*saṃyojana*)—i.e., conceit (*māna*), restlessness (*uddhacca*) and ignorance (*avijjā*)—arise in all levels of being—from the sensual realm (*kāmāvacara*) to the fine non-material sphere (*arūpāvacara*). As said before, mental proliferation (*papañca*) occurs through clinging (*upādāna*) to an object of experience that was approached with craving (*taṅhā*), conceit (*māna*) and views (*diṭṭhi*). Craving (*taṅhā*) and conceit (*māna*) form the core of an 'I' or a personality to which one clings with views (*diṭṭhi*). If all three—i.e., craving, conceit and views—appear together, they are known as the 'personality view' (*sakkāyadiṭṭhi*). Only when the meditator realises through mindfulness (*sati*) and wisdom (*paññā*) that the 'I' or personality is not real can conceit (*māna*) be overcome. The fetter of conceit (*māna*) occurs when we think that we are better, equal or worse than others.[111] In the *Vibhaṅga*, nine types of conceit are listed:

1. I am a superior person, the other is superior;
2. I am a superior person, the other is average;
3. I am a superior person, the other is inferior;
4. I am an average person, the other is superior;
5. I am an average person, the other is also average;
6. I am an average person, the other is inferior;
7. I am inferior, the other is superior;
8. I am inferior, the other is average;
9. I am inferior and so is the other person. (Vibh 389–390)[112]

If a person makes such comparisons, it means that she or he does not see or understand the cause (*hetu*) and effect (*phala*) of the phenomena experienced. When conceit (*māna*) occurs along with craving (*taṅhā*) and views (*diṭṭhi*), it may manifest in the nine comparisons listed above, which cause much harm to oneself and others. Only when the meditator reaches the knowledge of distinguishing materiality and mentality (*nāmarūpaparicchedañāṇa*)[113]—i.e., the stage of the purification of view (*diṭṭhivisuddhi*)—do these nine gross comparisons and discriminations stop occurring in the mind. However, conceit (*māna*) is still not overcome at that stage but remains present at a subtle level. Hence, it is difficult to notice; it can be seen as the subtle pride in medi-

111. The fetter of conceit (*māna*) is presented in the *Dhammasaṅgaṇi* as three kinds of thoughts: 'I am a superior person,' 'I am as good a person' and 'I am an inferior person.' Further on, it is described as 'conceit, conceitedness, pride, haughtiness, loftiness, [flaunting] flag, arrogance, self-advertisement' (Dhs 197–198: *Seyyo 'hamasmīti māno—sadiso 'hamasmīti māno—hīno 'hamasmīti māno—ye evarūpo māno maññaṇā maññitattaṃ uṇṇati uṇṇamo dhajo sampaggāho ketukamyatā cittassa—idam vuccati mānasaññojanaṃ*).

112. Vibh 389–390: *Seyyassa seyyo 'ham asmīti māno. Seyyassa sadiso 'ham asmīti māno. Seyyassa hīno 'ham asmīti māno. Sadisassa seyyo 'ham asmīti māno. Sadisassa sadiso 'ham asmīti māno. Sadisassa hīno 'ham asmīti māno. Hīnassa seyyo 'ham asmīti māno. Hīnassa sadiso 'ham asmīti māno. Hīnassa hīno 'ham asmīti māno. Ime navavidhā mānā.*

113. The knowledge of distinguishing materiality and mentality (*nāmarūpaparicchedañāṇa*) is presented under the purification of view (*diṭṭhivisuddhi*), which is the third of the seven stages of purification leading to final liberation. The seven stages are described in the *Rathavinītasutta* (M I 145–151). A detailed description of the purification of view (*diṭṭhivisuddhi*) is given in the *Visuddhimagga* (Vism 587–597).

tators who practise well and teach others.[114] The *Mūlapariyāyasutta* (M I 1–6) narrates how monks who listened to the Buddha's discourse on the root of all things 'did not rejoice in the teaching,' and as the *Papañcasūdani* commentary on this *sutta* explains, this was because of their conceit (*māna*) (Ps I 58–59). Even non-returners (*anāgāmin*) have conceit (*māna*) in relation to their meditation practice of the absorptions (*jhāna*) when comparing themselves with others; however, such conceit is harmless. When conceit (*māna*) arises, one should contemplate impermanence (*anicca*), as the Buddha advised his son Rāhula in the *Mahārāhulovādasutta*:

> Rāhula, cultivate meditation on the perception of impermanence; if you cultivate meditation on the perception of impermanence, the conceit 'I am' will be abandoned. (M I 424–425)[115]

Because of craving (*taṅhā*), views (*diṭṭhi*) and conceit (*māna*), we try to make objects of experiences stable or permanent and cannot accept when they inevitably pass away. For example, the meditator may have experienced a high level of concentration (*samādhi*) in the past. Now, however, she or he relates to the present objects of meditation from the position of these previous experiences, evaluating the present as worse than the past, thinking that something is wrong with the meditation practice. These kinds of comparisons are a form of conceit (*māna*), which creates an 'I.' If the meditator is not aware of conceit (*māna*), it can grow to such a level that she or he starts talking to others about past meditation experiences; this also happens to meditation teachers. Only when clearly seeing impermanence (*anicca*), the meditator does not try to maintain any experiences, because she or he understands that all objects momentarily cease, and with this insight, an 'I' cannot be created.[116]

The ninth fetter (*saṃyojana*) is restlessness (*uddhacca*), which arises along with all the other fetters. It is one of the mental concomitants (*cetasika*) that accompanies every unwholesome mental state. Apart from being a fetter, restlessness (*uddhacca*) is also listed in conjunction with remorse (*kukkucca*) as one of the five hindrances (*nīvaraṇa*).[117] Why is only restlessness (*uddhacca*) taken as a fetter while remorse (*kukkucca*) is not? The reason is that remorse (*kukkucca*) is linked to desire (*kāmarāga*) and aversion (*vyāpāda*); when the latter two are relinquished by the meditator at the stage of non-returner (*anāgāmin*), remorse (*kukkucca*) is also abandoned, whereas restlessness (*uddhacca*) remains until one reaches arahantship. However, the restlessness (*uddhacca*) of a non-returner (*anāgāmin*) is very slight, occurring mainly in relation to the meditative absorptions (*jhāna*) when the meditator cannot maintain a certain absorption (*jhāna*) in the way that she or he wishes.

The final fetter is ignorance (*avijjā*). Ignorance (*avijjā*) is the first link in dependent origination (*paṭiccasamuppāda*), positioned as the very root of suffering and rebirth. It is often defined in the texts as the absence of knowledge about the four noble truths.[118] Ignorance (*avijjā*) is different

---

114. The *Papañcasūdani* commentary similarly presents conceit (*māna*) in relation to meditation, saying: 'The fetter of pride arises in one who thinks, "Nobody but myself is able to clearly understand the object"' (Ps I 288: *Ṭhapetvā maṃ na koci añño etaṃ ārammaṇaṃ vibhāvetuṃ samattho atthī ti maññato mānasaṃyojanaṃ uppajjati*).

115. M I 424–425: *Aniccasaññaṃ Rāhula bhāvanaṃ bhāvehi, aniccasaññaṃ hi te Rāhula bhāvanaṃ bhāvayato yo asmimāno so pahīyissati.*

116. Many texts such as the *Avijjāsutta* of the *Saṃyuttanikāya* state that the fetters (*saṃyojana*) can be extinguished by seeing impermanence (*anicca*) (S IV 31: *tampi aniccato jānato passato saṃyojanā pahiyyanti*).

117. For a more detailed description, see Chapter V.1, under the subheading 'Restlessness and worry (*uddhaccakukkucca*).'

118. For example, in the *Nidānasaṃyutta*, ignorance (*avijjā*) is defined as 'not knowing suffering, not knowing the arising of suffering, not knowing the cessation of suffering and not knowing the path leading to the cessation

from delusion (*moha*): it is not classified as a mental concomitant (*cetasika*) and can arise along with unwholesome (*akusala*) and wholesome (*kusala*) mental states, whereas delusion is a mental concomitant (*cetasika*) that only arises with unwholesome (*akusala*) states. There is a link between the two: when delusion (*moha*) is present, it is always accompanied by ignorance (*avijjā*).

In fact, no such thing as ignorance (*avijjā*) exists in the world; we talk about it only because of the first nine fetters (*saṃyojana*). Ignorance (*avijjā*) can be compared to a house comprised of nine rooms that represent the first nine fetters (*saṃyojana*). Because there are nine rooms, the concept of a 'house' is created; if all nine rooms are destroyed one by one, the house will eventually no longer exist. Thus, ignorance (*avijjā*) refers to the first nine fetters (*saṃyojana*);[119] when they are relinquished, there is no experience or object that can arise only with ignorance (*avijjā*). In the *Avijjāsutta* it is said:

> Monks, a beginning of ignorance is not discerned, so that before a certain point, there was no ignorance and afterwards it came into being. However, ignorance has a condition. ...What is the nutriment for ignorance? The five hindrances ... (A V 113)[120]

This means that we cannot see the beginning of ignorance (*avijjā*), although it has nutrients as stated in the *sutta* above, beginning with the five hindrances (*nīvaraṇa*).[121] Since the meditator does not see or understand the first nine fetters (*saṃyojana*), ignorance (*avijjā*) arises; this means that with every object that she or he experiences, an 'I' emerges. Every occurrence of a personality or an 'I' is actually the arising of ignorance (*avijjā*). For example, if the meditator practises with the aim (no matter how subtle) to liberate her or himself, then the meditation is itself based on ignorance (*avijjā*), since it presumes that there is an 'I' to be liberated. It is impossible to attempt to overcome ignorance (*avijjā*); what must be overcome are views (*diṭṭhi*), meaning that one has to see the cause (*hetu*) and effect (*phala*), understand impermanence (*anicca*) and clearly comprehend the dependent origination of phenomena without perceiving them as 'me' and an 'object.' The *Paccayasutta* (S II 25–27) mentions that by seeing dependent origination (*paṭiccasamuppāda*) with the right wisdom (*sammapaññā*), the meditator is liberated.[122] This means that the meditator is free from an 'I,' with which she or he creates the past, future or present. Only when the meditator observes and understands the processes of dependent origination as they arise and pass away can her or his practice be called meditation (*bhāvanā*). In other words, the meditator should understand that all mental formations (*saṅkhāra*) are impermanent (*anicca*), subject to suffering (*dukkha*) and without self (*anattā*); this is understood through wisdom (*paññā*), which prevents the activation of ignorance (*avijjā*).

The complete elimination of the fetters (*saṃyojana*) takes place through relinquishment

---

of suffering (S II 4: *Yaṃ kho bhikkhave dukkhe aññāṇaṃ dukkhasamudaye aññāṇaṃ dukkhanirodhe aññāṇaṃ dukkhanirodhagāminiyā paṭipadāya aññāṇaṃ. Ayaṃ vuccati bhikkhave avijjā*).

119. The *Papañcasūdani* commentary says that ignorance (*avijjā*) arises with all the other fetters (Ps I 288: *Sabbeh' eva sahajātāññāṇavasena avijjāsaṃyojanaṃ uppajjati*), implying that it does not occur on its own.

120. A V 113: *Purimā bhikkhave koṭi na paññāyati avijjāya 'ito pubbe avijjā nāhosi, atha pacchā sambhavī ti, evañc' etaṃ bhikkhave vuccati. Atha ca pana paññāyati' idappaccayā avijjā' ti. Avijjam p' ahaṃ bhikkhave sāhāraṃ vadāmi, no anāhāraṃ. Ko cāhāro avijjāya? Pañca nīvaraṇā ti 'ssa vacanīyaṃ.*

121. For a more detailed description, see Chapter V.1, under the subheading 'Sloth and torpor (*thīnamiddha*).'

122. This *sutta* states that the noble disciple is free from personality views when he has 'clearly seen with right wisdom the dependently arisen phenomena and dependent origination as it is' (S II 27: *Tathā hi bhikkhave ariyasāvakassa ayañca paṭiccasamuppādo ime ca samuppannā dhammā yathā-bhūtaṃ sammapaññāya sudiṭṭhāti*).

(*vossagga*)—at this point, the mind enters *nibbāna*.[123] For example, it is said in the *Mettāsutta* that the path to liberation can be achieved through the cultivation of friendliness or loving kindness (*mettā*) in conjunction with the seven factors of awakening (*bojjhaṅga*):

> based on seclusion (*viveka*), dispassion (*virāga*) and cessation (*nirodha*), leading to relinquishment (*vossagga*) (S V 119).[124]

Here seclusion (*viveka*) means the secluded tranquillity of the body and mind[125] achieved through the experience of *nibbāna*, while dispassion (*virāga*) refers to the path and fruition knowledge (*maggaphalañāṇa*).[126] Cessation (*nirodha*) is difficult to explain. If we say that something does not exist, it implies that something existed before, but this is not the meaning of *nirodha*. For example, I had a cup and then I lost it; although it no longer exists, I can still think about it. But if I never had a cup or if it had never been manufactured, it would be impossible to know or think about it. We have the perception of the cup only because it existed in the past, but if there were no cup in the past, there would be no perception (*saññā*)—neither of the cup nor of its absence. Similarly, *nirodha* does not mean the cessation of something that had been there and then disappeared; after *nirodha* is reached, it is not possible to perceive it, since there is absolutely nothing to think about; it is a kind of 'non-experience' within which *nibbāna* is situated. Therefore, *nibbāna* is often described as the complete cessation of craving (i.e., *taṇhākkhayanirodha*),[127] because craving is always connected with perception (*saññā*), whereas perception does not exist in *nibbāna*.

V 4 Seven factors of awakening (*satta bojjhaṅgā*)

> *Puna ca paraṃ bhikkhave bhikkhu dhammesu dhammānupassī viharati* ***sattasu bojjhaṅgesu****. Kathañca bhikkhave bhikkhu dhammesu dhammānupassī viharati sattasu bojjhaṅgesu? Idha bhikkhave bhikkhu santaṃ vā ajjhattaṃ* ***satisambojjhaṅgaṃ****: atthi me ajjhattaṃ satisambojjhaṅgo ti pajānāti, asantaṃ vā ajjhattaṃ satisambojjhaṅgaṃ: natthi me ajjhattaṃ satisambojjhaṅgo ti pajānāti, yathā ca anuppannassa satisambojjhaṅgassa uppādo hoti tañca pajānāti, yathā ca uppannassa satisambojjhaṅgassa bhāvanāpāripūrī hoti tañca pajānāti. Santaṃ vā ajjhattaṃ* ***dhammavicayasambojjhaṅgaṃ*** *... Santaṃ vā ajjhattaṃ* ***viriyasambojjhaṅgaṃ*** *... Santaṃ vā ajjhattaṃ* ***pītisambojjhaṅgaṃ*** *.... Santaṃ vā ajjhattaṃ* ***passaddhisambojjhaṅgaṃ*** *... Santaṃ vā ajjhattaṃ* ***samādhisambojjhaṅgaṃ*** *... Santaṃ vā ajjhattaṃ* ***upekkhāsambojjhaṅgaṃ****: atthi me ajjhattaṃ upekkhāsambojjhaṅgo ti pajānāti, asantaṃ vā ajjhattaṃ*

123. In the *Sammohavinodanī*, relinquishment (*vossagga*) is presented in the sense of entering into *nibbāṇa* and related to the giving up of the defilements (Vibh-a 317: *kilesapariccāgavossaggatthaṃ nibbāṇapakkhandanavossaggatthañ ca*).

124. S V 119: *Kathambhāvitā ca bhikkhave mettācetovimutti ... Idha bhikkhave bhikkhu mettāsahagataṃ satisambojjhaṅgam bhāveti ... mettāsahagatam upekkhāsambojjhaṅgam bhāveti vivekavirāganirodhanissitam vossaggapariṇāmiṃ.*

125. Detachment or seclusion (*viveka*) is similarly described in the *Visuddhimagga* as bodily and mental seclusion as well as seclusion by elimination [of the defilements] (Vism 140: *tathā pi kāyaviveko cittaviveko vikkhambhanaviveko ti tayo eva idha daṭṭhabbā*).

126. Dispassion (*virāga*) is frequently mentioned in the *suttas* in relation to *nibbāna*; for example, in the *Brahmasaṃyutta*, it is linked to the calming of all mental formations (*saṅkhāra*), the relinquishment of all attachments, the destruction of craving, dispassion, cessation and *nibbāna* (*yad idaṃ sabbasaṅkhārasamatho sabbupadhipaṭinissaggo taṇhakkhayo virāgo nirodho nibbānaṃ*) (S I 136).

127. For example, in the *Aggappasādasutta*, the destruction of craving (*taṇhakkhaya*) is linked to *nibbāna*: 'In as much as phenomena are conditioned or not conditioned, of those phenomena dispassion excels as foremost, that is, the release from pride, the removal of thirst, the abolishment of attachment, the ending of the cycle of rebirths, the destruction of craving, dispassion, cessation, *nibbāna*' (A II 34: *Yāvatā bhikkhave dhammā saṅkhatā vā asaṅkhatā vā virāgo tesaṃ dhammānaṃ aggam akkhāyati yadidaṃ madanimmadano pipāsavinayo ālayasamugghāto vaṭṭūpacchedo taṇhakkhayo virāgo nirodho nibbānaṃ*).

upekkhāsambojjhaṅgaṃ: natthi me ajjhattaṃ upekkhāsambojjhaṅgo ti pajānāti, yathā ca anuppannassa upekkhāsambojjhaṅgassa uppādo hoti tañca pajānāti, yathā ca uppannassa upekkhāsambojjhaṅgassa bhāvanāpāripūrī hoti tañca pajānāti.

'And again, monks, a monk abides contemplating phenomena as phenomena in regard to the **seven factors of awakening.** And how does a monk abide contemplating phenomena as phenomena in regard to the seven factors of awakening? Here, monks, when the **mindfulness factor of awakening** is present in him, a monk knows: "There is the mindfulness factor of awakening in me"; when the mindfulness factor of awakening is not present in him, he knows: "there is no mindfulness factor of awakening in me"; and he also knows how the unarisen mindfulness awakening factor arises, and how the arisen mindfulness awakening factor is accomplished by cultivation. ... When the **investigation-of-*dhammas* factor of awakening** is present in him ... when the **energy factor of awakening** is present in him ... when the **joy factor of awakening** is present in him ... when the **tranquillity factor of awakening** is present in him ... when the **concentration factor of awakening** is present in him ... when the **equanimity factor of awakening** is present in him, a monk knows: "There is the equanimity factor of awakening in me"; when the equanimity factor of awakening is not present in him, he knows: "there is no equanimity factor of awakening in me"; and he also knows how the unarisen equanimity awakening factor arises, and how the arisen equanimity awakening factor is accomplished by cultivation.'

Recurring passage indicating the ways to approach the contemplation[128]

Iti ajjhattaṃ vā dhammesu dhammānupassī viharati, bahiddhā vā dhammesu dhammānupassī viharati, ajjhattabahiddhā vā dhammesu dhammānupassī viharati. Samudayadhammānupassī vā dhammesu viharati, vayadhammānupassī vā dhammesu viharati, samudayavayadhammānupassī vā dhammesu viharati. Atthi dhammā ti vā panassa sati paccupaṭṭhitā hoti yāvadeva ñāṇamattāya patissatimattāya, anissito ca viharati na ca kiñci loke upādiyati. Evam kho bhikkhave bhikkhu dhammesu dhammānupassī viharati sattasu bojjhaṅgesu.

'Thus he abides contemplating phenomena as phenomena internally, or he abides contemplating phenomena as phenomena externally, or he abides contemplating phenomena as phenomena both internally and externally. He abides contemplating the arising of phenomena in phenomena, or he abides contemplating the passing away of phenomena in phenomena, or he abides contemplating both the arising and passing away of phenomena in phenomena. Or, mindfulness that "there are phenomena" is established in him just to the extent necessary for knowledge and mindfulness. And he abides without attachment, not clinging to anything in the world. Monks, thus a monk abides contemplating phenomena as phenomena in regard to the seven factors of awakening.'

Pemasiri Thera's commentary

'Seven factors of awakening' (*satta bojjhaṅgā*)

We could say that meditation (*bhāvanā*) only truly begins with the arising of the seven factors of awakening (*satta bojjhaṅgā*). In this manner, meditation centres are meant to be a kind of factory for the production of the awakening factors.[129] These comprise:

---

128. For comments on the recurring passage, see Chapter II.1, under the subheading 'Recurring passage indicating the ways to approach the contemplation.'

129. The importance of the seven factors of awakening (*bojjhaṅga*) is reflected in the *Papañcasūdani* commentary, which dedicates much more attention to this section of the *sutta* (Ps I 289–301) than to the previous ones, i.e., on the contemplation of the five aggregates (Ps I 286–287) and the six sense spheres (Ps I 287–289). The commentary states that it is because of the seven factors of awakening (*bojjhaṅga*) that the meditator

1. mindfulness (*sati*)
2. investigation of *dhammas* (*dhammavicaya*)
3. energy (*viriya*)
4. joy (*pīti*)
5. tranquillity (*passaddhi*)
6. concentration (*samādhi*)
7. equanimity (*upekkhā*)

The meditator cultivates the first three factors (i.e., mindfulness, investigation of *dhammas* and energy), whereas the other four (i.e., joy, tranquillity, concentration and equanimity) result from the establishment of the first three. At the preparatory stage for the cultivation of the first three factors of awakening, the meditator begins with the practice of ardour or diligence (*ātāpa*), mindfulness (*sati*) and clear comprehension (*sampajañña*); it is thus said in the beginning of the *Satipaṭṭhānasutta* that the meditator should be 'ardent, clearly comprehending, mindful, having abandoned desires and discontent in regard to the world.'[130] When these three qualities—i.e., mindfulness (*sati*), clear comprehension (*sampajañña*) and diligence (*ātāpa*)—strengthen and mature, they can be called the first three factors of awakening—i.e., mindfulness (*sati*), investigation of *dhammas* (*dhammavicaya*) and energy (*viriya*), respectively (Figure 3).

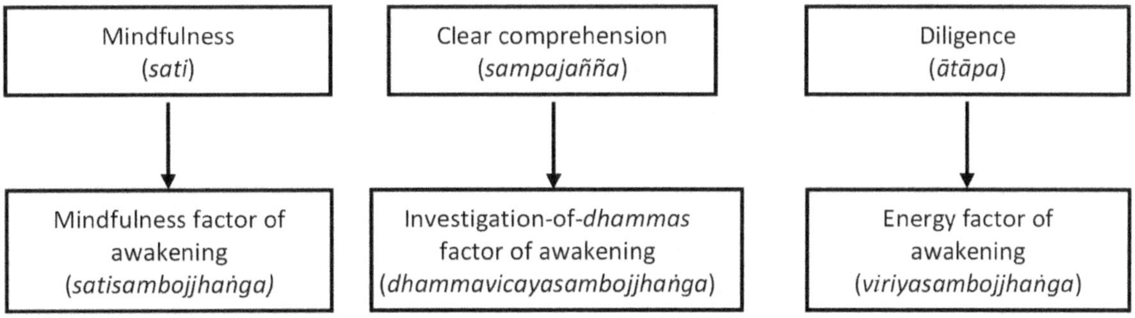

Figure 3 Stages in the cultivation of the first three factors of awakening (*bojjhaṅga*).

The presence of mindfulness (*sati*) indicates that desires and discontent are (temporarily) abandoned (*vineyya loke abhijjhādomanassaṃ*). Diligence (*ātāpa*) refers to the mental effort needed to relinquish the defilements, whereas energy (*viriya*) signifies that the mental states without defilements are maintained. In other words, at the beginning of meditation practice, the meditator should have the intention to be without the defilements, and once the mental states without defilements actually arise, they must then be maintained. Diligence (*ātāpa*),

becomes completely awakened; she or he rises from the sleep of defilements (*kilesa*) and penetrates the truths (Ps I 289: *Ettha hi, sambujjhati āraddhavipassakato paṭṭhāya yogāvacaro ti sambodhi. Yāya vā so sati-ādikāya sattadhammasāmaggiyā sambujjhati, kilesaniddāto uṭṭhāti, saccāni vā paṭivijjhati, sā dhammasāmaggī sambodhi*). The indispensable role of the seven factors of awakening (*bojjhaṅga*) on the path to liberation is further indicated by their inclusion in all textual versions of the *Satipaṭṭhāna* in the Pāli canon such as the *Satipaṭṭhānavibhaṅga* (Vibh 199–200), which includes only two areas—i.e., contemplation of the five hindrances (*nīvaraṇa*) and the seven factors of awakening (*bojjhaṅga*)—in the section on the contemplation of phenomena (*dhammānupassanā*).

130. M I 56: *ātāpī sampajāno satimā vineyya loke abhijjhādomanassaṃ.*

mindfulness (*sati*) and clear comprehension (*sampajañña*) are initially cultivated in all four domains of mindfulness (*cattāro satipaṭṭhānā*)—i.e., the contemplation of the body (*kāyānupassanā*), feeling (*vedanānupassanā*), the mind (*cittānupassanā*) and phenomena (*dhammānupassanā*)—while the practice encompasses both calm (*samatha*) and insight (*vipassanā*) meditation. However, when the seven factors of awakening (*bojjhaṅga*) are well established, the meditation takes place predominantly in the domain of the contemplation of phenomena (*dhammānupassanā*), and the practice becomes pure insight meditation (*vipassanā*). The meditator then no longer requires any advice or instructions from a teacher, and her or his life should be without displeasure or confusion irrespective of whether she or he has gained the path knowledges (*maggañāṇa*). At that stage, the meditator's mind is very clear and free; it is like a drop of mercury that never remains in the same place and cannot become stuck to any object or like a lotus flower from which any drop of water immediately slides off. In the mind that arises with well-developed awakening factors (*bojjhaṅga*), no object or experience remains, because the nature of phenomena—i.e., their impermanence (*anicca*), unsatisfactoriness (*dukkha*) and non-self (*anattā*)—is clearly observed and understood. Such a practitioner is already closely associated with the states of detachment or seclusion (*viveka*), dispassion (*virāga*) and cessation (*nirodha*) and therefore has no problems in relation to any object; this is the highest level of purity that can arise in regard to the mind and body (*nāmarūpa*).

The importance of the factors of awakening (*bojjhaṅga*) is emphasised in many *suttas*. For example, the *Sabbāsavasutta* says that the cultivation of the seven factors of awakening (*bojjhaṅga*) is the path to the abandonment of the taints (*āsava*):

> There are taints that should be abandoned by cultivation ... What taints should be abandoned by cultivation? A monk, reflecting wisely, develops the awakening factors of mindfulness, investigation of *dhammas*, energy, joy, tranquillity, concentration and equanimity based on seclusion, dispassion and cessation, leading to relinquishment. (M I 11)[131]

Likewise, the *Bojjhaṅgasutta* of the *Asaṅkhatasaṃyutta* (S IV 367–368) explains that the seven factors of awakening (*bojjhaṅga*) are the path leading to the 'unconditioned' (*asaṅkhatagāmimagga*). The word *saṅkhata* denotes anything that is conditioned and produced by causes; however, the factors of awakening (*bojjhaṅga*), though conditioned, do not produce effects.[132] Therefore, it is said in this *sutta* that they are based on detachment (*viveka*), dispassion (*virāga*) and cessation (*nirodha*), which leads to the unconditioned (*asaṅkhatagāmimagga*).[133]

131. M I 11: *atthi āsavā bhāvanā pahātabbā ... Katame ca bhikkhave āsavā bhāvanā pahātabbā: Idha bhikkhave bhikkhu paṭisaṅkhā yoniso satisambojjhaṅgaṃ bhāveti vivekanissitaṃ virāganissitaṃ nirodhanissitaṃ vossaggapariṇāmiṃ, paṭisaṅkhā yoniso dhammavicayasambojjhaṅgaṃ bhāveti ... pe ... viriyasambojjhaṅgaṃ bhāveti ... pītisambojjhaṅgaṃ bhāveti ... passaddhisambojjhaṅgaṃ bhāveti ... samādhisambojjhaṅgaṃ bhāveti ... upekhāsambojjhaṅgaṃ bhāveti.*

132. It is thus said in the *Atthasālinī* commentary that the seven factors of awakening (*bojjhaṅga*), though themselves *kamma* (which is neither pure nor impure, producing neither purity nor impurity), lead to the destruction of *kamma* (As 89: *Yadidaṃ satta bojjhaṅgā - satisambojjhaṅgo ... pe ... upekkhāsambojjhaṅgo, idaṃ vuccati, bhikkhave, kammaṃ akaṇhaṃ asukkaṃ akaṇhāsukkavipākaṃ kammakkhayāya saṃvattati*).

133. The *Bojjhaṅgasutta* says: 'Monks, what is the path to the unconditioned? Here a monk cultivates the awakening factors of mindfulness, investigation of *dhammas*, energy, joy, tranquillity, concentration and equanimity based on seclusion, dispassion and cessation, leading to relinquishment' (S IV 367: *Katamo ca bhikkhave asaṅkhatagāmimaggo. Idhabhikkhave bhikkhu satisambojjhaṅgam bhāveti ... viriyasambojjhaṅgaṃ bhāveti ... pītisambojjhaṅgaṃ bhāveti ... passaddhisambojjhaṅgaṃ bhāveti ... samādhisambojjhaṅgaṃ bhāveti ... upekkhāsambojjhaṅgam bhāveti vivekanissitaṃ virāganissitaṃ nirodhanissitaṃ vossaggaparināmi*).

The *Gilānasutta* of the *Bojjhaṅgasaṃyutta* (S V 97–80) narrates how the Buddha expounded the seven factors of awakening (*bojjhaṅga*) to his disciple Mahākassapa who was gravely ill; after hearing the teaching, Mahākassapa rejoiced and was cured of his illness. Because Mahākassapa was already a highly accomplished meditator, the awakening factors (*bojjhaṅga*) could easily arise in him. For those who were still in training and had not yet developed the awakening factors (*bojjhaṅga*), the Buddha would give different advice if they were ill; for example, in the *Girimānandasutta* (A V 108–112), the sick monk Girimānanda was instructed to contemplate the ten perceptions, which cured him of his illness.[134] The ten perceptions listed in this *sutta* include impermanence (*aniccasaññā*) and non-self (*anattasaññā*) but not the perception of suffering (*dukkha*); this is because suffering arises only when we approach an object of experience with the perception of permanence, which consequently creates problems, dissatisfaction or pain.

Among the seven factors of awakening (*bojjhaṅga*), mindfulness (*sati*) and investigation of *dhammas* (*dhammavicaya*) play a crucial role in the suppression and final elimination of the fetters (*saṃyojana*). The number of eliminated fetters (*saṃyojana*) depends on the strength of the investigation-of-*dhammas* factor of awakening (*dhammavicayabojjhaṅga*). Usually only some fetters (*saṃyojana*) are eliminated; it is much rarer to eradicate them all, as in the aforementioned story of Bāhiya who, upon hearing the Buddha's instructions, instantly became an *arahant* (Ud 8).

'Mindfulness factor of awakening' (*satisambojjhaṅga*)

Mindfulness (*sati*)[135] is listed as the first factor of awakening (*satisambojjhaṅga*). As discussed earlier, when wise attention (*yoniso manasikāra*) has been established for some time and has maintained the state of wholesomeness, mindfulness (*sati*) may arise.[136] When mindfulness (*sati*) is cultivated over and over again, it can reach the strength of the awakening factor (*bojjhaṅga*); at that stage, it is associated with detachment or seclusion (*viveka*), dispassion (*virāga*) and cessation (*nirodha*), and leads to the unconditioned (*asaṅkhata*), as said in the *Bojjhaṅgasutta* of the *Asaṅkhatasaṃyutta*:

> And what, monks, is the path leading to the unconditioned? Here, monks, a monk cultivates the mindfulness factor of awakening, which is founded on seclusion, dispassion and cessation, resulting in release. This is called the path leading to the unconditioned. (S IV 367)[137]

Detachment or seclusion (*viveka*) has three aspects: detachment from the body (*kāyaviveka*), detachment from the mind (*cittaviveka*) and detachment from defilements (*vikkhambhana-*

134. The ten perceptions listed in the *Girimānandasutta* are: (1) impermanence (*aniccasaññā*), (2) non-self (*anattasaññā*), (3) perception of unattractiveness (*asubhasaññā*), (4) danger (*ādīnavasaññā*), (5) relinquishment (*pahānasaññā*), (6) dispassion (*virāgasaññā*), (7) cessation (*nirodhasaññā*), (8) non-delight in the whole world (*sabbaloke anabhiratasaññā*), (9) impermanence of all formations (*sabbasaṅkhāresu aniccasaññā*) and (10) mindfulness of breathing (*ānāpānasati*) (A V 109).

135. For a detailed discussion on the concept of mindfulness (*sati*), see Chapter I, under the subheading 'Mindful (*satimā*).'

136. It is also stated in the *Papañcasūdani* commentary that wise attention 'nourishes' the arising of the mindfulness awakening factor (Ps I 289: *Tattha yoniso manasikārabahulīkāro, ayam āhāro anuppannassa vā satisambojjhaṅgassa uppādāya*). The commentary then lists four aspects that lead to the arising of the mindfulness awakening factor: (1) mindfulness and clear comprehension, (2) avoiding confused people, (3) associating with mindful people and (4) inclination towards mindfulness (Ps I 290: *apica cattāro dhammā satisambojjhaṅgassa uppādāya saṃvattanti: satisampajaññaṃ muṭṭhassatipuggalaparivajjanatā, upaṭṭhitasatipuggalasevanatā, tadadhimuttatāti*).

137. S IV 367: *Katamo ca bhikkhave asaṅkhatagāmimaggo. Idha bhikkhave bhikkhu satisambojjhaṅgam bhāveti vivekanissitaṃ virāganissitaṃ nirodhanissitaṃ vossaggapariṇā*mi. *Ayaṃ vuccati bhikkhave asaṅkhatagāmimaggo.*

viveka).[138] Detachment or seclusion from the body (*kāyaviveka*) refers to the body of mental concomitants (*cetasika*),[139] which become tranquil and arise in an appropriate way in relation to the objects of experience. This means that the meditator is secluded or detached from the defilements (*kilesa*) or free from their influence, and when the tranquillity of the mental concomitants (*cetasika*) is established, the seclusion from the mind (*cittaviveka*) automatically arises.[140]

The mindfulness factor of awakening (*satisambojjhaṅga*) is also associated with dispassion (*virāga*), which refers to freedom from desire or craving (*taṇhā*) as well as cessation (*nirodha*), which is the complete absence of defilements (*kilesa*). Cessation (*nirodha*) means that a particular experience will never arise again, since the object that ceased can no longer be contacted. This does not mean that the object has been destroyed or passed away, since what passes away is remembered and can arise again; in the case of cessation (*nirodha*), it is impossible for any thought or perception (*saññā*) about it to arise. For cessation (*nirodha*) to occur, dispassion (*virāga)* or seclusion (*viveka*) should already be well established. Cessation (*nirodha*), seclusion (*viveka*) and dispassion (*virāga*) lead to *nibbāna*. When mindfulness (*sati*) is supported by seclusion (*viveka*), dispassion (*virāga*) and cessation (*nirodha*) and results in relinquishment (*vossagga*), it is called the mindfulness factor of awakening (*satisambojjhaṅga*).[141]

A similar explanation is given in the *Ānāpānasatisutta* (M III 83): the meditator, while mindfully breathing in and out, contemplates impermanence (*anicca*) followed by dispassion (*virāga*), cessation (*nirodha*) and abandonment (*paṭinissagga*).[142] Thus, the meditator firstly contemplates impermanence (*aniccānupassī*), and when insight into impermanence and the other two characteristics of phenomena (i.e., unsatisfactoriness and non-self) is well established, dispassion

---

138. These three aspects of detachment or seclusion (*viveka*) are also listed in the *Atthasālinī* and *Visuddhimagga* (As 164; Vism 140: *tathā pi kāyaviveko cittaviveko vikkhambhanaviveko ti tayo eva idha daṭṭhabbā*). The *Sammohavinodanī* lists five aspects of detachment (*viveka*) that are developed through: (1) substitution of opposites (*tadaṅgaviveka*), (2) suppression [of defilements] (*vikkhambhana*), (3) relinquishment (*samuccheda*), (4) complete calming down (*paṭippassaddhi*) and (5) liberation (*nissaraṇa*) (Vibh-a 316: *so cāyaṃ tadaṅgaviveko, vikkhambhanasamucchedapaṭippassaddhinissaraṇavivekoti pañcavidho*).

139. As discussed earlier, the Pāli word *kāya* has a wide spectrum of meanings and also refers to the group of mental concomitants—i.e., the aggregates of feeling (*vedanā*), perception (*saññā*) and mental formations (*saṅkhāra*). It is thus interpreted in the *Dhammasaṅgaṇi* (Dhs 14–16) and *Abhidhammattha Saṅgaha* (Aung and Rhys Davids, 1910, 96; cf. also Bodhi 1993, 87). Conversely, commentaries like the *Atthasālinī* explain the seclusion of the body (*kāyaviveka*) as detachment from desires based on objects (As 164: ... *vatthukāmehipi viviccevāti attho yujjati. Tena kāyaviveko vutto hoti*). In the commentary on the *Visuddhimagga*, *kāyaviveka* is interpreted as physical seclusion (Vism-a, M I 219: *rahogatenāti rahasi gatena. tena kāyavivekaṃ dasseti*).

140. This is similarly explained in the *Sammohavinodanī*, saying that bodily tranquillity (*kāyapassaddhi*) in relation to distress (*daratha*) refers to the three [mental] aggregates (or the mental concomitants), while the tranquillity of the mind (*cittapassaddhi*) in relation to distress refers to the aggregate of consciousness (*viññāṇakkhandha*) (Vibh-a 314: *Kāyapassaddhīti tiṇṇaṃ khandhānaṃ darathapassaddhi. Cittapassaddhīti viññāṇakkhandhassa darathapassaddhi*).

141. In the *Vibhaṅga*, the mindfulness factor of awakening (*satisambojjhaṅga*) is defined as dependent on detachment, dispassion and cessation and resulting in relinquishment (Vibh 229: *Idha bhikkhu satisambojjhaṅgaṃ bhāveti vivekanissitaṃ virāganissitaṃ nirodhanissitaṃ vossaggapariṇāmiṃ*). The *Sammohavinodanī* says that the mindfulness awakening factor (*satisambojjhaṅga*) is cultivated for the purpose of relinquishment in the sense of giving up the defilements and entering into *nibbāna*. (Vibh-a 317: *Ayaṃ hi bojjhaṅgabhāvanam anuyutto bhikkhu yathā satisambojjhaṅgo kilesapariccāgavossaggatthaṃ nibbāṇapakkhandanavossaggatthañ ca paripaccati, yathā ca paripakko hoti, tathā naṃ bhāvetīti*).

142. M III 83: *Aniccānupassī assasissāmīti sikkhati; Aniccānupassī passasissāmīti sikkhati; Virāgānupassī assasissāmīti sikkhati; Virāgānupassī passasissāmīti sikkhati; Nirodhānupassī assasissāmīti sikkhati; Nirodhānupassī passasissāmīti sikkhati; Paṭinissaggānupassī assasissāmīti sikkhati; Paṭinissaggānupassī passasissāmīti sikkhati.*

(*virāga*) arises, meaning that the defilements (*kilesa*) no longer appear. When the meditator is firmly grounded in dispassion, cessation (*nirodha*) can occur, which refers, as mentioned earlier, to a state in which it is impossible for the perception (*saññā*) of an object to arise. For example, when the meditator reaches the stage of stream-winner (*sotāpanna*), the cessation (*nirodha*) of personality view (*sakkāyadiṭṭhi*), doubt (*vicikicchā*) and attachment to rites and rituals (*sīlabbataparāmāsa*) takes place; these three fetters (*saṃyojana*) cease and can never arise again, i.e., absolutely no thought in relation to these fetters can emerge.

The contemplation of cessation (*nirodha*) is followed by the contemplation of abandonment (*paṭinissagga*); this means that habitual tendencies are gradually lost.[143] For example, a fire was burning in a fireplace for a long time and then it was extinguished; the fireplace was cleaned and washed with water. Although the fire is no longer there, some heat may still be left, even though it is not possible for fire to arise again. Such is the experience of a stream-winner (*sotāpanna*) after cessation (*nirodha*): while certain fetters (*saṃyojana*) are eradicated, some inherent tendencies remain for a while—although they cannot arise again—until they are completely dispersed like the heat in the fireplace after the extinction of the fire. In this way, abandonment (*paṭinissagga*) occurs after path and fruition knowledge (*maggaphalañāṇa*), when various habitual tendencies are gradually relinquished. All defilements (*kilesa*) are in fact by-products of past habits and tendencies; when they emerge, they cause much trouble and suffering (*dukkha*). They can gradually be reduced and eventually completely relinquished through the practice of the four foundations of mindfulness (*cattāro satipaṭṭhānā*). However, this does not mean that the meditator should constantly examine whether the habitual tendencies, fetters (*saṃyojana*) or defilements (*kilesa*) are present or not, since such an examination only indicates that the defilements (*kilesa*) in question are still active. After cessation (*nirodha*), when the contemplation of abandonment (*paṭinissagga*) takes place, there is no more concern about whether a particular fetter (*saṃyojana*) or defilement (*kilesa*) is there or not.

To summarise, right mindfulness (*sammā sati*) developed to the strength of the awakening factor (*satisambojjhaṅga*) is the foundation for the gradual reduction and relinquishment or abandonment of the defilements (*kilesa*), which in turn leads to the unconditioned (*asaṅkhata*), to liberation.

'Investigation-of-*dhammas* factor of awakening' (*dhammavicayasambojjhaṅga*)

The investigation-of-*dhammas* factor of awakening (*dhammavicayasambojjhaṅga*) refers to the wisdom through which the mind and body (*nāmarūpa*) are investigated. Like the mindfulness factor of awakening (*satisambojjhaṅga*), it is also associated with detachment (*viveka*), dispassion (*virāga*) and cessation (*nirodha*), thus resulting in relinquishment (*vossaggapariṇāmi*).[144]

The investigation-of-*dhammas* factor of awakening (*dhammavicayasambojjhaṅga*) can be considered the highest level of wisdom. Several terms in Pāli can denote what we call wisdom,

143. The term *paṭinissagga* is presented in the *Visuddhimagga* as the path that involves the abandonment of the defilements (*kilesa*) and the mental formations that produce the aggregates by cutting them off. The meditator then enters *nibbāna*, taking it as the object (Vism 290: *Maggo samucchedavasena saddhiṃ khandhābhisankhārehi kilese pariccajati: ārammaṇakaraṇena ca nibbāne pakkhandatī ti pariccāgapaṭinissaggo ceva pakkhandanapaṭinissaggo ti ca vuccati*).

144. The *Bojjhaṅgasutta* of the *Asaṅkhatasaṃyutta* states that 'the investigation-of-*dhammas* factor of awakening is founded on detachment, dispassion, cessation, resulting in release. This is called the path leading to the unconditioned' (S IV 367: *dhammavicayasambojjhaṅgaṃ bhāveti vivekanissitaṃ virāganissitaṃ nirodhanissitaṃ vossaggapariṇāmi. ayaṃ vuccati bhikkhave asaṅkhatagāmimaggo*).

knowledge, discernment and understanding. All are interrelated, and each is described in the Buddhist texts in several ways. As discussed before, the earliest stage of wisdom developed by the meditator is clear comprehension (*sampajañña*),[145] as she or he sees objects changing and begins to understand impermanence (*anicca*), causes (*hetu*), effects (*phala*) and conditions (*paccaya*). When clear comprehension (*sampajañña*) matures, it conditions the arising of the investigative inquiry or discernment (*vimāṃsā*), which is one of the four bases for power (*iddhipāda*), presented as part of the Buddhist path to liberation:

> Monks, these are the four bases for power which, when developed and practised, lead to going beyond. What four? Here, monks, a monk develops the basis for power that possesses concentration due to the will to act and the mental formations of striving. He develops the basis for power that possesses concentration due to energy and the mental formations of striving. He develops the basis for power that possesses concentration due to the mind and the mental formations of striving. He develops the basis for power that has concentration due to investigative discernment and the mental formations of striving. These four bases for power, when developed and cultivated, lead to going beyond. (S V 254)[146]

The four bases for power (*iddhipāda*) refer to the concentration (*samādhi*) developed in meditation, which is based on the will to act or strong enthusiasm (*chanda*), energy (*viriya*), strength of the mind (*citta*) and investigative discernment (*vīmaṃsā*).[147] The final base for power with concentration based on discernment (*vīmaṃsā*) means that the meditator relates to the arising objects with understanding, investigation and an absence of delusion.[148] This involves understanding and striving to prevent unwholesome states from arising and instead cultivating wholesome ones.[149] For example, during certain stages in meditation practice, a particular feeling or mental state may keep arising, and the meditator is accordingly instructed by her or his teacher to ignore it and instead direct her or his attention elsewhere; this shift in focus should be done with discernment (*vīmaṃsā*). If one meditates with a lack of investigative discernment (*vīmaṃsā*) and certain unusual phenomena occur, the meditator may think that she or he has achieved high attainments, and consequently, strong conceit (*māna*) may arise; this deception could be prevented by discernment (*vīmaṃsā*). Thus, discernment (*vīmaṃsā*) can be seen as an aspect of wisdom.

145. For details, see Chapter I, under the subheading 'Clearly comprehending (*sampajāno*).'

146. S V 254: *Cattāro me bhikkhave iddhipādā bhāvitā bahulīkatā aparāparaṃ gamanāya saṃvattanti. Katame cattāro? Idha bhikkhave bhikkhu chandasamādhipadhānasaṅkhārasamannāgatam iddhipādam bhāveti, viriyasamādhipadhānasaṅkharasamannāgatam iddhipādam bhāveti, cittasamādhipadhānasaṅkhārasamannāgatam iddhipādam bhāveti, vīmaṃsāsamādhipadhānasaṅkhārasamannāgataṃ iddhipādam bhāveti. Ime kho bhikkhave cattāro iddhipādā bhāvitā bahulīkatā aparāparaṅgamanāya saṃvattantīti.*

147. For a detailed description of the four bases of spiritual power (*iddhipāda*), see the *Iddhipādasaṃyutta* (S V 254–293).

148. The *Vibhaṅga* similarly defines discernment (*vīmaṃsā*) as 'the absence of delusion, investigation of phenomena and right view' (Vibh 219: *Tattha katamā vīmaṃsā? Yā paññā pajānanā ... amoho dhammavicayo sammādiṭṭhi: ayaṃ vuccati vīmaṃsā*).

149. The *Vibhaṅga* comments that concentration based on discernment (*vīmaṃsa*) is cultivated by 'striving for the non-arising of unwholesome states that have not arisen, abandoning those that have arisen, striving for the arising of wholesome states that have not arisen and maintaining those that have arisen' (Vibh 219: *Ayaṃ vuccati vīmaṃsāsamādhi. So anuppannānaṃ pāpakānaṃ akusalānaṃ dhammānaṃ anuppādāya chandaṃ janeti vāyamati viriyaṃ ārabhati cittaṃ paggaṇhāti padahati, uppannānaṃ kusalānaṃ dhammānaṃ ṭhitiyā ...*).

The most frequent term for wisdom used in the *Tipiṭaka* is the Pāli word *paññā*, which is described variously in the Buddhist teachings.[150] It is often presented as the mental component that has insight into three characteristics (*tilakkhaṇa*), namely, impermanence (*anicca*), unsatisfactoriness (*dukkha*) and non-self (*anattā*), or as an understanding of and clarity about the Dhamma and the path to *nibbāna*.[151] Wisdom (*paññā*) also encompasses right view (*sammā diṭṭhi*) and right intention (*sammā saṅkappa*); the former is often presented as an understanding of the four noble truths[152] and the latter as renunciation.[153]

Although related, wisdom (*paññā*) differs from the concept of knowledge (*ñāṇa*); for example, the hindrances are cognised by wisdom (*paññā*), whereas knowing what the hindrances are and how to avoid them is called knowledge (*ñāṇa*). Knowledge (*ñāṇa*) can be understood and taught to others, whereas wisdom (*paññā*) cannot because it is an experiential realisation. There may be *arahants* who have attained the final realisation through wisdom (*paññā*), but they may not have ability to teach or share knowledge (*ñāṇa*). By contrast, others who have not realised liberation through wisdom (*paññā*) may have knowledge (*ñāṇa*) and are able to teach. When the *suttas* discuss knowledge (*ñāṇa*) in the context of meditation, they often refer to the special knowledges (*abhiññā*) that may occur after experiencing the meditative absorptions (*jhāna*) such as mind-penetrating knowledge (*cetopariyañāṇa*). The knowledges ascribed to the Buddha include the knowledge of the four noble truths (*dukkhañāṇa, samudayañāṇa, nirodhañāṇa, mārgañāṇa*), which are presented in his teachings as the foundation for awakening. For example, in the *Dhammacakkappavattanasutta*, it is said that the middle path discovered by the Buddha gives rise to knowledge (*ñāṇakaraṇī*), which leads to higher knowledge (*abhiññā*) and awakening (*sambodha*).[154]

Wisdom (*paññā*) is different from intelligence. What is called 'intelligence' may be described as a combination of five mental concomitants (*cetasika*) operating together, namely:

1. attention (*manasikāra*)
2. applied thought (*vitakka*)

150. According to numerous passages in the Pāli canon and its commentaries, *paññā* is viewed as a pivotal component of the path to liberation. It is a very broad concept without an exact English equivalent; for example, it is translated as 'understanding, discernment, insight, knowledge, absence of ignorance, right view' (PED, *s.v.*). As one of the faculties (*indriya*), wisdom (*paññā*) is presented in the *Dhammasaṅgaṇi* in a vast semantic field, referring to insight, understanding, inquiry, discernment, reflection, analysis, etc. (Dhs 11).

151. In the *Mahāvedallasutta*, wisdom (*paññā*) is equated with understanding the four noble truths (M I 292: *idaṃ dukkhan ti pajānāti, ayaṃ dukkhasamudayo ti pajānāti, ayaṃ dukkhanirodho ti pajānāti, ayaṃ dukkhanirodhagāminī paṭipadā ti pajānāti. Pajānāti pajānātīti kho āvuso, tasmā paññavā ti vuccatīti*). Likewise, in the *Indriyavibhaṅgasutta*, wisdom (*paññā*) is described as the insight into impermanence and the noble truths (S V 199): *Idha bhikkhave ariyāsāvako paññavā hoti udayatthagāminiyā paññāya samannāgato ariyāya nibbedhikāya sammādukkhakkhayagāminiyā. so idaṃ dukkhanti yathābhūtam pajānāti. Ayaṃ dukkhasamudayo ti yathābhūtam pajānāti. Ayaṃ dukkhanirodhagāminipatipadā ti yathā bhūtam pajānāti*). See also Vism 436–437; M III 245; S II 32.

152. Likewise, in the *Vibhaṅga*, right view (*sammā diṭṭhi*) is presented as understanding the four truths (Vibh 235: *dukkhe ñāṇaṃ dukkhasamudaye ñāṇaṃ dukkhanirodhe ñāṇaṃ dukkhanirodhagāminiyā paṭipadāya ñāṇaṃ: ayaṃ vuccati sammādiṭṭhi*). In the *Sammādiṭṭhisutta*, right view (*sammā diṭṭhi*) is explained as the understanding of wholesomeness and unwholesomeness and as an insight into the four truths, dependent origination and taints (M I 46–55).

153. The *Vibhaṅga* explains right intention (*sammā saṅkappa*) as the resolve to cultivate wholesome mental states, namely, renunciation, absence of all will and absence of cruelty (Vibh 235: *Nekkhammasaṅkappo, avyāpādasaṅkappo, avihiṃsāsaṅkappo: ayaṃ vuccati sammāsaṅkappo*).

154. S V 421: *majjhimā paṭipadā Tathāgatena abhisambuddhā cakkhukaraṇī ñāṇakaraṇī upasamāya abhiññāya sambodhāya nibbānāya saṃvattati.*

3. sustained thought (*vicāra*)
4. energy (*viriya*)
5. one-pointedness (*ekaggatā*)

The mental concomitants (*cetasika*) can arise in conjunction with wholesome (*kusala*) or unwholesome (*akusala*) states. Animals also possess intelligence; in this respect, they are not so different from humans, as they are also comprised of the five aggregates (*khandha*). However, the degree of intelligence varies among creatures depending on how the mental concomitants (*cetasika*) are combined and used. For example, mindfulness (*sati*) does not function in animals, although attention (*manasikāra*), contact (*phassa*), feeling (*vedanā*), perception (*saññā*), volition (*cetanā*) and one-pointedness (*ekaggatā*) operate effectively, as animals know how to hide, observe, wait and so on. Although humans have the potential to cultivate meditation (*bhāvanā*) and wisdom (*paññā*), most people never attempt to do so and instead live their lives at a level very similar to animals.

Intelligence can be used to study the *Tipiṭaka*, cultivate wholesomeness or teach the Dhamma; however, wisdom (*paññā*) cannot arise from such activities, and *nibbāna* cannot be attained therefrom. Wisdom (*paññā*) is more important than intelligence, because it is always wholesome and brings about an understanding of the nature of the five aggregates (*khandha*), elements (*dhātu*) and sense spheres (*āyatana*). For wisdom (*paññā*) to evolve, meditation (*bhāvanā*) should be cultivated; this means that apart from the five mental concomitants (*cetasika*) comprising intelligence, the faculties of trust (*saddhā*), energy (*viriya*), mindfulness (*sati*) and concentration (*samādhi*) must be established.[155] Only then can wisdom (*paññā*) arise, because the well-established first four faculties (*indriya*) reduce or suppress the hindrances (*nīvaraṇa*).

As the meditation practice progresses, wisdom emerges at the highest level, which is called the investigation of *dhammas* (*dhammavicaya*).[156] Here the word *vicaya* means 'investigation, examination,' while the word *dhamma* refers to all the phenomena within the mind and body or mentality and materiality (*nāmarūpa*). When all phenomena arising within the mind and body (*nāmarūpa*) are seen with wisdom at the highest level, this means that the three characteristics (*tilakkhaṇa*) are understood with each phenomenon, as it arises and passes away.[157] The investigation of *dhammas* (*dhammavicaya*) is like the tip of the elephant's trunk, which curls out and can pick up even the minutest object. Wisdom at the level of the investigation of

155. The *Papañcasūdani* commentary dedicates a large section to the importance of the five faculties—i.e., trust (*saddhā*), energy (*viriya*), mindfulness (*sati*), concentration (*samādhi*) and wisdom (*paññā*)—and discusses how they should be balanced for the investigation-of-*dhammas* factor of awakening (*dhammavicayasambojjhaṅga*) to arise; the text stresses the crucial role of mindfulness (*sati*) in balancing them all (Ps I 290–292).

156. The *Papañcasūdani* commentary (Ps I 290) lists several qualities that are conducive to the arising of the investigation-of-*dhammas* factor of awakening (*dhammavicayasambojjhaṅga*): (1) inquiry [into phenomena] (*paripucchakatā*), (2) the purification of the fundamentals (i.e., cleanliness of the body and environment) (*vatthuvisadakiriyā*), (3) balance of the five faculties (*indriyasamattapaṭipādanā*), (4) avoidance of ignorant people (*duppaññapuggalaparivajjanā*), (5) association with wise people (*paññavantapuggalasevanā*), (6) reflection on profound knowledge (in regard to the processes of the aggregates, elements and sense spheres) (*gambhīrañāṇacariyapaccavekkhaṇā*) and (7) inclination towards that (i.e., development of the investigation-of-*dhammas* factor of awakening) (*tadadhimuttatā*).

157. It is similarly stated in the *Ānāpānasatisutta* and *Ānāpānasaṃyutta* that the investigation-of-*dhammas* factor of awakening (*dhammavicayasambojjhaṅga*) arises when the meditator investigates and examines *dhamma* with wisdom (S V 331; M III 85: *tam dhammam paññāya pavicinati parivīmaṃsam āpajjati*), which may indicate the contemplation of the three characteristics (*tilakkhaṇa*). See Gethin (2001, 147).

dhammas is so strong that it is called one of the awakening factors (*sambojjhaṅga*). Any experience is seen as nothing but mind-body processes (*nāmarūpa*), and all defilements (*kilesa*), wrong view (*diṭṭhi*) and wrong intentions (*saṅkappa*) are absent. The processes within the body (*nāma*) and mind (*rūpa*) are clearly distinguished, and the distinction between the mind (*citta*) and mental factors (*cetasika*) is clearly comprehended. The meditator understands that the body (*rūpa*) and mind (*nāma*) are two different processes; for example, she or he can see how the body moves due to the influence of the mind. This is explained through the metaphor of the blind man (representing the body) and the cripple (representing the mind) who live together as friends and help each other. The blind man who cannot see but can easily walk carries on his shoulders the cripple who tells him where to walk.[158] Through the power of the investigation of *dhammas* (*dhammavicaya*), the cripple (mind) and the blind man (body) are clearly distinguished; this investigation of the mind (*nāma*) and body (*rūpa*) continues throughout the path up to arahantship.

When investigation of *dhammas* (*dhammavicaya*) emerges with the six other awakening factors—i.e., mindfulness (*sati*), energy (*viriya*), joy (*pīti*), tranquillity (*passaddhi*), concentration (*samādhi*) and equanimity (*upekkhā*)—at equal strength, the meditator may enter path knowledge (*maggañāṇa*). At that point, all thirty-seven *dhammas* of awakening (*bodhipakkiyādhammā*) are fully developed at the highest level; these include the following:

1. four foundations of mindfulness (*cattāro satipaṭṭhānā*)
2. four right strivings (*cattāro sammappadhānā*)
3. four bases of power (*cattāro iddhipādā*)
4. five faculties (*pañc'indriyāni*)
5. five powers (*pañca balāni*)
6. seven factors of awakening (*satta sambojjhaṅgā*)
7. noble eightfold path (*ariyo aṭṭhaṅgiko maggo*)[159]

As the meditation practice continues after attaining the first path knowledge (*maggañāṇa*), there comes a time when the thirty-seven *dhammas* of awakening are once again balanced and stronger than before. Then the meditator may enter the next path knowledge (*maggañāṇa*).

To recapitulate, when wisdom is at the level of clear comprehension (*sampajañña*), the meditator begins to see the arising and passing away of phenomena, albeit not yet consistently. Sometimes the objects are perceived in relation to oneself and sometimes without self. Hence, at this stage, the practice usually fluctuates between calm (*samatha*) and insight (*vipassanā*) meditation, while investigative inquiry or discernment (*vimāṃsā*) occurs with both types of meditation. But when the investigation of *dhammas* (*dhammavicaya*) emerges, the meditator clearly comprehends causes (*hetu*), effects (*phala*) and conditions (*paccaya*); then the sense of self or 'I' no longer arises, and it can be said that the practice has completely entered the domain of insight (*vipassanā*) meditation. At that level, the meditator has clearly realised and accepted that there is only mentality and materiality (*nāmarūpa*), or said otherwise, that there are only mental and material processes and nothing else. Once wisdom is at the level of the investigation of *dhammas* (*dhammavicaya*), it only inclines towards *nibbāna*.[160]

---

158. This metaphor about the relationship between the mind and body is narrated in the *Visuddhimagga* (Vism 596).

159. For a detailed study of the thirty-seven qualities of awakening (*bodhipakkhiyā dhammā*), see Gethin (2001).

160. The pivotal role of the investigation-of-*dhammas* factor of awakening (*dhammavicayasambojjhaṅga*) is well

'Energy factor of awakening' (*viriyasambojjhaṅga*)

In the beginning of the *Satipaṭṭhānasutta*, it is said that the meditator who cultivates mindfulness (*sati*) is 'ardent' (*ātāpī*), which means that she or he has the diligence or energy necessary to maintain the practice without letting it go.[161] Along with mindfulness (*sati*) and clear comprehension (*sampajañña*), ardour contributes to the right conditions for wisdom (*paññā*) to arise. When the practice becomes stable, ardour strengthens and can be called energy (*viriya*). The term energy (*viriya*) does not refer to the physical energy required to maintain the meditation posture but rather to the mental quality of sustained effort, which is necessary to burn the defilements.[162] Physical effort must be balanced with mental energy (*viriya*); if the physical effort is excessive, the meditator becomes physically unwell or exhausted and cannot focus on the meditation object. In this case, more mental energy (*viriya*) is needed, which means increasing the mental effort required to incline the mind towards wholesomeness and diligently sustain it. Mindfulness (*sati*) will then be supported and maintained, and wisdom (*paññā*) may arise, leading to the insight into the absence of self or 'I' in the process of meditation. Thus, energy (*viriya*) is essential in the cultivation of mindfulness (*sati*) and wisdom (*paññā*), which is why the final words of the Buddha related to diligence, as narrated in the *Mahāparinibbānasutta*: 'Strive on diligently' (D II 156: *appamādena sampādethā*).

Energy (*viriya*) is a component of several groups of qualities required on the Buddhist path. It is presented in the model of the thirty-seven *dhammas* relating to awakening (*bodhipakkhiyādhammā*), where it is a component of the four right endeavours or strivings (*cattāro sammappadhānā*).[163] It is also listed as one of the five faculties (*indriya*) and five powers (*bala*): the powers (*bala*) are much stronger than the faculties (*indriya*) and can suppress the hindrances and fetters for longer periods. The faculty of energy (*viriya*) in conjunction with the faculty of trust (*saddhā*) supports the cultivation and maintenance of mindfulness (*sati*). The effect of these three qualities—i.e., trust, energy and mindfulness—is the strengthening of concentration (*samādhi*), and all the four of them can then provide conditions for wisdom (*paññā*) to enter the process. Concentration (*samādhi*) is like a door: when open for some time, a visitor—in this case, wisdom (*paññā*)—may enter, but if nobody comes, the door may close again.

---

illustrated in the *Milindapañhā* in the following dialogue between King Milinda and the monk Nāgasena: 'The king said: "How many factors of awakening are there, Venerable Nāgasena?" "Seven, O king." "By how many factors does one awaken?" "By one factor, the investigation of *dhammas*." "Then why is it said that there are seven?" "Could the sword in your sheath cut anything if it was not taken up in the hand?" "No, Venerable Sir." "Just so, O king, without the other factors of awakening, the investigation of *dhammas* cannot awaken."' (Mil 83: *Rājā āha: Kati nu kho bhante Nāgasena bojjhangā ti. Satta kho mahārāja bojjhangā ti. Katihi pana bhante bojjhangehi bujjhatīti. Ekena kho mahārāja bojjhangena bujjhati: dhammavicayasambojjhangenāti. Atha kissa nu kho bhante vuccanti satta bojjhangā ti. Taṃ kim maññasi mahārāja: asi kosiyā pakkhitto aggahito hatthena ussahati chejjaṃ chinditun ti. Na hi bhante ti. Evameva kho mahārāja dhammavicayasambojjhangena vinā chahi bojjhangehi na bujjhatīti*).

161. For comments on the term 'ardent' (*ātāpī*), see Chapter I, under the subheading 'Ardent (*ātāpī*).'

162. The faculty of energy (*viriya*) is frequently presented as the four strivings (*padhāna*); for example, according to the *Saṅgītisutta*, it is comprised of (1) restraint (of the senses), (2) abandoning (of defilements), (3) cultivation (of the factors of awakening) and (4) preservation (of concentration) (D III 225: *Cattāri padhānāni. Saṃvarapadhānaṃ, pahānapadhānaṃ, bhāvanāpadhānaṃ, anurakkhaṇāpadhānaṃ*). In the *Indriyasaṃyutta*, the faculty of energy (*viriya*) is described as the energy required for the relinquishment of unwholesome states and the cultivation of wholesome ones, while being steady and firm in exertion and not avoiding the cultivation of wholesome states (S V 198: *akusalānaṃ dhammānaṃ pahānāya kusalānaṃ dhammānam upasampadāya thāmavā daḷhaparakkamo anikkhittadhuro kusalesu dhammesu*).

163. For an overview of the four right strivings (*cattāro sammappadhānā*), see Gethin (2001, 69–80).

Faculties (*indriya*)	Calm (*samatha*) meditation	Insight (*vipassanā*) meditation
To be cultivated	(1) trust (*saddhā*) (2) mindfulness (*sati*) (3) energy (*viriya*)	
Resulting from the cultivation of the first three	(4) concentration(*samādhi*)	(4) concentration(*samādhi*) (5) wisdom (*paññā*)

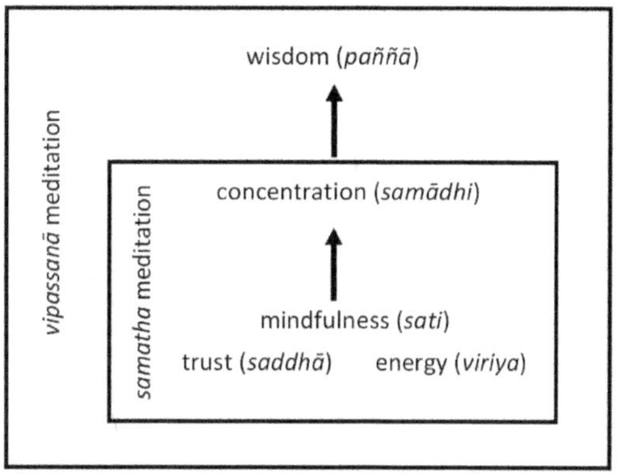

Figure 4 Cultivation of the faculties in calm and insight meditation.

As long as mindfulness (*sati*) is well maintained, wisdom (*paññā*) may enter through the door of concentration (*samādhi*), and then the practice becomes insight (*vipassanā*) meditation. However, if wisdom (*paññā*) does not emerge, the practice remains in the domain of calm (*samatha*) meditation (Figure 4).

To summarise, in meditation, the first three faculties (*indriya*) are cultivated, namely, trust (*saddhā*), energy (*viriya*) and mindfulness (*sati*), whereas the last two—concentration (*samādhi*) and wisdom (*paññā*)—are their fruits. Along with the gradual development of mindfulness (*sati*) and wisdom (*paññā*), energy (*viriya*) also strengthens and matures into an awakening factor (*sambojjhaṅga*). Several aspects help shift energy (*viriya*) to the level of a factor of awakening (*viriyasambojjhaṅga*) such as the wise reflections on the benefits of energy, fearfulness of miserable states and contemplations about the greatness of holy life.[164] The energy factor of awakening (*viriyasambojjhaṅga*) supports and maintains the continuity of the arising of the mindfulness factor of awakening (*satisambojjhaṅga*) and the investigation-of-*dhammas* factor of awakening (*dhammavicayasambojjhaṅga*), which in turn enhance and condition the energy

164. The *Papañcasūdani* commentary lists eleven qualities that are conducive to the arising of the energy factor of awakening (*viriyasambojjhaṅga*), which comprise reflections on: (1) fearfulness of lower states, (2) benefits [of energy], (3) path to be taken, (4) honouring of alms, (5) greatness of the tradition, (6) greatness of the master, (7) greatness of the lineage, (8) greatness of fellow renouncers, (9) avoidance of lazy people, (10) association with people who exert themselves and (11) inclination [towards the energy factor of awakening] (Ps I 292–296: *apāyabhayapaccavekkhaṇatā, ānisaṃsadassāvitā, gamanavīthipaccavekkhaṇatā, piṇḍapātāpacāyanatā, dāyajjamahattapaccavekkhaṇatā, satthumahattapaccavekkhaṇatā, jātimahattapaccavekkhaṇatā, sabrahmacārimahattapaccavekkhaṇatā, kusītapuggalaparivajjanatā, āraddhaviriyapuggalasevanatā, tadadhimuttatā*).

factor (*viriyasambojjhaṅga*).[165]

Meditation therefore mainly focuses on the cultivation of the first three factors of awakening (*sambojjhaṅga*), whereas the other four are their outcomes (Table 13).

Table 13 Cultivation of the factors of awakening (*sambojjhaṅga*) in insight (*vipassanā*) meditation.

Factors of awakening (*sambojjhaṅga*) to be cultivated	1. mindfulness factor of awakening (*satisambojjhaṅga*) 2. investigation-of-*dhammas* factor of awakening (*dhammavicayasambojjhaṅga*) 3. energy factor of awakening (*viriyasambojjhaṅga*)
Factors of awakening (*sambojjhaṅga*) resulting from the cultivation of the first three	4. joy factor of awakening (*pītisambojjhaṅga*) 5. tranquillity factor of awakening (*passaddhisambojjhaṅga*) 6. concentration factor of awakening (*samādhisambojjhaṅga*) 7. equanimity factor of awakening (*upekkhāsambojjhaṅga*)

'Joy factor of awakening' (*pītisambojjhaṅga*)

Joy or rapture (*pīti*) is a mental concomitant (*cetasika*) that arises along with various mental states.[166] It is often listed as the third of the following five *jhāna* factors:

1. initial thought (*vitakka*)
2. sustained thought (*vicāra*)
3. joy (*pīti*)
4. happiness (*sukha*)
5. one-pointedness (*ekaggatā*)

The joy (*pīti*) experienced in meditation is a component of high levels of concentration (*samādhi*). It is like the delight of a thirsty person who has been walking for a long time in the hot sun and then sees a shaded area with a well in the distance. After reaching the shade and quenching her or his thirst, the person experiences happiness, lightness and tranquillity. The meditative mind that arises along with joy (*pīti*) is accompanied by calmness (*passaddhi*) and softness (*mudutā*) and is (temporarily) free from the hindrances (*nīvaraṇa*) and fetters (*saṃyojana*), thus leading to strong concentration (*samādhi*).

Joy (*pīti*) is a component of both calm (*samatha*) and insight (*vipassanā*) meditation. It is called the awakening factor (*pītisambojjhaṅga*) only when the first three factors of awakening (i.e., mindfulness, investigation-of-*dhammas* and energy) are firmly established and maintained. Many conditions can enhance its development; for example, the meditator may try to avoid crude people with rough behaviour and instead seek the company of refined, restrained and gentle people who are trustworthy and whose qualities generate inspiration.[167] It is also helpful

165. The *Ānāpānasatisutta* (M III 85–87) describes how the mindfulness factor of awakening leads to the investigation-of-*dhammas* factor of awakening, which further leads to the arising of the energy factor of awakening and so on. This is similarly explained in the *Sīlasutta* of the *Bojjhaṅgasaṃyutta* (S V 67–68).

166. In the *Vibhaṅga* and *Dhammasaṅgaṇi*, joy (*pīti*) is described as 'rapture, rejoicing, delight, joy, laughter, felicity, elation and exultation of the mind' (Vibh 229; Dhs 10: *Yā pīti pāmojjaṃ āmodanā pamodanā hāso pahāso vitti odagyaṃ attamanatā cittassa pītisambojjhaṅgo: ayaṃ vuccati pītisambojjhaṅgo*).

167. The *Papañcasūdani* commentary mentions eleven qualities that are conducive to the arising of the joy factor of awakening (*pītisambojjhaṅga*), which comprise recollections on the following: (1) the Buddha, (2) Dhamma, (3) Saṅgha, (4) virtue, (5) generosity, (6) deities, (7) subsidence, (8) avoidance of rough people, (9) association with refined people, (10) reflection on discourses that inspire confidence and (11) inclination

for the meditator to recite the *suttas* mentioning the qualities of the Triple Gem such as the *Ratanasutta* (Sn 222–238), in which the qualities of the Buddha, the Dhamma and the Saṅgha are praised. The meditator may choose to contemplate one of the qualities listed in this *sutta* and thus develop joy (*pīti*) and concentration (*samādhi*). Meditators often recite the well-known *Mahāmaṅgalasutta* (Sn 46–47) in which thirty-eight different qualities, the so-called 'greatest blessings,' are listed, including association with wise people, generosity, self-discipline, respectfulness, patience, understanding the four noble truths and freedom from defilements. Any of these qualities can be taken as an object of contemplation to generate inspiration and joy (*pīti*).

The *Mahānāmasutta* (A V 328–334) also describes the qualities to be cultivated for the generation of joy (*pīti*), which in turn leads to tranquillity (*passaddhi*) and concentration (*samādhi*). These include the recollection (*anussati*) of the Tathāgata, Dhamma and Saṅgha, the recollection of one's own virtue (*sīla*) and generosity (*cāga*) and the recollection of deities (*devatānussati*). In the recollection of deities, the meditator contemplates the five qualities that make it possible for one to be born as a deity, namely, trust (*saddhā*), virtue (*sīla*), learning (*suta*), generosity (*cāga*) and wisdom (*paññā*). The *Mahānāmasutta* then says that following such practices, the meditator is free from greed (*lobha*), aversion (*dosa*) and delusion (*moha*), and becomes full of joy (*pīti*), tranquillity (*passaddhi*), happiness (*sukha*) and concentration (*samādhi*). Such a person is called a 'noble disciple' (*ariyasāvaka*) and the 'one who has entered the stream of Dhamma' (*dhammasotasamāpanna*) (A V 329), thus referring to the stream-winner (*sotāpanna*).[168]

'Tranquillity factor of awakening' (*passaddhisambojjhaṅga*)

Calm or tranquillity is already mentioned in the beginning of the *Satipaṭṭhānasutta* when mindfulness of breathing (*ānāpānasati*) is discussed; it is said that when the meditator is mindful of breath, she or he is 'calming the body formation' (*passambhayaṃ kāyasaṅkhāraṃ*).[169] This refers to the stage in meditation when the meditator does not apprehend the breath at all but experiences and contemplates tranquillity. This means that the practice of calm (*samatha*) meditation is now well established, and that the meditator may continue with it or turn to insight (*vipassanā*) meditation. In the latter case, tranquillity (*passaddhi*) increases and deepens, thus reaching the level of awakening factor (*passaddhisambojjhaṅga*). It is experienced as the calmness of the mental concomitants (*kāyapassaddhi*) and the mind (*cittapassaddhi*).[170]

Several conditions can enhance the development of the tranquillity factor of awakening (*passaddhisambojjhaṅga*).[171] For example, the meditator should live in an appropriate environ-

[towards the joy factor of awakening]' (Ps I 292–296: *api ca ekādasa dhammā pītisambojjhaṅgassa uppādāya saṃvattanti: buddhānussati, dhammasaṅghasīlacāgadevatānussati, upasamānussati, lūkhapuggalaparivajjanatā, siniddhapuggalasevanatā, pasādanīyasuttantapaccavekkhaṇatā, tadadhimuttatāti*).

168. The Abhidhammic texts and canonical commentaries explain the seven factors of awakening (*bojjhaṅga*) as those involved in the supramundane mental states (*lokuttara*). For example, in the *Vibhaṅga*, it is explained that the seven factors of awakening (*bojjhaṅga*) occur in the supramundane *jhāna* (Vibh 229: *Tattha katame satta bojjhaṅgā? Idha bhikkhu yasmiṃ samaye lokuttaraṃ jhānaṃ bhāveti*).

169. See Chapter II.1, under the subheading 'Calming the body formation (*passambhayaṃ kāyasaṅkhāraṃ*).'

170. Likewise, the *Sammohavinodanī* explains that the calmness of the body refers to the aggregates of feeling, perception and mental formations, while the calmness of the mind relates to the aggregate of consciousness (Vibh-a 314: *Kāyapassaddhīti tiṇṇaṃ khandhānaṃ darathapassaddhi. Cittapassaddhīti viññāṇakkhandhassa darathapassaddhi*).

171. The *Papañcasūdani* commentary lists seven qualities that contribute to the arising of the joy factor of awakening (*pītisambojjhaṅga*): (1) appropriate food, (2) convenient climate, (3) suitable posture,

ment and eat suitable food. There is a story in the commentary on the *Dhammapada* (Dhp-a 290–291) about Mātikamātā, the mother of a village headman, who cooked for and looked after sixty monks during their rainy season retreat. She also started to practise meditation at that time, attained the stage of a non-returner (*anāgami*) and obtained psychic powers. Through her ability to read other people's minds, she saw at the end of the retreat that the monks had not attained any path knowledge, because they had not had the appropriate food. She then prepared suitable meals for each of them, and consequently, they all attained arahantship. The story aims to stress the importance of food for the meditator.[172]

The texts also emphasise that the meditator should stop eating when she or he considers that another three or four mouthfuls would make them feel full and should instead drink water.[173] The best time for meditation is immediately after the noon meal; this is when the meditator can develop very strong concentration (*samādhi*). Another important condition for the cultivation of tranquillity (*passaddhi*) is the appropriate climate. In hot parts of the world, it is suitable to meditate inside a thick forest or jungle where it is always relatively cool. In very hot areas, the best time for practice is in the evening, at night, or very early in the morning. The meditator should choose the most suitable meditation posture; some people may choose walking and others sitting. Then the meditator should contemplate the causes (*kamma*) and results (*vipāka*) of phenomena arising:[174] after clearly seeing and understanding them, she or he cannot be attached to or repulsed from phenomena, and consequently, generates tranquillity (*passaddhi*), which in turn enhances concentration (*samādhi*).

'Concentration factor of awakening' (*samādhisambojjhaṅga*)

When the meditator's concentration (*samādhi*) matures and strengthens to the extent that it cannot be shaken, disturbed or lost under any circumstance, it can be called a factor of awakening (*sambojjhaṅga*). Several qualities contribute to the establishment of the concentration factor of awakening (*samādhisambojjhaṅga*).[175] Firstly, the meditator should live a simple life,

(4) mental balance, (5) avoidance of restless people, (6) association with calm people and (7) inclination [towards the tranquillity factor of awakening] (Ps I 297: *Api ca satta dhammā passaddhisambojjhaṅgassa uppādāya saṃvattanti: paṇītabhojanasevanatā, utusukhasevanatā, iriyāpathasukhasevanatā, majjhattapayogatā, sāraddhakāyapuggalaparivajjanatā, passaddhakāyapuggalasevanatā, tadadhimuttatāti*).

172. This story may convey other messages such as for lay supporters to provide good food to monks.

173. Moderation in food (*bhojane mattaññutā*) is frequently discussed in the Pāli canon and its commentaries such as the *Mahāssapurasutta* (M I 273) and *Doṇapākasutta* (S I 81–82). The point at which the meditator should stop eating before feeling full is called the 'grasping of the sign of overeating' (Ps 284; Vbh-a 273: *atibhojane nimittaggāha*). The *Theragāthā* (983) also recommends eating four or five mouthfuls less than the amount needed to feel full and then drinking water (Th 89: *cattāro pañca ālope abhutvā udakaṃ pive, alaṃ phāsuvihārāya pahitattassa bhikkhuno*); see also Vism 33.

174. The *Papañcasūdani* commentary similarly explains that the application of mental balance (*majjhattapayogatā*), which is one of the conditions for enhancing the tranquillity factor of awakening (*passaddhisambojjhaṅga*), refers to the reflection on one's own and other's *kamma* (Ps I 297: *majjhattapayogo vuccati attano ca parassa ca kammassakatāpaccavekkhaṇā*).

175. The *Papañcasūdani* commentary lists eleven qualities that lead to the arising of the concentration factor of awakening (*samādhisambojjhaṅga*): (1) purification of the fundamentals (i.e., cleanliness of the body and environment), (2) balance of the five faculties, (3) skill in taking up the sign of concentration, (4) skill in inciting the mind on the right occasion, (5) restraining the mind on the right occasion, (6) gladdening the mind on the right occasion, (7) taking care on the right occasion, (8) avoidance of distracted people, (9) association with people with concentration, (10) reflection on meditative absorptions and liberation and (11) inclination towards that (i.e., development of the concentration factor of awakening) (Ps I 298: *apica ekādasa dhammā*

while keeping her or his clothes and surroundings clean and tidy. Then it is very important for the meditator to balance the five faculties (*indriya*); concentration (*samādhi*) must be in balance with energy (*viriya*) and trust (*saddhā*) with wisdom (*paññā*), while mindfulness (*sati*) is the supporting faculty for all of them. Comparing the five faculties (*indriya*) to the five fingers, mindfulness (*sati*) is represented by the thumb. When we try to grasp an object with four fingers without the support of the thumb, we cannot pick up the object. Similarly, only with the support of mindfulness (*sati*) can the four other faculties function well. If the five faculties (*indriya*) are not properly balanced, clinging (*upādāna*) can arise, and the five hindrances (*nīvaraṇa*) can emerge.

The cultivation of the five faculties (*indriya*) is not an original Buddhist teaching, as it was known well before the Buddha. For example, it is narrated in the *Ariyapariyesanāsutta* (M I 160–175) that when the Buddha was still a *bodhisatta,* his teacher Āḷāra Kālāma had developed the five faculties, although the Buddha pursued the path further until reaching *nibbāna.* The first faculty (*indriya*) is trust (*saddhā*), which can be described as confidence in the cultivation of wholesomeness and trust in the existence of a state beyond wholesomeness; this faculty strengthens with the development of insight meditation.[176] Having strong trust (*saddhā*) in the pursuit of wholesomeness, the meditator increases her or his energy (*viriya*) to tirelessly continue seeking. Trust (*saddhā*) and energy (*indriya*) in turn enhance mindfulness (*sati*), which observes the phenomena without craving (*lobha*) or aversion (*dosa*). As the first three faculties (*indriya*) are well established and balanced, the other two—i.e., concentration (*samādhi*) and wisdom (*paññā*)—occur. It is important not to develop excessive energy (*viriya*), as it can generate restlessness (*uddhacca*) and thus reduce concentration (*samādhi*); therefore, it should be balanced with the help of mindfulness (*sati*). If the faculty of wisdom (*paññā*) does not arise, the meditator should contemplate the Buddhist teachings, the four noble truths (*cattāri ariyasaccāni*) or other aspects of the Dhamma,[177] which would also enhance concentration (*samādhi*).

When all five faculties (*indriya*) strengthen to the point that they become stable and unshakeable, they are called the five powers (*bala*); at that stage, defilements (*kilesa*) in relation to objects experienced no longer appear, even if the meditator occasionally fails to note an object with mindfulness (*sati*). Only when the faculties (*indriya*) are at the level of powers (*bala*) do the seven factors of awakening (*bojjhaṅga*) start to emerge, and the noble eightfold path (*ariyo aṭṭhaṅgiko maggo*) evolves, leading to liberation from the taints (*āsava*) and fetters (*saṃyojana*).[178] Therefore, it is crucial to cultivate and balance the five faculties (*indriya*).

---

samādhisambojjhaṅgassa uppādāya saṃvattanti vatthuvisadakiriyatā indriyasamattapaṭipādanatā nimittakusalatā samaye cittassa paggahaṇatā samaye cittassa niggahaṇatā samaye sampahaṃsanatā samaye ajjhupekkhanatā asamāhitapuggalaparivajjanatā samāhitapuggalasevanatā jhānavimokkhapaccavekkhaṇatā tadadhimuttatāti).

176. This is also mentioned in the *Visuddhimagga*: 'Trust is resolve; it arises along with insight as a very strong confidence of the mind and mental concomitants' (Vism 636: *Adhimokkho ti saddhā, vipassanāsampayuttā yeva hi 'ssa cittacetasikānaṃ atisayapasādabhūtā balavatī saddhā uppajjati*).

177. Among the factors that enhance the development of wisdom and the investigation-of-*dhammas* factor of awakening (*dhammavicayasambojjhaṅga*), the *Papañcasūdani* commentary similarly includes the inquiry into *dhamma* (*paripucchakatā*) and reflection on the profound knowledge [in regard to processes of the aggregates, elements and sense spheres] (*gambhīrañāṇacariyapaccavekkhaṇā*) (Ps I 290).

178. A similar sequence for the components developed on the path of liberation appears in several canonical texts. For example, the *Ānāpānasatisutta* (M III 80–81) describes the path, beginning with the development of the four kinds of striving (*sammappadhāna*), followed by the four bases for spiritual power (*iddhipāda*), five faculties (*indriya*), five powers (*bala*), seven factors of awakening (*bojjhaṅga*) and noble eightfold path (*ariyo aṭṭhaṅgiko maggo*), which leads to the destruction of taints (*āsava*) and fetters (*saṃyojana*) and finally, to complete liberation (*nibbāna*).

For the development of concentration (*samādhi*), a suitable object of meditation (*nimitta*) is required. The object should be chosen skilfully, usually by the teacher; sometimes it has to be changed during practice. For example, the meditator may begin with mindfulness of breathing (*ānāpānasati*) but may encounter difficulties after some time. For a certain period, she or he should practise the recollection of the Buddha (*buddhānusati*) or loving kindness (*mettā*) and only later return to mindfulness of breathing (*ānāpānasati*). The meditator should live in conducive circumstances for the development of concentration (*samādhi*) and associate with people who are restrained and have a gentle manner and good understanding of the Dhamma.

'Equanimity factor of awakening' (*upekkhāsambojjhaṅga*)

The equanimity factor of awakening (*upekkhāsambojjhaṅga*) refers to a balanced mental state of evenness when the mind arises with strong neutrality (*tatramajjhattatā*).[179] Equanimity (*upekkhā*) can arise out of ignorance (*avijjā*) or evolve from wisdom (*paññā*).[180] For example, at the higher levels of calm meditation (*samatha*), the meditator experiences equanimity (*upekkhā*) and (temporarily) removes greed (*lobha*) and aversion (*dosa*). Or, in the cultivation of the four 'divine abodes' (*cattāri brahmavihārā*), once loving kindness (*mettā*), compassion (*karuṇā*) and sympathetic joy (*muditā*) are well established, equanimity (*upekkhā*) gradually emerges by itself; the meditator experiences this as a peaceful and well-balanced state of mind. However, in calm meditation (*samatha*), this happens without wisdom (*paññā*), and therefore the taints (*āsava*) have not been relinquished.

Equanimity (*upekkhā*) can also stem from wisdom (*paññā*), which emerges due to several causes and conditions. Firstly, all five hindrances (*nīvaraṇa*) should be (temporarily) absent for the faculties (*indriya*) to begin to grow. It is important that the meditator reduces or (temporarily) suppresses all five hindrances equally; for example, she or he may stay without sense desire (*kāmacchanda*), but some aversion (*vyāpāda*) may still arise, which prevents the five faculties (*indriya*) from developing. When the five faculties are established and function well and in a balanced manner, equanimity (*upekkhā*) may arise. As wisdom (*paññā*) deepens, equanimity (*upekkhā*) strengthens and gradually reaches the level of an awakening factor (*bojjhaṅga*). Hence, the equanimity factor of awakening (*upekkhāsambojjhaṅga*) always results from wisdom, which emerges at its uppermost strength, namely as the investigation-of-*dhammas* factor of awakening (*dhammavicayasambojjhaṅga*). At this point, the meditator has reached the highest level of mindfulness practice. This is why it is also said at the end of the section on the contemplation of phenomena in the *Ānāpānasatisutta* that:

> Having seen with wisdom the abandoning of desires and discontent in regard to the world, [the meditator] comprehensively observes phenomena with equanimity. (M III 84–85)[181]

---

179. Neutrality (*tatramajjhattatā*) is one of the wholesome mental concomitants (*cetasika*), which is described in the *Visuddhimagga* as follows: 'It is neutrality in relation to the *dhammas*. Its characteristic is to convey the mind and mental concomitants evenly, its function is to control deficiency and excess or to cut off partiality and it is manifested as the state of neutrality. Because of its neutrality in relation to the mind and mental concomitants, it should be viewed like a charioteer who treats the well-bred horses that he is driving with neutrality' (Vism 466–467: *Tesu dhammesu majjhattatā tatramajjhattatā. Sā cittacetasikānaṃ samavāhitalakkhaṇā,* ūnādhikatā*nivāraṇarasā, pakkhapātupacchedanarasā vā, majjhattabhāvapaccupaṭṭhānā, cittacetasikānaṃ ajjhupekkhanabhāvena, samappavattānaṃ ājānīyānaṃ ajjhupekkhakasārathi viya daṭṭhabbā*). See also As 133.

180. For further details, see Chapter III, under the subheading 'Neither-unpleasant-nor-pleasant feeling (*adukkhamasukhavedanā*).'

181. M III 84–85: *So yaṃ taṃ abhijjhādomanassānaṃ pahānaṃ taṃ paññāya disvā sādhukaṃ ajjhupekkhitā hoti.*

This means that equanimity (*upekkhā*) arises at its highest strength at the level of the awakening factors as a result of profound understanding and wisdom.

Several factors contribute to the advancement of the equanimity factor of awakening (*upekkhāsambojjhaṅga*) such as associating with equanimous and detached people. Above all, however, the meditator should cultivate impartiality or neutrality in relation to any phenomenon that arises.[182] When the meditator progresses in insight meditation (*vipassanā*) and experiences the insight knowledges (*vipassanāñāṇa*), equanimity (*upekkhā*) is the highest and final stage of insight reached, called the 'knowledge of equanimity about formations' (*saṅkhār'upekkhāñāṇa*). The three characteristics (*tilakkhaṇa*) of every phenomenon are then clearly observed and understood from moment to moment and thereafter, the meditator may proceed to the path knowledge (*maggañāṇa*). To summarise, when the seven factors of awakening (*bojjhaṅga*) are well established and balanced, they are the very foundation and portal for liberation, inclined to and leading to *nibbāna*.

V 5 Four noble truths (*cattāri ariyasaccāni*)

Puna ca paraṃ bhikkhave bhikkhu dhammesu dhammānupassī viharati ***catusu ariyasaccesu****. Kathañca bhikkhave bhikkhu dhammesu dhammānupassī viharati catusu ariyasaccesu? Idha bhikkhave bhikkhu: idaṃ* ***dukkhan****ti yathābhūtaṃ pajānāti, ayaṃ* ***dukkhasamudayo*** *ti yathābhūtaṃ pajānāti, ayaṃ* ***dukkhanirodho*** *ti yathābhūtaṃ pajānāti, ayaṃ* ***dukkhanirodhagāminī paṭipadā*** *ti yathābhūtaṃ pajānāti.*

'And again, monks, a monk abides contemplating phenomena as phenomena in regard to the **four noble truths.** And how does a monk abide contemplating phenomena as phenomena in regard to the four noble truths? Here, monks, a monk knows as it actually is: "This is **suffering**"; he knows as it actually is: "This is the **arising of suffering**"; he knows as it actually is: "This is the **cessation of suffering**"; he knows as it actually is: "This is the **path leading to the cessation of suffering.**"'

Recurring passage indicating the ways to approach the contemplation[183]

Iti ajjhattaṃ vā dhammesu dhammānupassī viharati, bahiddhā vā dhammesu dhammānupassī viharati, ajjhattabahiddhā vā dhammesu dhammānupassī viharati. Samudayadhammānupassī vā dhammesu viharati, vayadhammānupassī vā dhammesu viharati, samudayavayadhammānupassī vā dhammesu viharati. Atthi dhammā ti vā panassa sati paccupaṭṭhitā hoti yāvadeva ñāṇamattāya patissatimattāya, anissito ca viharati na ca kiñci loke upādiyati. Evam kho bhikkhave bhikkhu dhammesu dhammānupassī viharati catūsu ariyasaccesu.

'Thus he abides contemplating phenomena as phenomena internally, or he abides contemplating phenomena as phenomena externally, or he abides contemplating phenomena as phenomena both internally and externally. He abides contemplating the arising of phenomena in phenomena, or he abides contemplating the passing away of phenomena in phenomena, or he abides contemplating both the arising and passing away of phenomena in phenomena. Or, mindfulness that "there are phenomena" is established in him just to the extent necessary for knowledge and mindfulness. And he abides without attachment, not clinging to anything in the world. Monks, thus a monk abides contemplating phenomena as phenomena in regard to the four noble truths.'

182. The *Papañcasūdani* commentary lists five qualities that lead to the arising of the equanimity factor of awakening (*upekkhāsambojjhaṅga*): (1) detachment or impartiality towards living beings, (2) detachment or impartiality towards things, (3) avoidance of people who are selfish in relation to living beings and things, (4) association with people who are impartial in relation to living beings and things and (5) inclination towards that (i.e., the development of the equanimity factor of awakening) (Ps I 299: *apica pañca dhammā upekkhāsambojjhaṅgassa uppādāya saṃvattanti sattamajjhattatā saṅkhāramajjhattatā sattasaṅkhārakelāyanapuggalaparivajjanatā sattasaṅkhāramajjhattapuggalasevanatā tadadhimuttatāti*).

183. For comments on the recurring passage, see Chapter II.1, under the subheading 'Recurring passage indicating the ways to approach the contemplation.'

Pemasiri Thera's commentary

'Four noble truths' (*cattāri ariyasaccāni*)[184]

The very last section of the contemplation of phenomena (*dhammānupassanā*) consists of the four noble truths (*cattāri ariyasaccāni*).[185] The path to liberation encompasses the cultivation of the thirty-seven qualities of awakening (*bodhipakkhiyā dhammā*), which include (as their last component) the fourth noble truth, namely, the noble eightfold path (*ariyo aṭṭhaṅgiko maggo*).[186] The four noble truths (*cattāri ariyasaccāni*) are regarded as the very core of Buddhist teachings.[187]

As shown in Figure 5 opposite, the four noble truths (*cattāri ariyasaccāni*) can be presented as two sets of results and causes: the first noble truth, which is about unsatisfactoriness or suffering (*dukkha*), is the result of the second noble truth about the arising of suffering (*dukkhasamudaya*), namely, craving (*taṇhā*). Similarly, the third noble truth about the cessation of suffering (*dukkhanirodha*) is the result of the fourth noble truth about the path leading to the cessation of suffering (*dukkhanirodhagāminī paṭipadā*), namely, the noble eightfold path (*ariya aṭṭhaṅgika magga*).

In meditation practice, the contemplation of the four noble truths (*cattāri ariyasaccāni*) is experienced in a different sequence, usually one comprehends the causes first and then the results. For example, when the meditator contemplates the processes arising in the mind and body (*nāmarūpa*) at the level of the contemplation of phenomena (*dhammānupassanā*) and observes the tendency to seek comfort or pleasure in experiences, she or he knows that the cause for this is craving (*taṇhā*). Having mindfully seen and comprehended craving (*taṇhā*), the meditator understands that if she or he had not known and noted the cause (i.e., craving), attachment would have arisen and suffering (*dukkha*) would have ensued. By seeing the cause of suffering (*dukkhasamudaya*), which is craving (*taṇhā*), the meditator clearly understands the consequence or result, which is suffering (*dukkha*). She or he then knows that this very insight prevented the arising of suffering (*dukkha*), or in other words, that mindfulness (*sati*) and clear understanding (*sampajañña*) are the path to freedom from suffering (*dukkhanirodhagāminī paṭipadā*).[188] By knowing that craving (*taṇhā*) has not arisen, the meditator can see the consequent

184. The most widely accepted English rendering of the Pāli term *sacca* is 'truth' (PED, *s.v.*, gives two meanings: 'truth, reality'). However, it should be highlighted once again that translating key Buddhist terminology is highly problematic, since English (as well as other modern European languages) has no clear equivalents for most technical terms in Pāli, thus reflecting the fundamental differences between the ancient Indian and modern Western discourses. For a discussion on the English translation of *sacca*, see Harvey (2009).

185. The *Papañcasūdani* commentary (Ps I 300–301) provides very brief comments on this section about the four noble truths and refers to the *Visuddhimagga* where they are discussed comprehensively (Vism 494–516).

186. Here Pemasiri Thera refers to the thirty-seven qualities of awakening (*bodhipakkhiyā dhammā*); they are listed in several texts such as the *Visuddhimagga* (Vism 678). For a detailed study, see Gethin (2001).

187. The four noble truths (*cattāri ariyasaccāni*) are discussed in numerous instances in the Pāli canon. According to the tradition, the Buddha expounded them in his first sermon, the *Dhammacakkappavattanasutta* (S V 420–424).

188. This is explained in a similar manner in the *Papañcasūdani* commentary: 'Having set aside craving, [the monk] understands that all phenomena of the three realms of being are suffering according to their nature and that previous craving has produced and caused this suffering; that the non-occurrence of both [suffering and its origin] is *nibbāna*, which is the cessation of suffering; and that the path to the cessation of suffering [comprises] the understanding of suffering, the abandoning of its origination, the realisation of cessation, the noble path' (Ps I 300–301: *ṭhapetvā taṇhaṃ tebhūmake dhamme, idaṃ dukkhan ti yathāsabhāvato pajānāti. Tass'eva kho pana dukkhassa janikaṃ samuṭṭhāpikaṃ purimataṇhaṃ, ayaṃ dukkhasamudayo ti, ubhinnaṃ appavattiṃ nibbānaṃ, ayaṃ dukkhanirodho ti, dukkhaparijānanaṃ samudayapajahanaṃ nirodhasacchikaraṇaṃ ariyamaggaṃ, ayaṃ dukkhanirodhagāminī paṭipadā*). Further explanations of this commentary are found in the *Visuddhimagga* (Vism 494–516).

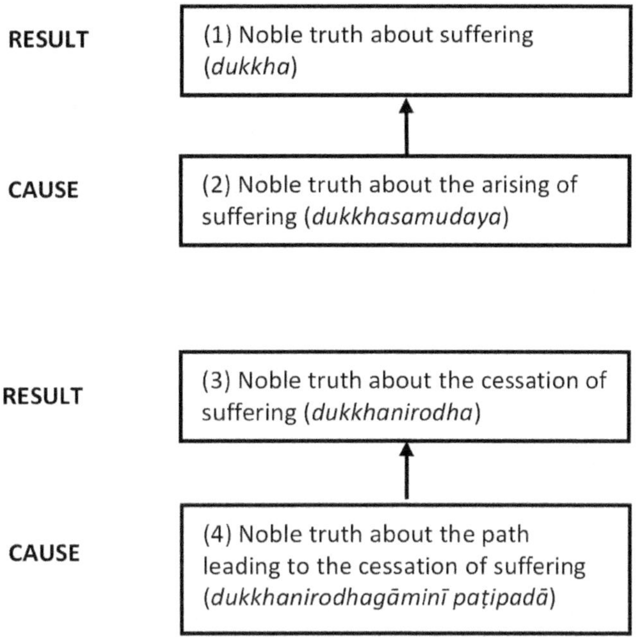

Figure 5 Four noble truths (*cattāri ariyasaccāni*).

cessation of suffering (*dukkhanirodha*). This is how the direct insight into the four noble truths (*cattāri ariyasaccāni*) takes place in regard to phenomena. Sometimes the meditator sees and comprehends one or two truths more prominently, but if her or his mindfulness (*sati*) and comprehension (*sampajañña*) are very strong, all four noble truths can clearly be seen with every arising phenomenon.[189]

There is a difference between the four truths (*cattāri saccāni*) and the four noble truths (*cattāri ariyasaccāni*). The four truths (*cattāri saccāni*) can be generally understood by ordinary people. For example, a glass of water on the table is intended for a monk who is speaking. He becomes thirsty; this is the cause or origin of suffering, which he experiences because of his thirst. Then he sees the glass of water and picks it up, which can be called the path; after drinking the water, his thirst disappears, which is the cessation of suffering. There are many other such examples, although explanation does not help one attain *nibbāna*. To understand the four truths at a deeper level and attain *nibbāna*, one must enter the practice of insight meditation (*vipassanā*). Then, having attained the path and fruition knowledges (*maggaphalañāṇa*), the meditator gains such an understanding of and insight into the four truths, which are then called the 'four *noble* truths.' Thus, the word 'noble' (*ariya*) implies that the four truths are manifested to or understood by a 'noble person' (*ariyapuggala*).[190]

189. In the *Sammohavinodanī*, this is expressed from the perspective of non-self (*anatta*): 'There is suffering but nobody suffers; there is doing but no doer; there is quenching but nobody quenched, there is a path but nobody is going' (Vibh-a 89: *Dukkham eva hi na koci dukkhito, kārako na kiriyāva vijjati. Atthi nibbuti, na nibbuto pumā. Maggam atthi, gamako na vijjatīti*).

190. A similar interpretation of the Pāli word *ariyasacca* is found in the commentary *Sammohavinodanī* (Vibh-a 84–85), which states that they are called the noble truths, because the noble ones comprehend them (*ariyā imāni paṭivijjhanti*), that they belong to the noble ones (*ariyassa saccāni*), because of the noble state accomplished through the perfect realisation (*abhisambuddhattā ariyabhāvasiddhito*) and because they are true

'Suffering' (*dukkha*)

Suffering or unsatisfactoriness (*dukkha*)[191] arises because of a variety of causes and conditions. However, most people do not examine the causes of suffering but instead find fault in their own circumstances or blame others. If the meditator clearly sees and comprehends suffering, its causes and the path to the cessation of suffering, right view (*sammā diṭṭhi*) develops. Then the meditator understands that holding onto anything at all is suffering (*dukkha*), because taking anything as permanent is the very cause of trouble and pain. More generally, whatever a person accumulates and grasps in this world generates suffering (*dukkha*). Or in other words, the cause of suffering (*dukkha*) is craving (*taṇhā*) and clinging (*upādāna*) to the five aggregates (*khandha*) or the mind and body (*nāmarūpa*), while clinging (*upādāna*) is based on and generates further ignorance (*avijjā*). The characteristic of suffering (*dukkha*) is oppression or trouble, experienced as a kind of torment or burning.[192] The *Paṭisambhidāmagga* describes four aspects of the truth about suffering (*dukkha*):

> Suffering has the meaning of oppression, the meaning of being compounded, the meaning of burning up and the meaning of change (*vipariṇāmaṭṭho*). Suffering has these four meanings, which are true, not untrue, not otherwise. (Paṭis II 104)[193]

As said in this passage, one aspect of suffering is change (*vipariṇāma*).[194] If one does not see that this change takes place because of the impermanence (*anicca*) of the five aggregates (*khandha*), then suffering (*dukkha*) inevitably ensues. Through ignorance (*avijjā*), we continuously create and condition the five aggregates (*khandha*), and by clinging (*upādāna*) to them, we create further suffering (*dukkha*), because we cannot see the impermanence (*anicca*) of everything. Simply put, taking objects as permanent (*nicca*) is the cause of trouble and pain (*dukkha*).

'Arising of suffering' (*dukkhasamudaya*)

The second noble truth relates to the arising of suffering (*dukkhasamudaya*). The first truth represents the effect and the second its cause; normally, we first speak of the cause followed by its result, but in the case of the four noble truths, suffering (*dukkha*), both physical and mental, is much more evident and easier to grasp than its causes.[195] According to the *Paṭisambhidāmagga*, the arising of suffering (*dukkhasamudaya*) has four aspects:

> The arising of suffering has the meaning of accumulation (*āyūhanaṭṭho*), the meaning of arising (*nidānaṭṭho*), the meaning of bondage (*saṃyogaṭṭho*) and the meaning of obstruction

and not unreal (*tathāni avitathāni*). See Vism 495 as well as Norman (1993).

191. The translation of the Pāli term *dukkha* is very challenging, as there is no appropriate English equivalent. The most commonly accepted rendering is 'suffering'; other frequently used translations are 'unsatisfactoriness' and 'pain' (for details, see DP; PED, *s.v.*).

192. Here Pemasiri Thera follows the *Visuddhimagga*, which describes the truth of suffering (*dukkha*) as having the characteristic of oppression, the function of burning and is manifested as occurrence (Vism 495–496: *Ettha hi bādhanalakkhaṇam dukkhasaccaṃ, santāpanarasaṃ, pavattipaccupaṭṭhānaṃ*).

193. Paṭis II 104: *pīḷanaṭṭho saṅkhataṭṭho santāpaṭṭho, vipariṇāmaṭṭho. Ime cattāro dukkhassa dukkhaṭṭhā tathā avitathā anaññathā.* See also Vibh-a 83.

194. For further comments on the term *vipariṇāma*, see the *Saṅgītisutta* (D III 216), *Sammohavinodanī* (Vibh-a 48; 93) and *Visuddhimagga* (Vism 360; 499).

195. The *Sammohavinodanī* also states that the truth of suffering is easy to understand, because it is gross and common to all beings (Vibh-a 86: *Ettha ca oḷārikattā sabbasattasādhāraṇattā ca suviññeyyanti dukkhasaccaṃ paṭhamaṃ vuttaṃ*).

(*palibodhaṭṭho*). The arising of suffering has these four meanings, which are true, not untrue, not otherwise. (Paṭis II 104)[196]

The origin of suffering (*dukkhasamudaya*) is craving (*taṇhā*), which is the compounding of many components that come together; it is like a cup of tea that combines water, tea leaves, sugar and milk. It manifests itself as an obstacle to freedom from suffering since we relate to objects with craving (*taṇhā*). In other words, the origin of suffering is the mind and body (*nāmarūpa*) or the accumulation of the five aggregates (*khandhas*) that generate craving (*taṇhā*), which in turn conditions clinging (*upādāna*).[197] When this happens, meditation becomes coarse or gross, and the meditator begins to relate to objects with much force in order to keep the attention focused on the object of practice, thus creating an 'I' and consequent suffering (*dukkha*).

Three types of craving (*taṇhā*) are described in the texts; for example, in the *Esanāsutta* of the *Maggasaṃyutta*, it is said:

> Monks, these are three kinds of craving (*taṇhā*). What three? Craving for sensual pleasures (*kāmataṇhā*), craving for existence (*bhavataṇhā*), craving for non-existence (*vibhavataṇhā*). These are the three kinds of craving. The noble eightfold path is to be cultivated for the direct knowledge and full understanding, for the destruction, and for the abandoning of the three cravings. (S V 58)[198]

Craving for sensuality (*kāmataṇhā*) arises in relation to the sense objects perceived through the six senses; craving for existence (*bhavataṇhā*) is the desire to be, to continue and to obtain the results from one's actions; and craving for non-existence (*vibhavataṇhā*) is craving for annihilation or hoping that there will be no results from one's actions. Craving for existence (*bhavataṇhā*) originates from fear and leads to the belief in an eternal soul and permanent heaven, whereas craving for non-existence (*vibhavataṇhā*) is born from doubt and creates a belief that the mind is annihilated at death.[199] The Buddhist teachings are not about extinguishing existence, since this would imply that we exist as individuals in the first place and that there is a self. This is also highlighted in the *Kaccānagotasutta*:

> For one who sees with right wisdom the origin of the world [of formations] as it is, there is no [notion of] non-existence in regard to the world. And for one who sees with right wisdom the cessation of the world [of formations] as it is, there is no [notion of] existence in regard to the world. (S II 17)[200]

We can say that there is neither existence (*atthitā*) nor non-existence (*natthitā*) in regard to the world. The aim of the Buddhist path is simply to extinguish suffering (*dukkha*), which can

196. Paṭis II 104: *āyūhanaṭṭho nidānaṭṭho saṃyogaṭṭho palibodhaṭṭho. Ime cattāro samudayassa samudayaṭṭhā tathā avitathā anaññathā. evaṃ samudayo tathaṭṭhena saccaṃ.* See also Vibh-a 83.

197. Here Pemasiri Thera again refers to dependent origination (*paṭiccasamuppāda*), highlighting the following links: (4) mentality and materiality (*nāmarūpa*) (8) craving (*taṅhā*) (9) clinging (*upādāna*) (10) becoming (*bhava*) (12) suffering (*dukkha*). The destruction of craving (*taṅhā*), which is conditioned by the first seven links of the formula of dependent origination, is presented as the very condition for the non-arising of the last five links that lead to suffering (*dukkha*).

198. S V 58: *Tisso imā bhikkhave taṇhā. Katamā tisso. Kāmataṇhā bhavataṇhā vibhavataṇhā, imā kho bhikkhave tisso taṇhā. Imāsaṃ kho bhikkhave tissannam taṇhānaṃ abhiññāya pariññāya parikkhayāya pahānāya ariyo aṭṭhaṅgiko maggo bhāvetabbo.*

199. Clinging to various views about existence and non-existence is described in the *Diṭṭhisaṃyutta* (S III 202–216).

200. S II 17: *Lokasamudayaṃ kho Kaccāyana yathābhūtaṃ sammappaññāya passato yā loke natthitā sā na hoti. Lokanirodhaṃ kho Kaccāyana yathābhūtaṃ sammappaññāya passato yā loke atthitā sā na hoti.*

be achieved by clearly seeing and understanding dependent origination (*paṭiccasamuppāda*), and the processes of numerous causes (*hetu*) and effects (*phala*). Only when ignorance (*avijjā*) is eradicated is suffering (*dukkha*) extinguished.

'Cessation of suffering' (*dukkhanirodha*)

The third noble truth concerns the cessation of suffering (*dukkhanirodha*). When people use the word cessation (*nirodha*), they usually refer to an object that must cease. For example, when we have an illness, we want to cure ourselves, because we like the five aggregates (*khandha*). But if we are very sick and suffer a great deal, we may think that it would be better to die, so we want the cessation of the five aggregates (*khandha*), because we cannot maintain them in the way that we want. If suffering (*dukkha*) becomes overwhelming, some people even commit suicide. The *suttas* include several stories about monks who killed themselves such as in the *Vakkalisutta* (S III 119–124) and the *Channasutta* (S IV 55–60) in which the ethical question of suicide is expounded. From the Buddhist perspective, taking one's life does not bring about the cessation of suffering (*dukkhanirodha*): because of the subsequent rebirth, suffering (*dukkha*) does not cease with suicide and death, and therefore it is not considered the right path.[201]

The true cessation of suffering (*dukkhanirodha*) encompasses the following four aspects, which are outlined in the *Paṭisambhidāmagga*:

> Cessation of suffering has the meaning of escape, the meaning of seclusion, the meaning of being unconditioned and the meaning of deathlessness. Cessation of suffering has these four meanings, which are true, not untrue, not otherwise. (Paṭis II 105)[202]

The cessation of suffering (*dukkhanirodha*) refers to the escape (*nissaraṇa*) from *saṃsāra*. It occurs when one no longer needs to look to anyone or anything for refuge, since only the path is needed until reaching cessation (*nirodha*). Furthermore, the cessation of suffering (*dukkhanirodha*) refers to the state of seclusion or separation (*viveka*), i.e., seclusion from or disposing of the defilements.[203] The cessation of suffering (*dukkhanirodha*) also has the meaning of being uncompounded or unconditioned (*asaṅkhata*), which denotes that it does not arise due to causes and conditions.[204] The fourth aspect of the cessation of suffering (*dukkhanirodha*) is deathlessness (*amata*), referring to the state beyond life and death, beyond change, the state that does not decay or die.[205] Such a state is described in the *Dhammapada* as unconditioned and empty:

---

201. See, for example, the *Vesālīsutta* (S V 320–322).

202. Paṭis II 105: *nissaraṇaṭṭho vivekaṭṭho asaṅkhataṭṭho amataṭṭho. Ime cattāro nirodhassa nirodhaṭṭhā tathā avitathā anaññathā*. See also Vibh-a 83.

203. Seclusion (*viveka*) is described in the *Visuddhimagga* as having three aspects: 'the seclusion of the body, the seclusion of the mind and the seclusion by elimination [of the defilements]' (Vism 140: *kāyaviveko cittaviveko vikkhambhanaviveko ti tayo eva idha daṭṭhabbā*). For more comments on seclusion (*viveka*), see Chapter V.4, under the subheading 'Mindfulness factor of awakening (*satisambojjhaṅga*).'

204. The unconditioned (*asaṅkhata*) state is defined in the *Dhammasaṅgaṇi* as the state without cause (Dhs 193: *Yo eva so dhammo appaccayo, so eva so dhammo asaṅkhato*). In the *Cūḷavagga* of the *Aṅguttaranikāya*, three characteristics of the unconditioned (*asaṅkhata*) state are listed: (1) absence of arising, (2) absence of passing away and (3) absence of alternations while it persists (A I 152: *Na uppādo paññāyati na vayo paññāyati na ṭhitassa aññathattaṃ paññāyati. Imāni kho bhikkhave tīṇi asaṅkhatassa asaṅkhatalakkhaṇānī ti*).

205. In the *Visuddhimagga*, the cessation of suffering (*dukkhanirodha*) is described as follows: 'Its characteristic is peace, its function is not to die or to comfort and its manifestation is signlessness or non-proliferation' (Vism 507: *Tayidaṃ santilakkhaṇaṃ, accutirasaṃ, assāsakaraṇarasaṃ vā, animittapaccupaṭṭhānam, nippapañcapaccupaṭṭhānaṃ vā*).

Those without accumulation, and having a full understanding [of the nature] of food,
And whose pasture is freedom, empty and without a sign,
Their trail is difficult to trace like that of the birds in the sky. (Dhp 26)[206]

Another metaphor for the cessation of suffering (*dukkhanirodha*) or *nibbāna* can be found in the *Pahārādasutta* (A IV 202), where it is compared to the ocean: no matter how many rivers flow into the ocean, it does not change, neither increasing nor decreasing. The cessation of suffering (*dukkhanirodha*) occurs because of the cessation of the arising of suffering (*dukkhasamudaya*), which is craving (*taṇhā*).[207] Cessation is experienced as ultimate peace, because craving (*taṇhā*) and defilements (*kilesa*) are extinguished. If the meditator has reached path knowledge (*maggañāṇa*), fruition (*phala*) resembles a sort of great quenching or a special kind of freedom. The object of path consciousness (*maggacitta*) *is nibbāna*, which eradicates some (or all) defilements (*kilesa*), and is followed by fruition consciousness (*phalacitta*), which is experienced as a kind of supramundane state that cannot be described since there is no perception (*saññā*).

The cessation of suffering (*dukkhanirodha*) results from deep insight into suffering (*dukkha*) and its origin (*dukkhasamudaya*). Such an insight is achieved through the practice of the noble eightfold path (*ariyo aṭṭhaṅgiko maggo*).

'Path leading to the cessation of suffering' (*dukkhanirodhagāminī paṭipadā*)

The path leading to the cessation of suffering (*dukkhanirodhagāminī paṭipadā*) is a way of life, which is cultivated with the aim to understand suffering and its causes (*dukkhasamudaya*) and reach the cessation of suffering (*dukkhanirodha*). As mentioned earlier, the entire path to liberation is described as the cultivation of the thirty-seven qualities of awakening (*bodhipakkiyā dhammā*), which include, as their last component, the noble eightfold path (*ariyo aṭṭhaṅgiko maggo*). The path is called 'noble' when the meditator gains clear insight into the process of cause (*hetu*) and effect (*phala*), dependent origination (*paṭiccasamuppāda*) and non-self (*anattā*).

For the development of the noble eightfold path (*ariyo aṭṭhaṅgiko maggo*), the meditator initially has to cultivate virtue (*sīla*), loving kindness (*mettā*), compassion (*karuṇā*), renunciation (*nekkhamma*) and understanding of the process of cause (*hetu*) and effect (*phala*). Friendliness or loving kindness (*mettā*) is the intention or wish that all beings live in amity and friendliness, free from anger, hatred, thoughts of revenge and similar negative states.[208] Compassion (*karuṇā*) refers to the desire to help those who suffer and alleviate their troubles and misery.[209] Sympathetic joy (*muditā*) is the appreciative joy at another person's happiness and success; it

206. Dhp 26: *yesaṃ sannicayo n'atthi ye pariññātabhojanā, suññato animitto ca vimokho yesaṃ gocaro, ākāse va sakuntānaṃ gati tesaṃ durannayā.*

207. This is also said in the *Visuddhimagga*: 'It is because suffering ceases only through the cessation of its origins that the Blessed One, when teaching the cessation of suffering, taught the cessation of the origin' (Vism 507: *Iti yasmā samudayanirodhen' eva dukkhaṃ nirujjhati, tasmā Bhagavā dukkhanirodhaṃ desento samudayanirodhen' eva desesi*).

208. In the *Vibhaṅga*, friendliness or loving kindness (*mettā*) is equated with the absence of ill will (*avyāpāda*) (Vibh 86: *Yā sattesu metti mettāyanā mettāyitattaṃ mettā cetovimutti: ayaṃ vuccati avyāpādadhātu*), while in the *Dhammasaṅgaṇi*, it is presented as the absence of anger (*adosa*) and regarded as the root of wholesomeness (*kusalamūla*) (Dhs 189: *Yo adoso adussanā adussitattaṃ mettaṃ mettāyanā mettāyitattaṃ ... adoso kusalamūlaṃ, ayaṃ vuccati adoso*). Friendliness (*mettā*) is also described in the *Karaṇīyamettāsutta* (Sn 25–26), while a detailed description of the loving kindness (*mettā*) meditation practice is given in the *Visuddhimagga* (Vism 295–314).

209. In the *Vibhaṅga*, compassion (*karuṇā*) is equated with the absence of cruelty (*avihiṃsā*) (Vibh 86–87: *Yā sattesu karuṇā karuṇāyanā karuṇāyitattaṃ karuṇā cetovimutti: ayaṃ vuccati avihiṃsādhātu*). The meditation practice on compassion (*karuṇā*) is briefly outlined in Vism 314–315.

counteracts envy and jealousy, which are frequently encountered not only in worldly life but also among meditators.[210] For the cultivation of these states, it is not sufficient to merely repeat the words: 'May all beings be free from suffering,' although such thoughts can make the meditator feel happy and joyful, but one really has to act on them and try to alleviate suffering. Only then are these three mental qualities—i.e., loving kindness (*mettā*), compassion (*karuṇā*) and sympathetic joy (*muditā*)—truly cultivated and put into practice. Thereupon, greed (*lobha*) or aversion (*dosa*) will no longer occur, and tranquillity (*passaddhi*), concentration (*samādhi*) and right view (*sammā diṭṭhi*) will develop.

In the *Paṭisambhidāmagga*, the path leading to the cessation of suffering (*dukkhanirodhagāminī paṭipadā*) is described with the following four aspects:

> The path has the meaning of deliverance (*niyyānaṭṭho*), the meaning of cause (*hetuṭṭho*), the meaning of seeing (*dassanaṭṭho*) and the meaning of mastery (*ādhipateyyaṭṭho*). The path has these four meanings, which are true, not untrue, not otherwise. (Paṭis II 105).[211]

The four aspects listed above must be directly seen and comprehended by the meditator in her or his practice while noting objects as they arise and pass away. This means that the meditator understands that the noble eightfold path (*ariyo aṭṭhaṅgiko maggo*) is the release or deliverance (*niyyāna*) from suffering or unsatisfactoriness (*dukkha*), because when the path is cultivated, no more problems arise but rather the opposite: great peace and relief are felt. If the meditator encounters obstacles and other issues in her or his practice, this indicates that she or he is not properly cultivating the noble eightfold path (*ariyo aṭṭhaṅgiko maggo*). As the practice evolves, the meditator realises that the eightfold path itself is the cause (*hetu*) of freedom from suffering and unsatisfactoriness (*dukkha*) and is thus required for the attainment of liberation. The meditator understands that the noble eightfold path (*ariyo aṭṭhaṅgiko maggo*) is in fact the path for developing insight (*dassana*) into suffering (*dukkha*), its origins (*dukkhasamudaya*) and its cessation (*dukkhanirodha*). And finally, the noble eightfold path is viewed as the highest mastery (*ādhipateyya*) that one can develop; this is the mastery over oneself, leading to the highest possible knowledge, namely, the path knowledge (*maggañāṇa*).[212] When the meditator follows the noble eightfold path (*ariyo aṭṭhaṅgiko maggo*), it can be said that she or he takes refuge in Dhamma.

The noble eightfold path (*ariyo aṭṭhaṅgiko maggo*) encompasses the following eight components, as illustrated opposite (Table 14). The eight components are often presented in three groups: the first two components comprise wisdom (*paññā*), the next three moral virtue (*sīla*) and the last three meditation (*samādhi*).[213] Moral virtue (*sīla*) is essential for the development of meditation

210. The *Visuddhimagga* describes sympathetic joy (*muditā*) as follows: 'Its characteristic is gladness (*pamodanā*), its function is the absence of envy (*anissā*), it is manifested as the removal of dislike and its proximate cause is seeing others' success' (Vism 318: *Pamodanalakkhaṇā muditā, anissāyanarasā, arativighātapaccupaṭṭhānā, sattānaṃ sampattidassanapadaṭṭhānā*).

211. Paṭis II 105: *niyyānaṭṭho hetuṭṭho, dassanaṭṭho ādhipateyyaṭṭho. Ime cattāro maggassa maggaṭṭhā tathā avitathā anaññathā.* The same four aspects of the four noble truths are listed in the *Visuddhimagga* (Vism 494; 691); see also Vibh-a 83.

212. In the *Visuddhimagga*, it is said that at the moment of path knowledge (*maggakkhaṇa*), all aspects of the four truths are discerned together (Vism 692: *maggakkhaṇe pana sabbe c'ete atthā eken'eva dukkhādisu catukiccena ñāṇena paṭivedhaṃ gacchantī ti*).

213. The components of the noble eightfold path are thus classified in several canonical texts; for example, in the *Cūḷavedallasutta* (M I 301: *sammāvācā yo ca sammākammanto yo ca sammāājīvo, ime dhammā sīlakkhandhe saṅgahītā; yo ca sammāvāyāmo yā ca sammāsati yo ca sammāsamādhi, ime dhammā samādhikkhandhe saṅgahītā; yā ca sammādiṭṭhi yo ca sammāsaṅkappo, ime dhammā paññākkhandhe saṅgahītā ti*).

Table 14 Noble eightfold path (*ariyo aṭṭhaṅgiko maggo*).

Right view (*sammā diṭṭhi*) Right thought (*sammā saṅkappa*)	Wisdom (*paññā*)
Right speech (*sammā vācā*) Right action (*sammā kammanta*) Right livelihood (*sammā ājīva*)	Virtue (*sīla*)
Right effort (*sammā vāyāma*) Right mindfulness (*sammā sati*) Right concentration (*sammā samādhi*)	Meditation (*samādhi*)

(*samādhi*), which is the very foundation for wisdom (*paññā*) to emerge. Thus, restraint in speech and bodily actions (*sīla*) has to be established before beginning meditation practice.

All eight components of the path have the attribute of 'right' (*sammā*) in the sense that they are appropriate or suitable; this means that if they are cultivated appropriately, they lead to liberation from suffering or unsatisfactoriness (*dukkhanirodha*). Through the practice of meditation (*samādhi*), which is founded on moral virtue (*sīla*), wisdom (*paññā*) emerges; this means that due to the (temporary) absence of greed (*lobha*) and aversion (*dosa*), right view (*sammā diṭṭhi*) develops. At this point, the five hindrances (*nīvaraṇa*) are (temporarily) absent, the five faculties (*indriya*) are well established and balanced, and the meditator no longer creates suffering (*dukkha*) but instead relates to others with friendliness (*mettā*) and compassion (*karuṇā*). When the meditator is free from greed (*lobha*) and aversion (*dosa*), she or he can clearly comprehend renunciation (*nekkhamma*),[214] which is an important component in the arising of right thought (*sammā saṅkappa*). With the emergence of right thought (*sammā saṅkappa*), moral virtue (*sīla*) becomes firmly established,[215] which in turn creates the foundation for the deepening of meditation practice. Thus, moral virtue (*sīla*) is the foundation for meditation (*samādhi*) and wisdom (*paññā*), and when wisdom (*paññā*) is well established, path knowledge (*maggañāṇa*) is realised. Because the meditator then sees all phenomena as impermanent, based on causes and conditions, she or he understands that they are unsatisfactory (*dukkha*) and that there is nothing in them to hold onto. It is only due to ignorance (*avijjā*) that we cannot see the three characteristics (*tilakkhaṇa*).

'Moral virtue' (*sīla*)

The noble eightfold path begins with moral virtue (*sīla*), which comprises right speech (*sammā vācā*),[216] right action (*sammā kammanta*)[217] and right livelihood (*sammā ājīva*).[218] In other words,

214. The term *nekkhamma* most frequently refers to renunciation of worldliness, detachment, or freedom from desires and aversions (PED, *s.v.*); it is stated that all wholesome states are components of renunciation (Vibh 86).

215. It is said in the *Visuddhimagga* that practitioners 'follow renunciation for perfection of moral virtue' (Vism 325: *sīlaparipūraṇatthaṃ nekkhammaṃ bhajanti*).

216. For example, the *Vibhaṅga* describes right speech (*sammā vācā*) as abstaining from false speech, slander, harsh speech, and frivolous talk (Vibh 105: *Musāvādā veramaṇī pisuṇāya vācāya veramaṇī pharusāya vācāya veramaṇī samphappalāpā veramaṇī: ayaṃ vuccati sammāvācā*).

217. The *Vibhaṅga* presents right action (*sammā kammanta*) as abstaining from killing beings, taking what is not given, and sensual misconduct (Vibh 105: *Pāṇātipātā veramaṇī adinnādānā veramaṇī kāmesu micchācārā veramaṇī: ayaṃ vuccati sammākammanto*).

218. Right livelihood (*sammā ājīva*) means making one's living in a non-harmful manner. In the *Vibhaṅga*, it is only briefly described as abandoning wrong livelihood (Vibh 105: *Idha ariyasāvako micchā-ājīvaṃ pahāya sammā-*

this involves taking five or eight precepts (*sīla*)[219] as well as the three refuges (*saraṇa*) in the Buddha, the Dhamma and the Saṅgha. Although the meditator may begin her or his practice without much belief in the Buddha, she or he must nevertheless have some level of trust (*saddhā*) in the process of meditation and the Buddhist teachings. Trust (*saddhā*) in the Dhamma then extends to those who previously discovered the path (i.e., the Buddha); thus, the *Vakkalisutta* (S III 120) narrates that the Buddha said: 'One who sees the Dhamma sees me and one who sees me sees the Dhamma.'[220] Having established confidence (*saddhā*) in the Buddha and his teachings about how to overcome the habits of becoming (*bhava*) and reach the end of the journey in *saṃsāra*, the meditator's trust can then extend to other practitioners who have followed the path of the Dhamma, namely, the Saṅgha.[221] The word Saṅgha refers to the assembly of monks and nuns (*sammutisaṅgha*), whereas the term 'noble Saṅgha' (*ariyasaṅgha*) refers to those who have partially or completely overcome greed (*lobha*), aversion (*dosa*), delusion (*moha*), views (*diṭṭhi*) and conceit (*māna*).

Contemplation of the Buddha, Dhamma and Saṅgha is described in many texts such as the *Mahānāmasutta* (A V 329–330), which includes the recollection of the qualities of the Buddha:

> an *arahant*, perfectly awakened, accomplished in knowledge and conduct, fortunate, knower of the worlds, unsurpassed trainer of those to be trained, teacher of deities and humans, the Awakened One and the Blessed One.[222]

The contemplation of the Dhamma refers to the teachings of the Buddha, which are:

> well taught by the Blessed One, visible, immediate, inviting everyone to come and see, applicable, to be personally realised by the wise.[223]

Although the term Dhamma has a wide range of meanings, in the context of recollection, it refers to the teachings of the Buddha, which are presented as wholesome; they can therefore protect the mind from sinking into unwholesomeness. For this reason, the commentaries such as the *Papañcasūdanī* state that the Dhamma maintains the mind at a high level of wholesomeness and does not allow it to fall into unwholesomeness,[224] instead leading the meditator to develop concentration (*samādhi*) and wisdom (*paññā*). Hence, the Dhamma is said to be well taught (*svākkhāta*) and can actually be grasped by oneself (*sandiṭṭhika*) right now (*akālika*).

---

ajīvena jīvitaṃ kappeti: ayaṃ vuccati sammā-ājīvo). In several texts such as the *Sucimukhīsutta* (S III 239), right livelihood (*sammā ājīva*) is discussed mainly for ascetics and renouncers who live on alms.

219. The five precepts (*pañcasīla*) include abstaining from: (1) taking life, (2) taking what is not given, (3) sensual misconduct, (4) false speech and (5) intoxicants. Lay people may also take eight precepts, which include the five aforementioned precepts while replacing rule (3) with celibacy, and in addition, three further abstinences from: (6) eating at the wrong time, (7) entertainment, dancing, wearing ornaments, etc. and (8) sleeping on luxurious beds. The five and eight precepts are described in the *Dhammikasutta* (Sn 66–70).

220. S III 120: *Yo kho Vakkali dhammam passati so mam passati, yo maṃ passati so dhammam passati.*

221. For example, according to the *Aṭṭhapuggalasutta*, the Saṅgha is described as eight worthy people who practise for the fruit of realisation or who have already attained one of the following four stages of awakening: stream-winner (*sotāpanna*), once-returner (*sakadāgāmin*), non-returner (*anāgāmin*) and *arahant* (cf. A IV 292: *Sotāpanno sotāpattiphalasacchikiriyāya paṭipanno, sakadāgāmī sakadāgāmiphalasacchikiriyāya paṭipanno, anāgāmī anāgāmiphalasacchikiriyāya paṭipanno, arahā arahattāya paṭipanno*).

222. A V 329: *itipi so Bhagavā arahaṃ sammāsambuddho vijjācaraṇasampanno sugato lokavidū anuttaro purisadammasārathi satthā devamanussānaṃ buddho Bhagavā' ti.*

223. A V 229: *svākkhāto Bhagavatā dhammo sandiṭṭhiko akāliko ehipassiko opanayiko paccattaṃ veditabbo viññūhī' ti.*

224. Ps I 131; Sv I 229; Mp II 107: *apatamāne dhāretīti dhammo.*

To express the immediacy of the Dhamma, the term 'timeless' (*akālika*) is used here rather than the word *paccuppanna*, which means 'present time' (or more precisely, 'what has arisen'). Since *paccuppanna* denotes something that no longer exists when it is noted, the concept of the present (*paccuppanna*) refers to experiencing an object that no longer exists and is already dead. This means that there is really no present; therefore, the Dhamma has no duration and does not occur within the bounds of time—it is timeless (*akālika*).

As narrated in the *Mahānāmasutta*, the recollection of the Saṅgha refers to the disciples of the Buddha:

> The Saṅgha of the Blessed One's disciples follows the good way (*supaṭipanna*), lives uprightly (*ujupaṭipanna*), follows the right path (*ñāyapaṭipanna*) and follows the proper course (*sāmīcipaṭipanna*); these are the four pairs of people, the eight types of individuals. (A V 330)[225]

The *sutta* describes those who contemplate the qualities of the Buddha, the Dhamma and the Saṅgha:

> Their mind is not obsessed by desire, aversion or delusion ... [it] gains delight ... joy ... tranquillity ... happiness ... and becomes concentrated. (A V 333)[226]

Thus, the recollection of the Buddha, the Dhamma and the Saṅgha leads to freedom from the defilements (*kilesa*), to increased concentration (*samādhi*) and consequently to all other aspects of the noble eightfold path (*ariyo aṭṭhaṅgiko maggo*).

Taking the three refuges (*saraṇa*)—in the Buddha, the Dhamma and the Saṅgha—can also be viewed as a practice of generosity (*dāna*), virtue (*sīla*) and meditation (*bhāvanā*).[227] Along with generosity (*dāna*), the practice of virtue (*sīla*) is an extremely important foundation of meditation practice; it discourages any physical and verbal unwholesome actions (*akusala kamma*), which are always based on delusion (*moha*) and may arise in conjunction with greed (*lobha*) or aversion (*dosa*). Unwholesome mental states and actions can also be observed in animals, which are not very different from humans. Unwholesome actions arise easily and very naturally in us; we do not need to be taught since they are an intrinsic part of human life. Through the cultivation of virtue (*sīla*), animal instincts can be kept at bay and wholesome actions encouraged. When physical and verbal actions become more wholesome, they contribute to the development of wholesome (*kusala*) mental states, which are the foundation for the development of all the other components of the noble eightfold path (*ariyo aṭṭhaṅgiko maggo*). Thus, from virtue (*sīla*), right view (*sammā diṭṭhi*) and other components arise, not the other way around.

To reiterate, before beginning with meditation (*bhāvanā*), it is important to cultivate generosity (*dāna*) and virtue (*sīla*), as these will help the practitioner to reduce—at least to some extent—the defilements (*kilesa*). Then one can take up the practice of meditation (*bhāvanā*) through which the defilements (*kilesa*) can be further diminished and eventually eradicated.

---

225. A V 330: *Supaṭipanno Bhagavato sāvakasaṅgho, ujupaṭipanno Bhagavato sāvakasaṅgho, ñāyapaṭipanno Bhagavato sāvakasaṅgho, sāmīcipaṭipanno Bhagavato sāvakasaṅgho, yad idaṃ cattāri purisayugāni, aṭṭha purisapuggalā.*

226. A V 333: *nev'assa tasmiṃ samaye rāgapariyuṭṭhitaṃ cittaṃ hoti, na dosapariyuṭṭhitaṃ cittaṃ hoti, na mohapariyuṭṭhitaṃ cittaṃ hoti ... labhati pāmujjaṃ, pamuditassa pīti jāyati, pītimanassa kāyo passambhati, passaddhakāyo sukhaṃ vediyati, sukhino cittaṃ samādhiyati.*

227. Generosity (*dāna*), virtue (*sīla*) and meditation (*bhāvanā*) are usually listed as the three bases of meritorious deeds (*puññakiriyavatthūni*); this is stated, for example, in the *Dānavagga* of the *Aṅguttaranikāya* (A IV 241: *Tīṇ' imāni bhikkhave puññakiriyavatthūni. Katamāni tīṇi? Dānamayaṃ puññakiriyavatthuṃ, sīlamayaṃ puññakiriyavatthuṃ, bhāvanāmayaṃ puññakiriyavatthuṃ*).

It can be said that the only purpose of taking the five or eight precepts (*sīla*) and the three refuges (*saraṇa*) is to free oneself from the unsatisfactoriness and suffering (*dukkha*) of *saṃsāra*. The mere reciting of the precepts and three refuges (*saraṇa*) in a ritual does not mean much unless they are understood and implemented in daily life. Only when the meditator becomes grounded in virtue (*sīla*) and the three refuges (*saraṇa*) can she or he progress on the path.

'Wisdom' (*paññā*)

All the components of the noble eightfold path (*ariyo aṭṭhaṅgiko maggo*) are important and interrelated, although right view (*sammā diṭṭhi*) holds a special place, since its role is to understand the four noble truths in the proper (*sammā*) way.[228] Right view (*sammā diṭṭhi*) begins to evolve when the meditator clearly distinguishes between materiality (*nāma*) and mentality (*rūpa*); this means that she or he experiences every moment of experience as an interaction between materiality (*nāma*) and mentality (*rūpa*), without craving (*taṅhā*), conceit (*māna*) or views (*diṭṭhi*).[229] However, if craving (*taṅhā*), conceit (*māna*) or views (*diṭṭhi*) arise, the four noble truths (*cattāri ariyasaccāni*) are instantly concealed; consequently, meditation practice becomes gross, and the contemplation of phenomena (*dhammānupassanā*) cannot take place. Once craving (*taṅhā*) arises, the meditator usually tries to increase concentration (*samādhi*), but mindfulness (*sati*), clear comprehension (*sampajañña*) and the path cannot evolve in this manner. Therefore, the noble eightfold path (*ariyo aṭṭhaṅgiko maggo*) only develops when the meditator has no expectations or any other kind of craving (*taṅhā*). Insight into impermanence (*anicca*) will then emerge with the understanding that when objects are not observed with mindfulness (*sati*) and clear comprehension (*sampajañña*), suffering or unsatisfactoriness (*dukkha*) will ensue. After gaining such an insight, the meditator becomes tranquil and can clearly see that there is no person (*anattā*) but simply a succession of objects arising and passing away along with the mind that understands them.

When right view (*sammā diṭṭhi*) is established, right thought (*sammā saṅkappa*) arises.[230] It can be said that meditation practice is the cultivation of right thought (*sammā saṅkappa*). For example, when the meditator practises mindfulness of breathing (*ānāpānasati*), she or he observes the object of contemplation with thought (*vitakka*),[231] which is applied to each in-breath and out-breath. After some time, when the meditator observes the breath without desire (*abhijjhā*)

228. Right view (*sammā diṭṭhi*) is defined in the *Vibhaṅga* as 'knowledge of suffering, knowledge of the arising of suffering, knowledge of the cessation of suffering and knowledge of the path leading to the cessation of suffering' (Vibh 104: *Tattha katamā sammādiṭṭhi? Dukkhe ñāṇaṃ dukkhasamudaye ñāṇaṃ dukkhanirodhe ñāṇaṃ dukkhanirodhagāminiyā paṭipadāya ñāṇaṃ*). Many canonical and commentarial texts discuss right view (*sammā diṭṭhi*); for example, a comprehensive discourse is given in the *Sammādiṭṭhisutta* (M I 46–55).

229. Craving (*taṅhā*) and conceit (*māna*) create an 'I' or a personality to which one clings with views (*diṭṭhi*). Therefore, when these three aspects occur simultaneously, they form what is called the 'personality view' (*sakkāyadiṭṭhi*).

230. Right thought (*sammā saṅkappa*) is usually described as thought associated with renunciation as well as the absence of ill will and cruelty (Vibh 104: *katamo sammāsaṅkappo? Nekkhammasaṅkappo, avyāpādasaṅkappo, avihiṃsāsaṅkappo*).

231. The term *vitakka* generally refers to 'thought, thinking' (PED, *s.v.*). In the *Abhidhamma* texts, it is presented as one of the mental concomitants (*cetasika*) whose characteristic is mounting the mind to its object (As 114: *Svāyaṃ ārammaṇe cittassa abhiniropanalakkhaṇo*). *Vitakka* is similarly described in the *Visuddhimagga*: 'Its characteristic is mounting the mind on its object, its function is striking at and impinging on [the object]. It is manifested as leading the mind to an object' (Vism 142: *Svāyaṃ ārammaṇe cittassa abhiniropanalakkhaṇo; āhananapariyāhananaraso. Arammaṇe cittassa ānayanapaccupaṭṭhāno*).

and discontent (*domanassa*) and can remain with the meditation object for some time, mindfulness (*sati*) and clear comprehension (*sampajañña*) emerge, and then the thought (*vitakka*) that observes the breathing is wholesome (*kusala*). At this point, right thought (*sammā saṅkappa*) arises. Now the meditator no longer creates the eight types of thoughts, which the *Padhānasutta* from the *Suttanipāta* describes as 'the armies of Māra,' namely:

> The first army is sense desire, the second is discontent, the third is hunger and thirst, the fourth is craving, the fifth is sloth and torpor, the sixth is fear, the seventh is doubt and the eighth is hypocrisy and stubbornness. (Sn 76)[232]

Instead, right thought (*sammā saṅkappa*) arises, which is the thought associated with renunciation (*nekkhamma*). Only then does clear understanding emerge, namely, that suffering (*dukkha*) is always linked to unwholesome (*akusala*) states. In other words, it can be said that the meditator then lives with loving kindness (*mettā*) and compassion (*karuṇā*) towards her or himself. Right thought (*sammā saṅkappa*) then enhances and increases right effort (*sammā vāyāma*), right mindfulness (*sammā sati*) and right concentration (*sammā samādhi*), while moral virtue (*sīla*), which has already been established, is further strengthened.

'Meditation' (*samādhi*)

When right thought (*sammā saṅkappa*) is present, and the meditator continues to practise, right endeavour or effort (*sammā vāyāma*)[233] develops. This means that the meditator continues to mindfully observe the meditation object without any attachment and aversion, thus maintaining wholesomeness. Right effort (*sammā vāyāma*) comprises the four bases of power (*cattāro iddhipādā*); as mentioned before, these refer to the concentration (*samādhi*) developed in meditation based on the will to act (*chanda*), energy (*viriya*), strength of mind (*citta*) and investigative discernment (*vīmaṃsā*).[234] Sometimes people equate right effort (*sammā vāyāma*) with the physical effort required to sit or walk in meditation for long hours. Although at the early stages of meditation, physical endeavours are helpful and quite necessary, right effort (*sammā vāyāma*) refers to the mental energy[235] required to keep the mind on a wholesome meditation object, thus stabilising mindfulness (*sati*) and providing the foundation for wisdom (*paññā*) to emerge. Vigorous physical exertion often becomes wrong effort, thus creating unwholesome mental states. For example, the meditator who sits in meditation for long hours may become irritable and overcome by hindrances (*nīvaraṇa*) or defilements (*kilesa*), which prevent the arising of energy (*viriya*) and other wholesome faculties (*indriya*). It is therefore essential to

232. Sn 76: *Kāmā te paṭhamā senā, dutiyā arati vuccati, tatiyā khuppipāsā te, catutthī taṇhā pavuccati, pañcamī thīnamiddhaṃ te, chaṭṭhā bhīrū pavuccati, sattamī vicikicchā te, makkho thambho te aṭṭhamo.*

233. Right effort (*sammā vāyāma*) is described in the *Vibhaṅga* as avoiding the arising of unwholesome states, abandoning already arisen unwholesome states, developing wholesome states and maintaining already arisen wholesome states (Vibh 105: *Idha bhikkhu anuppannānaṃ pāpakānaṃ akusalānaṃ dhammānaṃ anuppādāya chandaṃ janeti vāyamati viriyaṃ ārabhati cittaṃ paggaṇhāti padahati, uppannānaṃ pāpakānaṃ akusalānaṃ dhammānaṃ pahānāya ... anuppannānaṃ kusalānaṃ dhammānaṃ uppādāya ... uppannānaṃ kusalānaṃ dhammānaṃ ṭhitiyā asammosāya bhiyyobhāvāya vepullāya bhāvanāya pāripūriyā chandaṃ janeti vāyamati viriyaṃ ārabhati cittaṃ paggaṇhāti padahati: ayaṃ vuccati sammāvāyāmo*).

234. These four bases of power (*cattāro iddhipādā*) are described in Chapter V.4, under the subheading 'Investigation-of-*dhammas* factor of awakening' (*dhammavicayasambojjhaṅga*). For details, see the *Iddipādasaṃyutta* (S V 254–293).

235. Effort (*vāyāma*) is similarly explained in the *Vibhaṅga*: 'What is effort? It is a mental concomitant of energy' (Vibh 213: *tattha katamo vāyāmo? Yo cetasiko viriyārambho*).

balance any effort (*vāyāma*); if too much effort is exerted, clinging (*upādāna*), restlessness and worry (*uddhaccakukkuca*) can ensue, while too little effort creates sloth and torpor (*thīnamiddha*). The importance of balanced effort is described in the *Soṇasutta* (A III 374–375) using the metaphor of the lute: for the instrument to be well tuned and easy to play, its strings should be neither too loose nor too tight. Likewise, in meditation, energy should be balanced; excessive energy leads to restlessness, while overly lax energy leads to laziness. The meditator should balance her or his practice like a tightrope walker who moves very carefully—not too fast and not too slow—always focused on every step, in order to let go of the past, the future, craving, aversion, thinking, expectations, yearning for fast results or heedlessness.

Right effort (*sammā vāyāma*) should be cultivated until right mindfulness (*sammā sati*) has been properly established; only then is the practice well balanced.[236] Thereupon, mindfulness (*sati*) functions like the watchful gatekeeper of a city, checking who approaches the entrance;[237] the meditator not only observes the various objects arising but also knows when greed (*lobha*) or aversion (*dosa*) occur with the object. When mindfulness (*sati*) is present in every activity or process without greed (*lobha*) or aversion (*dosa*), it is called right mindfulness (*sammā sati*). Then, along with right thought (*sammā saṅkappa*), right effort (*sammā vāyāma*) and right mindfulness (*sammā sati*), right concentration (*sammā samādhi*)[238] can also evolve.

Right concentration (*sammā samādhi*) is thought (*vitakka*) based on wholesomeness, which is sustained (*vicāra*) and can continue arising with the same meditation object until the object disappears; it is accompanied by joy (*pīti*), happiness (*sukha*) and one-pointedness (*ekaggatā*).[239] When these mental concomitants (*cetasika*) are present and well established, then it is called right concentration (*sammā samādhi*). Now the meditator can remain with the chosen object of concentration (*samādhi*) for long periods and develop the progressive stages of the absorptions (*jhāna*). Alternatively, the meditator can pay attention, with a similar degree of concentration, to any other object that arises; in this case, she or he may begin observing impermanence (*anicca*) and understand that the object contemplated at the present moment is not the same as the object that arises in the next moment. In other words, the meditator gains an insight that any object that occurs immediately passes away, not lasting for even one second, and that the object that has arisen is not the same as the object that has ceased. After establishing right concentration (*sammā samādhi*) and clearly understanding impermanence (*anicca*), the meditator can contemplate objects without an 'I' or self (*anattā*); thus, right view (*sammā diṭṭhi*) emerges and becomes further strengthened. When the meditator reaches the level of the knowledge

236. In the *Satipaṭṭhānasutta* and many other Pāli canonical and post-canonical texts, the meditator who cultivates right mindfulness (*sammā sati*) is described as someone who cultivates the four foundations of mindfulness, being ardent (*ātāpī*), clearly comprehending (*sampajāno*), mindful (*satimā*) and having abandoned desires and discontent in regard to the world (*vineyya loke abhijjhādomanassaṃ*) (e.g., M I 56; M III 84; D II 94-95; D II 100; D II 276; S V 9; Vibh 105, 194).

237. This metaphor is explained in Chapter I, under the subheading 'Mindful (*satimā*).'

238. Right concentration (*sammā samādhi*) is frequently described as the state of meditative absorption (*jhāna*); for example, the *Vibhaṅga* describes it as the succession of absorptions up to the fourth *jhāna*: 'neither pain nor pleasure, [and] purity of mindfulness through equanimity' (Vibh 105: *adukkhamasukhaṃ upekhāsatipārisuddhiṃ catutthaṃ jhānaṃ*).

239. Here the five components of the first *jhāna* are listed: (1) applied thought (*vitakka*), (2) sustained thought (*vicāra*), (3) joy (*pīti*), (4) happiness (*sukha*) and (5) one-pointedness (*ekaggatā*). Many canonical and post-canonical texts provide detailed descriptions of the *jhānas* and their components (e.g., M I 40–41; A IV 438–448; S IV 217; D I 73–74; Dhs 31–56; Vism 137–169, 326–340).

of equanimity of formations (*saṅkhār'upekkhāñāṇa*) but before entering the path knowledge (*maggañāṇa*), her or his concentration is in fact stronger than in the meditative absorptions (*jhāna*); at that point, the mind has deeply penetrating clarity, and the most subtle phenomena are distinctly seen and comprehended.

This is how the noble eightfold path (*ariyo aṭṭhaṅgiko maggo*) is to be understood by the meditator. Only when right view (*sammā diṭṭhi*) is present, and all the components of the noble eightfold path (*ariyo aṭṭhaṅgiko maggo*) are evenly balanced, can the meditator see and understand the four noble truths (*cattāri ariyasaccāni*) with every object arising and passing away. She or he may thus reach the final liberation from unsatisfactoriness and suffering (*dukkha*), namely, the realisation of *nibbāna*.

— VI —

CONCLUSION

Yo hi koci bhikkhave ime cattāro satipaṭṭhāne evaṃ bhāveyya satta vassāni, tassa dvinnaṃ phalānaṃ aññataraṃ phalaṃ pāṭikaṅkhaṃ diṭṭheva dhamme aññā, sati vā upādisese anāgāmitā. Tiṭṭhantu ***bhikkhave*** *satta vassāni, yo hi koci bhikkhave ime cattāro satipaṭṭhāne evaṃ bhāveyya cha vassāni ... pañca vassāni ... cattāri vassāni ... tīṇi vassāni ... dve vassāni ... ekaṃ vassaṃ ... tiṭṭhatu bhikkhave ekaṃ* ***vassaṃ****, yo hi koci bhikkhave ime cattāro satipaṭṭhāne evaṃ bhāveyya satta māsāni, tassa dvinnaṃ phalānaṃ aññataraṃ phalaṃ pāṭikaṅkhaṃ diṭṭheva dhamme aññā, sati vā upādisese anāgāmitā. Tiṭṭhantu bhikkhave satta māsāni, yo hi koci bhikkhave ime cattāro satipaṭṭhāne evaṃ bhāveyya cha māsāni ... pañca māsāni ... cattāri māsāni ... tīṇi māsāni ... dve māsāni ... ekaṃ māsaṃ ... addhamāsaṃ ... tiṭṭhatu* ***bhikkhave*** *addhamāso, yo hi koci bhikkhave ime cattāro satipaṭṭhāne evaṃ bhāveyya sattāhaṃ, tassa dvinnaṃ phalānaṃ aññataraṃ phalaṃ pāṭikaṅkhaṃ diṭṭheva dhamme aññā, sati vā upādisese anāgāmitā.*

Ekāyano ayaṃ bhikkhave maggo sattānaṃ visuddhiyā sokapariddavānaṃ samatikkamāya ***dukkhadomanassānaṃ*** *atthagamāya ñāyassa adhigamāya nibbānassa sacchikiriyāya, yadidaṃ cattāro satipaṭṭhānā ti, iti yantaṃ vuttaṃ idametaṃ paṭicca vuttanti. Idamavoca bhagavā. Attamanā te bhikkhū bhagavato bhāsitaṃ abhinandunti.*

'Monks, if anyone thus developed the four foundations of mindfulness for seven years, he could expect one of two fruits: either final knowledge here and now, or if some clinging still remained, the state of non-return. Let alone seven years, monks, if anyone thus developed the four foundations of mindfulness for six years ... for five years ... for four years ... for three years ... for two years ... for one year, he could expect one of two fruits: either final knowledge here and now, or if some clinging still remained, the state of non-return. Let alone, monks, if anyone thus developed the four foundations of mindfulness for seven months ... for six months ... for five months ... for four months ... for three months ... for two months ... for one month ... for half a month, he could expect one of two fruits: either final knowledge here and now, or if some clinging still remained, the state of non-return. Let alone half a month, monks, if anyone thus developed the four foundations of mindfulness for seven days, he could expect one of two fruits: either final knowledge here and now, or if some clinging still remained, the state of non-return.'

In reference to this, it was said: 'Monks, the four foundations of mindfulness are the direct path for the purification of beings, for the overcoming of grief and sorrow, for the relinquishment of suffering and discontent, for the attainment of the true path, for the realisation of *nibbāna*.' This is what the Blessed One said. The monks were delighted and rejoiced in the words of the Blessed One.

Pemasiri Thera's commentary

The time required for the meditator to reach final liberation depends on the approach used for training. Most meditators in meditation centres are mindful for only very brief periods, although they may not think so. This is because they tend to spend so much time practising meditation with great expectations of progress and constantly evaluate their meditation, or otherwise they may think about other people and compare themselves with them. Indeed, the greater the expectations of progress or results, the less mindful they will be. This is why meditators are sometimes told to let the mind wander as much as it likes; the very desire to stop the mind wandering will make it wander even more.

People undertake meditation with various motives and expectations; they may want to calm the mind, gain more knowledge or wisdom, increase their ability to concentrate, perform better in their studies or work or heal themselves if they are sick. The range of motivations for engaging in meditation or joining the Saṅgha was similar in the Buddha's time. For example, as narrated in the *Theragāthā* commentary (*Paramatthadīpanī* V) (Th-a III 180–181), the monk Vaṅgīsa joined the Saṅgha with an initial intention to show off his ability to predict where a dead person would be reborn by tapping their skull; however, he eventually became an *arahant* and one of the most distinguished disciples of the Buddha.[1] Thus, irrespective of the initial expectations and intentions, the four foundations of mindfulness (*cattāro satipaṭṭhānā*) are always beneficial and useful for anybody who undertakes meditation and develops it properly, irrespective of their background.

Along with various expectations, meditators are often fooled or misled by various defilements (*kilesa*) such as greed (*lobha*), aversion (*dosa*), delusion (*moha*), conceit (*māna*) and views (*diṭṭhi*), which may arise in a very deceptive and subtle manner, and consequently, hamper any progress. For example, defilements (*kilesa*) may arise in the meditator along with thoughts such as 'Now I have good concentration; my meditation is progressing very well' or 'I have developed wisdom.' Such thoughts are rooted in the defilements (*kilesa*), but because they are accompanied by a pleasant feeling, the meditator is deceived. Sometimes the meditator may live with such false ideas and thoughts for many years and may even become a meditation teacher. This happens because she or he has well-developed attention (*manasikāra*) and can be aware and stay with the object of meditation without seeing the defilements (*kilesa*) such as conceit (*māna*) and views (*diṭṭhi*). Consequently, she or he is attached to past meditation experiences and views them as permanent.

But when right mindfulness (*sammā sati*) is developed, the meditator has no attachment or aversion. With clear comprehension (*sampajañña*), the meditator can then observe the experiences as impermanent (*anicca*), as a continuous flow of arising (*samudaya*) and passing away (*vaya*) of phenomena at the level of the aggregates (*khandha*), elements (*dhātu*) or sense spheres (*āyatana*). The most important aspect of meditation practice is the cultivation of mindfulness (*sati*). When it is well established, the meditator feels relaxed and no longer compares or evaluates her or himself or others but instead relates to people with compassion and detachment. Along with strong mindfulness (*sati*) and clear comprehension (*sampajañña*), the meditator can make very rapid progress and reach final liberation (or if some clinging still remains, attain the state of non-return) in seven years or even much faster, namely, in seven days or less, as

1. Vaṅgīsa was also a poet to whom the final section of the *Theragāthā*, the *Mahānipāta* comprised of fourteen poems, is ascribed (Ireland 1997).

said in the *Satipaṭṭhānasutta* and several other texts.[2] However, it is possible to make such rapid progress and reach arahantship in a day or less,[3] so long as right mindfulness (*sammā sati*) is fully established along with all other components of the noble eightfold path (*ariyo aṭṭhaṅgiko maggo*).

The very end of the *Satipaṭṭhānasutta* says: 'The monks were delighted and rejoiced in the words of the Blessed One' (*Attamanā te bhikkhū Bhagavato bhāsitaṃ abhinandunti*). The *sutta* does not conclude, like many other *suttas*, by stating that the monks attained path knowledge (*maggañāṇa*) and reached the end of suffering (*dukkha*). Instead, it outlines a plan or blueprint for monks, which describes the meditation path and shows how to develop their practice. It is like an architect's plan that needs to be completed by constructing the building. Similarly, the monks, after hearing the *sutta*, would then go off into solitude and meditate in order to realise the teachings through the practice of the four foundations of mindfulness (*cattāro satipaṭṭhānā*).

2. A similar timeframe ranging from seven days to seven years is provided in the *Udumbarikasīhanādasutta* (D III 55) for the attainment of final liberation.

3. In the *Bodhirājakumārasutta*, it is said that a monk, who has well established the five factors of striving (*pañcahi padhāniyaṅgehi samannāgato*) and is 'instructed in the evening, may attain in the morning; and being instructed in the morning, he may attain in the evening' (M II 96: *sāyam anusiṭṭho pāto visesaṃ adhigamissati, pātam anusiṭṭho sāyaṃ visesaṃ adhigamissatīti*). This passage is commented on in the *Papañcasūdanī* (Ps 302), which states that the meditator of acute wisdom (*tikkhapaññā*) can achieve liberation in such a short time.

Bibliography

Anālayo, Bhikkhu. 2003. *Satipaṭṭhāna: The Direct Path to Realization*. Birmingham: Windhorse.

Aung, Shwe Zan, trans., and Caroline Rhys Davids, rev. ed. 1910. *Compendium of Philosophy: Being a Translation Now Made for the First Time from the Original Pali of the Abhidhammattha-Sangaha: With Introductory Essay and Notes by Shwe Zan Aung*. London: Luzac and Company for the Pali Text Society.

Bodhi, Bhikkhu, trans. 1993. *Abhidhammattha Saṅgaha: A Comprehensive Manual of Abhidhamma: Pali Text, Translation and Explanatory Guide*. Kandy: Buddhist Publication Society.

———. 2000. *The Connected Discourses of the Buddha: A New Translation of the Saṃyutta Nikāya*. Boston, MA: Wisdom Publications.

———. 2012. *The Numerical Discourses of the Buddha: A Translation of the Aṅguttara Nikāya*. Boston, MA: Wisdom Publications.

Braun, Erik. 2013. *The Birth of Insight: Meditation, Modern Buddhism, and the Burmese Monk Ledi Sayadaw*. Chicago, IL: University of Chicago Press.

Bucknell, Roderick S. 1993. 'Reinterpreting the Jhānas.' *Journal of the International Association of Buddhist Studies* 16(2): 375–409.

Burlingame, Eugene Watson, trans. [1921] 1995. *Buddhist Legends: Translated from the Original Pali Text of the Dhammapada Commentary*. 3 vols. Reprint. Oxford: Pali Text Society.

Ditrich, Tamara. 2016a. 'Buddhism between Asia and Europe: The Concept of Mindfulness through an Historical Lens.' *Asian Studies: Religious and Spiritual Practices in Asia: Continuity and Change* 4(1): 197–213.

———. 2016b. 'Intepretations of the Terms Ajjhattaṃ and Bahiddhā: From the Pāli Nikāyas to the Abhidhamma.' In *Text, History and Philosophy: Abhidharma Across Buddhist Scholastic Traditions*, edited by Bart Dessein and Weijen Teng, 108–145. Leiden: Brill.

Gethin, Rupert. 1998. *The Foundations of Buddhism*. Oxford: Oxford University Press.

———. 2001. *The Buddhist Path to Awakening*. Oxford: Oneworld.

———. 2011. 'On Some Definitions of Mindfulness.' *Contemporary Buddhism* 12(1): 263–279.

———. 2012. '*Bhavaṅga* and Rebirth According to the Abhidhamma.' [Reprint of the Indian edition by Heritage Publishers in 1992.] In *The Buddhist Forum, Vol. III: Papers in Honour and Appreciation of Professor David Seyfort Ruegg's Contribution to Indological, Buddhist and Tibetan Comprehension Studies*, edited by Tadeuzs Skorupski and Ulrich Pagel, 11–35. Tring, Berkeley: The Institute of Buddhist Studies.

Goenka. 1999. *Discourses on the Satipaṭṭhāna Sutta*. Igatpuri: VRI.

Gyatso, Janet, ed. 1992. *In the Mirror of Memory: Reflections on Mindfulness and Remembrance in Indian and Tibetan Buddhism*. Albany: State University of New York.

Harvey, Peter. 2009. 'The Four Ariya-saccas as 'True Realities for the Spiritually Ennobled'—the Painful, its Origin, its Cessation, and the Way Going to This—Rather than 'Noble Truths' Concerning These.' *Buddhist Studies Review* 26(2): 197–227.

———. 2013. *An Introduction to Buddhism: Teaching, History and Practices*. Second ed. Cambridge: Cambridge University Press.

Ireland, J. D. 1997. *Vaṅgīsa: An Early Buddhist Poet: Pali Text Edited and Translated*. Kandy: Buddhist Publication Society.

Karunadasa, Y. 1967. *Buddhist Analysis of Matter*. Colombo: Department of Cultural Affairs.

———. 2010. *The Theravāda Abhidhamma: Its Inquiry into the Nature of Conditioned Reality*. Center of Buddhist Studies Publication Series. Hong Kong: Center of Buddhist Studies, University of Hong Kong.

Mahāsi Sayadaw. 2016. *Manual of Insight*. Somerville, MA: Wisdom Publications.

McMahan, David L. 2008. *The Making of Buddhist Modernism*. Oxford: Oxford University Press.

Ñāṇamoli, Bhikkhu, trans. 1999. *The Path of Purification: Visuddhimagga*. Onalaska, WA: BPS Pariyatti.

Ñāṇanamoli, Bhikkhu, and Bhikkhu Bodhi, trans. 1995. *The Middle Length Discourses of the Buddha: A New Translation of the Majjhima Nikāya*. Boston, MA: Wisdom Publications.

Nyanaponika. 1965. *Abhidhamma Studies: Buddhist Explorations of Consciousness and Time*. Fourth Revised Edition. Boston, MA: Wisdom Publications, in collaboration with the Buddhist Publication Society, Kandy, Sri Lanka.

Nyanatiloka. 2008. *Guide through the Abhidhamma Piṭaka: A Synopsis of the Philosophical Collection of the Theravāda Buddhist Canon, Followed by an Essay on Dependent Origination*. Fifth Revised Edition. Kandy: Buddhist Publication Society.

Norman, K. R. 1993. 'Why are the Four Noble Truths called 'Noble'?' In *Collected Papers*, Vol. IV, 171–174. Oxford: Pali Text Society.

Pa-Auk. 2003. *Knowing and Seeing*. Revised Edition. Kuala Lumpur: WAVE Publications.

Poddar, R.P. ed. 2013–2014. *A Comprehensive and Critical Dictionary of the Prakrit Languages with Special Reference to Jain Literature*. Pune: Bhandarkar Oriental Research Institute.

Rhys Davids, Caroline, trans. 2012. *A Buddhist Manual of Psychological Ethics*. PTS Translation Series 39. Bristol: Pali Text Society.

Soma, Thera. 1981. *The Way of Mindfulness: Being a Translation of the Satipaṭṭhāna Sutta of the Majjhima Nikāya; its Commentary the Satipaṭṭhāna Sutta Vaṇṇanā of the Papañcasūdanī of Buddhaghosa Thera; and Excerpts from the Līnatthapakāsanā Ṭīkā, Marginal Notes of Dhammapāla Thera on the Commentary*. 5th rev. ed. Kandy: Buddhist Publication Society.

Sujato, Bhikkhu. 2005. *A History of Mindfulness: How Insight Worsted Tranquillity in the Satipatthana Sutta*. Taipei: The Corporate Body of the Buddha Educational Foundation.

Thiṭṭila, trans. 2010. *The Book of Analysis (Vibhaṅga)*. PTS Translation Series 39. Bristol: Pali Text Society.

Tin, Pe Maung, trans. 2013. *The Expositor (Atthasālinī)*. PTS Translation Series 8, 9. Bristol: Pali Text Society.

Walshe, Maurice, trans. 1995. *The Long Discourses of the Buddha: A Translation of the Dīgha Nikāya*. Boston, MA: Wisdom Publications.

Warder, A. K. 1971. 'Dharmas and Data.' *Journal of Indian Philosophy* 1: 272–295.

Wijeratne, R. and Rupert Gethin. [2001] 2007. *Summary of the Topics of Abhidhamma (Abhidhammatthasaṅgaha) by Anuruddha. Exposition of the Topics of Abhidhamma (Abhidhammatthavibhāvinī) by Sumaṅgala: Being a Commentary to Anuruddha's 'Summary of the Topics of Abhidhamma.'* Reprinted with corrections. Lancaster: Pali Text Society.

Glossary

In this glossary arranged in English alphabetical order, the main Pāli terms discussed or mentioned are listed below with the English translations used in this book. For the whole range of meanings and translations, the reader may refer to PED or DP.

abhijjhā	desire
abhiññā	superior knowledge
ādīnavañāṇa	knowledge of danger
adukkhamasukhavedanā	neither-unpleasant-nor-pleasant feeling
āhāra	nutriment
ahirika	shamelessness
ajjhattam	internally
ajjhattabahiddhā	internally and externally
akālika	timeless
ākāsadhātu	element of space
akusala	unwholesome, unskilful
amahaggata	unexalted
amoha	non-delusion, wisdom
anāgāmin	non-returner
ānāpānasati	mindfulness of breathing
anattā	non-self
anicca	impermanence
anottappa	lack of fear of doing wrong
anuloma	conformity
anupassanā	contemplation

anusaya	underlying, latent tendency
anuttara	unsurpassable
appamāda	striving, diligence
āpodhātu	water element
arahant	one who has attained the final stage of *nibbāna*
asamāhita	unconcentrated
asaṅkhata	unconditioned, unconstructed
āsava	taint, mental contaminant
ātāpī	ardent
aṭṭhaṅgikamagga	eightfold path
avijjā	ignorance
avimutta	unliberated
āyatana	sense sphere
ayoniso manasikāra	unwise attention
bahiddhā	externally
bala	power
bhaṅgañāṇa	knowledge of dissolution
bhava	becoming
bhāvanā	cultivation, meditation
bhavarāga	desire for being
bhayañāṇa	knowledge of fear
bhikkhu	monk
bhikkhunī	nun
bojjhaṅga	factor of awakening
cakkhu	eye
cetanā	volition
cetasika	mental concomitant, mental factor
chanda	will to act
citta	mind, consciousness
cittānupassanā	contemplation of the mind
dāna	generosity
dhamma	phenomenon, Buddhist teachings
dhammānupassanā	contemplation of phenomena

dhammavicaya	investigation of *dhamma*
dhātu	element
diṭṭhi	view(s)
diṭṭhivisuddhi	purification of view
domanassa	discontent, displeasure
dosa	aversion
dukkha	unsatisfactoriness, suffering
dukkhavedanā	unpleasant feeling
ekaggatā	focus, one-pointedness
gandhā	smell
ghāna	nose
gotrabhū	change-of-lineage
iddhipāda	base of power
indriya	faculty
indriyasaṃvara	restraint of the senses
iriyāpatha	mode of movement
jaratā	decay
jhāna	meditative absorption
jīvita	life energy
jivhā	tongue
kalyāṇamitta	good friend, teacher
kāmacchanda	sense desire
kamma	action, cause and consequence, action having result
kammaññatā	adaptability
karuṇā	compassion
kāya	body
kāyagātasati	mindfulness directed to the body
kāyānupassanā	contemplation of the body
kāyasaṅkhāra	body formation
khandha	aggregate
kilesa	defilement
kukkucca	worry
kusala	wholesome, skilful

lahutā	lightness
lobha	greed
magga	path
maggañāṇa	path knowledge
maggaphalañāṇa	path and fruition knowledge
mahaggata	exalted
māna	conceit
manasikāra	attention
mano	mind
mettā	friendliness, loving kindness, benevolence
micchā diṭṭhi	wrong view
middha	torpor
moha	delusion
mudutā	tenderness
muñcitukamyatāñāṇa	knowledge of desire for deliverance
nāmakāya	mental body
nāmarūpa	mentality and materiality
ñāṇa	knowledge
nekkhamma	renunciation
nibbāna	cessation, liberation
nibbidāñāṇa	knowledge of disenchantment or disgust
nirodha	cessation
nisatta	non-being, non-essence
nissattanijjīvata	having no essence and no living being
nīvaraṇa	hindrance
pajānāti	clearly comprehends
pāmujja	gladness
pañcabalāni	five strengths
pañc'indriyāni	five faculties: (1) trust (*saddhā*), (2) energy (*viriya*), (3) mindfulness (*sati*), (4) concentration (*samādhi*), (5) wisdom (*paññā*)
paññā	wisdom
papañca	expansion, proliferation of obstacles

parimukham	in front, at the forefront
pasādaniya nimitta	pleasing object
passaddhi	peace, tranquillity
paṭhavīdhātu	earth element
paṭiccasamuppāda	dependent origination
paṭigha	anger
paṭikkūlamanasikāra	reflection on the troublesomeness
paṭinissagga	abandonment
paṭisaṅkhāñāṇa	knowledge of reobservation
phala	fruition
phassa	contact
phoṭṭhabbā	touch
pīti	joy
rāga	desire, lust, passion
rasa	taste
rūpa	matter, materiality, visible form
sadda	sound
saddhā	trust, faith
sadosa	with aversion
samādhi	concentration
samāhita	concentrated
samatha	calm
sammā diṭṭhi	right view
sammā sati	right mindfulness
sammā saṅkappa	right thought
samoha	with delusion
sampajañña	clear comprehension
saṃsāra	the round of rebirths
samudaya	arising
samudayadhammā	arising phenomena
samudayavayadhammā	arising and passing away phenomena
saṃyojana	fetter
saṅkhāra	mental formation

saṅkhār'upekkhāñāṇa	knowledge of equanimity of formations
saṅkhitta	contracted
saññā	perception
santati	continuity
sarāga	with desire
sati	mindfulness
satipaṭṭhāna	foundation of mindfulness
satta	being
sa-uttara	surpassable
sikkhati	trains, restrains oneself
sīla	virtue
somanassa	mental ease, pleasantness
sota	ear
sotāpanna	stream-winner
sukha	happiness
sukhavedanā	pleasant feeling
taṇhā	craving
thambha	grossness or roughness
thīna	sloth
tejodhātu	fire element
tilakkhaṇa	the three characteristics of all phenomena: impermanence (*anicca*), unsatisfactoriness (*dukkha*) and non-self (*anattā*)
udayabbayañāṇa	knowledge of arising and passing away
uddhacca	restlessness
ujugatacitta	straight mind
upacāra samādhi	access concentration
upacaya	arising
upādāna	clinging
upasaṃharati	approaches
upekkhā	equanimity
utu	temperature
vaya	passing away
vayadhammā	passing away phenomena

vāyāma	effort
vāyodhātu	air element
vedanā	feeling
vedanānupassanā	contemplation of feeling
vicāra	sustained thought
vicikicchā	doubt
vijjāvimutti	knowledge and liberation
vijjāvimuttiphala	the fruit of knowledge and liberation
vikkhitta	distracted
vīmaṃsa	investigative discernment
vimutta	liberated
viññāṇa	consciousness
vipassanā	insight
vipassanāñāṇa	insight knowledge
virāga	dispassion
viriya	energy, mental effort
vītadosa	applied thought
vitakka	without aversion
vītamoha	without delusion
vītarāga	without desire
viveka	detachment
vossagga	relinquishment
vyāpāda	ill will
yoniso manasikāra	wise attention

Discourse on the Foundations of Mindfulness (*Satipaṭṭhānasutta*)

Pāli Text and English Translation

The Pāli text used here is the *Satipaṭṭhānasutta* version from the *Majjhima Nikāya* (MN I 55–63). In the English translation, I have largely adopted the renderings of Ñāṇanamoli and Bodhi (1995, 145–155) though with a number of modifications.

Pāli Text

Evaṃ me sutaṃ. Ekaṃ samayaṃ Bhagavā Kurūsu viharati Kammāssadhammaṃ nāma Kurūnaṃ nigamo. Tatra kho Bhagavā bhikkhū amantesi Bhikkhavo ti. Bhadante ti te bhikkhū Bhagavato paccassosuṃ. Bhagavā etadavoca:

Ekāyano ayaṃ bhikkhave maggo sattānaṃ visuddhiyā sokapariddavānaṃ samatikkamāya dukkhadomanassānaṃ atthagamāya ñāyassa adhigamāya nibbānassa sacchikiriyāya yadidaṃ cattāro satipaṭṭhānā. Katame cattāro? Idha bhikkhave bhikkhu kāye kāyānupassī viharati ātāpī sampajāno satimā vineyya loke abhijjhādomanassaṃ, vedanāsu vedanānupassī viharati ātāpī sampajāno satimā vineyya loke abhijjhādomanassaṃ, citte cittānupassī viharati ātāpī sampajāno satimā vineyya loke abhijjhādomanassaṃ, dhammesu dhammānupassī viharati ātāpī sampajāno satimā vineyya loke abhijjhādomanassaṃ.

Kāyānupassanā

[*Ānāpānasati*]

Kathañca bhikkhave bhikkhu kāye kāyānupassī viharati? Idha bhikkhave bhikkhu araññagato vā rukkhamūlagato vā suññāgāragato vā nisīdati pallaṅkaṃ ābhujitvā ujuṃ kāyaṃ paṇidhāya parimukhaṃ satim upaṭṭhapetvā. So sato va assasati sato passasati. Dīghaṃ vā assasanto dīghaṃ assasāmīti pajānāti, dīghaṃ vā passasanto dīghaṃ passasāmīti pajānāti; rassaṃ vā assasanto rassaṃ assasāmīti pajānāti, rassaṃ vā passasanto rassaṃ passasāmīti pajānāti. Sabbakāyapaṭisaṃvedī assasissāmīti sikkhati, sabbakāyapaṭisaṃvedī passasissāmīti sikkhati. Passambhayaṃ kāyasaṅkhāraṃ assasissāmīti sikkhati, passambhayaṃ kāyasaṅkhāraṃ passasissāmīti sikkhati.

Seyyathā pi bhikkhave dakkho bhamakāro vā bhamakārantevāsī vā dīghaṃ vā añchanto dīghaṃ añchāmīti pajānāti, rassaṃ vā añchantorassaṃ añchāmīti pajānāti, evameva kho bhikkhave bhikkhu dīghaṃ vā assasanto: dīghaṃ assasāmīti pajānāti - pe - passambhayaṃ kāyasaṅkhāraṃ passasissāmīti sikkhati.

Iti ajjhattaṃ vā kāye kāyānupassī viharati, bahiddhā vā kāye kāyānupassī viharati, ajjhattabahiddhā vā kāye kāyānupassī viharat. Samudayadhammānupassī vā kāyasmiṃ viharati, vayadhammānupassī vā kāyasmiṃ viharati, samudayavayadhammānupassī vā kāyasmiṃ viharati. Atthi kāyo ti vā panassa sati paccupaṭṭhitā hoti yāvadeva ñāṇamattāya patissatimattāya, anissito ca viharati na ca kiñci loke upādiyati. Evampi bhikkhave bhikkhu kāye kāyānupassī viharati.

[*Iriyāpatha*]

Puna ca paraṃ bhikkhave bhikkhu gacchanto vā gacchāmīti pajānāti, ṭhito vā ṭhitomhīti pajānāti, nisinno vā nisinnomhīti pajānāti, sayāno vā sayānomhīti pajānāti, yathā yathā vā panassa kāyo paṇihito hoti tathā tathā naṃ pajānāti.

English Translation

Thus have I heard. Once the Blessed One was staying in the Kuru country, in a town of the Kurus called Kammāsadhamma. There he addressed the monks thus: 'Monks.' 'Venerable sir,' they replied. The Blessed One said this:

'Monks, this is the direct path for the purification of beings, for the overcoming of sorrow and lamentation, for the disappearance of suffering and grief, for the attainment of the right path, for the realisation of *nibbāna,* namely, the four foundations of mindfulness. What are the four? Here, monks, a monk abides contemplating the body as a body, ardent, clearly comprehending, mindful, having abandoned desires and discontent in regard to the world. He abides contemplating feelings as feelings, ardent, clearly comprehending, mindful, having abandoned desires and discontent in regard to the world. He abides contemplating mind as mind, ardent, clearly comprehending, mindful, having abandoned desires and discontent in regard to the world. He abides contemplating phenomena as phenomena, ardent, clearly comprehending, mindful, having abandoned desires and discontent in regard to the world.

Contemplation of the body

Mindfulness of breathing

'And how, monks, does a monk abide contemplating the body as a body? Here, monks, a monk, gone into the forest, or to the root of a tree, or to an empty hut, sits down having folded his legs crosswise, set his body erect, and established mindfulness in front, mindful he breaths in, mindful he breathes out. Breathing in long, he knows: "I breathe in long"; or breathing out long, he knows: "I breathe out long." Breathing in short, he knows: "I breathe in short"; or breathing out short, he knows: "I breathe out short." He trains thus: "I shall breathe in experiencing the whole body"; he trains thus: "I shall breathe out experiencing the whole body." He trains thus: "I shall breathe in calming the body formation"; he trains thus: "I shall breathe out calming the body formation."

'Just as a skilled turner or his apprentice, when making a long turn, understands: "I make a long turn"; or, when making a short turn, understands: "I make a short turn"; so too, monks, breathing in long, a monk knows: "I breathe in long" ... [the above paragraph repeated] he trains thus: "I shall breathe out calming the body formation."

'Thus he abides contemplating the body as a body internally, or he abides contemplating the body as a body externally, or he abides contemplating the body as a body both internally and externally. He abides contemplating the arising of phenomena in the body, or he abides contemplating the passing away of phenomena in the body, or he abides contemplating both the arising and passing away of phenomena in the body. Or, mindfulness that "there is a body" is established in him just to the extent necessary for knowledge and mindfulness. And he abides without attachment, not clinging to anything in the world. Monks, thus a monk abides contemplating the body as a body.

Ways of movement

'Again, monks, when walking, a monk knows: "I am walking"; when standing, he knows: "I am standing"; when sitting, he knows: "I am sitting"; when lying down, he knows: "I am lying down"; or he knows accordingly in whatever way his body is positioned.

Iti ajjhattaṃ vā kāye kāyānupassī viharati, bahiddhā vā kāye kāyānupassī viharati, ajjhattabahiddhā vā kāye kāyānupassī viharati. Samudayadhammānupassī vā kāyasmiṃ viharati, vayadhammānupassī vā kāyasmiṃ viharati, samudayavayadhammānupassī vā kāyasmiṃ viharati. Atthi kāyo ti vā panassa sati paccupaṭṭhitā hoti yāvadeva ñāṇamattāya patissatimattāya, anissito ca viharati na ca kiñci loke upādiyati. Evampi bhikkhave bhikkhu kāye kāyānupassī viharati.

[*Sampajañña*]

Puna ca paraṃ bhikkhave bhikkhu abhikkante paṭikkante sampajānakārī hoti, ālokite vilokite sampajānakārī hoti, samiñjite pasārite sampajānakārī hoti, saṅghāṭipattacīvaradhāraṇe sampajānakārī hoti, asite pīte khāyite sāyite sampajānakārī hoti, uccārapassāvakamme sampajānakārī hoti, gate ṭhite nisinne sutte jāgarite bhāsite tuṇhībhāve sampajānakārī hoti.

Iti ajjhattaṃ vā kāye kāyānupassī viharati, bahiddhā vā kāye kāyānupassī viharati, ajjhattabahiddhā vā kāye kāyānupassī viharati. Samudayadhammānupassī vā kāyasmiṃ viharati, vayadhammānupassī vā kāyasmiṃ viharati, samudayavayadhammānupassī vā kāyasmiṃ viharati. Atthi kāyo ti vā panassa sati paccupaṭṭhitā hoti yāvadeva ñāṇamattāya patissatimattāya, anissito ca viharati na ca kiñci loke upādiyati. Evampi bhikkhave bhikkhu kāye kāyānupassī viharati.

[*Paṭikkūlamanasikāra*]

Puna ca paraṃ bhikkhave bhikkhu imameva kāyaṃ uddhaṃ pādatalā adho kesamatthakā tacapariyantaṃ pūraṃ nānappakārassa asucino paccavekkhati: Atthi imasmiṃ kāye kesā lomā nakhā dantā taco maṃsaṃ nahāru aṭṭhī aṭṭhimiñjā vakkaṃ hadayaṃ yakanaṃ kilomakaṃ pihakaṃ papphāsaṃ antaṃ antaguṇaṃ udariyaṃ karīsaṃ, pittaṃ semhaṃ pubbo lohitaṃ sedo medo assu vasā kheḷo siṅghāṇikā lasikā muttanti. Seyyathā pi bhikkhave ubhato mukhā mutoḷī pūrā nānāvihitassa dhaññassa, seyyathīdaṃ: sālīnaṃ vīhīnaṃ muggānaṃ māsānaṃ tilānaṃ taṇḍulānaṃ, tamenaṃ cakkhumā puriso muñcitvā paccavekkheyya: ime sālī, ime vīhī, ime muggā, ime māsā ime tilā ime taṇḍulā ti, evameva kho bhikkhave bhikkhu imameva kāyaṃ uddhaṃ pādatalā adho kesamatthakā tacapariyantaṃ pūrannānappakārassa asucino paccavekkhati: Atthi imasmiṃ kāye kesā lomā nakhā dantā taco maṃsaṃ nahāru aṭṭhī aṭṭhimiñjā vakkaṃ hadayam yakanaṃ kilomakaṃ pihakaṃ papphāsaṃ antaṃ antaguṇaṃ udariyaṃ karīsaṃ, pittaṃ semhaṃ pubbo lohitaṃ sedo medo assu vasā kheḷo siṅghāṇikā lasikā muttanti.

Iti ajjhattaṃ vā kāye kāyānupassī viharati, bahiddhā vā kāye kāyānupassī viharati, ajjhattabahiddhā vā kāye kāyānupassī viharati. Samudayadhammānupassī vā kāyasmiṃ viharati, vayadhammānupassī vā kāyasmiṃ viharati, samudayavayadhammānupassī vā kāyasmiṃ viharati. Atthi kāyo ti vā panassa sati paccupaṭṭhitā hoti yāvadeva ñāṇamattāya patissatimattāya, anissito ca viharati na ca kiñci loke upādiyati. Evampi bhikkhave bhikkhu kāye kāyānupassī viharati.

[Recurring passage]

'Thus he abides contemplating the body as a body internally, or he abides contemplating the body as a body externally, or he abides contemplating the body as a body both internally and externally. He abides contemplating the arising of phenomena in the body, or he abides contemplating the passing away of phenomena in the body, or he abides contemplating both the arising and passing away of phenomena in the body. Or, mindfulness that "there is a body" is established in him just to the extent necessary for knowledge and mindfulness. And he abides without attachment, not clinging to anything in the world. Monks, thus a monk abides contemplating the body as a body.

Clear comprehension of bodily activities

'Again, monks, when going forward and returning, a monk acts with clear comprehension; when looking ahead and looking away, he acts with clear comprehension; when bending and stretching his limbs, he acts with clear comprehension; when wearing his robes, outer robe and bowl, he acts with clear comprehension; when eating, drinking, consuming food and tasting, he acts with clear comprehension; when defecating and urinating, he acts with clear comprehension; when walking, standing, sitting, falling asleep, waking up, talking and keeping silent, he acts with clear comprehension.

[Recurring passage]

'Thus he abides contemplating the body as a body internally, or he abides contemplating the body as a body externally, or he abides contemplating the body as a body both internally and externally. He abides contemplating the arising of phenomena in the body, or he abides contemplating the passing away of phenomena in the body, or he abides contemplating both the arising and passing away of phenomena in the body. Or, mindfulness that "there is a body" is established in him just to the extent necessary for knowledge and mindfulness. And he abides without attachment, not clinging to anything in the world. Monks, thus a monk abides contemplating the body as a body.

Reflection on the troublesomeness of the body

'And again, monks, a monk reflects on this very body up from the soles of the feet and down from the top of the hair, bounded by skin, as full of many kinds of impurity: "In this body there are head-hairs, body-hairs, nails, teeth, skin, flesh, sinews, bones, bone-marrow, kidneys, heart, liver, diaphragm, spleen, lungs, intestines, mesentery, stomach contents, faeces, bile, phlegm, pus, blood, sweat, fat, tears, grease, spittle, snot, oil of the joints and urine." Just as if there were a bag with an opening at both ends, full of many sorts of grain such as hill rice, red rice, beans, peas, millet, and white rice, and a man with good eyes were to open it and review it thus: 'This is hill rice, this is red rice, these are beans, these are peas, this is millet, this is white rice'; so too, a monk reflects on this very body up from the soles of the feet and down from the top of the hair, bounded by skin, as full of many kinds of impurity thus: "In this body there are head-hairs, body-hairs, nails, teeth, skin, flesh, sinews, bones, bone-marrow, kidneys, heart, liver, diaphragm, spleen, lungs, intestines, mesentery, stomach contents, faeces, bile, phlegm, pus, blood, sweat, fat, tears, grease, spittle, snot, oil of the joints and urine."

[Recurring passage]

'Thus he abides contemplating the body as a body internally, or he abides contemplating the body as a body externally, or he abides contemplating the body as a body both internally and externally. He abides contemplating the arising of phenomena in the body, or he abides contemplating the passing away of phenomena in the body, or he abides contemplating both the arising and passing away of phenomena in the body. Or, mindfulness that "there is a body" is established in him just to the extent necessary for knowledge and mindfulness. And he abides without attachment, not clinging to anything in the world. Monks, thus a monk abides contemplating the body as a body.

[*Catudhātumanasikāra*]

Puna ca paraṃ bhikkhave bhikkhu imameva kāyaṃ yathāṭhitaṃ yathāpaṇihitaṃ dhātuso paccavekkhati: Atthi imasmiṃ kāye paṭhavīdhātu āpodhātu tejodhātu vāyodhātūti. Seyyathā pi bhikkhave dakkho goghātako vā goghātakantevāsī vā gāviṃ vadhitvā cātummahāpathe bilaso paṭivibhajitvā nisinno assa, evameva kho bhikkhave bhikkhu imameva kāyaṃ yathāṭhitaṃ yathāpaṇihitaṃ dhātuso paccavekkhati: Atthi imasmiṃ kāye paṭhavīdhātu āpodhātu tejodhātu vāyodhātūti.

Iti ajjhattaṃ vā kāye kāyānupassī viharati, bahiddhā vā kāye kāyānupassī viharati, ajjhattabahiddhā vā kāye kāyānupassī viharati. Samudayadhammānupassī vā kāyasmiṃ viharati, vayadhammānupassī vā kāyasmiṃ viharati, samudayavayadhammānupassī vā kāyasmiṃ viharati. Atthi kāyo ti vā panassa sati paccupaṭṭhitā hoti yāvadeva ñāṇamattāya patissatimattāya, anissito ca viharati na ca kiñci loke upādiyati. Evampi bhikkhave bhikkhu kāye kāyānupassī viharati.

[*Navasīvathikā*]

Puna ca paraṃ bhikkhave bhikkhu seyyathāpi passeyya sarīraṃ sīvathikāya chaḍḍitaṃ ekāhamataṃ vā dvīhamataṃ vā tīhamataṃ vā uddhumātakaṃ vinīlakaṃ vipubbakajātaṃ, so imameva kāyaṃ upasaṃharati: Ayampi kho kāyo evaṃdhammo evaṃbhāvī etaṃ anatīto ti.

Iti ajjhattaṃ vā kāye kāyānupassī viharati, bahiddhā vā kāye kāyānupassī viharati, ajjhattabahiddhā vā kāye kāyānupassī viharati. Samudayadhammānupassī vā kāyasmiṃ viharati, vayadhammānupassī vā kāyasmiṃ viharati, samudayavayadhammānupassī vā kāyasmiṃ viharati. Atthi kāyo ti vā panassa sati paccupaṭṭhitā hoti yāvadeva ñāṇamattāya patissatimattāya, anissito ca viharati na ca kiñci loke upādiyati. Evampi kho bhikkhave bhikkhu kāye kāyānupassī viharati.

Puna ca paraṃ bhikkhave bhikkhu seyyathāpi passeyya sarīraṃ sīvathikāya chaḍḍitaṃ kākehi vā khajjamānaṃ kulalehi vā khajjamānaṃ gijjhehi vā khajjamānaṃ supāṇehi vā khajjamānaṃ sigālehi vā khajjamānaṃ vividhehi vā pāṇakajātehi khajjamānaṃ, so imameva kāyaṃ upasaṃharati: Ayampi kho kāyo evaṃ dhammo evaṃbhāvī etaṃ anatīto ti.

Iti ajjhattaṃ vā kāye kāyānupassī viharati ... upādiyati. Evam-pi bhikkhave bhikkhu kāye kāyānupassī viharati.

Puna ca paraṃ bhikkhave bhikkhu seyyathāpi passeyya sarīraṃ sīvathikāya chaḍḍitaṃ, aṭṭhikasaṅkhalikaṃ samaṃsalohitaṃ nahārusambandhaṃ, so imameva kāyaṃ upasaṃharati: Ayampi kho kāyo evaṃ dhammo evaṃbhāvī etaṃ anatīto ti.

Reflection on the four elements

'Again, monks, a monk reflects on this very body, however positioned and disposed, in terms of the elements thus: "In this body, there are the earth element, the water element, the fire element and the air element." Just as a skilled butcher or his apprentice, having killed a cow, were seated at a crossroads with the carcass cut up into pieces, so too a monk reflects on this very body, however positioned and disposed, in terms of the elements thus: "In this body, there are the earth element, the water element, the fire element and the air element."

[Recurring passage]

'Thus he abides contemplating the body as a body internally, or he abides contemplating the body as a body externally, or he abides contemplating the body as a body both internally and externally. He abides contemplating the arising of phenomena in the body, or he abides contemplating the passing away of phenomena in the body, or he abides contemplating both the arising and passing away of phenomena in the body. Or, mindfulness that "there is a body" is established in him just to the extent necessary for knowledge and mindfulness. And he abides without attachment, not clinging to anything in the world. Monks, thus a monk abides contemplating the body as a body.

Nine cemetery contemplations

'And again, monks, if a monk were to see a corpse discarded in a cemetery, one, two or three days dead, bloated, bluish and festering, he approaches this same body thus: "This body too is of the same nature, it will be like that, it is not exempt from that fate."

[Recurring passage]

'Thus he abides contemplating the body as a body internally, or he abides contemplating the body as a body externally, or he abides contemplating the body as a body both internally and externally. He abides contemplating the arising of phenomena in the body, or he abides contemplating the passing away of phenomena in the body, or he abides contemplating both the arising and passing away of phenomena in the body. Or, mindfulness that "there is a body" is established in him just to the extent necessary for knowledge and mindfulness. And he abides without attachment, not clinging to anything in the world. Monks, thus a monk abides contemplating the body as a body.[1]

'And again, monks, if a monk were to see a corpse discarded in a cemetery, being devoured by crows, hawks, vultures, dogs, jackals or various kinds of worms, he approaches this same body thus: "This body too is of the same nature, it will be like that, it is not exempt from that fate."

[Recurring passage]

'Thus he abides contemplating the body as a body internally ... thus a monk abides contemplating the body as a body.

'And again, monks, if a monk were to see a corpse discarded in a cemetery, a skeleton with flesh and blood, held together by sinews, he approaches this same body thus: "This body too is of the same nature, it will be like that, it is not exempt from that fate."

1. Since this section is very repetitious, most editions of the Pāli text (e.g., M I 58–59) and English translations (e.g., Ñāṇanamoli and Bodhi 1995, 148–49) are heavily abbreviated, perhaps to the detriment of clarity. The Pāli text and its translation here retain these significant repetitions to a large extent.

Iti ajjhattaṃ vā kāye kāyānupassī viharati ... upādiyati. Evam-pi bhikkhave bhikkhu kāye kāyānupassī viharati.

Puna ca paraṃ bhikkhave bhikkhu seyyathāpi passeyya sarīraṃ sīvathikāya chaḍḍitaṃ, aṭṭhikasaṅkhalikaṃ nimmaṃsalohitamakkhitaṃ nahārusambandhaṃ, so imameva kāyaṃ upasaṃharati: Ayampi kho kāyo evaṃ dhammo evaṃbhāvī etaṃ anatīto ti.

Iti ajjhattaṃ vā kāye kāyānupassī viharati ... upādiyati. Evam-pi bhikkhave bhikkhu kāye kāyānupassī viharati.

Puna ca paraṃ bhikkhave bhikkhu seyyathāpi passeyya sarīraṃ sīvathikāya chaḍḍitaṃ, aṭṭhikasaṅkhalikaṃ apagatamaṃsalohitaṃ nahārusambandhaṃ, so imameva kāyaṃ upasaṃharati: Ayampi kho kāyo evaṃ dhammo evaṃbhāvī etaṃ anatīto ti.

Iti ajjhattaṃ vā kāye kāyānupassī viharati ... upādiyati. Evam-pi bhikkhave bhikkhu kāye kāyānupassī viharati.

Puna ca paraṃ bhikkhave bhikkhu seyyathāpi passeyya sarīraṃ sīvathikāya chaḍḍitaṃ, aṭṭhikāni apagatasambandhāni disāvidisā vikkhittāni, aññena hatthaṭṭhikaṃ aññena pādaṭṭhikaṃ aññena jaṅghaṭṭhikaṃ aññena ūraṭṭhikaṃ aññena kaṭaṭṭhikaṃ aññena piṭṭhikaṇṭakaṃ aññena sīsakaṭāhaṃ, so imameva kāyaṃ upasaṃharati:Ayampi kho kāyo evaṃ dhammo evaṃbhāvī etaṃ anatīto ti.

Iti ajjhattaṃ vā kāye kāyānupassī viharati ... upādiyati. Evam-pi bhikkhave bhikkhu kāye kāyānupassī viharati.

Puna ca paraṃ bhikkhave bhikkhu seyyathāpi passeyya sarīraṃ sīvathikāya chaḍḍitaṃ, aṭṭhikāni setāni saṅkhavaṇṇūpanibhāni, so imameva kāyaṃ upasaṃharati: Ayampi kho kāyo evaṃ dhammo evaṃbhāvī etaṃ anatīto ti.

Iti ajjhattaṃ vā kāye kāyānupassī viharati ... upādiyati. Evam-pi bhikkhave bhikkhu kāye kāyānupassī viharati.

Puna ca paraṃ bhikkhave bhikkhu seyyathāpi passeyya sarīraṃ sīvathikāya chaḍḍitaṃ, aṭṭhikāni puñjakitāni terovassikāni, so imameva kāyaṃ upasaṃharati: Ayampi kho kāyo evaṃ dhammo evaṃbhāvī etaṃ anatīto ti.

Iti ajjhattaṃ vā kāye kāyānupassī viharati ... upādiyati. Evam-pi bhikkhave bhikkhu kāye kāyānupassī viharati.

Puna ca paraṃ bhikkhave bhikkhu seyyathāpi passeyya sarīraṃ sīvathikāya chaḍḍitaṃ, aṭṭhikāni pūtīni cuṇṇakajātāni, so imameva kāyaṃ upasaṃharati: Ayampi kho kāyo evaṃdhammo evaṃbhāvī etaṃ anatīto ti.

[Recurring passage]

'Thus he abides contemplating the body as a body internally ... thus a monk abides contemplating the body as a body.

'And again, monks, if a monk were to see a corpse discarded in a cemetery, a fleshless skeleton smeared with blood, held together by sinews, he approaches this same body thus: "This body too is of the same nature, it will be like that, it is not exempt from that fate."

[Recurring passage]

'Thus he abides contemplating the body as a body internally ... thus a monk abides contemplating the body as a body.

'And again, monks, if a monk were to see a corpse discarded in a cemetery, a skeleton without flesh and blood, held together by sinews, he approaches this same body thus: "This body too is of the same nature, it will be like that, it is not exempt from that fate."

[Recurring passage]

'Thus he abides contemplating the body as a body internally ... thus a monk abides contemplating the body as a body.

'And again, monks, if a monk were to see a corpse discarded in a cemetery, disconnected bones scattered in all directions—here a bone of the hand, there a bone of the foot, here a shin bone, there a thigh bone, here a hip bone, there a rib bone, here a skull, he approaches this same body thus: "This body too is of the same nature, it will be like that, it is not exempt from that fate."

[Recurring passage]

'Thus he abides contemplating the body as a body internally ... thus a monk abides contemplating the body as a body.

'And again, monks, if a monk were to see a corpse discarded in a cemetery, bones bleached white, the colour of shells, he approaches this same body thus: "This body too is of the same nature, it will be like that, it is not exempt from that fate."

[Recurring passage]

'Thus he abides contemplating the body as a body internally ... thus a monk abides contemplating the body as a body.

'And again, monks, if a monk were to see a corpse discarded in a cemetery, bones heaped up, more than a year old, he approaches this same body thus: "This body too is of the same nature, it will be like that, it is not exempt from that fate."

[Recurring passage]

'Thus he abides contemplating the body as a body internally ... thus a monk abides contemplating the body as a body.

'And again, monks, if a monk were to see a corpse discarded in a cemetery, bones rotted and crumbled to dust, he approaches this same body thus: "This body too is of the same nature, it will be like that, it is not exempt from that fate."

Iti ajjhattaṃ vā kāye kāyānupassī viharati, bahiddhā vā kāye kāyānupassī viharati, ajjhattabahiddhā vā kāye kāyānupassī viharat. Samudayadhammānupassī vā kāyasmiṃ viharati, vayadhammānupassī vā kāyasmiṃ viharati, samudayavayadhammānupassī vā kāyasmiṃ viharati. Atthi kāyo ti vā panassa sati paccupaṭṭhitā hoti yāvadeva ñāṇamattāya patissatimattāya, anissito ca viharati na ca kiñci loke upādiyati. Evampi kho bhikkhave bhikkhu kāye kāyānupassī viharati.

Vedanānupassanā

Kathañca bhikkhave bhikkhu vedanāsu vedanānupassī viharati? Idha bhikkhave bhikkhu ***sukhaṃ vedanaṃ*** *vediyamāno: sukhaṃ vedanaṃ vediyāmīti pajānāti,* ***dukkhaṃ vedanaṃ*** *vediyamāno: dukkhaṃ vedanaṃ vediyāmīti pajānāti,* ***adukkhamasukhaṃ vedanaṃ*** *vediyamāno: adukkhamasukhaṃ vedanaṃ vediyāmīti pajānāti,* ***sāmisaṃ*** *vā sukhaṃ vedanaṃ vediyamāno: sāmisaṃ sukhaṃ vedanaṃ vediyāmīti pajānāti, nirāmisaṃ vā sukhaṃ vedanaṃ vediyamāno: nirāmisaṃ vedanaṃ vediyāmīti pajānāti, sāmisaṃ vā dukkhaṃ vedanaṃ vediyamāno: sāmisaṃ vedanaṃ vediyāmīti pajānāti, nirāmisaṃ vā dukkhaṃ vedanaṃ vediyamāno: nirāmisaṃ vedanaṃ vediyāmīti pajānāti, sāmisaṃ vā adukkhamasukhaṃ vedanaṃ vediyamāno: sāmisaṃ adukkhamasukhaṃ vedanaṃ vediyāmīti, nirāmisaṃ vā adukkhamasukhaṃ vedanaṃ vediyamāno: nirāmisaṃ adukkhamasukhaṃ vedanaṃ vediyāmīti pajānāti.*

Iti ajjhattaṃ vā vedanāsu vedanānupassī viharati, bahiddhā vā vedanāsu vedanānupassī viharati, ajjhattabahiddhā vā vedanāsu vedanānupassī viharati. Samudayadhammānupassī vā vedanāsu viharati, vayadhammānupassī vā vedanāsu viharati, samudayavayadhammānupassī vā vedanāsu viharati. Atthi vedanā ti vā panassa sati paccupaṭṭhitā hoti yāvadeva ñāṇamattāya patissatimattāya, anissito ca viharati na ca kiñci loke upādiyati. Evampi kho bhikkhave bhikkhu vedanāsu vedanānupassī viharati.

Cittānupassanā

Kathañca bhikkhave bhikkhu citte cittānupassī viharati? Idha bhikkhave bhikkhu sarāgaṃ vā cittaṃ sarāgaṃ cittanti pajānāti, vītarāgaṃ vā cittaṃ vītarāgaṃ cittanti pajānāti, sadosaṃ vā cittaṃ sadosaṃ cittanti pajānāti, vītadosaṃ vā cittaṃ vītadosaṃ cittanti pajānāti, samohaṃ vā cittaṃ, samohaṃ cittanti pajānāti, vītamohaṃ vā cittaṃ vītamohaṃ cittanti pajānāti, saṅkhittaṃ vā cittaṃ saṅkhittaṃ cittanti pajānāti, vikkhittaṃ vā cittaṃ vikkhittaṃ cittanti pajānāti, mahaggataṃ vā cittaṃ mahaggataṃ cittanti pajānāti, amahaggataṃ vā cittaṃ amahaggataṃ cittanti pajānāti, sa-uttaraṃ vā cittaṃ sa-uttaraṃ cittanti pajānāti, anuttaraṃ vā cittaṃ anuttaraṃ cittanti pajānāti, samāhitaṃ vā cittaṃ samāhitaṃ cittanti pajānāti, asamāhitaṃ vā cittaṃ asamāhitaṃ cittanti pajānāti, vimuttaṃ vā cittaṃ vimuttaṃ cittanti pajānāti, avimuttaṃ vā cittaṃ avimuttaṃ cittanti pajānāti.[1]

Iti ajjhattaṃ vā citte cittānupassī viharati, bahiddhā vā citte cittānupassī viharati, ajjhattabahiddhā vā citte cittānupassī viharati. Samudayadhammānupassī vā cittasmiṃ viharati, vayadhammānupassī vā cittasmiṃ viharati, samudayavayadhammānupassī vā cittasmiṃ viharati. Atthi cittanti vā panassa sati paccupaṭṭhitā hoti yāvadeva ñāṇamattāya patissatimattāya, anissito ca viharati na ca kiñci loke upādiyati. Evam kho bhikkhave bhikkhu citte cittānupassī viharati.

1. Since this section is quite repetitious, the Pāli Text Society edition (M I 59–60) is heavily abbreviated, perhaps at the expense of clarity. Therefore, the Pāli text cited here retains the repetitions.

[Recurring passage]

'Thus he abides contemplating the body as a body internally, or he abides contemplating the body as a body externally, or he abides contemplating the body as a body both internally and externally. He abides contemplating the arising of phenomena in the body, or he abides contemplating the passing away of phenomena in the body, or he abides contemplating both the arising and passing away of phenomena in the body. Or, mindfulness that "there is a body" is established in him just to the extent necessary for knowledge and mindfulness. And he abides without attachment, not clinging to anything in the world. Monks, thus a monk abides contemplating the body as a body.

Contemplation of feeling

'And how, monks, does a monk abide contemplating feelings as feelings? Here, when feeling a pleasant feeling, a monk knows: "I feel a pleasant feeling"; when feeling an unpleasant feeling, he knows: "I feel an unpleasant feeling"; when feeling a neither-unpleasant-nor-pleasant feeling, he knows: "I feel a neither-unpleasant-nor-pleasant feeling." When feeling a worldly pleasant feeling, he knows: "I feel a worldly pleasant feeling"; when feeling an unworldly pleasant feeling, he knows: "I feel an unworldly pleasant feeling"; when feeling a worldly unpleasant feeling, he knows: "I feel a worldly unpleasant feeling"; when feeling an unworldly unpleasant feeling, he knows: "I feel an unworldly unpleasant feeling"; when feeling a worldly neither-unpleasant-nor-pleasant feeling, he knows: "I feel a worldly neither-unpleasant-nor-pleasant feeling"; when feeling an unworldly neither-unpleasant-nor-pleasant feeling, he knows: "I feel an unworldly neither-unpleasant-nor-pleasant feeling."

[Recurring passage]

'Thus he abides contemplating feelings as feelings internally, or he abides contemplating feelings as feelings externally, or he abides contemplating feelings as feelings both internally and externally. He abides contemplating the arising of phenomena in feelings, or he abides contemplating the passing away of phenomena in feelings, or he abides contemplating both the arising and passing away of phenomena in feelings. Or, mindfulness that "there is feeling" is established in him just to the extent necessary for knowledge and mindfulness. And he abides without attachment, not clinging to anything in the world. Monks, thus a monk abides contemplating feelings as feelings.

Contemplation of the mind

'And how, monks, does a monk abide contemplating the mind as the mind? Here, a monk knows a mind with desire as a desirous mind, a mind without desire as a mind without desire. He knows a mind with aversion as a mind with aversion, a mind without aversion as a mind without aversion. He knows a mind with delusion as a deluded mind, a mind without delusion as a mind without delusion. He knows a contracted mind as contracted, a distracted mind as distracted. He knows an exalted mind as exalted, an unexalted mind as unexalted. He knows a surpassable mind as surpassable, an unsurpassable mind as unsurpassable. He knows a concentrated mind as concentrated, an unconcentrated mind as unconcentrated. He knows a liberated mind as liberated, an unliberated mind as unliberated.

[Recurring passage]

'Thus he abides contemplating the mind as the mind internally, or he abides contemplating the mind as the mind externally, or he abides contemplating the mind as the mind both internally and externally. He abides contemplating the arising of phenomena in the mind, or he abides contemplating the passing away of phenomena in the mind, or he abides contemplating both the arising and passing away of phenomena in the mind. Or, mindfulness that "there is the mind" is established in him just to the extent necessary for knowledge and mindfulness. And he abides without attachment, not clinging to anything in the world. Monks, thus a monk abides contemplating the mind as the mind.

Dhammānupassanā

[*Pañca nīvaraṇāni*]

Kathañca bhikkhave bhikkhu dhammesu dhammānupassī viharati? Idha bhikkhave bhikkhu dhammesu dhammānupassī viharati pañcasu nīvaraṇesu. Kathañca bhikkhave bhikkhu dhammesu dhammānupassī viharati pañcasu nīvaraṇesu? Idha bhikkhave bhikkhu santaṃ vā ajjhattaṃ kāmacchandaṃ: atthi me ajjhattaṃ kāmacchando ti pajānāti, asantaṃ vā ajjhattaṃ kāmacchandaṃ: natthi me ajjhattaṃ kāmacchando ti pajānāti, yathā ca anuppannassa kāmacchandassa uppādo hoti tañca pajānāti, yathā ca uppannassa kāmacchandassa pahānaṃ hoti tañca pajānāti, yathā ca pahīnassa kāmacchandassa āyatiṃ anuppādo hoti tañca pajānāti. Santaṃ vā ajjhattaṃ vyāpādaṃ: atthi me ajjhattaṃ byāpādo ti ... pajānāti. Santaṃ vā ajjhattaṃ thīnamiddhaṃ: atthi me ajjhattaṃ thīnamiddhanti ... pajānāti. Santaṃ vā ajjhattaṃ uddhaccakukkuccaṃ: atthi me ajjhattaṃ uddhaccakukkuccanti ... pajānāti. Santaṃ vā ajjhattaṃ vicikicchaṃ: atthi me ajjhattaṃ vicikicchā ti pajānāti, asantaṃ vā ajjhattaṃ vicikicchaṃ: natthi me ajjhattaṃ vicikicchā ti pajānāti, yathā ca anuppannāya vicikicchāya uppādo hoti tañca pajānāti, yathā ca uppannāya vicikicchāya pahānaṃ hoti tañca pajānāti, yathā ca pahīnāya vicikicchāya āyatiṃ anuppādo hoti tañca pajānāti.

Iti ajjhattaṃ vā dhammesu dhammānupassī viharati, bahiddhā vā dhammesu dhammānupassī viharati, ajjhattabahiddhā vā dhammesu dhammānupassī viharati. Samudayadhammānupassī vā dhammesu viharati, vayadhammānupassī vā dhammesu viharati, samudayavayadhammānupassī vā dhammesu viharati. Atthi dhammā ti vā panassa sati paccupaṭṭhitā hoti yāvadeva ñāṇamattāya patissatimattāya, anissito ca viharati na ca kiñci loke upādiyati. Evam kho bhikkhave bhikkhu dhammesu dhammānupassī viharati pañcasu nīvaraṇesu.

[*Pañcas'upādānakkhandhā*]

Puna ca paraṃ bhikkhave bhikkhu dhammesu dhammānupassī viharati pañcas'upādānakkhandhesu. Kathañca bhikkhave bhikkhu dhammesu dhammānupassī viharati pañcas'upādānakkhandesu? Idha bhikkhave bhikkhu: iti rūpaṃ, iti rūpassa samudayo, iti rūpassa atthagamo; iti vedanā, iti vedanāya samudayo, iti vedanāya atthagamo; iti saññā, iti saññāya samudayo, iti saññāya atthagamo; iti saṅkhārā, iti saṅkhārānaṃ samudayo, iti saṅkhārānaṃ atthagamo; iti viññāṇaṃ, iti viññāṇassa samudayo, iti viññāṇassa atthagamo ti.

Iti ajjhattaṃ vā dhammesu dhammānupassī viharati, bahiddhā vā dhammesu dhammānupassī viharati, ajjhattabahiddhā vā dhammesu dhammānupassī viharati. Samudayadhammānupassī vā dhammesu viharati, vayadhammānupassī vā dhammesu viharati, samudayavayadhammānupassī vā dhammesu viharati. Atthi dhammā ti vā panassa sati paccupaṭṭhitā hoti yāvadeva ñāṇamattāya patissatimattāya, anissito ca viharati na ca kiñci loke upādiyati. Evam kho bhikkhave bhikkhu dhammesu dhammānupassī viharati pañcasu upādānakkhandhesu.

Contemplation of phenomena

Five hindrances

'And how, monks, does a monk abide contemplating phenomena as phenomena? Here, a monk abides contemplating phenomena as phenomena in regard to the five hindrances. And how does a monk abide contemplating phenomena as phenomena in regard to the five hindrances? Here, when sense desire is present in him, a monk knows: "There is sense desire present in me"; or when no sense desire is present in him, he knows: "There is no sense desire present in me"; and he also knows how the arising of unarisen sense desire comes to be, and how the abandoning of arisen sense desire comes to be, and how the future non-arising of abandoned sense desire comes to be. When ill will is present in him ... When sloth and torpor is present in him ... When restlessness and worry is present in him ... When doubt is present in him, a monk knows: "There is doubt present in me"; or there being no doubt present in him, he knows: "There is no doubt present in me"; and he knows how the arising of unarisen doubt comes to be, and how the abandoning of arisen doubt comes to be, and how the future non-arising of abandoned doubt comes to be.

[Recurring passage]

'Thus he abides contemplating phenomena as phenomena internally, or he abides contemplating phenomena as phenomena externally, or he abides contemplating phenomena as phenomena both internally and externally. He abides contemplating the arising of phenomena in phenomena, or he abides contemplating the passing away of phenomena in phenomena, or he abides contemplating both the arising and passing away of phenomena in phenomena. Or, mindfulness that "there are phenomena" is established in him just to the extent necessary for knowledge and mindfulness. And he abides without attachment, not clinging to anything in the world. Monks, thus a monk abides contemplating phenomena as phenomena in regard to the five hindrances.

Five aggregates of clinging

'And again, monks, a monk abides contemplating phenomena as phenomena in regard to the five aggregates of clinging. And how does a monk abide contemplating phenomena as phenomena in regard to the five aggregates of clinging? Here, monks, a monk (knows): "Such is materiality, such is its arising, such is its passing away; such is feeling, such is its arising, such is its passing away; such is perception, such is its arising, such is its passing away; such are mental formations, such are their arising, such are their passing away; such is consciousness, such is its arising, such is its passing away."

[Recurring passage]

'Thus he abides contemplating phenomena as phenomena internally, or he abides contemplating phenomena as phenomena externally, or he abides contemplating phenomena as phenomena both internally and externally. He abides contemplating the arising of phenomena in phenomena, or he abides contemplating the passing away of phenomena in phenomena, or he abides contemplating both the arising and passing away of phenomena in phenomena. Or, mindfulness that "there are phenomena" is established in him just to the extent necessary for knowledge and mindfulness. And he abides without attachment, not clinging to anything in the world. Monks, thus a monk abides contemplating phenomena as phenomena in regard to the five aggregates of clinging.

[*Cha āyatanāni*]

Puna ca paraṃ bhikkhave bhikkhu dhammesu dhammānupassī viharati chasu ajjhattikabāhiresu āyatanesu. Kathañca bhikkhave bhikkhu dhammesu dhammānupassī viharati chasu ajjhattikabāhiresu āyatanesu? Idha bhikkhave bhikkhu cakkhuñca pajānāti rūpe ca pajānāti, yañca tadubhayaṃ paṭicca uppajjati saṃyojanaṃ tañca pajānāti, yathā ca anuppannassa saṃyojanassa uppādo hoti tañca pajānāti, yathā ca uppannassa saṃyojanassa pahānaṃ hoti tañca pajānāti, yathā ca pahīnassa saṃyojanassa āyatiṃ anuppādo hoti tañca pajānāti; sotañca pajānāti sadde ca pajānāti ... ghānañca pajānāti gandhe ca pajānāti ... jivhañca pajānāti rase ca pajānāti ... kāyañca pajānāti phoṭṭhabbe ca pajānāti ... manañca pajānāti dhamme ca pajānāti, yañca tadubhayaṃ paṭicca uppajjati saṃyojanaṃ tañca pajānāti, yathā ca anuppannassa saṃyojanassa uppādo hoti tañca pajānāti, yathā ca uppannassa saṃyojanassa pahānaṃ hoti tañca pajānāti, yathā ca pahīnassa saṃyojanassa āyatiṃ anuppādo hoti tañca pajānāti.

Iti ajjhattaṃ vā dhammesu dhammānupassī viharati, bahiddhā vā dhammesu dhammānupassī viharati, ajjhatta-bahiddhā vā dhammesu dhammānupassī viharati. Samudayadhammānupassī vā dhammesu viharati, vaya-dhammānupassī vā dhammesu viharati, samudayavayadhammānupassī vā dhammesu viharati. Atthi dhammā ti vā panassa sati paccupaṭṭhitā hoti yāvadeva ñāṇamattāya patissatimattāya, anissito ca viharati na ca kiñci loke upādiyati. Evam kho bhikkhave bhikkhu dhammesu dhammānupassī viharati chasu ajjhattikabāhiresu āyatanesu.

[*Satta bojjhaṅgā*]

Puna ca paraṃ bhikkhave bhikkhu dhammesu dhammānupassī viharati sattasu bojjhaṅgesu. Kathañca bhikkhave bhikkhu dhammesu dhammānupassī viharati sattasu bojjhaṅgesu? Idha bhikkhave bhikkhu santaṃ vā ajjhattaṃ satisambojjhaṅgaṃ: atthi me ajjhattaṃ satisambojjhaṅgo ti pajānāti, asantaṃ vā ajjhattaṃ satisambojjhaṅgaṃ: natthi me ajjhattaṃ satisambojjhaṅgo ti pajānāti, yathā ca anuppannassa satisambojjhaṅgassa uppādo hoti tañca pajānāti, yathā ca uppannassa satisambojjhaṅgassa bhāvanāpāripūrī hoti tañca pajānāti. Santaṃ vā ajjhattaṃ dhammavicayasambojjhaṅgaṃ ... Santaṃ vā ajjhattaṃ viriyasambojjhaṅgaṃ ... Santaṃ vā ajjhattaṃ pītisam-bojjhaṅgaṃ .... Santaṃ vā ajjhattaṃ passaddhisambojjhaṅgaṃ ... Santaṃ vā ajjhattaṃ samādhisambojjhaṅgaṃ ... Santaṃ vā ajjhattaṃ upekkhāsambojjhaṅgaṃ: atthi me ajjhattaṃ upekkhāsambojjhaṅgo ti pajānāti, asantaṃ vā ajjhattaṃ upekkhāsambojjhaṅgaṃ: natthi me ajjhattaṃ upekkhāsambojjhaṅgo ti pajānāti, yathā ca anuppannassa upekkhāsambojjhaṅgassa uppādo hoti tañca pajānāti, yathā ca uppannassa upekkhāsambojjhaṅgassa bhāvanāpāripūrī hoti tañca pajānāti.

Iti ajjhattaṃ vā dhammesu dhammānupassī viharati, bahiddhā vā dhammesu dhammānupassī viharati, ajjhatta-bahiddhā vā dhammesu dhammānupassī viharati. Samudayadhammānupassī vā dhammesu viharati, vaya-dhammānupassī vā dhammesu viharati, samudayavayadhammānupassī vā dhammesu viharati. Atthi dhammā ti vā panassa sati paccupaṭṭhitā hoti yāvadeva ñāṇamattāya patissatimattāya, anissito ca viharati na ca kiñci loke upādiyati. Evam kho bhikkhave bhikkhu dhammesu dhammānupassī viharati sattasu bojjhaṅgesu.

Six sense spheres

'And again, monks, a monk abides contemplating phenomena as phenomena in regard to the six internal and external sense spheres. And how does a monk abide contemplating phenomena as phenomena in regard to the six internal and external sense spheres? Here, monks, a monk knows the eye, he knows forms, and he knows the fetter that arises dependent on both; and he also knows how there comes to be the arising of the unarisen fetter, and how there comes to be the abandoning of the arisen fetter, and how there comes to be the future non-arising of the abandoned fetter. He knows the ear, he knows sounds ... He knows the nose, he knows odours ... He knows the tongue, he knows flavours ... He knows the body, he knows tangibles ... He knows the mind, he knows mental phenomena, and he knows the fetter that arises dependent on both; and he also knows how there comes to be the arising of the unarisen fetter, and how there comes to be the abandoning of the arisen fetter, and how there comes to be the future non-arising of the abandoned fetter.

[Recurring passage]

'Thus he abides contemplating phenomena as phenomena internally, or he abides contemplating phenomena as phenomena externally, or he abides contemplating phenomena as phenomena both internally and externally. He abides contemplating the arising of phenomena in phenomena, or he abides contemplating the passing away of phenomena in phenomena, or he abides contemplating both the arising and passing away of phenomena in phenomena. Or, mindfulness that "there are phenomena" is established in him just to the extent necessary for knowledge and mindfulness. And he abides without attachment, not clinging to anything in the world. Monks, thus a monk abides contemplating phenomena as phenomena in regard to the six internal and external sense spheres. Monks, thus a monk abides contemplating phenomena as phenomena in regard to the six internal and external sense spheres.

Seven factors of awakening

'And again, monks, a monk abides contemplating phenomena as phenomena in regard to the seven factors of awakening. And how does a monk abide contemplating phenomena as phenomena in regard to the seven factors of awakening? Here, monks, when the mindfulness factor of awakening is present in him, a monk knows: "There is the mindfulness factor of awakening in me"; when the mindfulness factor of awakening is not present in him, he knows: "there is no mindfulness factor of awakening in me"; and he also knows how the unarisen mindfulness awakening factor arises, and how the arisen mindfulness awakening factor is accomplished by cultivation. ... When the investigation-of-dhammas factor of awakening is present in him ... when the energy factor of awakening is present in him ... when the joy factor of awakening is present in him ... when the tranquillity factor of awakening is present in him ... when the concentration factor of awakening is present in him ... when the equanimity factor of awakening is present in him, a monk knows: "There is the equanimity factor of awakening in me"; when the equanimity factor of awakening is not present in him, he knows: "there is no equanimity factor of awakening in me"; and he also knows how the unarisen equanimity awakening factor arises, and how the arisen equanimity awakening factor is accomplished by cultivation.

[Recurring passage]

'Thus he abides contemplating phenomena as phenomena internally, or he abides contemplating phenomena as phenomena externally, or he abides contemplating phenomena as phenomena both internally and externally. He abides contemplating the arising of phenomena in phenomena, or he abides contemplating the passing away of phenomena in phenomena, or he abides contemplating both the arising and passing away of phenomena in phenomena. Or, mindfulness that "there are phenomena" is established in him just to the extent necessary for knowledge and mindfulness. And he abides without attachment, not clinging to anything in the world. Monks, thus a monk abides contemplating phenomena as phenomena in regard to the seven factors of awakening.

[*Cattāri ariyasaccāni*]

Puna ca paraṃ bhikkhave bhikkhu dhammesu dhammānupassī viharati catusu ariyasaccesu. Kathañca bhikkhave bhikkhu dhammesu dhammānupassī viharati catusu ariyasaccesu? Idha bhikkhave bhikkhu: idaṃ dukkhanti yathābhūtaṃ pajānāti, ayaṃ dukkhasamudayo ti yathābhūtaṃ pajānāti, ayaṃ dukkhanirodho ti yathābhūtaṃ pajānāti, ayaṃ dukkhanirodhagāminī paṭipadā ti yathābhūtaṃ pajānāti.

Iti ajjhattaṃ vā dhammesu dhammānupassī viharati, bahiddhā vā dhammesu dhammānupassī viharati, ajjhatta-bahiddhā vā dhammesu dhammānupassī viharati. Samudayadhammānupassī vā dhammesu viharati, vaya-dhammānupassī vā dhammesu viharati, samudayavayadhammānupassī vā dhammesu viharati. Atthi dhammā ti vā panassa sati paccupaṭṭhitā hoti yāvadeva ñāṇamattāya patissatimattāya, anissito ca viharati na ca kiñci loke upādiyati. Evam kho bhikkhave bhikkhu dhammesu dhammānupassī viharati catūsu ariyasaccesu.

Yo hi koci bhikkhave ime cattāro satipaṭṭhāne evaṃ bhāveyya satta vassāni, tassa dvinnaṃ phalānaṃ aññataraṃ phalaṃ pāṭikaṅkhaṃ diṭṭheva dhamme aññā, sati vā upādisese anāgāmitā. Tiṭṭhantu bhikkhave satta vassāni, yo hi koci bhikkhave ime cattāro satipaṭṭhāne evaṃ bhāveyya cha vassāni ... pañca vassāni ... cattāri vassāni ... tīṇi vassāni ... dve vassāni ... ekaṃ vassaṃ ... tiṭṭhatu bhikkhave ekaṃ vassaṃ, yo hi koci bhikkhave ime cattāro satipaṭṭhāne evaṃ bhāveyya satta māsāni, tassa dvinnaṃ phalānaṃ aññataraṃ phalaṃ pāṭikaṅkhaṃ diṭṭheva dhamme aññā, sati vā upādisese anāgāmitā. Tiṭṭhantu bhikkhave satta māsāni, yo hi koci bhikkhave ime cattāro satipaṭṭhāne evaṃ bhāveyya cha māsāni ... pañca māsāni ... cattāri māsāni ... tīṇi māsāni ... dve māsāni ... ekaṃ māsaṃ ... addhamāsaṃ ... tiṭṭhatu bhikkhave addhamāso, yo hi koci bhikkhave ime cattāro satipaṭṭhāne evaṃ bhāveyya sattāhaṃ, tassa dvinnaṃ phalānaṃ aññataraṃ phalaṃ pāṭikaṅkhaṃ diṭṭheva dhamme aññā, sati vā upādisese anāgāmitā.

Ekāyano ayaṃ bhikkhave maggo sattānaṃ visuddhiyā sokapariddavānaṃ samatikkamāya dukkhadomanassānaṃ atthagamāya ñāyassa adhigamāya nibbānassa sacchikiriyāya, yadidaṃ cattāro satipaṭṭhānā ti, iti yantaṃ vuttaṃ idametaṃ paṭicca vuttanti. Idamavoca bhagavā. Attamanā te bhikkhū bhagavato bhāsitaṃ abhinandunti.

Four noble truths

'And again, monks, a monk abides contemplating phenomena as phenomena in regard to the four noble truths. And how does a monk abide contemplating phenomena as phenomena in regard to the four noble truths? Here, monks, a monk knows as it actually is: "This is suffering"; he knows as it actually is: "This is the arising of suffering"; he knows as it actually is: "This is the cessation of suffering"; he knows as it actually is: "This is the path leading to the cessation of suffering."

[Recurring passage]

'Thus he abides contemplating phenomena as phenomena internally, or he abides contemplating phenomena as phenomena externally, or he abides contemplating phenomena as phenomena both internally and externally. He abides contemplating the arising of phenomena in phenomena, or he abides contemplating the passing away of phenomena in phenomena, or he abides contemplating both the arising and passing away of phenomena in phenomena. Or, mindfulness that "there are phenomena" is established in him just to the extent necessary for knowledge and mindfulness. And he abides without attachment, not clinging to anything in the world. Monks, thus a monk abides contemplating phenomena as phenomena in regard to the four noble truths.

Conclusion

'Monks, if anyone thus developed the four foundations of mindfulness for seven years, he could expect one of two fruits: either final knowledge here and now, or if some clinging still remained, the state of non-return. Let alone seven years, monks, if anyone thus developed the four foundations of mindfulness for six years ... for five years ... for four years ... for three years ... for two years ... for one year, he could expect one of two fruits: either final knowledge here and now, or if some clinging still remained, the state of non-return. Let alone, monks, if anyone thus developed the four foundations of mindfulness for seven months ... for six months ... for five months ... for four months ... for three months ... for two months ... for one month ... for half a month, he could expect one of two fruits: either final knowledge here and now, or if some clinging still remained, the state of non-return. Let alone half a month, monks, if anyone thus developed the four foundations of mindfulness for seven days, he could expect one of two fruits: either final knowledge here and now, or if some clinging still remained, the state of non-return.'

In reference to this, it was said: 'Monks, the four foundations of mindfulness are the direct path for the purification of beings, for the overcoming of grief and sorrow, for the relinquishment of suffering and discontent, for the attainment of the true path, for the realisation of *nibbāna*.' This is what the Blessed One said. The monks were delighted and rejoiced in the words of the Blessed One.

Index

Entries in bold are the key terms or concepts given in the Glossary
n = footnote, e.g., 98n67 refers to page 98, footnote 67
f = Figure, e.g., 30*f* refers to page 30, in the Figure
t = Table, e.g., 48*t* refers to page 48, in the Table

A

abandonment (*paṭinissagga*) 98n67, 144–145, **183**
Abhidhamma 3–4, 28n48, 38n11, 45n24–25, 47n31–32, 52n44, 59n66, 60n72, 83n7, 84, 88n26, 89, 91n34, 104n11, 108n22, 111n37, 118n61, 119n65, 121n70, 122n71, 125n78, 128, 153n168, 168n231, 177–178
  categories 6–7, 45n45, 82n3, 123n5
  structure of 7, 13n1, 14, 83n7, 84, 123n5
Abhidhammapiṭaka 88n26, 112
abide (*viharati*) 11*t*, 13, 26–27, 33, 36–37, 39, 42, 44–47, 49–51, 53, 57, 63–65, 69, 73, 81, 99, 114–115, 119, 125–126, 139–140, 157, 188, 190–202
absorption (*jhāna*) 14, 18–20, 38, 40, 55n54, 56, 66n84, 74n19, 75–76, 77n30, 79–80, 86–87, 91–92, 94–88, 105, 109, 114n46, 119–120, 130, 135–137, 147, 152, 153n168, 170–171, **181**
action (*kamma*) 7, 60–61, 88n23, 115n50, 118, 120–123, 142n132, 154, 167, **181**
aggregates (*khandha*) 15–16, 25–26, 34, 46, 48*t*, 70, 100–101, 116–117, 134n103, 174
  as five aggregates (*pañca khandhā*) 6–7, 12*t*, 16n8, 32, 71, 73, 83n6, 92, 100–101, 116–119, 121, 122n71, 123n75, 125n78–79, 148, 160, 162
  See also contemplation of phenomena (*dhammānupassanā*)
Anālayo, Bhikkhu 1, 4, 31n56–57, 42n20, 84n9, 177
Ānāpānasatisutta 22, 39n14, 40, 72, 72n9, 74, 74n17, 79, 83, 96n58, 98, 144, 148n157, 152n165, 155n178, 156
arahant 19n23, 21, 23, 34, 47n31, 66, 67n88, 87n19, 90, 92, 98, 102, 107, 109–111, 120, 123, 132*t*, 134n101, 134n105, 137, 143, 147, 149, 154, 166, 174–175, **180**. *See also* path (*magga*)
ardent (*ātāpī*) 11*t*, 13, 27, 32, 40, 141, 150, 170n236, **180**, 188–189
arising (*samudaya*) 45–46, 71, 118–120, 122, 174, **185**. *See also* passing away (*vaya*)
attachment to rites and rituals (*sīlabbataparāmāsa*) 19n22, 48n34, 111n36, 129, 130n90, 132*t*, 133–135, 145. *See also* contemplation of phenomena (*dhammānupassanā*); fetters (*saṃyojana*)
attention (*manasikāra*) 6, 14–15, 17–18, 21, 28–29, 49, 82, 85*t*, 147–148, 174, **182**
  as wise attention (*yoniso manasikāra*) 6, 15n6, 21, 27–28, 30*f*, 56, 94, 105n13, 106n16, 143, **186**
  as unwise attention (*ayoniso manasikāra*) 28, 30*f*, 104n10, 106n15, 107n21, 108, 110, 111n35, 134n104, 135n109–110, **180**
aversion (*dosa*) 13–15, 17–18, 20, 22, 26, 27n42, 29–31, 36–38, 42, 49–50, 52, 54, 75, 77, 80, 85*t*, 86, 90–92, 93n42, 103, 105n14, 107–108, 111, 113–114, 118, 121, 123, 153, 155–156, 164–167, 170, 174, **181**
  non-aversion (*adosa*) 14n1, 85*t*, 163n208
  as state of mind. *See under* mind (*citta*)
  See also unwholesome states (*akusala*)
Avijjāsutta 22n33, 28, 35, 110, 137n116, 138

Aung, Shwe, and Caroline Rhys Davids 38n11, 144n139
awakening, seven factors of (*satta bojjhaṅgā*) 5, 12*t*, 22, 27n43, 28, 35, 43, 79, 132, 139–140, 141*f*, 142–143, 153n168, 155–157, **180**, 200–201
  cultivation of factors of (*sambojjhaṅga*) 149, 151–152, 154
  thirty-seven qualities of (*bodhipakkhiyā dhamma*) 149–150, 158, 163
  See also contemplation of phenomena (*dhammānupassanā*)

B

becoming (*bhava*) 7, 16n12, 19n20, 73, 77n28, 89, 104, 109, 124–125, 127, 130, 133, 135, 161n197, 166, **180**
  as cultivation (*bhāvanā*), 15n6, 54n47, 104, 148, 167, **180**. *See also* meditation (*bhāvanā*)
  as taint (*bhavāsava*), 125, 132–133
being (*satta*) 72–73, 139
  as mine (*mama*) 45n23, 47n30, 55n51, 63n80, 116–117, 129
  as myself (*me attā*) 45n23, 116–117, 129
  as self 5, 17, 44, 71, 78, 86, 114, 121, 125
  See also non-self (*anattā*)
Bhikkhuṇīvāsakasutta 73–74
body (*kāya*) 5, 16n10, 18n18, 26, 29, 32, 38, 40, 46, 58, 70, 78, 83, 127, 144n139, **181**
  body-consciousness (*kāyaviññāṇa*) 87n21, 127–128
  calming the body formation (*passambhayaṃ kāyasaṅkhāra*) 11*t*, 33, 39n14, 40–42, 74, 153, 188
  experiencing the whole body (*sabbakāyapaṭisaṃvedī*) 5–6, 11*t*, 33, 38–42, 188
  mental body (*nāmakāya*) 5, 38, 40, **182**
  tangible object and touch (*phoṭṭhabba*) 16n10, 59, 71–72, 78, 127, **183**
Bojjhaṅgasaṃyutta 2, 104n10, 106n16, 143, 152n165
Bodhi, Bhikkhu 3–4, 7n16, 13–14n1, 14n4, 15n6, 17n17, 38n11, 45n26, 60n73, 70n4, 79n37, 84n9, 84n12, 85n14, 86n15, 86–87n18, 88n26, 89n27, 91n34, 93n42, 109n28, 110n32, 111n37, 128n88, 144n139
Braun, Erik 1n1
Bucknell, Roderick S. 14n4, 109n28
Buddha 9n1, 19, 23, 27–28, 35, 45n25, 55–56, 62, 67, 74, 76, 84n13, 92n37, 97, 102, 107, 110n33, 112–115, 117, 120, 122, 134, 137, 143, 147, 150, 152n167, 153, 155–156, 166–167, 174
Burlingame, Eugene Watson 66n84

C

cause (*hetu*) 133, 136, 138, 146, 149, 163–164
cessation (*nirodha*) 15n6, 87, 98n67, 139, 142–145, 162, **182**
change (*vipariṇāma*) 46, 48*t*, 117, 160
change-of-lineage (*gotrabhū*) 95–96, 109n29, **181**
clear comprehension (*sampajañña*) 3, 6, 11t, 14–16, 18, 21–31, 34–35, 40, 43*t*, 49, 50–52, 54, 56–57, 62, 67, 70–72, 75–78, 82, 90–91, 93–94, 97, 102–103, 105, 107–110, 114, 117–118, 120, 128, 141–142, 146, 149–150, 158–159, 168–169, 174, **184**, 190–191
clinging (*upādāna*) 16n12, 72–73, 78, 89n30, 106, 114, 116, 118, 124, 127, 130n91, 134, 136, 155, 160–161, 170, **185**
  five aggregates of (*pañcas'upādānakkhandhā*) 12*t*, 43, 82n4, 115–125
compassion (*karuṇā*) 85*t*, 156, 163–165, 169, **181**
conceit (*māna*) 19n22, 20, 27n42, 45, 48*t*, 85, 86n16, 105n14, 111n36, 113, 122, 129–137, 146, 166, 168, 174, **182**. *See also* fetters (*saṃyojana*)
concentration (*samādhi*) 12*t*, 14, 16, 17n14, 19, 21, 23–4, 38, 51n43, 56, 79, 86, 105*f*, 112–114, 135, 137, 141, 146, 148–156, 164–170, **183**
  as access concentration (*upacāra samādhi*) 56, 95n51, **185**
  as calm (*samatha*) 6, 15, 18–22, 38, 40, 74, 75n21, 76–77, 79, 95*t*, 97n61, 130–131, 142, 149, 151–153, 156, **183**
  base of power (*iddhipāda*) 146, 149, 155n178, 169, **181**
  and insight (*vipassanā*). *See* insight (*vipassanā*)
  as right concentration (*sammā samādhi*) 94, 165*t*, 169–170
  as right effort (*sammā vāyāma*) 104, 165*t*, 169–170
  See also contemplation of phenomena (*dhammānupassanā*); four noble truths (*cattāri ariyasaccāni*)
conformity (*anuloma*) 95–96, **179**
consciousness (*viññāṇa*) 7, 12, 16n8, 16n12, 32, 66n86, 82n5, 83n7, 87–88, 89n29–30, 100–101, 103, 116, 118n63, 121, 123n75, 124–125, 127–129, **185**. *See also* aggregates (*khandha*)
contemplation (*anupassanā*) 18, 25–26, 46n29, 70, 100*t*, **180**
  as externally (*bahiddhā*) 5, 11*t*, 4–5, 48t, 49–50, 53, 57, 63, 65, 69, 81, 99, 115, 126, 140, 157, **180**, 188–202

as internally (*ajjhattam*) 5, 11*t*, 20n26, 42–45, 48*t*, 49–50, 53, 57, 63–65, 69, 81, 99, 115, 126, 139–140, 157, **179**, 188–202
as internally and externally (*ajjhattabahiddhā*) 5, 11*t*, 42–44, 48*t*, 49–50, 53, 57, 63, 65, 69, 81, 99, 115, 126, 140, 157, **179**, 188–202
contemplation of feeling (*vedanānupassanā*) 6, 11*t*, 26, 36, 42–43, 52, 62, 69–80, 82, 100, 142, **185**, 196–197
contemplation of phenomena (*dhammānupassanā*) 12*t*, 25–6, 42, 43*t*, 62, 72n9, 79, 83, 98, 99–171, **181**, 198–9
contemplation of the body (*kāyānupassanā*) 11*t*, 13, 16n9, 21, 26, 30, 33–67, 70, 72n9, 73–74, 100–101, 118, 142, **181**, 188–189
approaches (*upasaṃharati*) 11*t*, 63–66, **185**
gone to the forest (*araññagato*) 11*t*, 33, 35–37, 41*t*, 188
nine cemetery contemplations (*navasīvathikā*) 5, 11*t*, 43, 63
troublesomeness of (*paṭikkūlamanasikāra*) 11*t*, 34, 43, 53–54, **183**, 190–191
ways of movement (*iriyāpatha*) 11*t*, 43, 48–49, 51, **181**, 188–189
contemplation of the mind (*cittānupassanā*) 5, 12*t*, 26, 36, 42–43, 62, 72n9, 75, 81–98, 100, 102, 108, 129, 142, **180**, 196–197
contact (*phassa*) 7, 16n12, 71–72, 82n5, 85*t*, 87, 89n30, 93, 108, 120, 124, 127–128, 133n99, 148, **183**
craving (*taṇhā*) 7, 16n12, 31n56, 45, 61, 71–72, 78, 89n30, 116, 118, 122, 124, 127, 129, 130n91, 131–134, 136–137, 144, 158, 160–161, 163, 168–169, **184**

D

defilements (*kilesa*) 27, 37, 80, 92, 98, 105, 111, 113, 116, 119, 131, 140–141n129, 144–145, 149, 155, 163, 167, 169, 174, **182**
delusion (*moha*) 18, 22, 37–38, 42, 50, 75, 138, 153, **182**
as defilement (*kilesa*) 27n42, 80, 105n14, 113, 174
as state of mind. *See under* mind (*citta*)
as unwholesome state (*akusala*) 75, 85–86, 91, 92n37, 93, 108–111, 123, 166–167
dependent origination (*paṭiccasamuppāda*) 6–7, 15n6, 16, 26, 40n16, 47n31, 71n8, 73n11, 89, 92, 108n26, 115, 118n63, 120n66, 121n69, 123–124, 127, 130n91, 133n99–100, 137–138, 161n97, 162–163, **183**
desire (*rāga*) 5, 31n56, 86n16, 91, **183**
for material (*rūparāga*) and immaterial existence (*arūparāga*) 19n22, 48n34, 111n36, 129, 131–133, 135–136
as state of mind. *See under* mind (*citta*)
without desire (*vītarāga*) 91–92, 93n41, **185**
See also sense desire (*kāmacchanda*)
detachment (*viveka*) 139, 142–145, 162, **185**
Dhamma 1, 17, 20, 28, 45, 92, 102, 110, 112–113, 133, 134n106, 147–148, 152–153, 155–156, 164, 166–167
as timeless (*akālika*) 113, 166–167, **179**
dhamma. *See* phenomena (*dhamma*)
diligence (*appamāda*) 27, **180**
discontent (*domanassa*) 5, 31, 49, 51, 67, 70–72, 76n24, 78, 110, 169, **181**
dispassion (*virāga*) 98n67, 139, 142–145, **185**
Ditrich, Tamara 1n1, 44n21–22, 45n24
doubt (*vicikicchā*) **185**, 198
as fetter 19n22, 48n34, 111n36, 129–135, 145
as hindrance 12*t*, 21n28, 47n33, 84n13, 85*t*, 86, 99, 102, 105*f*, 111–115
See also contemplation of phenomena (*dhammānupassanā*); hindrances (*nīvaraṇa*)

E

ear (*sota*) 16n10, 127, **184**
ear-consciousness (*sotaviññāṇa*) 87n21, 127–128
sound (*sadda*) 16n10, 127, **183**
effect. *See* fruition or effect (*phala*)
elements (*dhātu*) 16, 25–26, 34, 39n12, 46, 48*t*, 58n60, 70, 118, 148, 174, **181**
air (*vāyodhātu*) **185**
earth (*paṭhavīdhātu*) **183**, 192
fire (*tejodhātu*) **184**, 192
six elements (*āpodhātu*) 11*t*, 16n9, 39, 58–61, 118n61
space (*ākāsadhātu*) 16n9, 58n60, 59–60, **179**
water (*āpodhātu*) 11*t*, 16n9, 39n12, 57–61, 118n59, **180**, 192
energy (*viriya*) 16–17, 23n37, 27, 79n34, 85*t*, 86, 105*f*, 107–108, 141, 146, 148–151, 155, 169, **185**
energy factor of awakening (*viriyasambojjhaṅga*) 12*t*, 27n43, 141*f*, 150–152
See also faculties (*indriya*)
equanimity (*upekkhā*) 6, 19, 24, 71n6, 76–79, 109, 141, 149, 156–157, **185**
knowledge of equanimity of formations (*saṅkhār'upekkhāñāṇa*) 20, 24–25, 96, 157, 171, **184**

eye (*cakkhu*) 16n10, 101, 127–128, 130, **180**
  eye-consciousness (*cakkhuviññāṇa*) 87n21, 101, 127–128
  See also six sense spheres (*saḷāyatana*)

F

faculties (*indriya*) 17n14, 27, 88n25, 105, 147n150, 148–151, 155–156, 165, 169, **181**
  as five powers (*bala*) 23n37, 27n43, 105, 150, 155, **180**
faith. *See* trust (*saddhā*)
feeling (*vedanā*) 6–7, 11*t*, 12*t*, 16n8, 16n12, 18n18, 20, 26, 29, 31n57, 32, 36, 38n11, 44, 47, 50, 52, 69–70, 71–73, 75–79, 82–83, 85*t*, 86–90, 93, 100–102, 108–109, 114n49, 115–121, 123–124, 127, 134n102, 144n139, 148, **185**, 198
  neither-unpleasant-nor-pleasant feeling (*adukkhamasukhavedanā*) 6, 11*t*, 70–71, 72n10, 76–79, **179**
  pleasant feeling (*sukhavedanā*) 11*t*, 26, 69, 70–76, **184**
  unpleasant feeling (*dukkhavedanā*) 11*t*, 70–77, 79, **181**
  See also aggregates (*khandha*); contemplation of phenomena (*dhammānupassanā*)
fetters (*saṃyojana*) 7n15, 12*t*, 19, 48, 77n28, 87, 111, 116, 127, 129–133, 134–139, 143, 145, 152, 155, **184**
  See also contemplation of phenomena (*dhammānupassanā*)
focus. *See* one-pointedness (*ekaggatā*)
four elements (*mahābhūta*) 58–61
  contemplation of the four elements (*cattāri mahābhūtāni*) 40n16, 118n60
  reflections on (*catudhātumanasikāra*) 11*t*, 39n12, 43, 57, 118n59, 192
four noble truths (*cattāri ariyasaccāni*) 12*t*, 16n13, 43, 47n31, 67n88, 114, 137, 147, 153, 155, 157–160, 168, 171, 203
friendliness. *See* loving kindness (*mettā*)
fruition or effect (*phala*) 70, 80n38, 109, 112n41, 113, 124, 133, 136, 138, 146, 149, 162–163, 173, **183**, 202–203
  as causality (*kammaphala*) 115
  as cause and effect (*hetuphala*) 78
  as fruition mind. *See under* mind (*citta*)
  and knowledge. *See under* knowledge (*ñāṇa*)

G

generosity (*dāna*) 17–18, 21, 167, **181**
  as *caga* 153
Gethin, Rupert 7n16, 23n38, 88n26, 89n28, 148n157, 149n159, 150n163, 158n186
Goenka 38n9
greed (*lobha*) 13–15, 17–18, 20, 22, 26, 27n42, 29–30, 31n56, 36–38, 42, 49–50, 52, 75, 77, 80, 153, 155–156, 164–167, 170, **182**
  as defilement 105n14, 113–114, 174
  as unwholesome 85*t*, 86, 90–93, 103, 107–108, 111, 121–123
Gyatso, Janet 124n77

H

happiness (*sukha*) 19, 56, 71n6, 74–75, 78–79, 105*f*, 152–153, 170, **184**. *See also* absorption (*jhāna*)
Harvey, Peter 7n16, 113n45, 158n184
hindrances (*nīvaraṇa*) 21, 24, 38, 76, 79, 82, 90, 95, 98, 103, 105, 108–111, 130, 137–138, 141n129, 148, 152, 155–156, 165, 169, **182**
  five hindrances (*pañca nīvaraṇāni*) 12*t*, 21–22, 28, 43*t*, 83, 99, 102, 198

I

ignorance (*avijjā*) 7, 16n12, 19n20, 26, 46, 48n34, 61, 77n28, 86n16, 89n30, 90–91, 103, 108–111, 118, 120n66, 121n69, 123–125, 129, 132*t*, 133, 135–138, 156, 160, 162, 165, **180**
  as taint (*avijjāsava*) 108n26, 125, 132–133
  See also fetters (*saṃyojana*); hindrances (*nīvaraṇa*)
ill will (*vyāpāda*) **186**
  as fetter 19n22, 48n34, 111n36, 129, 132*t*, 133–134, 136–139, **186**
  as hindrance 12*t*, 21n28, 31, 47n33, 76, 82, 84n13, 101–2, 104–5, 106, 137, 156, **186**
  See also contemplation of phenomena (*dhammānupassanā*); hindrances (*nīvaraṇa*)
impermanence (*anicca*) 16n11, 16n13, 20, 23, 25, 30, 46–49, 61, 70n3, 75–76, 96, 98n67, 101, 105n13, 117–120, 122, 137–138, 142, 144, 146–147, 160, 168, 170, **179**, 184
insight (*vipassanā*), 1, 6, 14–16, 18–23, 28, 30*f*, 39–41, 44, 56, 75, 78–79, 82, 94–95, 97–98, 109, 120–121, 130–131, 142, 149, 151–153, 157, 159, **185**
investigative discernment (*vīmaṃsā*) 6, 146, 149, 169, **185**
Ireland, J. D. 174n1

J

joy (*pīti*) 56, 74–75, 79, 85*t*, 105*f*, 141, 149, 152–153, 167, **183**
  factor of awakening (*pītisambojjhaṅga*) 12*t*, 152, 153*t*, 153n171
  See also absorption (*jhāna*)

K

Karunadasa, Y. 7n16, 14n1, 58n61, 58n63, 59n65, 59n67, 60n72, 70n4, 84n12, 86n15, 88n26, 89n28, 91n35, 93n42, 108n22, 111n37, 118n59, 128n88

Khandhasaṃyutta 46, 89n29, 117, 121n69

knowledge (*ñāṇa*) 3, 20, 23–24, 25n40, 35, 47, 72, 139, 145, 147, 157, 159, **182**

- path and fruition knowledge (*maggaphalañāṇa*) 70, 98, 139, 145, 159, **182**
- knows or knows well (*pajānāti*) 11*t*, 27, 33 36–37, 39, 40–41, 48–52, 69, 71–72, 81, 91–92, 95, 99, 101, 117, 125–126, 139–140, 157–158, **182**, 188–202
- purification by knowledge and vision (*ñāṇadassanavisuddhiniddesa*) 98n62
- reviewing knowledge (*paccavekkhaṇañāṇa*) 98
- *See also* perception (*saññā*); wisdom (*paññā*)

L

lack of restraint or shamelessness (*ahirika*) 27n42, 85*t*, 105n14, 111, **179**

liberation (*nibbāna*) 13–14, 18–19, 21, 23, 35, 40, 45n25, 47, 56, 70, 80n38, 83n7, 84, 87, 91n34, 96n56, 112, 121–123, 129, 131, 139, 144–145, 147–149, 155, 157, 158n188, 159, 163, 171, 173, 180, **182**, 189, 203

loving kindness (*mettā*) 74, 106n16, 110, 139, 156, 163–165, 169, **182**

M

Mahāsi Sayadaw 5, 23, 41, 178

Majjhima Nikāya 3, 9, 187

materiality (*rūpa*) 12*t*, 14, 16n8, 16n10, 32, 45–46, 58–61, 71, 78, 79n37, 83n7, 84, 86–87n18, 91n34, 100–101, 103, 116, 118–119, 122, 123n75, 127–128, 130, 149, 168, **183**

- as derived materiality (*upādāyarūpa*) 99, 118
- fine material form or sphere (*rūpāvacara*) 95–97, 109, 135–136
- as formless (*arūpa*) 14n4, 79n37, 86, 109
- *See also* aggregates (*khandha*); contemplation of phenomena (*dhammānupassanā*)

McMahan, David L. 1n1

meditation (*bhāvanā*) 12*t*, 14, 31n55, 32, 37–38, 40–41, 44, 46, 66, 74n16, 82–83, 89–90, 92, 97, 102, 104, 107–108, 110, 113–115, 118–119, 128–130, 138, 140–143, 147–148, 151–154, 161, 175, **180**

- calm meditation (*samatha*). *See under* concentration (*samādhi*)
- insight meditation (*vipassanā*). *See* insight (*vipassanā*)
- object of 14–15, 21–23, 27, 36–37, 39, 49–50, 51n43, 54–56, 66–67, 74, 94, 96n58, 98, 134, 137, 156, 169–170, 174
- as practice 1–2, 4–7, 17–27, 28–29, 35–36, 51–52, 56, 61–63, 72–76, 79, 86, 90–91, 93, 105, 137, 146, 148–149, 158, 163n208-209, 165–168, 170, 174
- posture 21n30, 27, 34–35, 48n37, 49–51, 54, 58, 108n24, 150, 153n171, 154

mental concomitants (*cetasika*) 5–7, 13–14n1, 15, 17n7, 31, 38, 45–46, 70–71, 82n5, 83–87, 91n34, 93n44, 94, 98, 101–102, 104, 107–111, 119n65, 120, 122–123, 128, 137–138, 144, 147–149, 152, 168n231, 170, **180**

- as wholesome (*sobhana cetasika*) 86, 156n79

mental expansion or proliferation (*papañca*) 86–87, 91–92, 128, 131, 136, **183**

mental formations (*saṅkhāra*) 7, 12*t*, 16n8, 16n12, 19, 32, 38n11, 83, 89n30, 100–101, 109, 115–125, 128, 138–139, 144, **184**, 198. *See also* aggregates (*khanda*); contemplation of phenomena (*dhammānupassanā*)

mentality (*nāma*) 13, 76n25, 78, 88n23, 101, 103, 128n86, 149, 168, 188

mentality and materiality (*nāmarūpa*) 16n12, 32, 40n16, 89n30, 118n63, 121n70, 124, 127, 142, 145, 148–149, 158, 160–161, **182**

mind (*citta*) 6, 12*t*, 14n1, 18n18, 26, 29, 32, 45–47, 60–61, 70, 75, 78, 83–86, 88–95, 101–102, 107–109, 118, 122–123, 146, 149, 169, **180**

- with aversion (*sadosacitta*) and without aversion (*vītadosacitta*) 12*t*, 81, 91*t*, 92, 93n41, **183**, **185**, 196–197
- as contracted (*saṅkhittacitta*) and distracted (*vikkhittacitta*) 12*t*, 81, 91*t*, 93–94
- as concentrated (*samāhitacitta*) or unconcentrated (*asamāhitacitta*) 12*t*, 81, 91, 96–97
- with desire (*sarāgacitta*) and without desire (*vītarāgacitta*) 12*t*, 75n22, 81, 91–93, 197
- with delusion (*samohacitta*) and without delusion (*vītamohacitta*) 12*t*, 81, 91*t*, 93
- as fruition (*phalacitta*) 70n5, 86, 98, 163
- as exalted (*mahaggatacitta*) and unexalted (*amahaggatacitta*) 12*t*, 81, 91*t*, 94–95, 196–197
- as liberated (*vimuttacitta*) and unliberated (*avimuttacitta*) 12*t*, 81, 91*t*, 98
- as path mind (*maggacitta*) 19n23, 70n5, 87n19, 95–96, 163

as surpassable (*sa-uttaracitta*) or unsurpassable (*anuttaracitta*) 12*t*, 81, 91, 95–96, **184**, 196–197
See also contemplation of the mind (*cittānupassanā*)
mind, as sense (*mano*) 6, 16n10, 59, 87–88, 127–128, **182**
mental phenomena (*dhamma*). *See* phenomena (*dhamma*)
mind-consciousness (*manoviññāna*) 16n9, 58n60, 59n66, 87n21, 88–89, 127–128
mind door (*manodvāra*) 88n25, 90, 128n88
mind-sphere (*manāyatana*) 88, 128–129
See also sense sphere (*āyatana*)
mindfulness (*sati*) 1, 6, 9n1, 34, 36, 40–42, 46–54, 56–57, 62–63, 65, 67, 69–72, 74–79, 81–82, 85*t*, 102–105, 108–111, 114–115, 118, 126, 128, 132, 136, 140–145, 148–151, 155, 157–159, 168–170, 173–174, **184**
of breathing (*ānāpānasati*) 11*t*, 21–22, 26, 33, 39, 41–44, 50, 54, 67, 70, 74, 79, 83, 96n58, 110, 119, 143n134, 153, 156, 168, **179**, 188
directed at the body (*kāyagātasati*) 34–35, **181**
at the forefront (*parimukham satim upaṭṭhapetvā*) 11*t*, 33, 36, 41*t*, 188–189
foundations of (*satipaṭṭhanas*) 3n3, 7, 42
four foundations of (*cattāro satipaṭṭhāna*) 6, 11*t*, 13–32, 33, 35–36, 39n14, 42, 45–46, 61–63, 70n3, 72, 76, 77n30, 92, 94, 96n58, 97, 100, 102, 106, 117, 130, 145, 149, 170, 173–175, **184**, 188, 202
as mindful (*satimā*) 6n8, 11*t*, 13–21, 32, 143n135, 170n236, 188
as recollections (*anussati*) 111, 153

N

Ñāṇanamoli, Bhikkhu, and Bhikkhu Bodhi 3, 4, 9, 31n56–57, 63n82, 66n85, 187, 193n1
non-returner (*anāgāmin*) 111, 132, 134n101, 135, 137, 166n221, **179**
non-self (*anattā*) 16n11, 21, 30, 47, 52, 70n3, 96, 98n67, 105n13, 117–119, 125n78, 147, 159n189, 163, **179**, 184. *See also* being (*satta*)
Norman, K. R. 159–160n190
nose (*ghāna*) 16n10, 127, **181**
nose-consciousness (*ghānaviññāṇa*) 87n21, 127–128
smell (*gandhā*) 16n10, 127, **181**
Nyanaponika 7n16, 14n1

O

one-pointedness (*ekaggatā*) 14, 18–19, 56, 74n19, 85*t*, 86, 97n61, 105*f*, 148, 152, 170, **181**

P

Pa-Auk 55n52
Pāli texts
structure of 2–7, 15n6, 16n12, 22n33, 48n37, 109n27, 119n64, 123n75, 132
terms 2–4, 6, 16n13, 25n40, 31, 35n7, 38n11, 39n14, 41, 58n60, 66, 70n6, 84n9, 85n14, 87, 116n53, 121n69, 144n139, 145, 147n150, 158n184, 159n190, 160n191
See also translation
Pali Text Society (PTS) 4, 9, 81n1, 196n1
passing away (*vaya*) 45–46, 71, 75n21, 117, 124, **185**
as passes away (*atthagama*) 118–120, 122
path (*magga*) 1, 20, 87, 89, 95–96, 109, 112n41, 113, **182**
as eightfold path (*aṭṭhaṅgika magga*) 34, 44, 47–48, 102, 132, 135, 149, 155, 158, 161, 163–165, 167–168, 171, 175, **180**
path knowledge (*maggañāṇa*) 19, 24, 25, 47, 48, 92, 96, 102, 120, 122, 132, 142, 149, 157, 163, 164, 165, 171, 175, **182**
peace. *See* tranquillity (*passaddhi*)
perception (*saññā*) 7, 12*t*, 16n8, 20, 32, 38n11, 71, 87, 90–93, 98, 100–102, 108–109, 115–117, 119–121, 123, 125, 139, 144–145, 148, 163, **184**, 198–199
and contemplation of the mind (*cittānupassanā*) 82–83, 85*t*, 86–87, 90–93, 98
and contemplation of phenomena (*dhammānupassanā*) 100–102, 108–109, 144–145, 148, 163
and feeling (*vedanā*) 119–121
and five aggregates of clinging (*pañcas'upādānakkhandhā*) 115–116, 117n55
and mental formations (*saṅkhāra*) 123, 124n75, 125
ten perceptions 143n134
phenomena (*dhammas*) 6–7, 12*t*, 14n1, 16n13, 25n40, 45n26, 79, 83n7, 122n71, 123n75, 140–143, 145, 149, 150, 155, 156n79, **181**
arising (*samudayadhamma*) and passing phenomena (*vayadhamma*), 11*t*, 33, 45–47, 48*t*, 49–50, 53, 57, 63, 65, 69, 81, 99, 115, 126, 140, 157, 188–202
investigation of *dhammas* (*dhammavicaya*) 6–7, 12*t*, 25, 31n53, 79, 141, 143, 145, 148–152, 156, 169n234, **181**, 201

investigation factor of awakening (*dhammavicayasambojjhaṅga*) 12*t*, 16n13, 31n53, 139, 141*f*, 142n131, 145–149, 151, 152*t*, 155n177, 156, 169n234, 200–201
three characteristics of (*tilakkhaṇa*) 16n13, 21, 23–25, 28, 31, 40n16, 47, 49n40, 52, 56, 76, 96, 98, 104, 117–118, 130, 147–148, 157, 165, **184**
Pemasiri Thera 1–7, 9–10, 13–32, 33–42, 43–49, 49–51, 51–53, 54–57, 58–65, 66–67, 70–80, 82–98, 100–116, 116–26, 126–140, 140–157, 158–173, 174–175
Poddar, R. P. 9n1

R

renunciation (*nekkhamma*) 5n6, 101, 163, 165, **182**
restlessness (*uddhacca*) 19n22, 20–21, 27n42, 48n34, 85*t*, 93–94, 105n14, 108, 111, 129, 132t, 133*t*, 135–137, 155, **184**
as restlessness and worry (*uddhaccakukkucca*) 12*t*, 21n28, 47n33, 82, 84n13, 86, 102, 105*f*, 111, 112n38
See also contemplation of phenomena (*dhammānupassanā*); hindrances (*nīvaraṇa*); worry (*kukkucca*)
Rhys Davids, Caroline 84n9

S

Saṅgha 110n33, 112–113, 134, 152n167, 153, 166–167, 174
Satipaṭṭhānasutta 1–3, 4–5, 9, 11–12, 13, 16n9, 21n30, 25–26, 29, 31, 33–34, 39, 42, 48, 54n48, 66–67, 70–71n6, 76–77, 79
areas of contemplation 58–59, 62
seclusion. *See* detachment (*viveka*)
sense desire (*kāmacchanda*) 11*t*, 19n22, 21n28, 31n56, 47n33, 48n34, 77n28, 82, 84n13, 102, 104–106, 111n36, 129, 132–135, 156, **181**
as taint (*kāmāsava*) 125, 132–133
See also contemplation of phenomena (*dhammānupassanā*); hindrances (*nīvaraṇa*)
sense spheres (*āyatana*) 7, 12*t*, 16, 25–26, 34, 43*t*, 46, 48*t*, 59, 70, 88, 118, 119n65, 121n70, 125–129, 131–132, 134n103, 148, **174**, 200–201
internal and external 16n10, 100, 127*t*, 128, 130
mind-sphere. *See under* mind, as sense (*mano*)
sense base (*saḷāyatana*) 124, 127*t*, 130n91
sense object (*dhammāyatana*) 128–129
See also contemplation of phenomena (*dhammānupassanā*); perception (*saññā*)
sit with legs bent crosswise (*pallaṅkaṃ ābhujitvā*) 11*t*, 35, 41, 188
sloth and torpor (*thīnamiddha*) 12*t*, 47n33, 84n13, 86, 94, 102, 105*f*, 107–111, 170, **184**. *See also* contemplation of phenomena (*dhammānupassanā*); hindrances (*nīvaraṇa*)
suffering (*dukkha*) 12*t*, 16n11, 21, 25, 30, 47–48, 54, 57, 70n3, 71, 76, 78, 86, 96, 98, 104, 105n13, 117–118, 121, 138, 142–143, 145, 147, 157–158, 160–165, 168–169, 171, 179, **181**
arising or origin of (*dukkhasamudaya*) 158, 159*t*, 160–161, 163–164
cessation of (*dukkhanirodha*) 12*t*, 130n93, 157–159, 162–165, 202–203
path to the cessation of (*dukkhanirodhagāminī paṭipadā*) 12*t*, 114n47, 147n151, 157–158, 159*t*, 163–164, 202–203
See also contemplation of phenomena (*dhammānupassanā*); four noble truths (*cattāri ariyasaccāni*)
Sujato, Bhikkhu 1n1
Suttapiṭaka 45n24, 89, 112
stream-winner (*sotāpanna*) 132, 135, 145, 153, 166n221, **184**

T

taint (*āsava*) 19, 21n29, 28n47, 34n4, 77, 125, 132–133, 142, 155–156, **180**
Tapussasutta 19, 76–77, 20n24
three refuges (*saraṇa*) 166–168. *See also* virtue (*sīla*)
three trainings (*sikkhā*) 112–115
thought or intention
applied thought (*vitakka*) 55–56, 74, 85*t*, 87, 101, 103, 105*f*, 147, 152, 168–170, **185**
right intention or thought (*sammā saṅkappa*) 101–102, 147, 165, 168–170, **183**
sustained thought (*vicāra*) 56, 74, 85*t*, 105*f*, 148, 152, 170, **185**
volition or intention (*cetanā*) 7, 82n5, 83n7, 85*t*, 88n23, 93, 108, 116, 120n68, 121n69, 123–125, 148, **180**
See also absorption (*jhāna*); mental concomitants (*cetasika*)
Tipiṭaka 2, 3n3, 5n5, 44n22, 83n7, 89n29, 92n37, 97n60, 98n63, 102, 112, 125n81, 147–148
tongue (*jivhā*) 16n10, 127, **181**
taste (*rasā*) 16n10, 127, **183**
tongue-consciousness (*jivhāviññāṇa*) 87n21, 127–128
training or restraint (*sikkhati*) 11*t*, 27, 33, 38–41, 74n17, 113n44, **184**, 188

tranquillity (*passaddhi*) 14, 79n34, 85*t*, 141, 149, 152–154, 164, **183**
factor of awakening (*passaddhisambojjhaṅga*) 12*t*, 152*t*, 153, 154n174
translation
interpretive process of 3, 5, 9n1, 31, 36, 41n18, 58n60, 66, 84n9, 87–89, 104, 121n69, 130n93, 147n150, 158n184, 160n191
processes of 1, 3–6, 45n26, 54n47, 63n82, 82n4, 86n16, 95–96n55, 101n4, 106n17, 107n19–20, 108n25, 109n29, 119n65, 121n70, 134n104
trust (*saddhā*) 14n1, 16–17, 23, 26, 28, 47, 85*t*, 86, 105*f*, 148, 150–1, 153, 155, 166, **183**

U

ultimate reality (*paramattha*) 45n25, 46n27, 91n34, 122n71
unconditioned state (*asaṅkhata*) 16n9, 58n60, 87, 139n127, 143, 145, 162, **180**
unsatisfactoriness. *See* suffering (*dukkha*)
unwholesome states (*akusala*) 15, 28n47, 49n39, 77n30, 85–86, 93n42, 107, 119n65, 121n70, 123, 138, 148, 167, 169, **179**. *See also* wholesome states (*kusala*)

V

views (*diṭṭhi*) 19n20, 27n42, 45, 77n28, 86n16, 93, 105n14, 111n37, 113, 115, 122, 130n90, 131–132, 134, 136–138, 166, 168, 174, **181**
personality or identity view (*sakkāyadiṭṭhi*) 19n22, 125, 129, 132*t*, 133–136, 145, 168n229
purity of (*diṭṭhivisuddhi*) 47n31, 78, 136, **181**
right views (*sammā diṭṭhi*) 39, 147, 160, 164–165, 167–168, 170–171, **183**
as taint (*diṭṭhāsava*) 125, 132–133
wrong view (*micchā diṭṭhi*) 23, 85*t*, 93, 108, 149, **182**
virtue (*sīla*) 12*t*, 17–18, 21, 39, 51n43, 153, 167–168, **184**
cultivation of 104, 110, 112–114, 163, 167
as moral precepts 39, 135, 164–169
See also contemplation of phenomena (*dhammānupassanā*); four noble truths (*cattāri ariyasaccāni*)

W

Walshe, Maurice 3, 4, 45, 178
Warder, A. K. 45n26
wholesome states (*kusala*) 5n6, 13, 15, 21, 28–29, 34, 77n30, 85, 104n12, 114, 123, 138, 148, 167, 169, **182**. *See also* unwholesome states (*akusala*)
Wijeratne, R., and Rupert Gethin 89n27
Wiles, Royce 7, 9n1
will to act (*chanda*) 85*t*, 104, 146, 169, **180**
wisdom (*paññā*) 3, 6–7, 12*t*, 15n6, 16–17, 19n23, 20–21, 23n37, 25n40, 26–28, 31, 34, 37n8, 47, 49–50n40, 52, 77–78, 85*t*, 90, 102, 105–106, 111–114, 118, 120, 130, 132, 135–136, 138, 147–148, 150–151, 153, 155–156, 164–166, 168–169, **183**
as absence of delusion (*amoha*) 25n40, 47n31, 75n21, 86, **179**
See also contemplation of phenomena (*dhammānupassanā*); four noble truths (*cattāri ariyasaccāni*)
as emptiness 72, 104
insight into non-self 6–7, 25, 40–1, 44n22, 47, 49, 51n43, 57, 62, 63n79
non-being (*nisatta*) 49–50n40, 62, 72, 138, **182**
no living being (*nissattanijjīvata*) 73, **182**
as perception of non-self (*anattasaññā*) 143
See also being (*sattā*); non-self (*anatta*)
worry (*kukkucca*) 85*t*, 111–12, 137, **185**. *See also* restlessness (*uddhacca*)

www.ingramcontent.com/pod-product-compliance
Lightning Source LLC
Chambersburg PA
CBHW081351230426
43667CB00017B/2791
* 9 7 8 1 8 0 0 5 0 3 9 4 6 *